FRENCH COOKING

Classic Recipes and Techniques

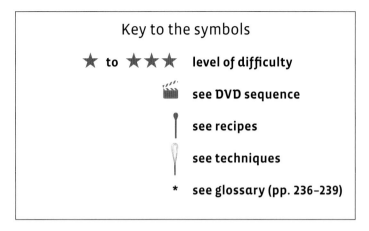

Key to the symbols

★ to ★★★ **level of difficulty**

see DVD sequence

see recipes

see techniques

* **see glossary (pp. 236–239)**

This book could not have been published without the support of Éditions LT Jacques Lanore.

Translated from the French by Carmella Abramowitz-Moreau
Graphics and design: Alice Leroy and Audrey Sednaoui
Editorial assistance: Rebecca Parsons
Copyediting: Penelope Isaac
Typesetting: Gravemaker+Scott
Proofreading: Helen Woodhall
Indexing: Carmella Abramowitz-Moreau
Color Separation: IGS, Limoges
Printed in China by Toppan Leefung

Distributed in North America by Rizzoli International Publications, Inc.
Originally published in French as *Encyclopédie de la gastronomie française*
© Flammarion, SA, Paris, 2009
English-language edition
© Flammarion, SA, Paris, 2010

Vincent Boué · Hubert Delorme · Photographs by Clay McLachlan

FRENCH COOKING
Classic Recipes and Techniques

Foreword by
Paul Bocuse

Flammarion

Contents

Practical Guide

Recipes

Foreword

By Paul Bocuse

This book will be an invaluable companion in the kitchen. Whether we are professionals or amateurs, whether we need to check the proportions or the processes involved in a recipe, prepare a forgotten classic, or reinvent a dish, there is always a time when we need to return to our books and consult the culinary advice of experts. Yet books alone are not enough, and therein lies the complexity of our profession, one that is both manual and scientific. Books certainly perpetuate recipes but, without the requisite skills, there can be no fine cuisine. Knowing that an onion must be chopped or how to prepare sweetbreads is no guarantee that we will actually achieve what we set out to accomplish. A great deal of training is required, as well as regular practice, to transform the theory in books into know-how. In times past, mothers transmitted precious culinary heritage to their daughters. The youth of today have to seek out other mentors. Fortunately, opportunities abound, and what better starting point than *French Cooking: Classic Recipes and Techniques*? It will soon prove to be indispensable for everyone, including aspiring cooks intent on learning the basics, or those honing their skills to master the fundamentals of French cuisine.

There is no doubt that this exceptional work is a continuation of the tradition of reference books that will contribute to the prestige of French cuisine worldwide. Many of these already occupy a prominent place in the kitchens of all self-respecting chefs. Notable examples are *L'Art de la cuisine française au XIXᵉ siècle* (*The Art of French Cooking in the Nineteenth Century*) by Antonin Carême, as well as the key work, the 1903 *Guide culinaire d'Auguste Escoffier* (*Culinary Guide of Auguste Escoffier*), *La Gastronomie pratique* (*The Encyclopedia of Practical Gastronomy*) by Ali-Bab (1907), and the 1992 *L'Art culinaire français par les grands maîtres de la cuisine* (French Culinary Art by the Great Masters of Cuisine). It is no coincidence that Flammarion published the three latter works. Today, once again, Flammarion is taking a bold step in this book by bringing together the two dimensions of cuisine: knowledge and know-how. *French Cooking* is divided into two distinct sections and, with its numerous photos, takes you through the basics step by step, before presenting more than one hundred recipes that make up the very foundation of French cuisine. The DVD adds another dimension by demonstrating, in detail, twenty-four complex methods, showing you how to "turn" vegetables, prepare fresh fruit mousses, fillet fish, and make puff pastry.

This book is distinctive in another way, too. Instead of calling on only renowned chefs for information, it also asks the teachers at a professional school for the hospitality industry to explain the techniques to enable you to prepare the thousands of recipes of the French *terroirs* successfully. A number of great chefs have contributed to the work, opening each recipe section: Anne-Sophie Pic for appetizers, Alain Passard for vegetables, Gérald Passédat for fish, Jean-François Piège for poultry, Régis Marcon for meat, Xavier Thuret for cheese, Yves Thuriès and Didier Stéphane for desserts, and Stéphane Augé for iced desserts. Their contributions may be interpreted as a homage to the men and women who are at the forefront of today's cuisine. *French Cooking* is, in essence, the transmission of the anonymous techniques and recipes that have built up the framework of French cuisine since the nineteenth century.

The publication of a book of this scope gives me more than one reason for profound satisfaction: it pays tribute to our ability to transmit our unique savoir-faire. For me, the passing on of knowledge is one of the fundamental values of the cooking profession. In my restaurant, I have a constant intake of apprentices and cooks from the world over. They come for hands-on learning experience: how to truss* a chicken, prepare a fillet, put together elaborate desserts, and make a perfect soufflé. They observe my chefs, who are officially acknowledged to be some of the finest artisans in France, and repeat their every action. At the Institut Paul Bocuse, founded twenty years ago in Écully, cooking instructors teach all these techniques to young students, who also train in management and the art of the hospitality industry.

Who could have imagined, when Jack Lang, Minister of Culture at the time, and I launched the project, that gastronomy would inspire such passion in the twenty-first century? Even the most optimistic were convinced that technology would reduce cuisine to little more than mechanized "ready meals," dealing a fatal blow to flavorsome food. Technology has certainly made its presence felt, but in no way like the imaginary food synthesizers of *Star Trek*. On the contrary, it has widened our creativity and extended our range of possibilities. The food processors, siphons, slow-cooking ovens, *sous vide**, and *planchas* (electric griddles) that come to us from agri-business have not only facilitated the work of cooks, they have also raised to new heights a profession that was so disparaged after World War II.

This book is part of a movement that is fighting for authentic taste. Significant changes in outlook mean that people from all walks of life are now happy to spend hours busying themselves in the kitchen with the sole aim of delighting a table of guests. Television programs, cooking lessons given in an ever-increasing number of cooking schools, practical and teaching books, lectures, debates, cartoons, and gastronomical encounters all inevitably lead back to the home kitchen. We are all seeking to take control of what is on our plates, selecting the healthiest and tastiest ingredients. Never before have cooks and those who consume their food had such a close relationship.

With this new culinary bible, there are no more secrets! At last, the intricacies of how to prepare the great classics of French cuisine are explained from A to Z. So peel, chop, slice, grill, braise, prepare stocks and sabayon, cook a sea bass in a salt crust, tuck goat cheese into pastry pouches, and put together unforgettable vol-au-vents. As long as you wield your kitchen utensils, cooking will live. And as long as there is cooking, there is hope!

Paul Bocuse

Basic
Techniques

Basic doughs and batters

Firm doughs

Shortcrust pastry (*pâte brisée*) ★

Pâte brisée is very often baked simultaneously with the filling, and is used both for savory and sweet dishes. This shortcrust pastry is used mainly to hold a relatively liquid filling, so is used for dishes such as quiches, flans, pies, or fruit tarts such as apple and pear. For sweet tarts, add 3 ½ tablespoons (40 g) sugar.

Ingredients

2 ¾ cups (250 g) cake flour
1 generous teaspoon (5 g) table salt
3 ½ tablespoons (40 g) sugar (for sweet tarts)
1 stick (125 g) unsalted butter, room temperature
1 egg yolk
4 ½ tablespoons (50 ml) water

Sift the flour and add the salt and sugar if using. Blend the butter and the flour together with your fingertips until the mixture forms coarse crumbs. Incorporate the egg yolk and water, working lightly with your hands (1). Do not overwork the dough as it will become too elastic. Form the dough into a ball and chill, covered in plastic wrap, for about 30 minutes. Cut in half and roll each half into a ball. Lightly sprinkle your working surface with flour and roll the dough into a disk shape with a thickness of about ⅙ inch (3 mm).
Roll the dough over your pastry roller to transfer it from the working surface to line your circle or tart dish (2). Decorate the edges.

● Chef's notes

Alternatively, the egg yolk and water may be mixed with the sifted flour, salt, and sugar (if using) first, followed by the butter (as shown on the DVD).
Make sure you leave time to chill the dough to reduce elasticity; it will be far easier to roll out.
Leftover pieces of dough may be used for other purposes.

❗ Recipe ideas

Quiche Lorraine ››p.271
Roquefort and caramelized pear tartes fines ›› p. 414
Apple upside-down cake (tarte Tatin) ›› p. 452
Apricot tartlets ›› p. 428

1

2

Sweetened short pastry (crumbled) (*pâte sablée*) ★

Because the butter and flour are worked together, this is a crumbly pastry. It is often baked blind* before being filled or topped. It is used for sweet pastry making only. You may also use it on its own, in individual portions, to make shortbread cookies. Many regions and towns in France, such as Brittany, Normandy, and Nantes, have their own specialty shortbread cookies.

Ingredients
2 ³/₄ cups (250 g) cake flour
1 generous teaspoon (5 g) table salt
1 stick (125 g) unsalted butter, softened*
²/₃ cup (125 g) sugar
1 egg

Sift the flour with the salt. Dice* the butter and blend it in with your fingers until it forms coarse crumbs (1, 2). Incorporate the sugar, make a well, and then work in the egg (3, 4).
Chill for around 30 minutes. Roll out the dough to form a disk about ¹/₁₀ inch (3 mm) thick.
Place it in a tart dish and bake blind* at 350°F (180°C) for about 20 minutes (if making a tart for 8 servings).

● Chef's notes
For an optimal crumbly texture, do not work the butter in for too long.
Add variety to your recipes by adding spices such as cinnamon or allspice, or candied ginger, dry ingredients such as shredded coconut, citrus zest, or cocoa powder, or liquid ingredients such as orange-blossom water, honey, or other flavor essences.

❙ Recipe ideas
Lemon meringue tartlets ≫ p. 435

Sweetened short pastry (creamed) (*pâte sucrée*) ★

This dough is used as a sweet tart base. Bake it blind* or fill it with almond cream, custard filling, or other sweet cream filling for baking.

Ingredients
1 stick (125 g) unsalted butter, softened*
¹/₂ cup (100 g) granulated sugar
1 egg
2 ³/₄ cups (250 g) cake flour
1 teaspoon (5 ml) salt

Place the butter, sugar, and egg in the bowl of a food processor (1) and cream together until smooth. Sift the flour and add it with the salt (2) to process for 1-2 minutes further, until smooth.
Press down the dough with the palm of your hand, pushing it away from you, until the ingredients are thoroughly blended. Chill, covered, for about 30 minutes.
Roll out the dough very thinly (to about ¹/₆ inch or 3 mm) to form a disk. Use your rolling pin to transfer it from the working surface to the baking pan or circle: drape it round the pin and then unroll it over the tart mold (3).
Make decorative patterns around the edge (4).

● Chef's note
This method uses creaming to combine the butter with the egg and sugar, which means it has a softer texture than the crumbly pastry dough in the previous method. If you make it ahead of time, keep it covered in plastic wrap so that it does not absorb any tastes or odors.
If you use just the egg yolk you may need to add a little water (about 3 ¹/₂ tablespoons [50 ml]).

❙ Recipe ideas
Mirabelle plum tart, a specialty of Alsace ›› p. 476
Mixed berry tart ›› p. 446
Raspberry ganache tart ›› p. 460

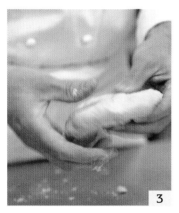

Pasta and noodle dough ★

Pasta has played an important role in the history of food for humankind. China is the country with the highest consumption of noodles in the world. In Europe, Italy is the leading consumer and producer, exporting a wide variety, including spaghetti, cannelloni, ravioli, fusilli, pappardelle, and tortellini. Several regions in France—Alsace, Savoy, Dauphiné—have traditional dishes that use pasta like *spätzles* (small dumplings), *crozets* (small squares of dough made with either wheat or buckwheat), and the *ravioles* of Royans (small stuffed pockets of dough).

This recipe gives a smooth, dry dough. It is rolled out very thinly for its various uses.

Ingredients
2 eggs
1 ¼ tablespoons (20 ml) oil
1 teaspoon (5 g) table salt
2 ½ cups (220 g) cake flour

Beat the eggs and combine with the oil and salt. Sift the flour, then make a well in the center and pour in the liquid ingredients.
Rapidly knead* the ingredients so that they form a ball. Do not overwork or else the dough will become too elastic (2, 3).
Chill, covered, for 30 to 45 minutes.
Roughly spread the dough out using a pastry roller, then process it through a pasta maker (4).
Use a cutter or laminator to cut the desired shapes (5, 6).
Allow the pasta to dry for several hours before using it.

● **Chef's notes**
To make ravioles, *pass the dough through a pasta maker until it is very thin. This will prevent it from having a floury taste when eaten. The dough can be prepared ahead of time, but it will lose its elasticity. If you wish to prepare it ahead, cover it in plastic wrap to protect it from other tastes and odors.*

● **Did you know?**
Using a flavored oil in the dough gives it an original touch.
Pasta dough may also be colored:
• black: cuttlefish ink
• red: tomato paste
• yellow: turmeric
• orange: ground saffron
• green: parsley chlorophyll

❙ **Recipe idea**
Snail ravioles and garlic cream ›› p. 267

Puff pastry ★★★ 🎬

Puff pastry is made by creating successive layers of fat (here, butter) and dough, each one as thin and even as possible. This is done by making a series of folds. The pastry puffs up because of the steam caught in the leaves of dough mixture that have been softened by the addition of fat or butter.

Ingredients
2 ³/₄ cups (250 g) cake flour
1 teaspoon (5 g) salt
¹/₂ cup (125 ml) water
10 ¹/₂ tablespoons (185 g) unsalted butter

Sift the flour and add the salt. Make a well in the center and pour the water into the flour. Blend the ingredients together rapidly until thoroughly mixed. You should have a smooth paste, known as the *détrempe*. Form it into a ball and chill, covered, for about 20 minutes.
Check that the butter has the identical consistency of the dough mixture. Flatten it, if necessary, between 2 sheets of parchment paper, using your rolling pin. This enables it to be incorporated more easily into the dough, and gives it a longer rectangular shape.
Now roll out the dough mixture to form a cross shape, leaving the center–where you will place the butter–thicker (about ¹/₃ inch or 8 mm) than the four other parts. The butter should fit over this part of the dough.
Place the butter in the center of the dough **(1)** and fold over each of the four parts of the cross (similarly to the back of an envelope).
Lightly dust your cool working counter with flour (use as little as possible each time, so that the pastry does not become too hard). Roll out the dough (called a *paton*) to form a rectangle whose length is three times greater than its width **(2)**.
Fold this into three, starting at each end (three layers) **(3)**. Rotate the folded dough a quarter-turn and roll out again to form the same shape as previously, a rectangle three times its width. Repeat the folding operation. Cover with plastic wrap and chill again for about 20 minutes.
Repeat this procedure–rolling out and folding–five more times (a total of six times), chilling for 20 minutes between each stage.

● Chef's notes
The quantity of fat to incorporate into this pastry is equal to half the weight of your dough mixture (water and flour).
Not all puff pastries are made with six turns. The fewer turns you make, the more it will puff up. However, the end result after baking will be less regular.
There are three other types of puff pastry:

• inverted puff pastry (feuilletage inverse), where the dough is incorporated into a mixture of fat and flour
• quick puff pastry, where the fat is cubed and incorporated into the dough mixture and four turns are made;
• Viennese puff pastry, using a slightly sweet dough to which milk is added.

● Did you know?
A simple form of puff pastry has been in existence for a long time. The Arabs and Greeks prepared it using oil. The French artist known as Claude Lorrain is said to have invented it in the seventeenth century when he was working as a pastry maker's apprentice. In the eighteenth century, Feuillet, a cook working for the princely Condé family, used and improved the recipe, as did Antonin Carême, recognized as the founder of French haute cuisine, some decades later.

Does a mille-feuille have one thousand leaves?
Mille-feuilles means, literally, one thousand leaves, and basing our calculations on a six-turn puff pastry, it is possible to calculate the number of leaves created by layering dough and fat.
After the first folding into three, there are three layers of butter and six layers of dough. However, two layers of dough are in direct contact and so form only one layer. Here's the calculation:
1st turn: 3 × 3 = 9 – 2 = 7
2nd turn: 7 × 3 = 21 – 2 = 19
3rd turn: 19 × 3 = 57 – 2 = 55
4th turn: 55 × 3 = 165 – 2 = 163
5th turn: 163 × 3 = 489 – 2 = 487
6th turn: 487 × 3 = 1,461 – 2 = 1,459
Three layers of pastry are normally used to make a mille-feuille, so altogether there will be
1,459 × 3 = 4,377 leaves.

▌ Recipe ideas
Provençal-flavored sardine *tartes fines* ›› p. 280
Cheese straws ›› p. 278
Sweetbread vol-au-vents with cider and apples ›› p. 272
Kings' cake (*galette des rois*) ›› p. 445
Diplomat-filled mille-feuille ››p. 479
Gâteau Saint-Honoré ›› p. 451

1 2

3

Batters

Crêpe batter ★

In France, crêpes are a special treat for the Candlemas festival in February, and may be enjoyed plain, sweet, or savory. Use them, too, as a base for other recipes. The batter is smooth, liquid, and a yellow color.

Ingredients

2 ¾ cups (250 g) cake flour
1 teaspoon (5 g) table salt
3 eggs
2 cups (500 ml) low-fat (semi-skimmed) milk, room temperature
Your own choice of flavoring, such as vanilla, orange-blossom water, or a hint of rum
3 tablespoons (40 g) unsalted butter, melted until brown
Oil for the skillet

Sift the flour and salt into a mixing bowl (1). Crack the eggs into the mixture one by one. Incorporate the melted butter into the milk without heating. Whisk the mixture briskly while pouring on a little of the milk and melted butter (2).
Incorporate the remaining milk, beating energetically until the batter is smooth and fluid.
Add the flavor of your choice and strain through a fine-mesh sieve (3).
Chill for about 30 minutes.
Heat a skillet or crêpe pan over high heat. Drizzle a little oil in and cook the crêpes one by one, turning them over when they go golden-brown at the edges (4).

● Chef's notes

To avoid lumps forming, use a whisk as you gradually pour the milk into the mixture of flour, eggs, and salt. If lumps form nevertheless, strain the batter through a fine-mesh sieve.
You may replace some or all of the milk with beer or hard cider: you may also substitute wheat flour with other types of flour such as buckwheat or spelt.*
For savory crêpes, think of adding finely chopped herbs, spices, or even finely shredded vegetables to the batter.
You can also add the melted brown butter at the end of the preparation, after straining.

1

2

● Did you know?

Plain, simple galettes date back to approximately 7,000 BCE. Crêpes as we know them were first made considerably later, in the thirteenth century. Blinis come to us from Russia. They are thick, leavened crêpes made with wheat and buckwheat.
In France, savory crêpes are known as galettes. They are of Celtic origin, and in Brittany are made using buckwheat flour, water, and salt.

● How to use them:

Aumonière (almoner's purse): sweet or savory filling in a crêpe that is tied up to form a pouch shape.
Crêpe Suzette: a crêpe flavored with curaçao and caramelized with sugar cubes rubbed on the skin of unsprayed tangerines.
Crêpe soufflée: a crêpe filled with a soufflé batter and then baked.
Gâteau de crêpes (crêpe cake): a pile of crêpes interspersed with a garnish, such as preserves, pastry cream, almond cream, ganache, and so on, to form a cake shape.
Pannequet: a crêpe holding a sweet or savory filling and folded into four, forming a small cushion shape.

❦ Recipe idea
Rolled Picardy crêpes >> p. 400

Choux pastry ★ ★ 🎬

Choux pastry may be used for sweet or savory recipes, on its own or with a purée, béchamel sauce, pastry cream, and so on. It is cooked by frying, poaching, or baking. This pastry is firm and sticky but smooth, and swells when cooked or baked.

Ingredients

1 ¼ cups (125 g) all-purpose flour
1 cup (250 ml) water
1 teaspoon (5 g) table salt
1 scant tablespoon (15 g) sugar (optional)
7 tablespoons (100 g) unsalted butter, diced*
4 eggs, and an additional egg for basting*

Sift the flour. In a saucepan, bring the water, salt, sugar (if using), and diced butter to the boil.
Pour all the sifted flour in (1) and beat energetically with a rubber spatula until the moisture has evaporated.
Transfer the mixture to a mixing bowl. Spread it out with the spatula so that it adheres (it will not stick, however) to the sides of the bowl.
Add the four eggs, one by one, using the spatula to mix (2). Stir in thoroughly each time.
Spoon the batter into a piping bag and pipe out the shapes you will need (puffs, éclairs, or profiteroles) (3).
Beat the remaining egg with a small pinch of salt and baste the shapes with a pastry brush.
Dip the tines of a fork into water and lightly press them in, in a cross pattern, to smooth out the surface of the choux pastry so that it bakes evenly (4).
Choux pastry bakes in two stages, first at 350°F (180°C) for 15 minutes (until the pastry is nicely swelled and is uniformly golden), and then at 325°F (160°C), for 10 minutes (the all-important drying-out stage). The exact time will of course depend on the size of the pastries you are baking. During the second stage, leave the oven door slightly ajar (use the handle of a wooden spoon) to facilitate the evaporation of the moisture in the pastries.

● Did you know?

An Italian pastry chef, Popelini, is said to have created choux pastry. He was employed by Catherine de Médici (1519–1589), the Italian-born queen of France. The choux pastry as we know it today has only been prepared since the eighteenth century.

● Use for:

Cream puffs, éclairs, chouquettes (small, sugar-coated puffs), religieuses, glands (small acorn-shaped pastries), soufflé doughnuts, and cakes such as the croquembouches, Paris-Brest, and Saint-Honoré.

● Chef's notes

For best results, have your butter at room temperature so that it melts as the same time as the water starts boiling. If too much evaporation occurs at this stage, the pastry will be too hard.
If your batter is not sufficiently dried out, only use three eggs so that you will be able to pipe it out with a pastry bag.

❙ Recipe ideas

Gnocchi, Florentine-style ›› p. 388
Mushroom gougères ›› p. 279

Basic doughs and batters

Waffle batter ★

Waffles are light, airy, honeycomb-shaped delicacies with a
rectangular form.
Enjoy them on their own or with fruit preserves, Chantilly cream,
or chocolate sauce.

Ingredients
3 ³/₄ cups (340 g) cake flour
Scant ¹/₂ cup (80 g) sugar
Scant ¹/₂ teaspoon (2 g) table salt
2 ³/₄ teaspoons (10 g) baking powder
2 eggs
1 cup (¹/₄ liter) milk
7 tablespoons (100 g) butter, melted and cooled
A few drops of vanilla extract

Combine the flour, sugar, salt, and baking powder in a mixing
bowl. Make a well in the center.
Break the eggs into the well and whisk them into the dry
ingredients with a little milk.
Gradually add the rest of the milk, whisking so that there are
no lumps.
Stir in the melted butter and vanilla extract.
Chill the batter for about 30 minutes. Cook your waffles in a
waffle maker according to instructions.

● **Chef's notes**
If you wish, you may substitute beer or hard cider for some or all
of the milk.*
*You can also use beaten egg whites to make waffles, or even
baking powder or yeast. Follow the instructions according to the
weight of your ingredients.*
*Try out different flavors, such as orange-blossom water, rum, and
so on.*

● **Did you know?**
*The ancestor of the waffle was the oublie, a small, flat wafer.
Like waffles, they were cooked between two hot iron plates by
oubloyeurs or oublieux, members of the guild who sold oublies.
When irons were made with a honeycomb indentation, the
resulting offerings became known as gaufres after the word for
honeycomb; the Old French version of this word, wafla, is the
origin of the name by which we know them today.*

❗ **Recipe idea**
Tutti-frutti waffles ≫ p. 464

1

Frying batter ★ ★

Batter for frying is light and airy. It is used to coat food before it is dipped in oil.

Ingredients

2 cups (200 g) all-purpose flour
1 teaspoon (5 g) table salt
2 eggs
4 teaspoons (20 ml) sunflower seed oil
$^3/_4$ cup (200 ml) milk or beer
3 egg whites

Sift the flour into a mixing bowl and add the salt (1). Break the whole eggs one by one, and whisk them in to the dry ingredients. Incorporate the oil.
Pour in the liquid (milk or beer) and whisk until the mixture is smooth. Stiffly beat the egg whites.
Gently fold* in the beaten egg whites using a flexible rubber spatula (2).

● **Chef's notes**

Fold in the egg whites just before you coat the food you will be frying so that it does not deflate.
The pan or pot must be perfectly clean. If you have prepared fish or fruit in it beforehand, make sure there are no traces left as the taste could permeate what you are frying.

● **Did you know?**

Fritters appeared in France as early as the thirteenth century. Each region had its own specialty with a specific shape, batter, and filling. Some examples are the bugne *of Lyon, the* bottereau *of the Charentes regions, the* roussette *of Strasbourg, the* merveilles *of Gascony, the* tourtisseau *of Anjou, the* bignes *of the Auvergne region, and the* oreillette *of Montpellier.*

❢ **Recipe idea**
Apple fritters and apricot coulis ›› p. 449

2

Yeast doughs

● Chef's note

Yeast doughs should be left to rise at a temperature of 77°F–82°F (25°C–28°C). They may be left in an oven heated only by the pilot light, with a bowl of water, over a pan of gently steaming water, or in a warm draft-free place such as an airing cupboard.

● Did you know?

There are two types of yeast:
• Fresh yeast. This is living yeast with a light color, from creamy white to ivory. Its smell is mild and it has no acid taste. It must be firm but malleable, and its texture crumbly. It must be stored in the refrigerator at a temperature between 37.4°F–44.6°F (3°C–7°C). It will keep for about ten days after purchase.
• Dried yeast: either dry active yeast, in granules, to be rehydrated in approximately five times its weight in water at a temperature of 95°F–108°F (35°C–42°C), or instant dried yeast, sold in vacuum packs, which is mixed directly into the dough. These two types of yeast must be stored at room temperature in an airtight container. In the US, fresh yeast is usually sold in compressed cakes of either 0.6 ounces (³/₅ oz. [17g]) or 2 ounces (57g), and dried yeast in ¼-ounce (7g) sachets. In the UK, fresh yeast is a little harder to come by, being sold mainly in bakeries or health food shops; dried yeast is more readily available and comes in ¼-ounce (7g) sachets, or in larger tubs. Dried yeast may be substituted for fresh, but dried is approximately twice as strong as fresh. When converting from fresh to dry, multiply the quantity of fresh yeast specified by 0.4; inversely, if the recipe calls for dried yeast and you wish to use fresh, divide the quantity of dried yeast indicated by 4 and multiply by 10. If using dried yeast, you will also need to leave your dough longer to rise.
Baking powder, a chemical leavening agent, is a mixture of bicarbonate of soda or ammonium bicarbonate, tartaric acid or sodium aluminum phosphate, all combined with an inert filler, such as flour or starch. This raising agent is easy to use and is convenient for homemade baked goods.

Brioche dough ★★

This is a yeast dough that gets its lovely yellow color from the eggs and fat included. The proportion of each determines just how delicate the brioche is.

Ingredients

¹/₆ oz./¹/₃ cake (5 g) fresh (compressed) yeast
2 teaspoons milk or water
2 ¹/₂ cups (250 g) all-purpose flour
1 teaspoon (5 g) table salt
2 tablespoons (25 g) granulated sugar
3 eggs
1 stick (125 g) unsalted butter, softened*

Dilute the yeast in 2 teaspoons (10 ml) milk or water at room temperature. Sift the flour onto a flat surface and make a well in the center. Sprinkle the salt and sugar outside the well so that they do not come into direct contact with the yeast (1). Beat the eggs and incorporate them into the mixture using a rubber scraper (2).

Knead* the dough energetically to give it elasticity. You may use the hook attachment of an electric beater to do this. If you opt for the electric beater, use medium speed for about 10 minutes. Then knead in the butter at room temperature until it is completely incorporated and the dough is smooth (3), and place the dough in a mixing bowl.

Cover with plastic wrap or a slightly damp tea towel and leave to rise for 30 to 40 minutes at a temperature of 77°F-82°F (25°C-28°C) with a bowl of water. (If left uncovered the dough will form a crust.) When the dough has doubled in volume, remove from the bowl and turn out onto a lightly floured surface. Flatten it and fold into three. This is known as deflating (or knocking back in the UK). Form a ball and then make the desired shapes. Leave to rise again (covered with a damp tea towel or plastic wrap) until it reaches the top of the mold (4), which should take 30 to 40 minutes.

Preheat the oven to 375°F (190°C), or slightly hotter, if you know your oven well, as high heat gives the impetus for the best result. Bake the brioche. Allow about 40 minutes for a single brioche using this recipe, less for smaller ones. It should be well risen and the crust will have a nice golden color. Test for doneness: the tip of a knife should come out dry.

4

● **Chef's notes**

The dough will also rise at a lower temperature than that stated in the recipe but will take more time. For a faster rising, all the ingredients should be at room temperature. Never allow the salt to come into direct contact with the yeast as this will kill it.

● **Did you know?**

The brioche has a long history. There are numerous regional specialties in France, and it is one of the Viennoiserie pastries that has the most variations. Kugelhopf dough is closely related to brioche dough.

Brioches differ in both shape and filling. Some examples are:
• the Nanterre brioche, made of two parallel lines of balls in a rectangular baking pan;
• the braided brioche, made with two, three, or four strands;
• the Swiss brioche, rolled with raisins, a type of raisin loaf made with brioche dough and pastry cream;
• the Parisian brioche, which has a little "head," and is probably the best-known type, popular for breakfast;
• the Bordelaise brioche, a crown shape with candied fruit and incisions on the top.

❙ Recipe idea
French brioche toast and vanilla-scented stewed rhubarb ≫ p. 459

Savarin or baba dough ★★

This leavened dough differs from brioche dough: different quantities of egg and fat are used, and it is shaped differently. For the babas, you will need to soak the raisins in the rum one day before baking.

Ingredients

³/₅ oz. /1 cake (17 g) fresh (compressed) yeast
Scant ¹/₂ cup (100 ml) water
2 ³/₄ cups (250 g) cake flour
1 teaspoon (58 g) table salt
2 ¹/₂ teaspoons (10 g) sugar
2 eggs, room temperature, beaten
7 tablespoons (100 g) unsalted butter, plus a little extra to grease the pan
For rum babas, add
Generous ³/₄ cup (125 g) currants or raisins
3 tablespoons (50 ml) amber rum

Syrup

2 cups (500 ml) water
1 ¹/₄ cup (250 g) granulated sugar
³/₄ cup (200 ml) amber rum

A day ahead: If you are making babas, plump up the raisins by soaking them in the rum.

Prepare the yeast by diluting it in a scant ¹/₂ cup (100 ml) water at room temperature. Sift the flour and make a well in the center.

Sprinkle the salt outside the well so that it does not come into direct contact with the yeast.

Add the sugar, combine the ingredients using a scraper, and gradually pour in the beaten eggs.

Knead* the dough energetically to give it elasticity. You may do this with the hook attachment of an electric beater. Stop kneading when the dough detaches either from your fingertips or from the sides of the bowl.

Melt the butter (ensure it is warm, not hot) and mix it into the dough.

Cover with plastic wrap and set aside to rise for 30-40 minutes at a temperature of 77°F-82°F (25°C-28°C).

When the dough has doubled in volume, remove it from the bowl and turn out onto a lightly floured surface. Flatten it and fold into three, punching it to remove the air. This is known as deflating. If you are making rum babas, stir in the rum-soaked raisins.

Butter the baking pans* (1). Spoon the dough into a pastry bag, or use a scraper to fill the buttered pans halfway (2).

Leave to rise, covered with a cloth or plastic wrap, until the dough reaches the top of the pan.

Preheat the oven to 375°F (190°C). When the dough has doubled in volume, place the pan or pans in the oven. Bake for about 40 minutes; check for doneness with the tip of a knife, which should come out dry. Keep a close eye on your cakes as they bake: the crust must be a nice golden color.

Prepare a syrup (see page 169).

For best absorption of the syrup, prepare it while the cake cools, and pour it over while still warm. You may place your baba or savarin in a special grid, known as a *candissoire*, to glaze* it. This equipment is convenient for glazing with sugar.

● **Chef's notes**

The dough will also rise at a lower temperature than 77°F–82°F (25°C–28°C) but will take more time. For a faster rising, all the ingredients should be at room temperature.

Never allow the salt to come into direct contact with the yeast, as this will kill it.

If you cannot plump your raisins in cool liquid (rum, water, tea) a day ahead, soak them in tepid liquid for 2 hours.

● **Did you know?**

Savarins are completely open in the center, forming a crown shape (4), whereas baba molds are not, and are indented (3). Stanislaw Leszczynski (1677–1766), King of Poland and father-in-law of Louis XV, found the kugelhopf too dry for his liking, so thought it would be a good idea to soak it with rum. He is said to have given it the name of "baba" in honor of Ali Baba, the hero of One Thousand and One Nights, *since the book was a favorite of his. Auguste Jullien created the savarin in 1845 in homage to Brillat-Savarin, the renowned author of a work on gastronomy,* La Physiologie du goût *(The Physiology of Taste), published twenty years earlier.*

3

4

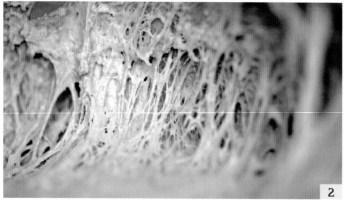

Bread dough ★★ 🎬

This is a dough that rises twice. It comes out of the oven with a lovely crust and a soft crumb.

Ingredients
⁴/₅ oz./1 ¹/₂ cakes (25.5 g) fresh (compressed) yeast
2 cups plus 1 scant ¹/₂ cup (600 ml) water
2 ¹/₄ lb. (1 kg) all-purpose flour
4 teaspoons (20 g) table salt
5 teaspoons (20 g) sugar (optional)

For best results, prepare this recipe using a kneading machine or the dough hook of an electric beater.
Dilute the yeast in tepid water, or slightly warm water, i.e., around 85°F (30°C).
Sift the flour onto a flat surface and make a well. Pour the yeast into the center. Add the sugar, if using. Knead* the dough on low speed for 3 minutes until it is smooth and slightly elastic. Continue kneading the dough at medium speed for about 10 minutes, adding the salt 5 minutes before the end.
Form the dough into a ball and cover the bowl with plastic wrap or a clean, slightly damp tea towel.
Heat the oven to a temperature of 77°F-82°F (25°C-28°C) and place a bowl of water at the bottom. Place the dough in the oven to rise until it doubles in volume (1, 2).
Split the dough into pieces and shape it to make individual rolls, loaves, or baguettes (3).
Cover the shaped dough and return to the oven until it again doubles in volume.
Make regular, shallow incisions, ¹/₁₀-¹/₅ inch (0.3-0.5 cm) deep at the top using the blade of a cutter or scissors. This will allow the bread to expand without cracking.
Preheat the oven to 450°F (230°C). When you are ready to place the bread in the oven, spray the bottom of the oven with water and immediately put the loaves in to bake. When baked, the crust will be golden brown and crisp.
Test for doneness by rapping on the bottom of the bread: this should make a hollow sound.
Remove the bread from the baking tray immediately so that it does not reabsorb any moisture.

● Chef's notes
The dough will rise also at a lower temperature than 77°F–82°F (25°C–28°C) but will take more time. For a faster rising, all the ingredients should be at room temperature.
Never allow the salt to come into direct contact with the yeast, as this will kill it.
Experiment with different types of flour, wholewheat or other, whatever you enjoy best. Should you want to add ingredients such as nuts, chopped onions, bacon bits, and so on, incorporate them when you split up the dough after the first rising.

● **Did you know?**

There are three main techniques in bread-making:
• the use of leaven or sourdough culture as a starter. This involves natural fermentation of flour and water at room temperature. It is a slow technique.
• the use of a poolish, or wet starter. This involves two stages: a dry flour-and-water paste (la détrempe) is added to a liquid paste that is fermented with yeast.
• the direct technique: the flour, water, and yeast are fermented together. This is the easiest and fastest of the methods.
Yeast is a live organism and its Latin name is Saccharomyces cerevisiae.

Sandwich loaf ★★

A yeast dough whose white crumb has fine, closely knit holes.

Ingredients (for one 15-inch [38-cm] loaf)
¼ cup (25 g) powdered milk
1 ¼ cups (300 ml) water, room temperature
¾ oz./1 ⅓ cakes (22 g) fresh (compressed) yeast
5 ½ cups (500 g) cake flour
5 teaspoons (20 g) sugar
5 ¼ tablespoons (75 g) unsalted butter, softened*, plus a little extra to grease the pan
2 ½ teaspoons table salt
Special equipment: a covered loaf pan (a Pullman pan), or aluminum foil, a baking sheet, and a weight to cover the loaf pan
For best results, make this recipe using a kneading machine or the dough hook of an electric beater.

Combine the milk powder with the water at room temperature and dilute the yeast in the liquid. Sift the flour, make a well in the center and pour in the liquid. Add the sugar.
Knead* the dough at low to medium speed until the mixture is smooth and slightly elastic (1).
Knead for about 5 minutes. Add the softened butter and the salt and knead for a further 5 minutes.
Shape the dough into a ball and cover it with a clean, damp cloth or plastic wrap.
Heat the oven to a temperature of 77°F-82 °F (25°C-28°C) and place a bowl of water at the bottom. Place the dough in the oven to rise until it doubles in volume.
Butter a baking pan. Now break the dough and punch it down to evacuate any air. Shape it to fit into the loaf pan.
Return it to the oven, cover with a damp cloth or plastic wrap, and leave it to double in volume with the cover slightly open (2). When it has reached this volume, preheat the oven to 425°F (220°C).
If you wish, you may make regular, shallow incisions, ¹⁄₁₀-¹⁄₅ inch (0.3-0.5 cm) deep at the top using the blade of a cutter or scissors. This will allow the bread to expand without cracking.
When you are ready to bake the bread, spray the bottom of the oven with water and immediately put the loaf in with the lid closed or the top of the pan covered to prevent the bread from rising. Bake for about 30-40 minutes.
Test for doneness by rapping on the bottom of the bread. It should make a hollow sound. Turn it out of the pan so that it does not reabsorb any moisture.

● **Did you know?**
A French sandwich loaf and brioched bread differ in that the brioched bread has more fat.
In France, sandwich loaves are used as a base for canapés, for toasts, and to make croutons. They are also used for croque monsieur, a popular toasted ham and cheese sandwich snack served in cafés.

● **Chef's notes**
The dough will also rise at a lower temperature than 77°F–82°F (25°C–28°C) but will take more time. For a faster rising, all the ingredients should be at room temperature.
Never allow the salt to come into direct contact with the yeast, as this will kill it.

Croissant dough ★★★

This quintessentially French breakfast treat is a yeast-based puff pastry, cut out into triangles and rolled from the base to the top, then shaped into a crescent. The same dough is used for many of the other pastries, collectively known as Viennoiseries, such as pains au chocolat (chocolate rolls) and pains au raisin (raisin rolls, usually made with pastry cream).

Ingredients (for about 25 croissants)

5 cups (500 g) all-purpose flour
2 teaspoons (10 g) table salt
1/4 cup (50 g) granulated sugar
1 1/4 cups (300 ml) whole milk, at room temperature
3/5 oz. cake (17 g) fresh (compressed) yeast
2 2/3 sticks (300 g) unsalted butter

Sift the flour and salt together and combine with the sugar. Dissolve the yeast in the milk. Make a well in the center of the flour. Rapidly work the liquid into the dry ingredients until the mixture is smooth. (If you are using an electric beater or heavy-duty mixer, this will take 4-5 minutes at medium speed.) Chill for about 20 minutes.

Then allow the dough to rise for 40 minutes in a warm, draft-free place at 77°F-86°F (25°-30°C). It should double in volume. Fold the dough over itself and rap to evacuate any air. Cover in plastic wrap and chill again for 30 minutes.

The butter should be at the same temperature as the dough. Roll the dough out into a cross shape, leaving the center thicker than the four sides, about 1/5 inch (5 mm).

Place the slab of butter between two sheets of parchment paper and flatten it with a rolling pin until it takes on a square shape. Place the butter in the center of the cross and wrap the four sides of the dough around it.

Roll out the dough until it forms a rectangle. The length should be three times the width.

Fold it into three, rotate the folded dough a quarter-turn and roll out again to form the same shape as previously. Repeat the folding and rotating operation three times, chilling between each stage. The dough will be folded a total of six times, just as for the basic puff pastry recipe.

Roll the dough out to a thickness of 1/5 inch (0.5 cm). Cut out triangles measuring about 4 inches at the base with sides about 6 inches long (10 cm base/15 cm sides). Roll up the croissants (**1, 2, 3**) starting from the base.

Leave to rise again for at least 40 minutes and bake for about 20 minutes at 350°F (180°C).

● Did you know?

Croissants were created in Austria, and introduced in France when Marie-Antoinette arrived, around 1770. With the Universal Exhibition of 1889, their popularity really took off.

1

2

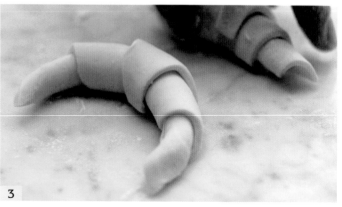

3

Batters with chemical raising agents

French fruit cake ★

In French, this loaf cake is simply known as *un cake*. It has less fruit than the traditional holiday or dark fruit cake baked in the English-speaking world, and a light batter.

Ingredients

1 ½ sticks (6 oz. or 175 g) unsalted butter, softened*, and a little extra for the pan
²/₃ cup (125 g) granulated sugar
½ teaspoon (3 g) fine sea salt
3 eggs
A few drops of fruit brandy or other strong alcohol
2 ½ cups (250 g) all-purpose flour
1 slightly heaped teaspoon (5 g) baking powder
7 oz. (200 g) candied fruit
3 ½ oz. (100 g) sultanas or raisins
A little flour or confectioners' sugar for coating the fruit

Place a baking tray in the center of the oven and preheat it to 400°F (200°C). Butter a loaf pan and/or line it with parchment paper.
Cream the butter, sugar, and salt together very thoroughly. Add the eggs, one by one, and combine. Flavor with fruit brandy.
Sift the flour and salt together into the batter and combine (1) until just mixed.
Coat the fruit lightly in flour or confectioners' sugar so that the pieces don't fall to the bottom of the pan during baking. Add the candied fruit and sultanas or raisins (2). Pour the batter into the loaf pan and place it on the baking tray.
Bake for 5 minutes, then reduce the temperature to 300°F (150°C). Bake for a further 40-50 minutes, depending on the size and shape of the cake pan, or until the tip of a knife comes out clean.
Turn out onto a rack to cool.

● Chef's notes

In general, allow 4 teaspoons (20g) of baking powder for 4 ¼ cups (1 kg) of flour.
Place the loaf pan on a well-heated baking pan in the oven, not on a rack.
You can also make savory versions of this recipe. Loaves with olives, diced* ham, onions, cheese, and bacon bits are popular in France at buffets, for picnics, or with drinks.

❚ Recipe idea
French fruit loaf ≫ p. 432

1

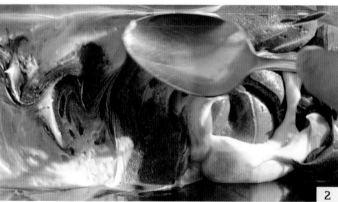

2

3

Marble cake ★★

Each portion of the batter is colored and flavored differently, then piped alternately into the loaf tin to create an attractive "marbled" effect.

Ingredients
1 stick (125 g) unsalted butter, softened*, plus extra for the mold
1 scant cup (125 g) confectioners' sugar
3 eggs
1 ³/₄ cups (160 g) cake flour
1 teaspoon (4 g) baking powder
A few drops of vanilla essence
Grated zest of 1 unsprayed or organic lemon
3 tablespoons (20 g) cocoa powder, unsweetened

Preheat the oven to 400°F (200°C). Place a baking tray on the middle rack on which to set the loaf pan for baking. Butter a loaf pan and/or line it with parchment paper.
Cream the softened butter with the sugar in a mixing bowl. Add the eggs, one by one, and mix thoroughly.
Sift the flour and baking powder together into the mixture and blend.
Divide the batter into two parts.
Flavor one half with the vanilla essence and lemon zest (the color should remain light).
Incorporate the cocoa powder into the other half.
Spoon the mixtures into two pastry bags. Pipe the two mixtures into the loaf pan alternately (1) and smooth the top with the back of a spoon (2).
Bake immediately for 5 minutes at 400°F (200°C), then lower the temperature to 300°F (150°C). Continue baking for 40-50 minutes depending on the size of the pan. Test for doneness: the tip of a knife should come out clean.
When done, turn out and cool on a rack (3).

● Chef's notes
For optimal flavor contrast and so that the batter does not become too liquid, use dry flavoring ingredients such as cocoa powder, and/or very concentrated essence.
Cakes that use chemical leavening agents should be baked as soon as the batter is in the loaf pan.

Madeleines ★

A raised dough that is baked to form small cakes in a special mold. The grooved base of each mold resembles a scallop shell. Nothing is added to the basic madeleine batter—madeleines are not filled, just flavored.

Ingredients (for about 30 standard-sized madeleines)
4 eggs
1 scant cup (175 g) granulated sugar
2 scant cups (175 g) cake flour
1 stick (125 g) unsalted butter, softened*, plus extra for molds
2 ¾ teaspoons (10 g) baking powder
A few drops of vanilla essence
Zest of ½ unsprayed or organic lemon or orange (optional)
Special equipment: a madeleine baking pan

Preheat the oven to 375°F (190°C). Place a baking tray large enough to hold your madeleine pan on the middle rack while the oven heats up. (If possible, use two trays, one on top of the other, to increase the amount of heat the madeleines come into contact with.) Whisk the eggs and sugar together until the mixture becomes pale and thick. Sift in the flour and combine. Then add the butter, followed by the baking powder, the vanilla essence, and the citrus zest if using. The consistency should be thick. Place the batter in the refrigerator; grease the molds and fill them to two-thirds with a pastry bag or a spoon (1).
Place the baking pan on the hot tray to ensure that the characteristic mound on top of the cakes forms. To ensure that the madeleines do not dry out, lower the oven temperature to 350°F (170°C) as soon as you place them in the oven, or spray a little water on the oven wall. Baking time will depend on the size of your madeleines. For the standard size, allow about 10 minutes. They are done when the top is a nice golden-brown color. Remove from the oven, test for doneness, and turn out from the pan immediately. Leave to cool on a rack.

● **Chef's notes**
It is best to place the filled madeleine baking pan on a tray that is already hot in the oven.
Turn them out of their molds as soon as you remove them from the oven so that no condensation forms between the cakes and the mold.

● **Did you know?**
The first madeleines are commonly believed to have been baked by Madeleine Paumier at the Château of Commercy in the Lorraine region around 1730. She made them for Stanislaw Leszczynski, King of Poland and father-in-law of Louis XV, who later made them famous.
The tops of the cakes are shaped like a scallop shell, a symbol of the pilgrims' route on Saint James's Way, El Camino de Santiago.

1

Eggs

How to choose eggs

The color of the eggshell—white or brown—depends on the breed of the hen, and is not a result of the hen's feed.

An egg is composed of:
• the white (1 oz. or 28 g on average): 87 percent water, 11 percent albumen;
• the yolk (0.98 oz. or 20 g on average): 50 percent water, 31 percent lipids, and 16 percent protein.

Eggs are not only a good, reasonably priced source of nutrition, delicious served on their own as in the recipes set out here, they are also a multipurpose foodstuff with a wide range of uses. Well beaten, they help cakes and soufflés rise; whisked into sauces, they prevent them from separating; they also play a key role in pastry making.

Eggs must always be stored in the refrigerator once they are bought, preferably in their cartons and with their larger end facing upward. For optimal quality, both in terms of taste and culinary use, use them within a week of their laying date, but if their shells are in perfect condition you may store them for up to one month.

Hard-boiled eggs ★

Ingredients
2 fresh eggs per person
A few drops of vinegar

Bring water to boil in a saucepan or pot. Add a few drops of vinegar just as you immerse the eggs (1). Allow them to cook for 11 to 12 minutes from the moment the water starts to boil again.
Remove them from the water and cool immediately under cold running water.
Remove the shells, taking care to remove the thin membrane covering the egg along with the shells (2, 3, 4).
Rinse the eggs to remove any remaining pieces of shell.
If storing them, leave them still slightly damp, on a tray or plate, covered with plastic wrap, in the refrigerator.

● Chef's note
Keep an eye on cooking times for eggs; an overcooked egg will have a greenish streak around the yolk.

❙ Recipe idea
Salad Niçoise ≫ p. 395

Soft-boiled eggs (*oeufs mollets*) ★

See hard-boiled eggs (p. 39). Use the same method but shorten the cooking time so that the yolk does not cook and remains runny.

Cooking time
5 to 6 minutes from the time the water starts to boil again. Shell the eggs before serving.

Recipe idea
Soft-boiled eggs on a bed of artichokes with eggplant caviar ›› p. 392

Lightly boiled eggs in their shells (*oeufs à la coque*) ★

See soft-boiled eggs (above).
Lightly boiled eggs are served in their shells to crack open at the table, hence their French name (coque means "shell").

Cooking time
3 minutes from the time the water starts to boil again.

● **Chef's note**
Do not bring the water to a fast boil as this causes the eggs to move around too much. If they come into contact with one another, or with the sides of the pot, they may crack, causing the white to escape during the cooking process.

3

1

2

Shirred eggs ★

Ingredients
2 fresh eggs per person
A little butter
Fine sea salt, white pepper

If you are using the traditional oven method, preheat the oven
to just below 195°F (90°C). Butter two egg dishes (they should
have small handles) using a pastry brush. Use one dish per
person (1). Otherwise, melt the butter in a frying pan.
Season the cooking dishes (2).
Break the eggs carefully, one by one, into the dish or frying
pan, ensuring that you do not break the yolks. If using dishes,
place two eggs in each.
Cook gently without coloring the white. It should coagulate,
and the yolk should remain runny (3).

● **Chef's notes**
*The low temperature (below 195°F [90°C]) of the oven ensures that
the eggs will not dry out or form unsightly bubbles.*
*Brush your eggs with butter just before serving to give them an
attractive sheen.*
*Season the dish or pan rather than the top of the eggs so that
there are no white or black spots.*

Scrambled eggs ★★ 🎬

Ingredients
2 fresh eggs per person
2 teaspoons (10 g) butter, cubed, and/or cream, plus a little butter
for the pan

To garnish: chopped fresh herbs, mushrooms, chopped tomatoes.
Salt, pepper

Break the eggs into a mixing bowl. Season and beat them with
a fork or a whisk.
Melt some butter in the pan over low heat. Pour the eggs into
the hot pan. Stir constantly with a spatula or wooden spoon.
The last moments of cooking are crucial. The eggs should not
be completely cooked, so remove the skillet from the heat
and add the butter cubes and/or a drizzle of cream to stop the
cooking. The final texture should be creamy.
Add your garnish and serve immediately.

● **Chef's note**
*You can also add the garnish (herbs, chopped tomatoes, or
minced meat) before you cook the eggs if you prefer.*

❙ **Recipe idea**
❙ Scrambled eggs and a mini-ratatouille >> p. 403

Eggs en cocotte ★

Ingredients

A little butter, melted
Fresh eggs

To garnish: port sauce, sautéed mushrooms, tomato sauce, etc.
Salt, pepper
Special equipment: ramekins, a large flameproof dish or pan

Grease the ramekins with the butter using a pastry brush (1).
Season the bottom of the ramekins with salt and pepper.
Break the eggs carefully, one into each ramekin, making sure you do not break the yolks (2).
Line a shallow flameproof baking dish with parchment paper and place the ramekins in this.
Half fill the dish with water.
Begin cooking the eggs on low heat, until the water simmers.
Remove from the heat when the white is coagulated, but the yolk still creamy (3).
Pour your sauce over the eggs, or add the garnish, and serve immediately.

● Chef's notes

The egg white should not be colored at all, and the yolk should not be covered by a dry film. It must be shiny, and this is why the result is called miroir—mirror—*in French.*
Eggs en cocotte may be accompanied by many sauces and side dishes. They are a real treat for breakfast.
Quail eggs are also excellent when cooked using this method.

1

2

3

Deep-fried eggs ★★

Ingredients
Oil for frying
Very fresh eggs
Special equipment: oil thermometer
Accompany with: bacon, eggplant caviar, fried mushroom, etc.

Heat the oil in a deep pan to a temperature of 350°F (180°C). Check the temperature with a thermometer.
Break the eggs, one by one, into separate ramekins or small cups. Be careful not to break the yolks (1).
Use two spatulas, one in each hand, to gently immerse each egg into the hot oil. Roll them gently so that they maintain an oval shape in the pan (2).
When the egg turns a nice light yellow color, remove it from the pan with a slotted spoon (3). Repeat the procedure with the remaining eggs. Drain on kitchen paper. Place on the plate with the accompaniment of your choice and serve immediately.

● Chef's notes
These eggs should be cooked only at the last minute, just before serving.
Be careful of the hot oil, which may splatter during cooking.
Only cook one egg at a time.

Eggs in aspic ★★

Serves 4

Aspic powder for 1 scant cup (200ml) aspic
4 fresh eggs
To garnish: a slice of ham, leek greens, tomato skin, black olives,
carrot, long turnip, etc.

Prepare the aspic according to the directions.
Bring salted water to the boil and poach the eggs for about 3
minutes (see p. 47).
Drain them and allow them to cool. Trim the eggs so that the
edges are regular.
Prepare the differently colored elements you will be using for
decoration, either raw or cooked (1).
Pour a thin layer of aspic into the bottom of the ramekins and
put them in the refrigerator to set. Make sure the dishes are
placed perfectly horizontally.
To decorate, place the various elements on the set aspic,
bearing in mind that this will be uppermost when the dish is
unmolded.
Pour in another thin layer of aspic and chill to set.
Place the egg at the center of the ramekin and pour in the
remaining aspic.
Return to the refrigerator to set.
Dip the ramekins briefly in boiling water to unmold them.
Arrange attractively on a plate (2).

1

2

1

2

Omelet ★★

Ingredients
2-3 fresh eggs per person
A little butter or oil for the pan
A little clarified butter* to brush the omelet
To garnish: chopped fresh herbs, cheese, sautéed mushrooms,
slow-cooked bell peppers with tomatoes, etc.
Salt, pepper

Take 2-3 eggs per person (1) and break into a mixing bowl.
Season with salt and pepper and whisk with a fork.
If you are making a flat omelet, add the garnish at this stage.
Melt a little butter or pour the oil into a hot pan and pour the
mixture in. Keeping the heat high, cook the omelet, drawing
the cooked edges towards the center so the still-liquid part can
cook. The texture should be creamy.
Place a plate over the pan and turn it over with a rapid
movement. Slip the other side of the omelet into the pan to
finish cooking.
Brush with clarified butter for a nice shine and serve on a plate.
If you are making a rolled omelet, heat the pan with butter or
oil and pour the beaten eggs in. Cook over high heat, drawing
the cooked edges towards the center so that the still-liquid eggs
can cook. The texture should be creamy.
Add the garnish (2), tilt the pan downward (handle upward)
and, using a fork, roll the omelet downward over itself. Brush
with clarified butter for a nice shine and serve on a plate.

● **Chef's note**
*The best omelet is a pale color. When omelets are overdone, they
become dry and rubbery.*

● **Did you know?**
*Omelets and hard-boiled eggs are probably the oldest dishes
made only with eggs. Mention is made of them in a book written
in 1398,* Le Mesnagier de Paris *(The Good Wife's Guide, translated
by Gina L. Greco and Christine M. Rose, Ithaca: Cornell University
Press, 2009), a medieval treatise for women.*

❘ **Recipe idea**
❘ Rolled mushroom omelet ›› p. 259

Poached eggs ★★

Ingredients
1 fresh egg per person
A few drops of vinegar

Bring the water to the boil (1).
Break the eggs, one by one, into individual ramekins. Take care not to break the yolks (2).
Add the vinegar to the water and gently slip the eggs in. Use a skimmer to shape the white as evenly as possible.
Cook for about 3 minutes.
Remove with a skimmer, refresh* very briefly under cold water, drain (3), and trim so that the edges are nice and neat.

● **Did you know?**
Eggs may be poached in red wine (the dish is called oeufs meurette *or* oeufs à la bordelaise*) as well as in milk.*
Poached eggs go well with very different accompaniments, from mushrooms, bacon bits, and croûtons to shellfish and salad.

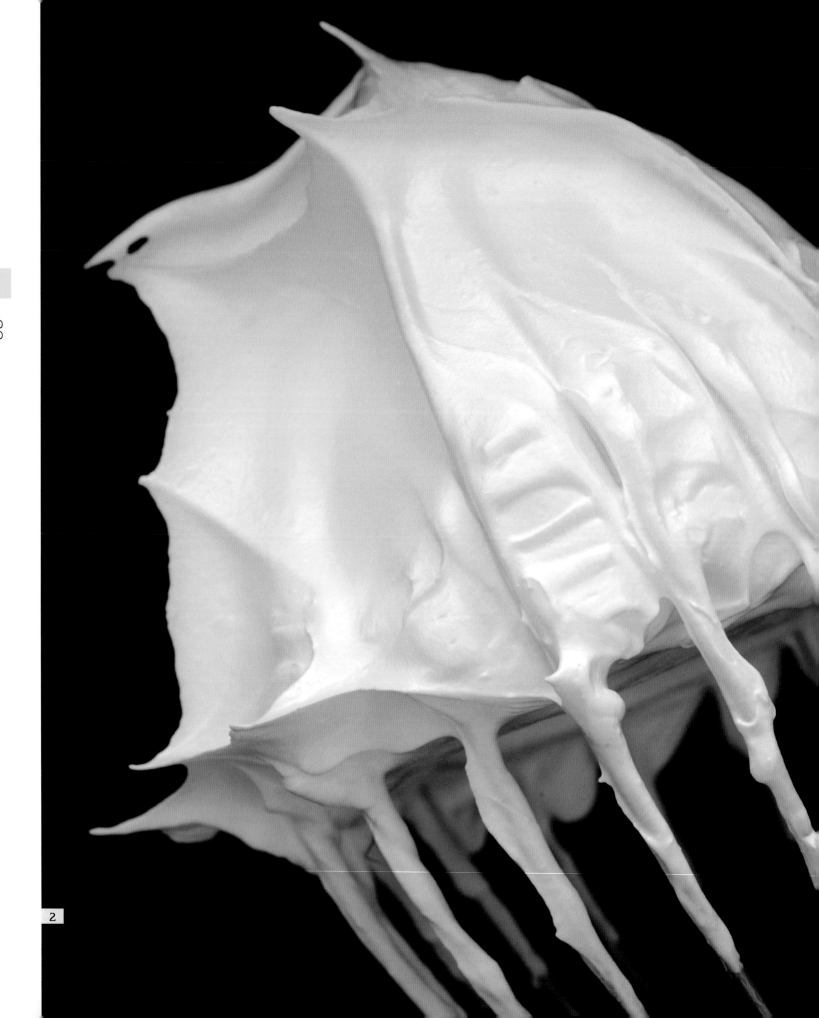

French meringue ★

This is also known as simple meringue. It is prepared cold, that is to say without cooking the sugar, and then usually baked.
French meringue is used to make plain or flavored meringues, and for the shells that hold ice cream in the dessert, vacherin.
The French meringue technique is also used to make mousses: the eggs are whisked stiffly and sugar is added to make them very firm and shiny.

Ingredients
4 egg whites
Scant ¹/₂ cup (80 g) sugar
1 pinch salt

First, liquefy the egg whites by beating them in a semi-spherical bowl with a pinch of salt.
Whisk them energetically, making sure to lift the beaters or whisk high to incorporate as much air as possible.
Briskly whisk the sugar in with a circular movement so that the mixture takes on a firm texture.
The meringue must be compact and smooth, and peaks must form when you lift it up with the whisk.

Recipe ideas
Floating islands with spun caramel ›› p. 463
Iced blackberry vacherin ›› p. 498

Italian meringue ★ ★ 🎬

This is a hot preparation, made with cooked sugar, and is widely used for decoration because of its firm texture. It is also used for making ice cream, and is an essential component of almond macaroons.

Ingredients
2 tablespoons (30 ml) water
²/₃ cup (120 g) granulated sugar
4 egg whites
1 pinch of salt
Special equipment: sugar thermometer

To prepare the syrup: heat the water and sugar in a saucepan (1). Meanwhile, put the egg whites in the bowl of a heavy-duty mixer, ensuring it is perfectly clean and dry first.
When the temperature of the syrup reaches 230°F (110°C), begin beating the egg whites with a pinch of salt. When the temperature of the syrup reaches 243°F-250°F (117°C-120°C), take the pan off the heat and start pouring it in a slow, steady stream into the egg whites. Continue beating until the meringue has cooled down completely. It will be dense and shiny, and will form many small peaks (2).

Recipe ideas
Lemon meringue tartlets ›› p. 435
Baked Alaska ›› p. 502
Iced banana soufflé ›› p. 501

Swiss meringue ★

This is a hot preparation made over a bain-marie*. It is firm meringue used for the small pastries known as rochers (rocks) and for decoration.
The origins of this dish are disputed, but one version claims that it was invented in 1720 in the town of Meiringen, Switzerland, giving meringues their name.

Ingredients
4 egg whites
1 pinch of salt
1/2 cup (100 g) granulated sugar
Special equipment: sugar thermometer

Prepare a pot half filled with hot water to make a bain-marie. The water should be between 122°F and 131°F (50°C-55°C) when you are ready to use it.
Liquefy the whites by beating them with a pinch of salt in a semi-spherical bowl. Pour the sugar in and whisk energetically, making sure you lift the whites high into the air. When the mixture begins to foam, place the bowl over the hot water. Whisk continuously until the mixture thickens, increases to three times its volume, and becomes shiny. At this point, the meringue should be at a maximum temperature of 113°F (45°C). When it reaches this temperature, remove it from the heat and continue to whisk until it cools down completely to room temperature.

Sabayon (*Zabaglione*) ★★

Ingredients
6 egg yolks
Generous 1/2 cup (150 ml) liquid, for example water, liqueur, or wine
2/3 cup (125 g) sugar (optional)

Place the egg yolks in a saucepan. Add the liquid and sugar (1), if using, and whisk energetically.
Place the saucepan over a low heat (low flame or hot water bath). Whisk the mixture continuously until it is creamy (2).

● **Did you know?**
Sweet sabayon is excellent with strawberries or as a base for a fruit gratin.
Savory sabayon pairs well with asparagus and fish.

❚ **Recipe idea**
Strawberry gratin with sabayon ›› p. 475

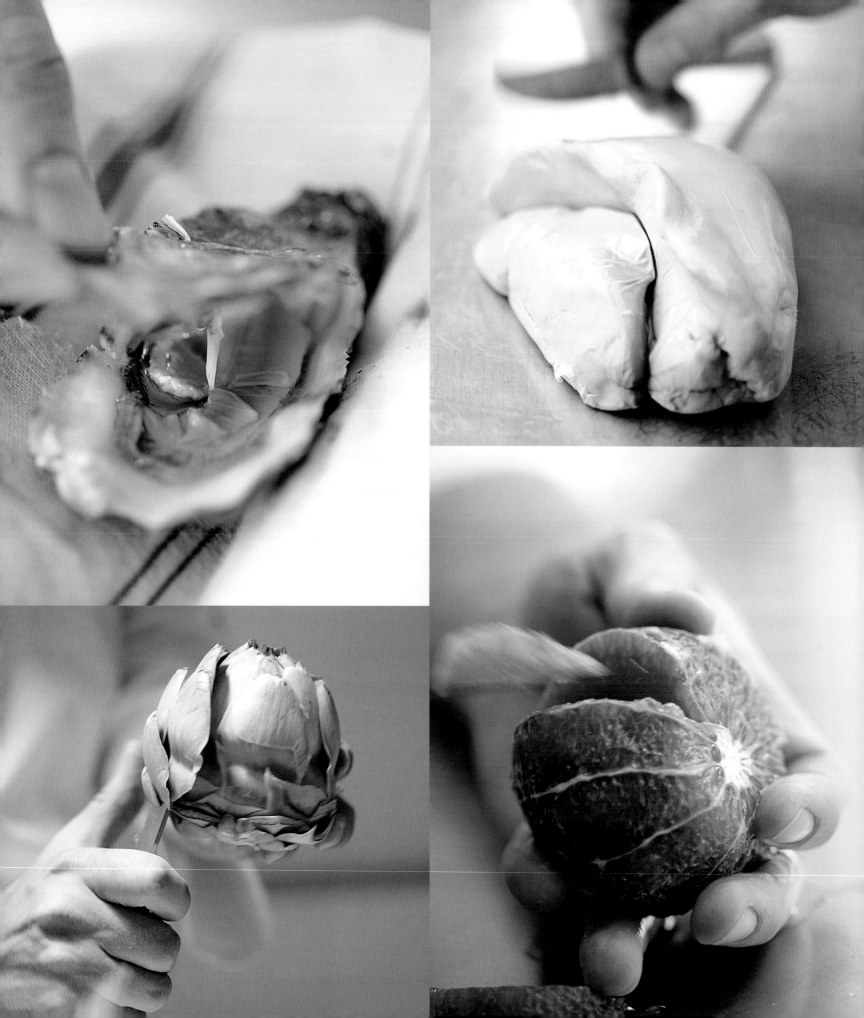

Garnishes

Fish, shellfish, and crustaceans

Meat and offal

How to prepare
garnishes, fish, and meat

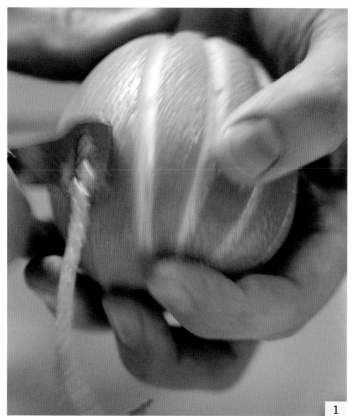

Canelling ★

Use this for decorative elements and aromatic ingredients (for example in a court bouillon).

Use this technique for carrots, zucchini, citrus fruits, and so on.
Wash, dry, and trim the ends of the fruit or vegetable. Using a canelle knife, make regular incisions lengthwise along the fruit or vegetable (1, 2, 3).

Dicing* ★★ 🎬

It is important to dice regularly to obtain pieces that are uniformly sized. This ensures even cooking.
If, however, you do find you have some large pieces, do not chop them any further as they will lose their juice and flavor.

Use this technique for shallots, large onions, and so on.
Cut the product in half through its thickest part, i.e. vertically, from top to bottom, to the root (1).
Taking each half separately, slice regularly lengthwise, but stop before you reach the base. (2).
Make two or three horizontal incisions, depending on the thickness of the product, without going as far as the root (3).
Hold the vegetable firmly and slice finely from top to root through the other cuts to create dice.

Chopping tomatoes ★★

The technique of rough chopping involves chopping food such as parsley, nuts, etc.

Remove the tomato skin using the boiling water technique (see p. 61), not forgetting to make a cross incision at the base. Cut in half from the stem to the cross you have made. Remove the seeds by gently squeezing each half in the palm of your hand. Cut and cube the tomato halves into the size that suits your recipe.

❗ **Recipe idea**
Provençal-flavored sardine *tartes fines* ›› p. 280

1

2

3

Simple slicing
(*émincer à la paysanne*) ★

This cutting technique is used for several aromatic bases. Depending on the vegetable, you can make shapes such as squares and triangles.

Use this technique for leeks, carrots, turnips, and so on.
Cut the vegetable into chunks, depending on its length (1).
Slice it lengthwise in two, or four if it is thick.
Hold the vegetable firmly and cut finely at right angles to the slices (2).

1

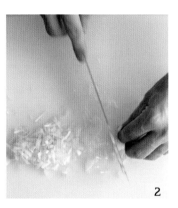

2

Cutting into rings
(*émincer en bracelets*) ★

Rings are fine cuts, used as garnish and as an aromatic base. It is important to keep to the cooking time specified in the recipe so that they maintain their shape.

Use this technique for large onions, shallots, and so on.
Choose a vegetable with a nice round shape.
Hold it firmly and cut regular fine slices. (1)
Detach the rings (2, 3).

● **Did you know?**
You can also use a Japanese mandolin to prepare rings.

Shredding (chiffonade) ★

Use for leafy vegetables such as lettuce, spinach, and cabbage.
Remove the central part (rib or stalk) (1) and place several leaves on top of one another (2).
Fold them over themselves.
Shred them as finely as you need for your recipe (3).

● **Chef's note**

Use the shredded vegetables as soon as you have cut them, whether raw or cooked, because they will wilt rapidly.

Recipe ideas
Creamed lettuce soup (*velouté Choisy*) ≫ p. 396
Sweetbread vol-au-vents with cider and apples ≫ p. 272

Cutting round slices ★

Use this technique for vegetables such as carrots, zucchini, and long turnips.
Slice rounds to the thickness required for your recipe using either a Japanese mandolin (1) or a vegetable slicing knife (2).

● **Did you know?**

The thickness of the slices depends on whether you are using the vegetable as an aromatic base or for garnish. If using several vegetables, it's best to cook them separately and combine them when you serve them, as each one has a specific cooking time and a particular taste that should be preserved.

Recipe ideas
Provençal shoulder of lamb and vegetable *tian* ≫ p. 359

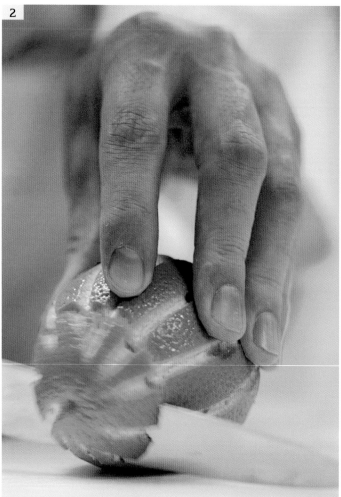

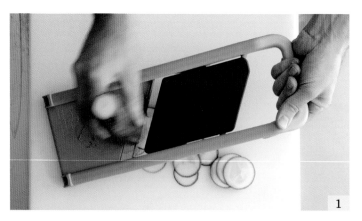

Cutting on the oblique ★

This technique is widely used for garnishes of mixed vegetables.

Use for vegetables such as carrots, zucchini, and long turnips.
Cut or slice the vegetables at a slight angle. Make regular slices of a thickness suitable for the recipe you will be preparing. Use either a Japanese mandolin (1) or a vegetable slicing knife (2). For an added attractive touch, canelle the product beforehand.

1

2

Peeling ★

Use this technique for fruit and vegetables such as carrots, large onions, asparagus, apples, and pears.
Remove the skin from a raw fruit or vegetable using a paring knife, a double-bladed vegetable peeler, or a peeler with a single blade.
Special care should be paid when preparing asparagus, black salsify (black oyster plant), and white salsify (white oyster plant).
Hold the vegetable firmly at its base.
Asparagus should be peeled from the tip towards the base, which should then be broken off. Asparagus is a fragile vegetable, so tie a bunch together and trim them before cooking so that they are all the same height.

● **Chef's notes**
Lemon juice should be squeezed over certain fruit, such as apples and pears, as soon as they are peeled so that they do not go brown. Potatoes should simply be left in water to await cooking.

Quartering button mushrooms ★

Use this technique for button mushrooms.
Separate the stalk from the cap by cutting just below the cap
(1).
Cut the cap in half, holding the blade of the knife at an angle.
This will ensure that you have an esthetically pleasing cut, not
one that is too straight or severe.
Rotate the cap a quarter turn and cut at an angle as before (2).

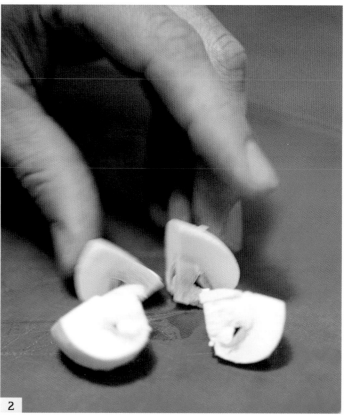

● **Chef's note**
*Squeeze a little lemon juice over the cut mushrooms so that they
do not darken. Even with the lemon juice, it is important to use
them rapidly.*

❘ **Recipe idea**
❘ Rolled mushroom omelet >> p. 259

Rubbing with kosher salt ★

Use this technique for Chinese artichokes.
Top and tail the Chinese artichokes. Place them on a tea cloth
with a handful of kosher salt. Wrap them up in the cloth and
rub them briskly.
Kosher salt eliminates the thin skin and any remaining earth
between the folds.
Rinse well under running water.

● **Chef's note**
*You may also leave the Chinese artichokes to soak overnight,
brush them, and then top and tail them.*

1

2

3

1

2

Zigzag cut (Vandyke technique) ★

This technique is mainly used for citrus fruits, but is very similar to fruit and vegetable sculpture.

Wash and dry the citrus fruit and slice off the two ends (1). Insert the blade of the knife at the widest point of the fruit, and make your way around the circumference by creating zigzag incisions. The size of the angle will depend on the number of zigzags you wish to make (2).
Continue round the fruit, cutting right into the center so the halves will come apart easily.
Separate the two halves carefully and remove the pips (3).

● Chef's note
It is possible to form many shapes—let your imagination inspire you.

Julienne strips ★★

Julienne strips must be very finely sliced. Julienned citrus zests may be up to 1 ¹/₂ in. (4 cm) in length, but they should always be very fine.

Use this technique for vegetables such as carrots, turnips, the whites of leeks, and pickled cucumbers.
Thinly slice the vegetable using a Japanese mandolin (1). You may use a slicing knife instead.
Place the slices one on top of another. Then cut very fine strips with a slicing knife (2).

Special case: the leek
First, cut chunks about 4 in. (10 cm) long. Cut them in half lengthwise.
Flatten the halves well so that you can place them on top of one another. Slice fine strips lengthwise with the same slicing knife.

● Chef's note
To prepare citrus zests, remove the skin with a double-bladed vegetable peeler (see below for the technique of preparing segments) and then slice it very finely.

❘ Recipe idea
Mixed garden vegetables >> p. 391

Scooping ★

Use this technique for fruits and vegetables such as potatoes, apples, melon, turnips, carrots, zucchini, and so on. Place the scoop on the surface of the fruit or vegetable and press it right in, pivoting it as you do so. This will form a ball that you can then scoop out.

● **Did you know?**
Apple balls make a nice change from apple slices on a tart, and may also be used to garnish a poultry dish.

❗ **Recipe idea**
Fish papillotes with vegetable scoops >> p. 295

Citrus segments ★

A fan of citrus segments and other cut fruits makes a spectacular platter, or you can use citrus segments as decoration on a dish.

Wash and dry your fruit. Cut off the top and bottom of the fruit, and stand it firmly on one of the cut ends.
Use a knife with a flexible edge. Hold it at an angle so that it follows the curve of the fruit. Make sure that all the pith is removed from the outside of the fruit (it tastes bitter and looks unattractive).
Using the same knife, remove the segments of flesh between the white membranes.
Arrange the segments and drizzle with the juice that has come out from the fruit.

● **Chef's note**
The segments of citrus fruit are very fragile once they are cut, and do not hold together when cooked.

❗ **Recipe idea**
Duckling à l'orange with sautéed potatoes and artichokes >> p. 333

Peeling using hot water ★ 🎬

Use this technique for fruits such as plums, tomatoes, almonds, and peaches.
Remove the stalk of the fruit (1) and make a cross-shaped incision at the other end with a kitchen knife.
Prepare a saucepan of boiling water and drop the fruit in for about ten seconds, or until the skin begins to peel off at the cross incision (2).
Remove from the water using a slotted spoon (3) and place immediately in a bowl of ice water. The difference in temperature will prevent the fruit from cooking further (4).

Peel with a paring knife (5) and place on paper towel to drain any excess water.

● Chef's note
The skin may be kept to use for decoration (fried), and the seeds can be added to a stock.

🍴 **Recipe idea**
Provençal-flavored sardine *tartes fines* ›› p. 280

Peeling using oil ★★

Use this technique for bell peppers.
Preheat the oven to 480°F-520°F (250°C-270°C), or to the maximum temperature your oven will reach.
Place the bell peppers on a baking tray and drizzle with oil (1). Cook until the skin begins to separate from the flesh and form bubbles.
Remove from the oven; allow to cool sufficiently that you are able to handle them, and remove the skin using a paring knife (2). Don't wait until they are completely cool as the skin will be hard to remove.

1

2

3

1

2

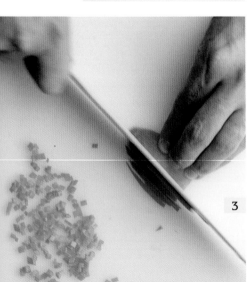
3

4

Cutting into batons (*jardinière*) ★

Use this technique for vegetables such as carrots and turnips.

Cut chunks about 4 in. (10 cm) long (**1**). Place the chunks lengthwise against the mandolin to make slices $^1/_6$-$^1/_5$ in. (4 mm-5 mm) thick (**2**).

Place the slices one above another and cut sticks about $^1/_6$-$^1/_5$ in. (4-5 mm) wide (**3**).

● **Chef's note**

Use good-sized vegetables to facilitate cutting.

❘ **Recipe idea**
❘ Roasted rack of lamb with garden vegetables ›› p. 368

Fine cubes (*brunoise*)* ★

Use this technique for all fruits and vegetables with firm flesh.

Cut chunks about 4 in. (10 cm) long (**1**).

Place the chunks lengthwise against the mandolin to make slices that are about $^1/_{10}$ in. (2-3 mm) thick (**2**).

Place the slices above one another and cut sticks about $^1/_{10}$ in. (2-3 mm) wide (**3**).

Cut them into regularly shaped $^1/_{10}$-in. (2-3-mm) cubes.

● **Did you know?**

To make a macédoine (mixed diced vegetables or fruit), use the method above for brunoise but make slightly larger cubes, with cuts about $^1/_5$ in. (4-5 mm).*

A mirepoix is a mixture of vegetables such as carrots, onions, and celery, in larger cubes measuring about $^1/_2$ in.–$^2/_3$ in. (1.5 cm) and often used as an aromatic base.*

❘ **Recipe idea**
❘ Rabbit terrine with pistachios and exotic fruit chutney ›› p. 260

Cutting wafers ★

Use this technique for vegetables such as potatoes, turnips, zucchini (courgettes), and celery root (celeriac).
Place a medium-sized vegetable on a mandolin with a wavy blade (1).
Each time you scrape the vegetable against the blade, rotate it a quarter-turn to obtain the fine open-work result (2).

● **Chef's note**
Rinse the wafers well, then dab them to dry thoroughly so that they don't stick together when fried.

❙ **Recipe idea**
Grilled cockerel and *diable* sauce ›› p. 348

1

2

3

4

Turning vegetables ★★ 🎬

Use this technique for vegetables such as potatoes, turnips, zucchini (courgettes), and carrot.

Cut chunks and then cut them lengthwise into two or four pieces, depending on the size (1, 2).

Hold the vegetable piece firmly between the thumb and index of one hand and, with the other, use a paring knife or a special shaping knife to shape curved sides, like the oval shape of a rugby or American football ball (3, 4).

● Chef's notes

For zucchini (courgettes), keep one side flat.

When using turning vegetables as a garnish, allow seven to nine pieces per person.

Generally, the trimmings are puréed to be used for another dish, so that there's no wastage.

Special case: the artichoke

Break off the stems of the artichokes. Remove the outside leaves using a knife with a short, rigid blade (1, 2).

Trim the base neatly to remove any traces of green–these parts are very bitter (3).

Trim the head an inch or so (a few centimeters) from the bottom, where the feathery "choke" is.

Remove the choke using a spoon or scoop if need be (4). You can also remove it after cooking.

Sprinkle the entire artichoke bottom with lemon juice so it does not oxidize. You may also tie a slice of lemon to the base for cooking (5).

Reserve the bottoms in water with lemon juice until you need them. To cook: in a *blanc* (salted water with lemon juice and flour) (p. 106) or braised (p. 98).

🥄 Recipe idea

Soft-boiled eggs on a bed of artichokes with eggplant caviar ›› p. 392

1

2

3   4   5

Fish, shellfish, and crustaceans

What to keep in mind when selecting seafood

A checklist for fresh, whole fish:
• the eyes must be shiny, bulging, and transparent; the gills should be damp and bright pink or red.
• the scales must be shiny and adhere to the flesh. They should be covered with a transparent, film of mucus.
• the smell should be fresh and inoffensive—not "fishy."

A whole fish often yields little flesh.
For fish such as John Dory, sea bream, and flat varieties, there may be as much as two-thirds wastage. The same is true of shellfish.

Type	Variety	Characteristics	Substitutes	Recipes
Cod Family	Cod	Dense white flesh, mild flavor	Halibut, Pollock, Hake, Haddock	Puréed salt cod with mashed potatoes (p. 296)
	Pollock/Black cod	Firm white flesh	Cod, Haddock, Halibut, Hake	Pollack fillets *bonne femme* (p. 303)
	Whiting	Delicate sweet flavor	Cod, Pollock, any white fish	Fish papillotes with vegetable scoops (p. 295)
Bony	Gurnard	Firm white dense flesh	Cod	Bouillabaisse (p. 307)
	Salmonette/Dogfish/Rock Salmon/Huss	Well flavored firmish pink flesh	Any firm white fish	Dogfish stew in red wine with brussel sprouts (p. 288)
Freshwater	Trout	Pink tender flesh, mild nutty flavor	Salmon	Trout with almonds (p. 291)
	Salmon	Pink oily flesh, distinctive flavor	Trout	Grilled salmon steaks with braised fennel (p. 308)
	Pike and Pickerel	Sweet and fine-textured flesh	Any firm white fish	Pike quenelles and crayfish sauce (p. 263)
	Sea Bass	White flesh with a medium sweet flavor and medium texture	Sea Bream, Snapper	Sea Bass in a salt crust (p. 300)
Small	Sole	Mild, buttery sweet flavor	Halibut, Lemon Sole, Flounder, Plaice	Sole meunière and potatoes cocotte (p. 320)
	Plaice	Mild sweet flavor and soft texture	Dab, Flounder, Sole	Plaice *goujonnettes* with sauce tartare (p. 315)
Large	Turbot	Bright white firm flesh, delicate flavor	Halibut, Dover Sole	Turbot poached in cardamom-flavored milk with hollandaise sauce (p. 319)
	John Dory/St Pierre	Nutty, sweet flavor with flaky meat	Sole, Turbot, Halibut	Sautéed fillets of John Dory with seaweed (p. 313)
Meaty	Monkfish	Firm, meaty texture	Lobster	Bacon-wrapped braised monkfish (p. 312) Monkfish medallions *à l'américaine* and rice pilaf (p. 323)
	Tuna	Oily, rich dark pink flesh, meat-like texture	Swordfish, Marlin, or other firm-fleshed fish	Tuna rillettes with horseradish p. 251)
Thin-bodied	Sea Bream	Medium sweet flavor, texture similar to Bass	Sea Bass, Snapper	Aniseed-flambéed* sea bream (p. 292)
	Mackerel	Pale and firm oily flesh	Herring, Sardines	Mackerel in *escabèche* (p. 316)
Long-bodied	Eel	Firm flesh, distinctive flavor	Alaskan or Canadian Black Cod	Rockfish soup (p. 268)
Other	Anchovy	Very strong salty flavor (preserved)	Sardines (if using fresh)	Salad niçoise (p. 395)

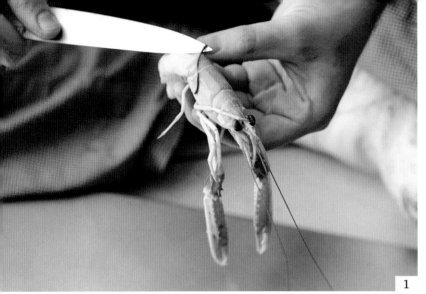

Shelling crustaceans ★★

The procedure is far easier when the crustacean is still alive.

Use this technique for shellfish such as langoustine and crayfish.
Hold the crustacean in the palm of your hand with the abdomen facing upward.
Remove the central intestinal vein by pulling on the central part of the tail (1).
Use a pair of pointed scissors to make an incision all along the membrane of the abdomen.
Pull the abdominal shell away from the flesh and remove it (see photo 2 for each step).
Rinse, drain, and chill.

● Chef's note
You may remove the gut or intestinal vein after you shell the crustacean: make a small incision on the back to expose it.

❚ Recipe ideas
Langoustine and pineapple skewers » p. 299

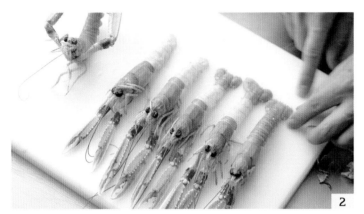

Preparing monkfish ★★

In French, there is a specific name for the whole fish (*baudroie*) and another name for the edible part of the monkfish (*lotte*). You won't see a whole fish at the fish seller's, but the cheeks are considered a delicacy and are sometimes available for sale.

Firmly grasp the black skin and use a knife to remove it, starting from the tail and moving toward the top of the bone (1, 2).
Cut the fillets away from the spine, and remove the thin membranes and violet-colored parts of the tails (these are very elastic) using a sole filleting knife (3).
Trim the rest of the tail so that it is as white as possible.

❚ Recipe idea
Monkfish medallions *à l'américaine* and rice pilaf » p. 323

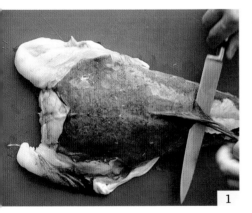
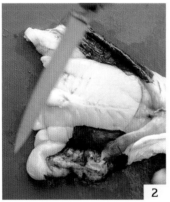

Cutting fish steaks ★

Use this technique for large fish such as salmon, conger or sea eel, and hake.

Take a prepared fish (scaled, gutted, fins removed, and washed) with the skin still on. Start at the head and work toward the tail, cutting perpendicularly to make thick slices weighing about 7 oz. (200 g).
Reserve the tail for other uses, such as *escalopes* (scaloppine), rillettes or terrines, cubes, or small morsels.
Tie the steaks with twine so that they hold together when cooked.
Remove the skin when they are ready to eat.

● **Chef's note**
If possible, do not rinse the steaks, particularly if they are to be grilled.

● **Did you know?**
In French, these steaks are called darnes, from the Breton word for "piece."

❗ **Recipe idea**
Grilled salmon steaks with braised fennel ›› p. 308

Cutting medallions ★★

A medallion should, as its name indicates, be round.

Use this technique for most firm varieties of fish.

Using a fish steak
Take a fish steak, cut it in two, and remove the central bone. Fold the abdominal section over the fleshy section. Tie them together with twine so that you have a nice, round piece.

Using a fillet
Remove the bones from the fillet. If you wish, you may remove the skin.
Use a round pastry cutter to cut out pieces. An average piece should weigh about 3 oz. (80 g). Allow two medallions per person for a main dish.

❗ **Recipe idea**
Monkfish medallions *à l'américaine* and rice pilaf ›› p. 323

1

Cutting fish and shellfish into chunks ★★

Use this technique for thick flat fish such as turbot, brill, and halibut.

Take a flat fish that is already prepared (scaled, gutted, fins removed, and washed) and remove its head, working carefully so that you remove the least possible amount of flesh.

Using a large knife with a rigid blade, slice the fish in two along the fine mark that indicates the central bone (a lateral line) (1). Begin cutting from the tail.

Cut chunks weighing about 10 to 12 oz. (300 to 350 g) taking into account the variable thicknesses of the two quarters (back and belly) (2).

Elongated fish (eel-shaped): eel, lamprey, and dogfish.

Remove the head and skin of the fish.

Cut thick slices, 3-4 ¹/₂ in. (8-12 cm) long, depending on the diameter of the fish.

The average weight of a chunk should be between 7-9 oz. (200-250 g) for a main dish.

Crustaceans such as lobster, crayfish, royal langoustine, large prawns, and so on.

Split the head (cephalothorax) in two.

Separate it from the abdomen and remove the pouch on one side of the head. Set aside the greenish matter (known as the tomalley) for another use–a sauce, for example.

Remove the legs and claws.

Slice the abdomen along the segments using a knife with a rigid blade (3).

Recipe ideas
Turbot poached in cardamom-flavored milk with hollandaise sauce ≫ p. 319
Tarragon-scented langoustines ≫ p. 311

2

3

Cutting strips (*goujonnettes*) ★

Use this technique for average-sized flat fish, such as sole, plaice, and lemon sole.
Take a flat fish that is already prepared (scaled, gutted, fins removed, and washed) and skinned.
Fillet it as explained below.
Hold your knife to cut thin, angled slices in the fillets.

● Did you know?

The French word for these strips, goujonnettes, *is derived from their resemblance to the* goujon, *a small, spindle-shaped freshwater fish.*

❙ Recipe idea

Plaice *goujonnettes* with tartare sauce >> p. 315

Filleting a fish (two round, flat fillets) ★ ★ 🎬

Use this technique for fish such as salmon, cod, trout, sea bass, sea bream, and pollack.
Take a fish that is already prepared (gutted, trimmed, and washed). Descale it with a knife (1) and make an incision along the back through to the central bone. Cut around the head, then cut through the side facing upward along the central bone, pressing on it as you work toward the tail (2).
Turn the fish around and repeat the procedure on the other side to make the other fillet.
Trim the fillets so that they are neat and clean. If necessary, remove the skin: place the fillet skin side downward and, starting from the tail, slip the blade of a flexible knife between the skin and the flesh. Make back- and forward movements with the knife as you work toward the head (3).
Use tweezers to remove the bones from the fillets.
Rinse, drain, and chill until needed.

● Chef's notes

If there is any flesh remaining along the central bone, scrape it off with a teaspoon and use it for stuffing, rillettes, and so on.
Use fillets to make escalopes (scaloppine), medallions, strips, and thick slices.
John Dory is the only fish in this category to yield two flat fillets.

❙ Recipe idea

Pollack fillets *bonne femme* >> p. 303

Filleting a fish (four flat fillets) ★ ★ 🎬

Use this technique for fish such as sole, lemon sole, plaice, and turbot.

Dress* the fish (1) and, if preparing sole, remove the skin at this stage. Starting at the tail, slip the blade of a flexible knife between the skin and the flesh and then pull away the skin (2). Using a knife with a flexible blade, make an incision along the sides, from the head to the tail. Take special care when rounding the head, so that there is minimum wastage. Starting from the central bone, cut away the fillets (3).
Turn the fish over and repeat the procedure.
Trim the fillets neatly: remove the barbell, an elongated, hair-like projection, usually around the mouth, chin, or nose, as well as any part that has bloody stains, and any fatty flesh.
If working with lemon sole, plaice, and turbot, remove the skin now. If there are any sinews left, make incisions with your knife. This will prevent the fish from retracting or twisting during cooking. If you need to flatten them, particularly if you are going to roll the fillets, use the smooth side of a tenderizer.

1   2

3

● Chef's notes

The four fillets will not be identically sized.
Choose good-sized fish to make fillets using this technique.
These fillets have no bones and so children will like them!

● Did you know?

Flat fish like sole, lemon sole, turbot, and plaice only spend the first four weeks after hatching in a vertical position. After this, they adopt their distinctive horizontal position.

🍴 Recipe idea

Plaice *goujonnettes* with sauce tartare >> p. 315

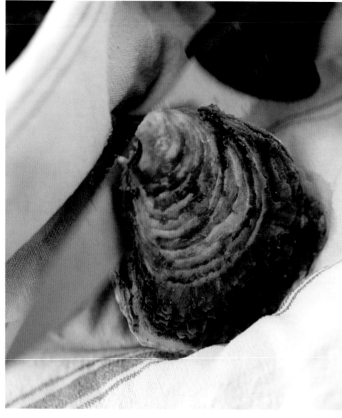

Opening oysters
and other shellfish ★★

Opening at the side (use this technique for hollow oysters and mussels)
Don a protective glove or use a folded tea towel to cover your hand and place the oyster in your palm with the hinge toward you.
Using a rigid oyster knife, insert the tip on the right-hand side, two-thirds of the way along, between the two shells.
Use a horizontal, small in-and-out movement with the knife to cut through the connecting muscle.
Lift the upper shell and separate the two shells at the hinge.
Check that no flesh is left on the upper shell. Check the oyster for freshness, and ensure that there are no shards of shell remaining.
For the finest taste, we recommend that you discard the brine in the shell and leave the oyster for 3 to 5 minutes while it secretes more liquid.

● **Did you know?**
To check that oyster are fresh, the first rule is to buy them live. Their shells must be closed, or else they must close as soon as they are tapped. Discard any that don't meet this criterion. Today, oysters are almost always eaten live, but they may be baked or poached, and served hot or cold.

Opening from the hinge (flat oysters, mollusks, and varieties of clams)
Don a protective glove or use a folded tea towel to cover your hand and place the oyster in your palm with the hinge facing away you.
Place the center of the blade of the rigid shucking knife at the hinge and press hard, bending your fingers to lever the knife. You must also cut the connecting muscle joining the oyster to the shell, which is to the right of its center.
Ensure that no flesh is left on the upper shell. Check the oyster for freshness, and ensure that there are no shards of shell remaining.
For the finest taste, we recommend that you discard the brine in the shell and leave the oyster for 3 to 5 minutes while it secretes more liquid.

● **Chef's note**
If you are going to replace the mollusks in their shells to cook them, clean them first and boil them for 2 minutes to eliminate any debris.

Recipe idea
Hot oyster gratin >> p. 256

Opening scallops ★★

Don a protective glove or use thick fabric to protect your hand.
Place the scallop shell in the cup of your hand with the hinge
facing away from you and the flat side facing up.
Insert the tip of a rigid knife into one of the two openings on
either side of the hinge.
Cut the connecting muscle (the scallop), keeping the knife
as close as possible to the flat part of the upper shell to avoid
wasting flesh. Lift off the upper shell and discard it (1).
Scoop out the scallop, the corral, the beards, and black innards
with a spoon (2).
Take the beards and rinse them several times. They can be used
later to make a sauce.
Discard the black innards (3).
Separate the scallop from the coral (4). You may want to use the
coral for another recipe .
Remove the white muscle at the end of the scallop.
Rinse, drain, and chill the coral and the scallop.

● **Did you know?**
*You can cook the coral in exactly the same way as the scallop
itself, or incorporate it in the sauce.*

Recipe idea
Luted scallops on a bed of gently cooked vegetables ›› p. 275

1

2

3

4

Meat and offal*

Barding a fillet ★

Barding meat prevents it from drying out when it is cooked, and enriches it with fat. Another, less frequently used method involves larding it—threading small strips of fat through the lean flesh of meat using a larding needle (one with a large eye).
Bard is made from fatback, a thick piece of fat that covers the back of a pig.

Prepare the meat to be barded and remove any nerves and sinews.
Cut the bard into strips. If you're cooking individual pieces of meat, such as tournedos or medallions, wrap the meat completely (1), or if you're using large pieces such as the tenderloin (filet) or a sizeable roast, envelop it only partially with bard, and tie it with individual pieces of kitchen twine (2).

● **Did you know?**
You can decorate the bard by making cut-out patterns before you drape it round your meat.
Do not keep bard in the freezer for more than three months: it goes rancid, oxidizes, and absorbs smells.

❘ **Recipe idea**
❘ Beef tournedos with foie gras ›› p. 381

1

2

Encrusting poultry ★

This involves slipping flavorsome ingredients such as truffle slices or bay leaves between the skin and the flesh of poultry.

❘ **Recipe idea**
❘ Bay-scented young guinea hen with canapés ›› p. 330

Cutting up raw, dressed* poultry ★ ★ ★

Pull away the wings and thighs from the carcass. Hold the bird firmly and make an incision in the skin between the thigh and the abdomen. Then disjoint the thigh at the articulation (1, 2). Cut along the backbone to separate the thigh from it. Make sure you include the choice morsel known as the oyster, which is found in the cavity just in front of the thigh.
Repeat the procedure for the other thigh. Turn the bird over. Cut along both sides of the wishbone to separate the fillets and the wings (3, 4).
Trim off the tips of the wings and thighs.

Recipe idea
Stuffed chicken legs with chestnuts ›› p. 344

1

2

3

Jointing rabbit ★ ★ 🎬

Rabbit meat is low in fat and is used much like most poultry and small game. Hare is cooked in the same way as rabbit, but it is best in dishes with a red wine sauce. These are known as *civets*, game stews. An average rabbit weighs between 3 lb. 5 oz. and 4 lb. 6 oz. (1.5–2 kg).

Remove the head and take out the giblets (heart, liver, and lungs).
Cleave the hind legs at the hip. Separate the two hind legs by removing the tip of the backbone (the coccyx). If the hind legs are a good size, you may want to cut each of them into two. Make a cut at the base of the rib cage, then cleave the backbone in half to separate the two forelegs. Cut the saddle into two or three pieces, depending on its size.

● **Chef's notes**
Ensure that you make clean, sharp cuts so that there are no bone splinters in the flesh.
The saddle can be boned and stuffed like a saddle of lamb.

Recipe idea
Rabbit stew with puréed Golden Hubbard squash ›› p. 340

4

Boning a shoulder of lamb ★★

When preparing a shoulder of lamb, bear in mind that
3 ¹/₂ lb.–4 ¹/₂ lb. (1.6–2 kg) will serve five to six people.

Place the shoulder of lamb on a chopping board (1). Remove the
thin membrane on the outside of the shoulder.
Turn the shoulder over. Take a boning knife and make an
incision in the flat part of the shoulder blade to free the meat
below (2).
Cut round the shoulder bone (it has a triangular shape) and
remove it by sectioning the nerve at the articulation.
Scrape the two remaining bones so that there is a minimum
amount of meat left on them, and remove them (3).
The shoulder can be used whole, rolled and tied (either roasted
or pan-cooked) or cut into 2oz.- (50 g-) pieces to make a stew.

❙ **Recipe idea**
❙ Provençal shoulder of lamb and vegetable *tian* >> p. 359

Boning a saddle of lamb ★★

Choose a saddle (loin) weighing 3 lb.–3 ¹/₂ lb. (1.2–1.6 kg) to serve four. In the USA, the term "saddle" may mean the whole loin, the hip, and the leg. Here, you will need the top of the hind leg.

Release the tenderloin (filet mignon) from the backbone, leaving it attached to the skin. Cut carefully around each vertebra. Be careful not to pierce the meat or make open holes in it.
Trim the flanks so that they are all the same length.
The saddle of lamb may be used plain, trussed* and roasted. You may also stuff it (see recipes for duxelles, mousseline, and so on).

Cooking times for a boned saddle of lamb
Pink: 20-25 minutes at 350°F-370°F (180°C-190°C).
Well done: approximately 40 minutes at 350°F-370°F (180°C-190°C).

In order for the meat not to shrink during cooking, remove the sciatic nerve on the backbone.

● **Did you know?**
In France, the finest lamb is salt marsh lamb. They graze on the grasses and plants on the coast of the Atlantic and the Channel. The plants, sprayed by the sea, are rich in iodine and impart a particular, much appreciated flavor to the meat.

Preparing foie gras ★★

Mistakenly termed "removing the nerves" of the foie gras, this technique involves removing the blood vessels, not the nerves.
If you are preparing a hot recipe (such as a sautéed slice), it is not necessary to remove the veins.
Allow 2 ½–2 ¾ oz. (70–80 g) per person for a cold terrine served as a starter, and 3 ½–4 ¼ oz. (100–120 g) for a sautéed scaloppine served as a hot starter.

Remove the foie gras from the refrigerator about 1 hour before you begin preparing it (1).
Separate the two lobes and remove any traces of green matter, the bile.
Make an incision along the length of the long vein so that you can remove it. Use your thumb or a round-tipped knife to adjust the movement of the knife, keeping it as precise as possible (2).
To make a terrine, marinate the deveined foie gras in milk in the refrigerator for 12 hours to remove any bitterness (there is always a little bitterness in foie gras). You may then soak it in a sweet wine or a stronger alcoholic beverage.
A foie gras terrine must be weighted down and cooked at about 175°F (80°C). The core temperature must reach 131°F (55°C). A terrine will keep no longer than a few days in the refrigerator.

● Chef's notes

Whether you prefer duck or goose foie gras, make sure that it is light colored, stain free, and firm. An average duck liver weighs between 1–1 lb. 2 oz. (450–500 g). An average goose liver is larger, between 1 ½–1 ¾ lb. (700–800 g).

● Did you know?

In ancient times, geese were force-fed with figs. Today, ducks are force-fed for two weeks and geese for three weeks, mainly with corn.

Recipe idea
Terrine of foie gras >> p. 264

1

2

1

2

3

Tying up a roast ★

Tying a roast makes the meat look attractive and ensures that it cooks evenly.

Separate ties
This method is usually used for individual pieces of meat, such as medallions, tournedos, and chateaubriand steak.
Prepare pieces of kitchen twine sufficiently long to go round the piece of meat and tie a knot.
Slide each length of kitchen twine under the meat, bring the ends round to the top and tie a knot.
Trim the excess twine closely.

With one piece of string
This method is used for large pieces of meat, such as a shoulder or leg of lamb, and loin.
Make a loop around one end of the meat and tie a knot. Do not cut the twine **(1)**.
Loop the string around your hand and slip the loop around the meat at about 1 ¼ in. (3 cm) from the first loop **(2)**. Tighten as necessary.
Repeat the procedure until you reach the other end of the piece of meat. Then tie the last loop to the first by looping the string under the meat to tie it on top **(3)**.

❗ Recipe idea
Provençal shoulder of lamb and vegetable *tian* ›› p. 359

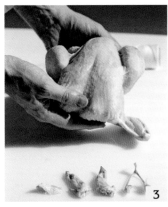

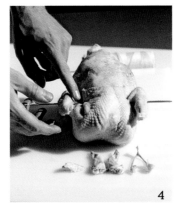

Dressing* and trussing* poultry ★★★ 🎬

This involves all the procedures that transform a raw product into a ready-to-cook ingredient.

To dress a fowl, stretch it out and burn off any remaining traces of feathers (1).
Cut the legs at the "knee" articulation, remove the tips of the wings and the gland located above the rump (parson's nose). Remove the neck and set it aside to use for stocks and/or a roasting gravy (2).
Remove the wishbone at the base of the neck (3).
Check that there are no giblets or other innards left. Season and stuff the cavity if your recipe calls for it.
Place the bird breast side down and thread twine–leaving about 4 in. (10 cm) loose at the entry point–through the wing, between the two bones, using a trussing needle. Continue through the skin of the neck and under the backbone (4).
Repeat the operation in the reverse order on the other side. Turn the fowl onto its back and pull the needle through the leg, between the drumstick and the thigh (5, 6).
Knot the two ends of twine together (7). Pierce the belly skin and thread the twine above the two legs. Make a loop around them.
Hold the legs firmly and make a knot so that the cavity is tightly closed (8).

● Chef's notes
You may place a strip of bard on the scaloppine of some poultry (squab [pigeon], guinea hens, and game birds) before trussing them. This will ensure that they do not dry out during cooking. You can also insert an aromatic ingredient under the skin before trussing (see page 76).
Baste* the poultry regularly while it cooks so that it does not dry out.

● Did you know?
Poultry from the Bresse region is famous, and is the only kind to have its own AOC (Appellation d'Origine Contrôlée, see p. 222). Turkeys, chickens, and capons (a fattened, castrated cock traditionally eaten during the festive season) are raised there. Fine restaurants often serve poultry from Bresse, and will specify its origin on their menus.

Mincing meat ★

This involves cutting meat more or less finely with a knife or a mincing machine. When meat is minced, it can be mixed with other types of meat, shaped, and seasoned throughout.

Preparing a rack (pork, veal, lamb) ★★★ 🎬

This preparation involves removing the vertebrae and removing the fat (and any meat) from the tips of the rib bones so that cutting the meat after it is cooked becomes easy. It is known as frenching a rack. When preparing lamb, allow two chops per person. For pork and veal, one chop or sirloin steak is enough.

Remove the fat and, if necessary, trim the top of the rack. Make a few incisions so that the meat does not shrink too much during cooking.
Trim the meat and fat between the tips of the ribs, about 1 1/4-1/1/2 in. down (3-4 cm), leaving them clear. Scrape all remains off the rib tips with a boning knife so that they do not color during cooking (1, 2).
Remove the meat by cutting along the flat side of the vertebrae until you reach the backbone (3).
Turn the rack over and separate the vertebrae one by one, cutting round each one. Pull on the base of each vertebra (4). Cut off the backbone. Only the ribs will remain joined to the loin. Tie the ribs together with the backbone to hold the rack.
The rack may be covered with a crust, such as herbs, garlic and parsley breadcrumbs, gingerbread crumbs, and so on, and then browned.
To reach a pale pink color, a rack of veal must be cooked gently until a drop–or "pearl"–of exuded juice appears when it is cut after its post-cooking resting time.

🍴 **Recipe idea**
Roasted rack of lamb and garden vegetables >> p. 368

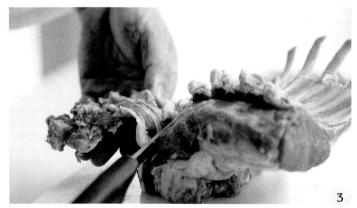

Preparing a leg of lamb ★★

The US and UK equivalent of a French *gigot d'agneau* is the leg. To serve 8, allow 2 lb. 10 oz.–3 lb. (1.2–1.4 kg) of meat with the bone.

Remove the thin membrane on the outside of the leg and trim any fat **(1)**.
If the pelvic bone is still there, remove it by cutting round it and sectioning off the joint.
Sever the tendons at the knee, making as small a hole as possible, to remove the hip bone **(2, 3)**. All that will remain is the shank bone.

● Did you know?

In France, lamb is often combined with typically Mediterranean flavors and studded with garlic cloves.
A slow-roasted leg of lamb, known in French as a gigot de sept heures, a seven-hour leg of lamb, is first slowly braised and then cooked in a luted (sealed with dough) cooking pot. The meat is so tender that it can be removed with a fork. Lamb is widely available at Easter time, and has a particularly tender, tasty meat.
The meat of the foreleg around the shank is considered a morsel of choice. In French, it is known as the souris, literally, the mouse. The term "leg" is reserved for lamb and mutton. The equivalent on a game animal is known as a "haunch."

⦿ Recipe idea
Braised leg of lamb, Breton-style >> p. 377

1

2

3

Preparing chops ★

Let us take the example of a rib roast, with an average weight of 2 lb. 10 oz.–3 ½ lb. (1.2–1.6 kg). Veal and pork chops constitute individual portions, while it takes two or three lamb chops to make one serving.

Cut the meat away from the top of the rib bone, down about ½ in. (3-4 cm), leaving it visible. Scrape away any remains so that it does not color during cooking. Remove any excess fat. Remove the vertebrae with the boning knife. If you are preparing a rib-eye roast, it is easier to saw the bone.
Make a ½-in. (a few millimeters) incision on the nerve on the outside (curved side) so that the meat does not shrink during cooking.
If your chop is very thick, tie it: start with a knot at the trimmed bone. Loop the string around and tie it at the starting point. Wrap the tip of the bone in foil so that it does not burn.
For chops, it is best to use high heat (grill, roast, or sauté), and it is important to let the meat rest once it has been cooked. This enables the juices to penetrate the meat, which becomes more tender.
Use high, dry heat (grilling, roasting, or sautéing) and allow your meat to rest after cooking so that the juices can reabsorb into the meat, thereby making it tender.

● Did you know?
The entrecote is a piece of meat located between two ribs. It is usually cut off a rack of boned ribs.

Recipe ideas
Veal chops, Normandy-style ›› p. 371
Grilled rib roast and béarnaise sauce ›› p. 356

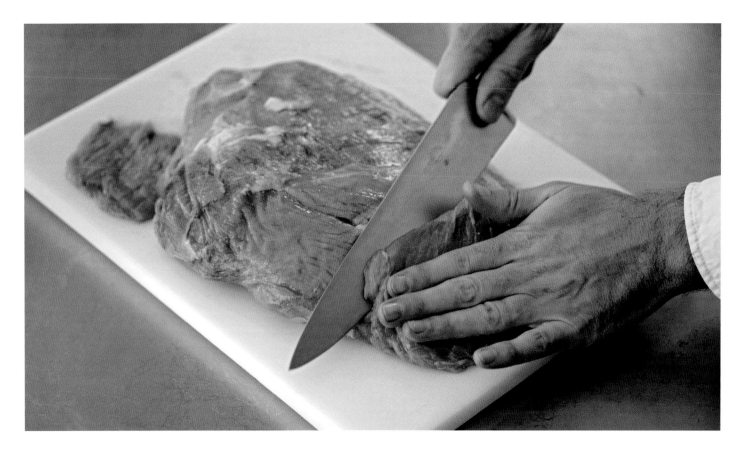

Preparing *escalopes* (scaloppine) ★

Cut thin slices of meat in a prime cut. The best pieces to use
for veal scaloppine are the leg and hind shank (UK silverside,
topside, and hind shank).
Place them between two sheets of plastic wrap and flatten them
by bashing on them with a mallet or meat tenderizer. If you
don't have one, use the bottom of a clean saucepan.
Trim the edges of the scaloppine with a kitchen knife.

● **Did you know?**
*Piccatas are 0.4 in.- (1 cm-) thick slices cut from the fillet. Allow
three pieces, each weighing about 2 ¹/₂ oz. (40 g) per person.
A* paillarde *is a thin scaloppine of veal or beef that has been
completely flattened and then grilled or fried.*

Recipe idea
Crumbed turkey scaloppine with sautéed potatoes ›› p. 337

Preparing veal sweetbreads ★★

The sweetbread is the thymus gland of young animals. In fact, there are two glands, one near the heart and one near the throat. Sweetbreads are one of the few animal foods to contain Vitamin C. Allow approximately 10–12 oz. (250–300 g) of unprepared sweetbread, either lamb or veal, per person.

Soak the sweetbreads in water in the refrigerator for 4-6 hours to rid them of all blood. Change the water at regular intervals. Drain the sweetbreads and blanch* them: place them in cold water (1) and bring to the boil. Allow to boil for 4-5 minutes. Skim the water frequently during this process.
Remove the sweetbreads from the water and refresh* them briefly in cold water with ice cubes.
Drain carefully.
Using a paring knife, remove the skin, fat, and cartilage, if any (2).
Place the sweetbreads on a clean cloth (3) between two plates. Apply pressure with a weight for a minimum of 3 hours, overnight if possible (3).

● **Chef's notes**
Transferring the sweetbreads into very cold water after they have been blanched not only stops the cooking process, it also makes them firmer for trimming.
The more pressure you apply to them, the more pink liquid they will exude. This will enable them to stay white.

🍴 **Recipe idea**
Sweetbread vol-au-vents with cider and apples ›› p. 272

Preparing kidneys ★★

Allow approximately 10 oz. (250 g) of unprepared kidneys per person.

Remove the fat from the kidneys and pull off the fine, transparent membrane that adheres to them.
Remove all the white parts, blood vessels, and the urinary tract.
You may either leave the kidney whole or cut it into small lobes, depending on your recipe.
To prevent the kidneys from becoming rubbery or elastic, it is essential to cook them rapidly on high heat and to ensure they remain pink inside.

● **Chef's notes**
It is best to buy kidneys in their fat as this helps maintain freshness.
They should not have a strong smell.

● **Did you know?**
Veal kidneys are considered to have the finest taste of all types of kidney.

Recipe idea
Kidneys in mustard sauce >> p. 367

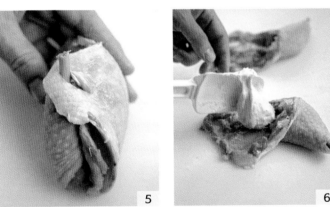

Boning and stuffing
a chicken leg ★★ 🎬

This technique creates a small, plump-looking leg that is firm and easy to eat, since most of the bone is removed.

Using dressed* thighs (1), remove the femur bone by scraping around it until you have freed it from the meat (2).
Remove the knee cap and continue to scrape around the other bone, the tibia.
Halfway down, cut the tibia, making sure you do not leave any bone shards (3). If you do not plan to stuff the leg, replace the remaining part of the tibia (4, 5) now, and season.
Otherwise, season the meat and fill it with a spoonful of mousseline stuffing (see p. 157) (6).
Fold the meat over the stuffing (7) and sew up with a trussing* needle (8).
You may also wrap the legs in caul* to hold the meat together and prevent it from drying out during cooking (9).

🍴 **Recipe idea**
Stuffed chicken legs with chestnuts ›› p. 344

Preparing terrines and pâtés
(terrine stuffing) ★★★

These stuffings or forcemeats can be used for vegetables, fish, and meat. They go under names as varied as *galantine*, terrine, pâté, *ballottine*, and more.

The delicacy of your stuffing will be determined by how finely you chop your ingredients. Bear in mind, however, that meat chopped too finely will lose its distinctive taste and will tend to dry out, particularly if you have removed too much fat.

Allow about 3 oz. (80 g) of terrine per person.

Ingredients (for 1 country-style terrine
[terrine de campagne] for 8 people)

14 oz. (400 g) pork side belly (*poitrine* cut in France)
7 oz. (200 g) pork picnic shoulder (hand [UK], *épaule* cut in France)
2 scant teaspoons (9-10g) salt
1 pinch (1 g) pepper
1 egg
1 generous pinch of fresh herbes de Provence*
1 ⅓ tablespoons (20 ml) cognac
6 ½ tablespoons (40 g) flour
5 oz. (150 g) larding strips
3 oz. (80 g) caul*
3 ½ oz. (100 g) strips smoked bacon
¾ cup (200 ml) prepared clear aspic (optional)
Special equipment: a meat thermometer

Trim the meat. Remove some of the fat and all the sinews and nerves. Cut into cubes or strips weighing about 2 oz. (50 g). Mince (1) and season the meat (2).

Mix with the remaining ingredients (for this recipe, use the egg, herbs, cognac, and flour).

Line the terrine mold with bard, caul, or dough, should you prefer, and fill it, pressing down regularly to eliminate any air. You may insert ingredients such as foie gras, fruit, or truffles. For this recipe, insert strips of smoked bacon (3).

Use whatever you have lined your mold with (in the photo, caul) to cover the terrine (4). Cook at a temperature of 275°F-285°F (140°C), in a water bath, until the center of the terrine reaches a temperature of 154°F-160°F (68°C-70°C).

When the terrine is done, you may pour the clear aspic over it so that it does not dry out. This will make it more tender and shiny.

● Chef's note

Opt for curing salt to enhance the pinkish color of the meat and prevent oxidation.

You may marinate the meat before preparing the terrine.

If you prepare other terrines with different quantities of meat, bear in mind that you should use 3-3 ½ teaspoons (14–16 g) salt and 1 pinch (1 g) pepper for every 2.2 lb. (1 kg) of the total meat used.

● **Did you know?**

In the late Middle Ages, only the corporation of chair-cuitiers saulcissiers (cookers of meat and sausage) were authorized to prepare and cook pork in all its forms. The generic French term for products that use pork meat and offal* as a base, charcuterie, derives from this.
The rules governing the pork cooking guild apparently date back to Roman times.
The pastissiers, makers of pastry, were allowed to cook pâtés that were wrapped in pastry.

❙ **Recipe idea**
❙ Rabbit terrine with pistachios and exotic fruit chutney ›› p. 260

Cutting medallions and noisettes ★

Allow 3 × 2 oz. (50 g) small cuts per person.

Remove the sinews from the small end of the tenderloin (*filet mignon*).
Roll it up and tie with kitchen twine every 1 ¹/₂-2 in. (4-5 cm) **(1, 2)**.
Cut the medallions between each loop of twine **(3)**.
The best way to cook them is to sauté them; cooking time will be very short.

● **Did you know?**

If the cut is a well-rounded shape and not particularly thick, you will find it in French restaurants under the name "medallion." Medallions of beef are also known as "tournedos."
If you leave the filet mignon whole and tied, on the other hand, the cylindrical shape gives it its name of "canon."

❙ **Recipe ideas**
❙ Lamb medallions with licorice-flavored foamed milk and duchess potatoes ›› p. 382
❙ Medallions of veal, green lentils, and horn of plenty mushrooms ›› p. 360

1

2

3

Cooking techniques
for accompaniments, fish, and meat

Low-temperature cooking

This is a recently developed cooking technique that is mainly used for meat and consists in cooking it either in direct contact —with a grill, oven grill, flat-top grill (plancha), etc—or in indirect contact (vacuum packed or sous vide*) at a temperature of 136°F (58°C). This method takes longer than traditional methods (about 20 percent more cooking time), and requires impeccable hygiene in all respects—in the products used, the material, and on the part of the cooking staff. It results in tender, juicy food that has undergone very little color change and is hence slightly less flavorful. To compensate, the meat may be browned before or after cooking with the sous-vide method.

Browning quickly in hot fat before cooking

Dress* the main ingredient (here, meat) and preheat the oven to 136°F (58°C).
Rapidly brown the meat over high heat and season it.
Place it on a rack with a dish below to catch the juices it exudes when cooked. Place in the oven. Insert a meat thermometer as near to the center of the meat as possible and set it to 136°F (58°C). Do not exceed this temperature.
Remove from the oven when the desired temperature is shown on the thermometer and serve.

Browning quickly in hot fat after cooking

Dress the main ingredient (here, meat) and preheat the oven to 136°F (58°C). Insert a meat thermometer as near to the center of the meat as possible and set it to 136°F (58°C). Do not exceed this temperature. Place in the oven on a rack with a dish below to catch the juices it exudes during cooking. Remove from the oven when the desired temperature is reached and rapidly brown the meat over high heat.
Season it and serve.

● Chef's notes

It is essential to place the thermometer at the center of the meat to check for doneness.
No resting time is required for this method, which results in little weight loss caused by evaporation. There is only about 15 percent shrinkage.

Brown braising (meat, poultry, offal*) ★★

A whole piece of meat, or a large-sized piece, is browned in fat in a pan with a tight-fitting lid over an aromatic base. Cooking liquid, which may or may not be thickened, is added.
If the cooking is done in the oven at a low temperature, it will take longer for the meat to be tenderized and the flavors of the cooking liquid and the product to meld. The cooking liquid, called a braising stock, is used to glaze* the meat and as an accompanying sauce.

Dress* and prepare the main ingredient.
Cut (dice*) the aromatic base into a mirepoix*. Prepare a bouquet garni*.
Begin cooking in the braising pan and brown all sides evenly in the fat you are using (1).
Transfer the meat to a dish and discard the fat from the cooking pot.
Add the aromatic base and sweat* it (2).
Pour in the marinade or wine (3). Reduce* it by half over high heat.
Preheat the oven to 350°F-400°F (180°C-200°C).
Return the meat to the braising dish and pour in enough cooking stock to half cover it.
Place the braising dish in the oven. Allow about 1 1/2 hours for pieces of offal, at least 2 hours for poultry, and 3 hours for a large piece of meat. Halfway through, turn the meat and vegetables over. This is particularly important for smaller pieces such as vegetables and legs.

Make the sauce:

Remove the pieces of meat or offal and tent under aluminum foil. Reserve in a warm place.
Skim the fat off the braising stock.
Return the braising pot to the stove top and, over high heat, reduce the stock until it reaches a thick consistency.
Strain it through a fine-meshed sieve.
Adjust the seasoning and flavor it with ingredients of your choice, such as wine or other alcohols, extracts, strongly flavored jus*, and so on.
Pour the sauce over the dish and place it in the oven so the glaze can coat it (4).

● Chef's note

To make sure that no moisture escapes, the braising pan or stew pot may be luted (see technique, p. 103). In this case, the meat will obviously not be turned over halfway through the cooking process.

● Did you know?

There is considerable loss of weight with the braising method. Some types of offal should be blanched* before being braised. You may also marinate your ingredients prior to braising them. The term "braise" comes from when dishes of meat were cooked in a closed pot that was surrounded and covered by braises, or embers.

❙ Recipe idea
Boeuf bourguignon with fresh pasta >> p. 363

1 **2**

3 **4**

1

Braising vegetables ★

Use raw or blanched* vegetables (1). Place over the aromatic base without browning them. Fill three-quarters way up with your cooking liquid, such as stock (see pp. 136, 138) (2). Cover with the lid and cook slowly in the oven.

● **Other types of stewing or braising**

Whole fish are placed raw over the aromatic base without being browned. Fill three-quarters way up with fish stock or velouté. Put the lid on and cook in the oven at 250°F (120°C). Small fish or fish pieces will take a maximum of 30 minutes.
For meat, sear it first without allowing it to brown. Place the meat over the aromatic base and pour in your white stock. Cover with the lid and cook at a low temperature in the oven at 325°F–350°F (160°C–170°C). Meat may take as long as 2–3 hours.*

2

Slow cooking in oil or fat ★

This involves slow cooking at a temperature of 136°F (58°C) in fat in order to preserve it. In French, the process is known as *confire*, and the final result is a confit (for example confit of duck, a dish particularly popular in the southwest of France).
Cooking time will depend on the size of the piece you are preparing. This method takes a considerable time (from 20 minutes for unpeeled garlic cloves to about 2 hours for duck thighs). Hygiene is all-important here.

If you wish, you may start by pickling or brining the main ingredient. If you have done so, rinse it well and dry it.
Dress* and prepare the main ingredient.
Place it in a bath of liquid fat (oil or clarified butter*).
Bring the temperature of the ingredients very slowly up to a core temperature of 136°F (58°C). The temperature of the fat should also not exceed 136°F (58°C), and must be checked with a thermometer.
Drain if necessary.
If a dish or foodstuff has not been sterilized, it is fragile and must be consumed within a short time. Use various types of oil or fat, and flavor them if you wish : see chapter on Basic preparations and sauces p. 125.
See also the table of fats p. 233.

🥄 **Recipe idea**
Duck confit and potatoes sarladaises ›› p. 338

Candying (crystallizing) ★★

This involves cooking a food in a sugar and water syrup, whose sugar concentration is progressively increased. It is traditionally used for fruit and vegetables.

Prepare the fruit or vegetables (1). If using products like citrus fruit or chestnuts, they will need to be blanched* at this stage.
Prepare a sugar syrup with an equal weight of water and sugar and bring it to 225°F (107°C).
Immerse the ingredients into the hot syrup (2) (you may want to lower them in using a metal basket), leave to simmer for 10 minutes, and remove from the heat. Strain the syrup into another receptacle and add 25 percent more sugar than you used initially (first sugar bath) to this syrup and return the ingredients to be candied. Repeat the procedure three to seven times, adding 25 percent of the original weight of sugar to each sugar bath, bringing the syrup to the boil each time and leaving to simmer for about 10 minutes.
The more sugar baths you candy your fruit in, the longer it will be preserved.
Drain the fruit and dust with confectioners' sugar.

● **Did you know?**
To enhance the flavor, add an ingredient like cinnamon, vanilla, star anise, or ginger to the syrup.

Gentle stewing

This is a method of cooking without browning that uses low heat and requires a tight-fitting lid. Little or no fat or cooking liquid is required. It is mainly used for vegetables, with the vegetables cooking in their own liquid.

Peel, wash, and finely slice the vegetables.
Heat any fat you may be using over a low heat (1) and add the vegetables (2).
If using cooking liquid, such as water, fumet*, or stock, pour it in now to create steam. Cover with a parchment paper lid (3), which will allow you to keep an eye on the cooking, and simmer over low heat until done (4). See the DVD for how to make a lid of parchment paper and poaching fish.

● **Did you know?**
A vegetable fondue involves similar preparation.
Sweating* means softening a vegetable in its own liquid. The pan is covered and placed over low heat. Very little fat is used. Cooking time is brief (2–3) minutes, and the vegetable retains its crunch.
Stewing to make a compotée is a variation on this technique; the cooking time is extended until the ingredients are particularly soft.

Recipe idea
Fish papillotes with vegetable scoops ›› p. 295

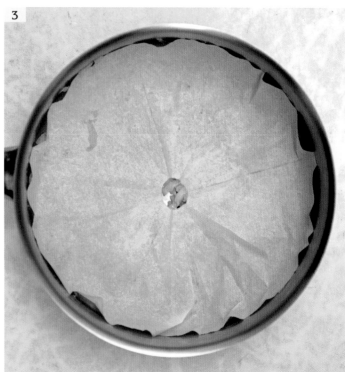

Cooking in a crust ★★

This involves cooking an ingredient in an oven, totally or partially covered in a crust, which may be of varying thickness. The coating may be a dough (brioche, puff pastry, bread, etc), a crust (herb mixture, flavored breadcrumbs, salt, gingerbread, flavored butter, etc), or other foodstuffs.
This cooking method results in the flavors blending between the main ingredient and the coating. It also keeps the main ingredient moist, and, in certain cases, such as a salt crust, results in cooking by steaming. This is what occurs when the ingredient is coated in kosher or other coarse salt.

Prepare the coating as required (crust, dough, flavored butter, etc) and set aside.
Dress* and trim the main ingredient. If necessary, pre-cook it and allow it to cool completely. (This is particularly important if you are using dough, which must not be softened or partially baked before it goes into the oven.) Season with salt and pepper.
If using dough, roll it out and place the accompanying ingredients of your choice on it. Wrap the main ingredient partially or wholly.
If you are using a yeast dough, allow it to rise, decorate it if necessary, and baste* with egg.

Preheat the oven as required. Place on a baking tray and cook until the crust is nicely colored.

● Chef's notes

To intensify flavors, we recommend you pre-cook your main ingredient. If you are preparing a fillet of beef in a pastry case, for example, brown the beef. For sausage in brioche pastry, poach the sausage.
Use this technique for both small and large pieces of meat or fish, and give free rein to your imagination when it comes to the coating.

Recipe ideas

Sea bass in salt crust ›› p. 300
Fillet of beef in a brioche crust ›› p. 372
Steamed fillets of bib (pouting) in a green robe ›› p. 304

1

2

Glazing* vegetables ★

Glazing vegetables gives them a shine thanks to a cooking method that uses butter, water, and sugar. Vegetables such as turnips may be blanched*, and carrots may be pre-cooked. Baby vegetables are particularly well suited for this cooking technique. Instead of water, try using stock.

Cut the vegetables into regular shapes. For pearl onions, this step is not necessary.
Place the vegetables, butter, sugar, and fine salt in a sauté pan and cover with water **(1)**.
Cut out a circle of parchment paper the size of the pan and cover the vegetables **(2)** (see DVD for method of making this cover). Cook over low heat.
As soon as all the water has evaporated, hold the pan with both hands and whirl the contents around to coat the vegetables in a shiny glaze.
"White" glazing is the result of cooking the vegetables without browning them. If you cook them further so that they caramelize, the glaze will at first be light colored and then brown.

● Did you know?
White sauce = white glaze (for a blanquette)
Blond (straw-colored) sauce = blond glaze (for a fricassee)
Brown sauce = brown glaze (for boeuf bourguignon)

❙ Recipe idea
Boeuf bourguignon with fresh pasta ›› p. 363

Frying ★

Frying involves immersing an ingredient in hot fat.
It is essential to choose the appropriate fat for your recipe (see table of fats p. 233).
Fragile products such as fish should be dipped in milk and then in flour to form a fine surrounding crust. This will prevent the flesh from falling apart.
You may also make a crumb preparation (see p. 122), frying batter (see p. 23), crêpe batter (see p. 18), or choux pastry (see p. 20).
Certain varieties of potato need to be fried in two stages. The first stage, at 300°F (150°C) cooks them; the second stage, at 350°F (180°C), browns them. Only souffléd potatoes require three successive immersions.

Prepare the ingredients and preheat the fryer to 350°F (180°C).
Make sure the food is carefully dried.
Immerse the food into the deep fryer or oil bath.
Turn until all the sides are evenly colored.
Remove from the fryer, drain, and use a paper towel to absorb any excess fat.

● Chef's notes
It is important to stir whatever you are cooking, particularly if you are preparing fritters.
It is preferable to season your ingredients before cooking them, as seasoning will not penetrate the crust formed during frying. Potatoes are the exception to this rule.
Never sprinkle salt over the deep fryer.
Don't fry different types of food, such as meat, fish, vegetables, and fruit, in the same oil, and discard your oil after it has been used ten times.
When not using your deep fryer, protect it from air and light so that the fat does not oxidize.

❙ Recipe ideas
Brie fritters with spicy stewed black cherries ›› p. 408
Apple fritters with apricot coulis ›› p. 449

Gratin ★

When preparing a gratin, the surface of the dish is browned and acquires a crusty texture. This develops as the dish cooks or can be done afterwards.
There are three types of gratins:
• Glazing: superficial color formed under high heat (oven broiler, salamander, caramelizing blowtorch).
• Blond gratin: a crust of cheese, breadcrumbs, flavored butter, and so on, placed on already cooked foods to brown and become crisp.
• Full gratin: the dish is cooked in the oven from beginning to end. The crust forms on the surface and is browned.

● Chef's note
Browning the crust of a blond gratin won't be enough to reheat an entire dish. To reheat, you will have to bring the various elements to a suitable temperature.

● Did you know?
The term "gratin" originates from the term for the crust that formed on the cooking pot, which was then scratched (gratter) off to be eaten.

❙ Recipe ideas
Onion soup ›› p. 399
Gnocchi, Florentine-style ›› p. 388
Rolled Picardy crêpes ›› p. 400
Hot oyster gratin ›› p. 256

Grilling ★

Grilling involves cooking a food in contact with a grilling rack or a very hot grill pan heated from below. The term also applies to food that is rapidly exposed to high, dry heat, and this is actually more like the roasting one does for almonds, hazelnuts, coffee beans, and so on.

If using an electric grill pan, turn it on; otherwise heat your pan on the stove top or the barbecue.
Rub the ridges with a slightly oiled cloth.
Dry, and apply a little oil to the food you are preparing.
To obtain a regular diamond pattern–this is called branding–(see photo, right), put the pieces you are grilling at an angle to the grill bars, and turn through 90 degrees halfway through the cooking process.
Season when done.
Remove from the heat.

● Chef's notes
Dust sole with flour before cooking for better browning.
When cooking red meat, allow the same amount of resting time as cooking time.
If you are cooking a thick item that is not done to your satisfaction after grilling, finish cooking in the oven.
The crisscross design is more attractive in a diamond shape than a square shape and, more importantly, easier to achieve.
Use an instant marinade prior to grilling (see p. 141) to tenderize and flavor the meat or fish.

❙ Recipe ideas
Grilled salmon steaks with braised fennel ›› p. 308
Grilled rib roast and béarnaise sauce ›› p. 356

Luting ★

Luting is a method providing a hermetic seal between a cooking receptacle and its lid.
It is made of a mixture of water and flour and rolled out to a strip or cord shape, which is placed around the cooking receptacle and overlaps both the lid and the container.
Luting is a technique mainly used for dishes with sauces, as it prevents too-rapid evaporation of the cooking liquid and allows the food to remain tender.

Sift 2 cups (200 g) all-purpose flour and make a well in the center. Pour in a scant $1/2$ cup (100 ml) water and combine until the mixture has a smooth texture.
Cover in plastic wrap and chill for 20-30 minutes.
Roll out into a strip or cord shape about $1/4$-$1/3$ in. (5 mm-1 cm), depending on the size of the container.
Make sure that the lid and the container are cold so that the dough does not dissolve. Seal them with the dough and check that there are no gaps.
Begin cooking, following the recipe.
Remove the lute at the very last moment, unless you are braising. Discard it, as it is not meant to be eaten.

● Chef's notes

You can use leftover puff pastry for luting. If your dish requires no more than 30 minutes' cooking, baste* it with egg yolk before putting it into the oven.
Resting time for the dough depends on the quantity and elasticity of your paste (détrempe). Bear in mind that insufficient resting time results in an elastic pastry.

❗ Recipe idea

Luted scallops on a bed of gently cooked vegetables ›› p. 275

Marinière ★

This is used only for seafood, and involves cooking it with white wine and finely sliced shallots. It is often used for shellfish, particularly for mussels. Allow 2 cups (0.5 liters) of mussels per person. This works out to approximately 1 lb. (450 g) for a main dish. For an appetizer, prepare ¼ lb. (250 g) per person, as below.

Ingredients
Serves 4
2 lb. (1 kg) mussels
2 shallots
1 large sprig of parsley
2 plus 1 tablespoons (50 g) unsalted butter
6 cups (1.5 liters) white wine
Pepper

Scrape and clean the mussels.
Finely dice* the shallots and chop the parsley.
Sweat* the shallots in 2 tablespoons (30 g) of the butter.
Add the mussels (1), white wine (2), and half the chopped parsley.
Cover and bring to a fast boil over high heat, stirring regularly (3).
Check that all the mussels have opened. Discard those that are still closed, and transfer the rest to a warm dish using a slotted spoon.
Filter the cooking liquid to remove any traces of sand.
Reduce* the liquid by half and then whip in the remaining butter.
Adjust the seasoning and pour the liquid over the hot mussels.

● Traditional mussel recipes
Different regions in France have their own regional specialties:
• *Biarritz style (à la biarrote): with finely diced bell peppers*
• *Bonne femme (home-style cooking): with julienned mushrooms and celery*
• *Provençal: with garlic and tomatoes*
• *Normandy style (à la normande): with heavy cream and hard cider**
• *Poulette sauce (a light white sauce): with shallots and mushrooms. The lemony sauce is reduced and then bound with heavy cream and egg yolk.*
• *Mouclade: this is a specialty of the Poitou-Charentes region. The mussels are first cooked marinière style and, when they open, cream is added to the sauce, butter is whipped in, and it is thickened. Cultured mussels from this region are flavored with a hint of curry and saffron.*

● Chef's note
Never leave mussels for more than 15 minutes in their soaking water. Remove all those you find floating. Do not eat a mussel that remains shut after cooking.

● Did you know?
In 2006, the first appellation for a sea product was awarded to the cultured mussel of the bay of Mont Saint-Michel. A bouchot is a wooden post that stands on the seabed. Mussels are attached to these posts by the cultivators. In France, you will often find recipes for moules de bouchot.

Recipe idea
Mussel mouclade ›› p. 255

Cooking en papillote ★

To cook en papillote is to wrap ingredients in a sheet of greased parchment paper. The aim is to blend the flavors of the aromatic ingredients and the main ingredient, ensuring all the while that they remain moist.

The contents of a papillote are done when the parchment paper parcel has puffed up due to the steam that comes from the food inside.

Open the papillote at the last moment; it is best to allow guests to do it themselves so that they can fully appreciate the aroma that will emerge from inside.

Dress* and prepare the main ingredients (fish, crustaceans, poultry, fruit, vegetables, etc) and finely slice the accompanying garnish.

Prepare the sheets of parchment paper (approximately notebook or foolscap sized). Grease one side with oil to prevent the contents sticking. If you wish, lightly beat an egg white with a pinch of salt and brush the edges of the paper with it (1).

Prepare the papillote: arrange the main ingredient and the garnish attractively on one half of the oiled side of the paper. If you wish, drizzle over a little liquid such as fish stock, wine, syrup, or whatever complements your recipe, and season.

Fold over the other half of the paper (2) and press the edges together, then turn them over, making several tight folds. Press down hard on the edges and use paper clips to ensure that your papillote is properly closed.

Cook in an oven heated to a medium temperature. If the heat is too high, the paper will brown before the ingredients are cooked.

When the papillote has puffed up, allow an extra 5-6 minutes for cooking.

● Did you know?

Today, aluminum paper is not in favor for papillotes: it causes the food to oxidize if an acidifier like lemon juice or vinegar is used. It also tears more easily than parchment paper.

The bed of vegetables under the main ingredient should be pre-cooked or cut very finely—use a julienne or diced* brunoise* technique.

Recipe idea
Fish papillotes with vegetable scoops >> p. 295

Shallow poaching (hot start) ★

This cooking technique is reserved for vegetables such as button mushrooms or turned (shaped) vegetables. They are cooked in water to which lemon juice has been added. This preserves their color and prevents oxidation.

Ingredients
A scant $^1/_2$ cup (100 ml) water
Juice of $^1/_2$ lemon
Salt
About 1 $^1/_2$ tablespoons (20 g) butter
$^1/_4$ lb. (250 g) button mushrooms

Place the water, lemon juice, salt, and butter in a pot. Bring to the boil.
Prepare the mushrooms and put them in the water.
Cover the pot with a parchment paper lid (see technique on DVD).
Leave to boil until the vegetables are completely done. Allow 3-5 minutes, depending on the size.
Leave to cool in their cooking liquid.

● Did you know?
The button mushroom is the most widely cultivated mushroom in the world. It is inexpensive and available all year round. Its mild, light taste makes it an easy-to-use, much-liked ingredient for many recipes.

Deep poaching (hot start) ★

In a blanc
A *blanc* (literally, white), is a solution of water with salt, lemon juice, and flour added.
The technique preserves the light color of certain foods, like artichoke bottoms, salsify, white asparagus, calf's head, cardoons, Swiss chard, and white offal*.

Ingredients
Main ingredient to be poached (e.g salsify, white asparagus)
1 lemon, or more if required
4 cups (1 liter) water, plus a little more to dilute the flour
Scant $^1/_4$ cup (50 ml) oil
Seasoning of your choice
$^1/_2$ cup (50 g) flour

Drizzle lemon juice all over the food you are about to cook. Bring the water, lemon juice, seasoning, and oil to the boil. Dilute the flour in a little cold water (1) and pour it into the boiling mixture. Allow the mixture to thicken until it reaches a light, velvety texture.
Place the food into the *blanc* (2) and cook. Depending on what you will be using it for, you may need it to cool in the liquid when it is done.

1

2

In water (pasta, rice, fruits, shellfish served in cooking liquid)

This is a way of cooking food in a large volume of boiling liquid (water, broth, fish stock, etc). Pasta and rice should be cooked in ten times their volume of water.

Bring a large volume of liquid (water, syrup, court bouillon, etc) to the boil.

Season according to the recipe and add a drizzle of oil if you are cooking a starchy food (1).

Add the food and quickly bring the liquid back to the boil (2).

Cook for required time.

Check for doneness (al dente for pasta) (3).

If preparing starches or other foods that must have the cooking process stopped, refresh* immediately in cold water. Items such as pears, however, should be allowed to cool in the cooking liquid.

● **Chef's note**
Drizzle a little oil over pasta after refreshing so that the pieces do not stick together.

 Recipe idea
Soft-boiled eggs on a bed of artichokes with eggplant caviar » p. 392

Shallow poaching (cold start) ★★

This cooking method uses the least possible liquid. For vegetables, grains, pulses, and fish.

Greek-style vegetables

To prepare Greek-style vegetables, the cooking is carried out on the stove top. The flavors of the vegetables meld with those of the cooking liquid.

Ingredients

Serves 6
3 tablespoons (50 ml) olive oil
3 oz. (80 g) onion
$^1/_2$ cup (100 ml) white wine
2 lb. (900 g) button mushrooms
1 lemon
1 bouquet garni*
Peppercorns, coriander seeds, and fennel seeds

Finely slice the onions and sweat* them in the olive oil. Cut up vegetables into pieces of identical size and add them to the pot (1).
Fill to halfway with white wine and the juice of a lemon (2).
Add a bouquet garni* (3) and a muslin bag containing peppercorns, coriander seeds, and fennel seeds.
Season with salt and leave to boil with the lid on.
Test the vegetables for doneness. The liquid exuded by the vegetables and the cooking liquid should have partially evaporated, as the lid is not hermetically sealed.
Serve cold.

● Chef's notes

Even when preparing mixed vegetables cooked Greek-style, each vegetable should be cooked separately.
As a variation, you may add chopped tomatoes.

Rice and other grains

When it comes to cooking grains, allow all of the poaching liquid to evaporate.

Rice pilaf is a classic preparation of cooked rice with sliced onions sweated* in butter and covered with stock. It is often accompanied by a garnish.

Sweat a white aromatic base in butter. It is a good idea to use aromatic ingredients of the same color (leek whites, onions, shallots, etc) as the grain you are preparing.

Coat the grains with the fat and cook until they become translucent (1).

If you are cooking long-grained white rice, add one and a half times its volume in cold liquid (water, stock, broth, etc) (2).

Add the seasonings and the bouquet garni*.

Preheat the oven to 250°F (120°C).

Bring to the boil and cover with parchment paper or aluminum foil (3).

Leave the rice in the oven until it is cooked and the liquid has evaporated (35-40 minutes).

Separate the grains of rice with the tines of a fork and serve.

● Did you know?

Rice is a grain of the Poaceae or Gramineae family. It is the main foodstuff of a large proportion of the world's population. It is found in various forms, long or round grains; the long grains stay separate when cooked while round grains tend to stick together. Its colors range from white through yellow and red to black and it may be fragrant, such as Basmati and Thai (also known as jasmine).

1

2

3

Pulses

Pulses should be cooked until practically all of the cooking liquid has evaporated (35–40 minutes).

Sweat the aromatic base (carrots, mushrooms, and celery).

Add the pulses.

Pour in twice their volume of cold liquid, using water, stock, or broth.

Add the seasonings, except for the salt, which should only be added when cooking is completed.

Bring to the boil over the stove top and cover.

Simmer until the consistency of the pulse is sufficiently soft.

● Chef's notes

Soak the pulses for a few hours or overnight in cold water, except lentils and split peas, which might ferment if soaked.

● Did you know?

In France, two pulses carry the AOC label:
• AOC coco de Paimpol: a semi-dry white bean, originally from South America, which is grown in the Paimpol region of Brittany. It is harvested by hand.
• AOC lentille verte du Puy: green lentils of the Puy-en-Velay region in Auvergne. They are dark green, marbled lentils that are tasty and fine-textured.

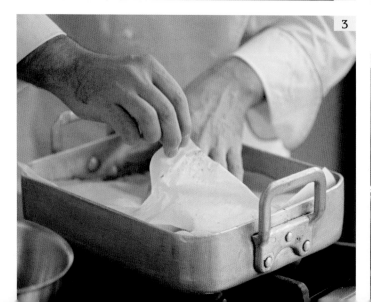

Fish

For fish, a small quantity of the poaching liquid can be used after cooking to prepare an accompanying sauce.

Butter the base of a high-sided cooking dish. Arrange the appropriate aromatic base at the bottom (1). Place the fish (whole or in fillets) on this, skin-side down to avoid shrinkage, and half cover with fumet* and/or white wine (2).
Preheat the oven to 250°F (120°C).
Place the dish on the stove top and bring to the boil. Cover with parchment paper (3) (see DVD for technique) and transfer immediately to the oven for a few minutes to finish the cooking. Pour the cooking liquid into a saucepan and reduce* it to make a sauce (4). You may, for example, whip cubed butter into it.

● **Chef's notes**

Select firm-fleshed fish, such as pollack, sole, salmon, and plaice. Use your imagination when choosing the cooking liquid. Try hard cider, beer, or red wine, for example.*

● **Did you know?**

Some well-known recipes:
• Turbot slices with Dugléré sauce (light butter sauce named for the revered nineteenth-century chef). Poach the fish briefly with a fish fumet, white wine, shallots, and paprika. Reduce the cooking liquid and whip in cubed butter.
• Lemon sole fillet à la hongroise. Briefly poach the fillets in fish fumet with white wine, shallots, and paprika. Reduce the cooking liquid and whip in cubed butter.
• Sole fillet Marguery. Marguery (1834–1910) was another famous chef whose signature dish this was: poach fillets of sole briefly with fish fumet, white wine, and shallots. Garnish with shelled shrimp and mussels prepared marinière style. Reduce the cooking liquid and whip in cubed butter. Pour the sauce over the sole fillets and broil them briefly. Garnish with puff pastry cut in the shape of flowers.

Recipe ideas
Pollack fillets *bonne femme* » p. 303
Monkfish medallions *à l'américaine* and rice pilaf » p. 323
Langoustine and pineapple skewers » p. 299

Deep poaching (cold start) ★

This method is mainly used for meats and fish, and involves completely covering the ingredient with cold water to which aromatic ingredients have been added. (In some cases, an even greater volume of liquid is required.) The flavors of the food and the aromatics blend.

Peel, wash, and roughly cut the vegetables used for the aromatic base.
Place them with the main ingredient in a suitably sized cooking pot and cover with the cold cooking liquid (water, court bouillon, stock, etc).
Bring to the boil over high heat and then reduce to a simmer.
Remove the cooked food, and reserve the cooking liquid to make an accompanying sauce for your recipe.

● **Chef's note**
If you are making a ragout or stew in a white stock, blanch* the pieces of meat before poaching.

● **Use this method for:**
Pot-au-feu, poached salmon in aspic, poached ham Parisian-style, poached hen, etc.

🍴 **Recipe idea**
Pot-au-feu >> p. 378

Thickened soups (*potages liés*)

A liquid preparation made from raw or cooked ingredients, served hot or cold.

Names of the main consommés and soups

Type	Name	Cooking liquid	Main ingredients
Consommé	Hochepot	Clear brown stock	Oxtail and aromatic garnish
	Brunoise	Clear brown stock	Vegetable brunoise*
	Printanier	Clear brown stock	Carrot and turnip scoops and garden peas
	Jacobine	Clear brown chicken stock	Diced* potatoes, green beans, turnips, peas, julienned truffles
	Chasseur	Clear brown game stock	Port wine, julienned mushrooms, chervil leaves
	Vatel	Fish fumet*	Crayfish flans, small sole fillet shapes
Soup	Parmentier	*Blanc* or water	Leek, potatoes
	Champenoise	*Blanc* or water	Creamed potatoes plus celery root and carrot and celery brunoise
	Julienne Darblay	*Blanc* or water	Creamed potatoes plus julienned vegetables
	Freneuse	*Blanc* or water	Creamed potatoes plus turnips
	Crécy	*Blanc* or water	Creamed potatoes plus carrots

Creamed soup ★

This is a soup made from a thickened white stock.
It is thickened again with crème fraîche or heavy cream just before serving, which makes it even more creamy and smooth.

Peel, wash, and cut your chosen vegetables (aromatic base and main ingredients).
Sweat* the aromatic base (1).
Cover it with some thickened white stock and bring to the boil.
Add the main vegetables (3).
Cook about 30 minutes, checking from time to time for doneness.
Blend and strain.
Add some crème fraîche. Return to the pot, bring to a simmer, and season.

● Chef's note

If you are using a clear white stock, sprinkle flour over the aromatic base once it has been sweated and before it is covered with liquid (2).

Velouté soups ★

A velouté (literally, velvety) soup is a creamed soup that is thickened a second time with a mixture of crème fraîche and egg yolk.

Make a creamed soup (see above).
Remove from the heat. Combine crème fraîche and egg yolks and pour the mixture into the creamed soup. Do not bring the velouté back to the boil once you have bound it with egg yolk.
Mix and serve immediately.

● Chef's note

As for the creamed soup, if you are using a light white stock, sprinkle flour over the aromatic base once it has been sweated and before it is covered with liquid (2).

❙ Recipe idea
Creamed lettuce soup (*velouté Choisy*) >> p. 396

Bisque ★★

A bisque is a shellfish soup based on the *américaine* sauce (sautéed live lobster, flambéed* in cognac, and simmered with wine, aromatic ingredients, and tomatoes) and bound with rice. Allow 1 cup (¼ liter) of soup per person.

Rinse some small crabs under running water. Rinse the shells of shellfish.
Peel, wash, and finely dice* (make a mirepoix*) of aromatic vegetable ingredients.
Color the small crabs and the shells in olive oil. Crush them finely using a pestle. Add the aromatic ingredients and flambé with cognac.

Deglaze* with white wine and allow to reduce* a little, about 10 percent.
Cover with fish fumet*.
Add tomato paste, a bouquet garni*, and garlic cloves from which the shoot has been removed.
Cook, uncovered, and skim regularly.
Blend (if possible in a food processor with a lid, so that the shells do not splatter) and strain through a sieve.
Mix rice flour with the fumet or cold water and pour the liquid into the boiling bisque.
Bind using a whisk and thin with a little crème fraîche.
Adjust the seasoning.
See p. 133 for the full recipe for a crayfish bisque.

● Did you know?
To use the classic method, cook some round-grain rice in the cooking liquid.
Use the flesh of the shellfish to make a side dish of a salpicon, a medallion, flaked crab, or in a mini-raviole (tiny filled pasta).*
Be creative and concoct a poultry or game bisque using the same technique.

Soups and consommés

Soup ★
This is a hot or cold liquid made of vegetables, fish, or meat, and classically thickened with bread.

Peel, wash, and cut the vegetables for the aromatic base and the main ingredients.
Sweat* the vegetables in oil or fat.
Add fish or meat, depending on the recipe you are preparing.
Cover with stock, water, wine, or beer, and simmer.
Season and skim if necessary.
Prepare the ingredients for the garnish.
Blend the soup, particularly if you are making a fish soup, or leave as is.
Serve very hot accompanied by bread (fresh, or as croûtons, toast, grissini, etc).

● Chef's note
Drizzle a little olive oil over the bread and/or rub it with a garlic clove.

● Did you know?
In the southwest of France, a major wine-producing area, it was customary to pour some red wine into the last of the soup to finish it; this was known as "faire chabrot."
In the Middle Ages, "soup" meant the thick slices of bread on which broths were poured.

● Fish soups
• Bouillabaisse: older books on cooking define it as a fish soup served as a main dish. Found on the Mediterranean coast from Marseille to Toulon using many different species of local fish, such as scorpion fish, conger or sea eel, and red gurnet, it is made in two stages. First the stock is made and then the bouillabaisse itself. A rouille, a sauce made of red chilies, garlic, and saffron, always accompanies it.
• Cotriade. This is a pot-au-feu with pieces of fish, potatoes, and herbs to which a dash of vinegar is added. Examples of the name are found from 1877 onward. It is thought to derive from the Breton word "kaoter" meaning a cauldron, or else from the Provençal.
• Chaudrée. A popular seafood pot-au-feu in the Charentes region. The word has the same origin as the cotriade.

Consommé ★★
A consommé is a broth made of vegetables, poultry, or meat that has not been thickened and is clarified*. It is clear and the color—usually brown—is determined by the main ingredient.

Peel, wash, and cut the vegetables for the aromatic base and the main ingredients.
Blanch* the meat and the bones, if using. Skim the top.
Place all the ingredients in a pot of cold water.
Add kosher salt and bring to a simmer. Leave to simmer for a long time, a minimum of 2 hours, for instance, for poultry or beef.
Prepare the garnish.
Strain the soup through a fine-mesh sieve and allow the broth to cool.

To clarify ★★★
Clarifying eliminates the particles in suspension in a broth or consommé and makes it clear. The method here is actually a double clarification.

Chop the meat or fish.
Finely slice the aromatic base (carrots, leeks, celery, and so on).
In a pot, mix the chopped meat, the aromatic base, and the egg whites. Use 4 egg whites and 5 oz. (150 g) in total of aromatic vegetables and meat for every 4 cups (1 liter) of liquid.
Pour the cold broth over the mixture and combine thoroughly. The aromatic base adds taste to the broth that is to be clarified.
Bring slowly to a simmer until a thick layer forms on the surface. This will take roughly 45 minutes.
Make a hole in the center.
Carefully remove the coagulated matter with a slotted spoon.
Ladle out the broth and strain it through cheesecloth (muslin) to remove all suspended matter.

⬧ Recipe ideas
Rockfish soup ›› p. 268
Onion soup ›› p. 399

Fricassee ★★

This is chiefly used for cut meat, such as rabbit, chicken, and veal; firm fish, such as conger or sea eel, John Dory, and monkfish; and vegetables. The pieces are cooked slowly in a thickened, creamed white liquid with the lid on.
It is usual to serve a side dish with it. Let us take the example of meat here.

Prepare and cut the meat, and prepare a white aromatic garnish of onions, leek whites, and celery.
Quickly sauté the pieces of meat in butter over a low heat, making sure they do not brown (1). If you are cooking delicate fish, lightly sauté them so they do not brown and coat them in a velouté sauce.
Place the aromatic base in the pot and leave to sweat* (2).
Sprinkle some flour over and cover with a cold white stock. Season and add a bouquet garni* if you wish.
Simmer gently with the lid on, or place in the oven at 350°F (180°C). If you are cooking small or delicate pieces, finish the cooking with the lid on, either on low heat or in a moderate oven, at 250°F (120°C).
Remove the pieces of meat when they are cooked and keep warm under aluminum foil or plastic wrap so they do not dry out.
Stir in the cream (3), and reduce* the sauce until it is thick enough to coat the back of a spoon*.
Adjust the seasoning and strain the sauce through a sieve.
Return the pieces of meat to the cooking dishes, along with other ingredients, if the recipe calls for them, such as glazed pearl onions, thinly sliced mushrooms, bacon bits, and so on.

● **Chef's note**
Searing* the meat (in the case of chicken) prevents it from sticking to the pot.
The pieces of meat may be removed from the pot before the flour is added. In this case, a white roux is made.

● **Did you know?**
Some regional specialties, like eel fricassee and Limoux pork fricassee, call for white wine to be added in addition to the white stock.
A rabbit stew cooked in white wine is known as a gibelotte.

Recipe ideas
Squab fricassee and garden peas *à la française* ›› p. 347
Chicken breasts with baby vegetables ›› p. 351
Rabbit stew with puréed Golden Hubbard squash ›› p. 340

Browned stews
(sautéed dishes in sauce) ★★

Preparing stews is comparable to braising, but the pieces of meat are smaller and there is more sauce.

Dress*, prepare, and cut the pieces of meat (1).
Cut the aromatic base into a mirepoix*.
Prepare a bouquet garni*.
Sauté the meat evenly on all sides (2).
Remove the excess fat from the cooking pot and add the aromatic base.
If you wish, add tomato paste and garlic cloves with the shoot removed.
Heat the oven to 350°F-400°F (180°C-200°C).
Cover with wine (3). Reduce* by half over high heat. Cover with stock (4).
Add the bouquet garni.
Place in the oven with the lid on.

Make the sauce:
Remove the pieces of meat from the pot and spoon off any fat from the surface of the sauce.
Place the pot over high heat and reduce* until the sauce is thick enough to coat the back of a spoon*.
Strain through a fine-mesh sieve and adjust the seasoning.
Put the meat back in the pot and pour the sauce over. Bring back to the boil quickly to dissolve the salt just added.
Add the garnish and serve.

● Chef's notes
To make a game stew (a browned stew), use the animal's blood to bind the sauce. Once you have added this, it must not boil again. Do not sprinkle flour over your ingredients if you are using a thickened stock.
When making lamb stew, add the potatoes 30 minutes before the cooking process is finished.

● Did you know?
The word for ragout, a stew, comes from the French verb ragoûter, *which means to give taste (goût) to small sautéed pieces by placing them in a sauce that will tenderize them. The first known recipes for ragout in France were used for mutton. In Old French, an* estouffade *referred to a slow cooking process in a hermetically sealed pot. It is now the name of a type of stew, usually beef. To make a daube, a traditional braised joint of beef, the pieces are cooked in their marinade. Curry, matelote (fish stew with wine), and navarin (a lamb stew) all call for a brown sauce to be used.*

▮ Recipe idea
Boeuf bourguignon with fresh pasta >> p. 363

2

3

4

Roasting ★

To roast is to cook in a dry oven or rotisserie, or on a spit, adding a little fat to the food so that it browns evenly to the desired color. You may, if you wish, brown your meat over high heat before placing it in the oven.

Dress* and prepare your main ingredient (1). Preheat the oven to about 400°F (200°C).
Brown all the sides over high heat using a little fat (oil and/or clarified butter*).
Place in the oven.
Baste* regularly during cooking with the fat and juices that exude from the meat. This prevents it from drying out and gives it a good color.
Check for doneness and transfer to a rack to drain. Season and tent under aluminum foil.

Prepare the gravy
Reduce* the juices remaining in the pan over high heat to caramelize them. Remove the excess fat from the roasting dish.
Sweat* the aromatic base (onions, carrots, mushrooms, celery, and so on) in the roasting dish.
Deglaze* the dish with wine (optional) and/or water (2).
Strain through a fine-meshed sieve and adjust the seasoning.
Serve while still very hot.

● Chef's notes
To give a personal touch to your gravy, add an aromatic base and a bouquet garni to the liquid in the roasting dish just before the estimated end of cooking time.*
Red meats should be allowed to rest a few minutes before serving. This makes the flesh tender because it allows the juices to return to and penetrate the muscle fiber.
Season all your ingredients when cooking is done.

❙ Recipe ideas
Aniseed-flambéed sea bream ›› p. 292
Roasted rack of lamb and garden vegetables ›› p. 368
Provençal shoulder of lamb and vegetable *tian* ›› p. 359

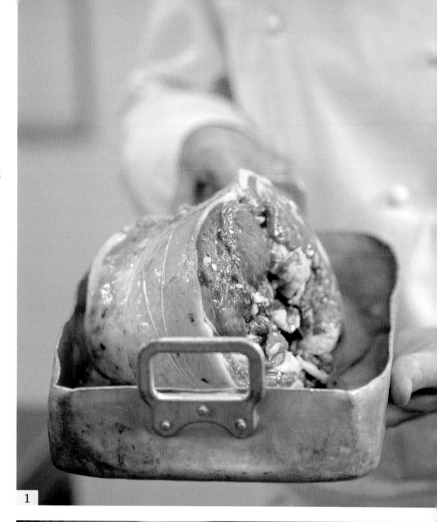
1

2

Internal temperatures for doneness for beef and lamb	
Very rare	113°F (45°C)
Rare	113°F (45°C)
Medium	136°F (58°C)
Well done	149°F (65°C) and higher

Average roasting times in an oven at 400°F (200°C)	
White meats (pork, veal)	35 min/lb., 60–70 min/kg
Red meats (beef, lamb)	15–17 min/lb., 25–35 min/kg
Poultry (chicken, turkey, capon)	30 min/lb., 45–60 min/kg

1

2

Game stews (salmis) ★★★

This involves two stages of cooking and is used for feathered game. They are initially roasted whole, and then cut up and stewed in brown stock.

Dress* and prepare the bird. Preheat the oven to about 400°F (200°C).
Brown the bird on all sides in oil and/or clarified butter* over high heat.
Place in the oven immediately.
Baste* regularly with the fat and juices from the bird to moisturize the meat and ensure a good color.
Halfway through the cooking process, cut up the bird and set aside the carcass to prepare a thickened brown stock (see p. 138) (1).
Flambé* the pieces and cover with the thickened brown stock (2).
Lower the oven temperature to 325°F-350°F (160°C-180°C) and place the dish in the oven with the lid on. Alternatively, cook over low heat.
Add the garnish required for the recipe and serve.

● Chef's note
In French, this is called a salmis. It is made using wild duck, pheasant, and partridge, but you will also find guinea fowl and squab (pigeon) salmis.

Recipe idea
Quail stew and potatoes *à la boulangère* >> p. 334

Sautéing ★

This means cooking food in direct contact with a smooth, flat, hot pan using fat. It is a cooking method to be used at the last minute.

Prepare, dress*, and cut up the food to be sautéed.
Preheat the sauté pan or cast-iron flat-top grill (*plancha*) with a little oil or butter.
Sear* the food, browning it.
Turn it over and season.
Transfer to a rack to allow the juices to flow out.
Prepare a sauce by deglazing* the pan according to your recipe.

● Chef's notes
It is best to salt smaller pieces after they have been cooked because salt dries out the meat.
Avoid pricking red meat so that the juice remains within the pieces.

❚ Recipe idea
Sesame-coated rabbit liver salad ›› p. 276

Sauté meunière ★

The food is kept whole or cut up, dusted in flour, and cooked by exposing it to high heat with fat. This cooking method is used at the last minute, and is most suitable for fragile fish, as it forms a crust that protects the flesh and holds it in place.

Prepare, dress*, and cut up (if necessary) the food that is to be sautéed.
Use paper towel to dry it, ensuring there is no moisture left.
Season with salt and pepper (1).
Quickly dip the pieces in flour and tap them to remove the excess (2).
Preheat the sauté pan with a little oil and/or butter.
Sear* the fish with the skin side downward. Brown evenly.
Turn over and finish cooking (3).
Make the sauce for your recipe.

● Did you know?
It is the flouring of the fish that gives the dish its name meunière, *which is French for "miller's wife." Confusingly,* beurre meunière *does not contain flour but is browned butter* to which lemon juice and chopped parsley have been added.*

❚ Recipe ideas
Sole meunière and potatoes cocotte ›› p. 320
Trout with almonds ›› p. 291

Crumbed sauté technique ★

The food is dusted with flour, dipped in egg, and then coated in crumbs. The cooking is identical to simple sautéing. Use the technique at the last moment to ensure that the crumbed coating remains crisp.

Prepare, dress*, and cut up the food to sauté.
Remove any remaining moisture with paper towel.
Dust the pieces with flour and tap them to remove the excess (1).
Dip them in a mixture of beaten egg, salt, and oil (2).
Coat in crumbs, such as breadcrumbs, ground hazelnuts, sesame seeds, and so on (3).
To decorate, make a grid pattern using the back of a slicing knife.
Sear* and brown evenly (4). Turn over and finish cooking.
Make the sauce for your recipe.

● **Chef's note**
If you use the same sauté pan several times, wipe it off and change the oil and/or butter.
Use a dry bread of your choice to make your own tasty breadcrumbs in a food processor.

Recipe ideas
Plaice *goujonnettes* with sauce tartare ›› p. 315
Crumbed turkey scaloppine with sautéed potatoes ››p. 337

Steaming ★

The food is cooked in air moistened by the steam given off by boiling liquid. This cooking method preserves the taste, texture, and aroma of the food.
A fat-free sauce is an ideal accompaniment to food that is steamed. Steam cooking involves either high or low pressure.

Place a small piece of food in a steaming basket or on a rack.
Place it in a pot holding a liquid (usually water), which you may flavor if you wish.
Close the steam cooker and heat.
Check for doneness and serve immediately.

● Chef's notes
This cooking technique is principally used for vegetables and fish.
Since they are not soaked in water, they maintain their taste, smell, and texture.

❘ Recipe idea
Steamed fillets of bib (pouting) in a green robe >> p. 304

Basic savory
preparations and sauces

Emulsified sauces

These sauces combine two ingredients, a watery substance and a fatty substance, which do not naturally mix. The emulsion may be stabilized for a certain time by adding an emulsifying ingredient. The resulting taste depends on the choice of basic components. Try flavored vinegars, for example, and vary the oils—think of walnut or olive.

Emulsified sauces—unstable emulsions

Base	Basic recipe	Additional ingredients	Name	Uses
Vinaigrette (Salad dressing) (see p. 150)	• 1 part vinegar • 2 parts oil • salt • freshly ground pepper	+ mustard*	= mustard vinaigrette	Serve cold or warm Salad seasoning
		+ sliced onion, capers, chopped herbs	= *ravigote* sauce	
		+ crème fraîche or heavy cream (no oil)		
		+ verjuice (no vinegar)	= *aigrelette*/sharp sauce	
Tomato coulis (see p. 134)	• peeled fresh tomatoes • vinegar or lemon juice • oil • salt • freshly ground pepper • chopped fresh herbs	+ locally produced honey	= sweet-sour tomato sauce	Ideal condiment for fish, shellfish, and summer crustaceans. Good with terrines, salads, mousses, and so on. N.B. Use tomatoes when they are in season and choose the tastiest varieties.
		+ whipped cream and cubed tomatoes	= sauce *aurore*	
		+ slow-roasted pink garlic and rosemary	= sauce *à la Gasconne*	
Raw, crushed ingredients (condiments)	• basic components (olives, anchovies, bell peppers, etc) • aromatics (basil) • garlic • oil • vinegar or lemon juice • salt • freshly ground pepper	+ salted anchovies	= *anchoïade*	Mainly used for Provençal dishes (carpaccio, croutons, and so on) and to accompany grilled fish and meat, or in crusts.
		+ basil, grated Parmesan and pine nuts	= pesto (see p. 144)	
		+ basil	= *pistou* (see p. 144)	
		+ puréed anchovies, cloves, thyme	= *pissalat*	
		+ olives	= tapenade	
Melted butter (see p. 132)	• butter • water • lemon juice • salt • freshly ground pepper	+ saffron threads	= saffron sauce	These sauces enhance steamed, poached, and sautéed fish, and vegetables.
		+ julienned smoked bacon	= smoked sauce	
		+ Roquefort cheese	= Roquefort butter	
		+ browned butter*	= meunière butter	
		+ reduced* citrus juice	= citrus butter	
Beurre blanc (see p. 132)	• butter • shallot • white wine (to be reduced) • wine vinegar	+ cream	= *Nantais* butter	Replace white wine with beer, red wine, or hard cider*. N.B. If you use an electric blender, the emulsion will take longer to prepare.
		+ softened sorrel	= beurre blanc with sorrel	
		+ dill	= beurre blanc with dill	

Emulsified sauces—stable emulsions

Raw egg yolk (lecithin)

Basic recipe	Additional ingredients	Name	Uses
Mayonnaise (p. 143) Egg yolk + mustard* + sunflower seed oil + table salt + freshly ground pepper	+ tomatoes, finely cubed sweet bell peppers	= Andalusian sauce	Serve with cold fish and crustaceans (*chauds-froids*, aspics, seafood platters), meat, cold poultry, vegetable sticks, and so on. N.B. This recipe requires careful preparation because of its use of raw egg yolk. Attention must be taken to avoid any risk of salmonella contamination. Insufficient liquid will make the mayonnaise unstable.
	+ olive oil, garlic, chopped cilantro, chervil, and parsley	= Antibes sauce	
	+ whipped cream	= Chantilly sauce	
	+ cognac, ketchup, Worcestershire sauce	= cocktail sauce	
	+ gelatin	= aspic	
	+puréed herbs and pistachios	= genoise sauce	
	+ sour cream, lemon juice, chopped fennel	= Gloucester sauce	
	+ reduction* of white wine and shallots, chives, chili	= mousquetaire sauce	
	+ mustard, gherkins, capers, chopped fine herbs, anchovy extract	= *rémoulade*	
	+ puréed lobster, caviar, mustard	= Russian sauce	
	+ apple and white wine condiment, shredded horseradish	= Swedish sauce	
	+ reduced red wine and shallot	= *vendangeur* sauce	
	+ *jus** of herbs	= green sauce	
	+ puréed herbs and boiled egg yolks	= Vincent sauce	

Basic recipe	Additional ingredients	Names	Uses
Mashed potato + egg yolk + oil + table salt + freshly ground pepper	+ puréed garlic	= aioli	Traditionally accompanies soups and fish soups.
	+ puréed garlic, soft bread, saffron, red chili	= rouille	

Hard-boiled egg yolk (lethicin)

Basic recipe	Additional ingredients	Names	Uses
Hard-boiled egg yolk + mustard + oil + vinegar + table salt + freshly ground pepper	+ anchovy fillets, capers, chervil, tarragon, chives	= Cambridge sauce	Mainly used with fried and grilled foods.
	+ puréed chives and spiced onion	= tartare sauce (see p. 149)	
	+ chopped gherkins, capers, parsley, chervil, tarragon, and julienned hard egg white	= *gribiche* sauce	

Semi-coagulated egg yolk (lecithin)

Basic recipe	Additional ingredients	Names	Uses
Hollandaise sauce (see p. 148) Water + butter + lemon juice + table salt + Cayenne pepper	+ reduction of white wine and vinegar, shallot, mignonette pepper, tarragon, and chervil	= béarnaise sauce (see p. 147)	Fish, shellfish, meat, poached and grilled poultry, terrines, and so on.
	+ juice and zest of blood orange	= Maltese sauce	
	+ juice and zest of mandarin	= Mikado sauce	
	+ whipped cream	= mousseline sauce	
	+ mustard	= mustard sauce	
	+ browned butter*	= noisette sauce	
	+ reduced fumet* and white wine, crayfish coulis, and anchovy sauce	= Rubens sauce	
Béarnaise sauce (see p. 147)	+ reduced fumet	= white wine sauce	
	+ tomato (no chervil or tarragon)	= Choron sauce	
	+ crustacean coral	= coral sauce	
	+ meat glaze*	= Foyot sauce	
	+ mint (no tarragon)	= *paloise* sauce	
	+ tomato whisked with oil over heat	= Tyrolean sauce	

Thickened sauces

Thickened sauces are liquids whose stable, coating consistency is achieved through the use of one or several binding ingredients—stabilizers, thickeners, and jelling agents. The texture (liquefied or solidified) depends on the temperature at which they are used. The thickeners or liaison agents are either starches or proteins.

Thickened sauces—starch liaisons

Base	Technique	Name	Uses
Dry starch	Sprinkling with flour	Tomato sauce. Aromatic base and smoked bacon are browned, flour is sprinkled over. Add fresh tomato or tomato concentrate and cover with liquid. Simmer (see p. 149).	Stews and ragouts, not frequently used for fish and other seafood.
Starch and fat	Roux: white, blond (straw-colored), and brown (identical quantities of butter and flour, cooked depending on the desired color and taste) (see p. 150)	Velouté fumet* or white wine sauce and white roux: seafood stew (see p. 150)	Poached, sautéed fish and shellfish, whole or cut. Glazed* or gratin fish and shellfish. To make creams and veloutés.
		Béchamel sauce and derived sauces: milk and white roux (p. 131).	
		Nantua sauce: béchamel sauce or velouté with cream, crayfish butter whipped in.	
		Soubise sauce: béchamel sauce or velouté with blanched*, chopped onions.	
		Sauce américaine: crustacean coulis and blond roux (see p. 146)	
		Oriental sauce: sauce américaine with curry.	
		Livonienne sauce: julienned vegetables and a fumet velouté with butter whipped in.	
		Sauce normande: velouté with sole fumet, oyster *jus*, and mushrooms.	
		Diplomat sauce: normande sauce with lobster butter whipped in.	
		Joinville sauce: normande sauce with crayfish and shrimp butter whipped in.	
	Beurre manié (paste): identical quantities of softened raw butter* and flour (see p. 153)	Cardinale sauce: béchamel sauce + fumet, truffle essence, and lobster butter.	Enables the creamy texture of sauces to be adjusted: fish stew
Starch and cold liquid	Cornstarch, potato starch, arrowroot, rice flour, etc, diluted in cold liquid before being used for a cold liquid (water, fumet, wine, etc)	Shellfish bisque: shellfish coulis with a rice liaison.	Dishes in sauce, creams, and veloutés. Thickened sauces.
		Soubise: same technique as above, but replace the béchamel sauce with a consommé thickened with rice flour.	
Polysaccharides	Pectin, alginates, agar-agar, and carrageen (seaweed extract)	Mousses	Bavarian cream, seafood terrine, aspic, and so on.

Thickened sauces—protein liaisons

Base	Technique	Name	Uses
Eggs	Whole or with egg yolks, cream, milk, and so on.	Seafood quiche Hot eel pâté Pike quenelles with Nantua sauce Seafood timbale Layered fish dishes Sole soufflé Paupiettes of sole	Flans, stuffing, creamed batter for baking, pâtés, quenelles, veloutés, soufflés, and so on.
Coral: crustaceans, sea urchins, scallops	Reduce to a paste, thin with a hot liquid, and add gradually to the preparation. Do not bring to the boil unless combined with a starch.	Sea urchin sauce or soup Scrambled eggs with sea urchin coral Lobster stew	Dishes with sauce, accompanying sauces
Lamprey blood N.B. The blood of eel and conger or sea eel is toxic if it comes in contact with open wounds or the eyes.	Mix immediately with a little vinegar. Do not bring to the boil unless combined with a starch.	Sturgeon stew Conger eel, Bordelaise style Tuna stew	Dishes with sauce
Liver: red mullet, monkfish, cod	Reduce to a paste, thin with a hot liquid, and add gradually to the preparation. Do not bring to the boil unless combined with a starch.	Red mullet soup with fennel Sea casserole Sauce with red mullet liver Cod and tomato soup	Sauces, soups, stuffing, and so on.

Savory cream mixture for baking ★

This is a mixture that includes milk and egg, and that coagulates when baked. It is used for quiches, pies, and flans.

Ingredients (makes 1 quiche)
Scant $^1/_2$ cup (100 ml) milk
Scant $^1/_2$ cup (100 ml) whipping cream
2 eggs
1 egg yolk
Pinch grated nutmeg
Salt, freshly ground pepper

Whisk all the ingredients together lightly, ensuring that the mixture does not form bubbles.
Strain through a chinois* or sieve, cover with plastic wrap, and chill until needed.

● **Chef's note**
Use moderate heat to bake this mixture. If the oven is too hot, a brown, dry crust will form on the surface. Increase the number of eggs if using a garnish of vegetables that produce water.

❙ **Recipe ideas**
❙ Quiche Lorraine ›› p. 271

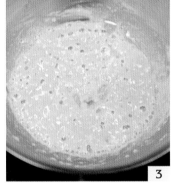

Basic savory preparations and sauces

Béchamel or white sauce ★

The béchamel is a velouté sauce with a milk base (a thickened sauce).

Ingredients (for 4 cups or 1 liter)
4 tablespoons (60 g) butter
²/₃ cup (60 g) flour
4 cups (1 liter) milk, divided
Pinch grated nutmeg
Scant ¹/₂ cup (100 ml) crème fraîche or thick cream (optional)
Salt, freshly ground pepper, to taste

Make a white roux with the butter and flour (see p. 150) (1, 2, 3).
Add 2 cups (¹/₂ liter) milk and the grated nutmeg (4).
Bring the mixture to boil over high heat, whisking constantly.
Pour in the remaining milk, bring to the simmer again, and season. Check the consistency, which should be thick enough to coat the back of a spoon* (5).
Stir in the cream, if using.
Transfer to a bowl and cover with plastic wrap flush with the surface. This will prevent a film from forming.

● Chef's note
Use a whisk to prepare your sauce to prevent lumps from forming.

● Did you know?
Traditionally, a béchamel is seasoned with fine salt, white pepper, and nutmeg. If you wish, replace the nutmeg with other spices like four-spice powder (pepper, nutmeg, cloves, and ginger), paprika, or old-fashioned French mustard* with seeds.*
This sauce comes to us from Marquis Louis de Béchameil, maître d'hôtel to King Louis XIV.

● Derived sauces
Mornay (egg yolk and grated Emmental cheese), half-milk and half-cream (very creamy béchamel), soubise (softened onions and béchamel sauce), Scottish sauce (light béchamel with chopped hard-boiled eggs).

❙ Recipe ideas
Rolled Picardy crêpes ›› p. 400
Gnocchi, Florentine-style ›› p. 388

Beurre blanc ★★

A cold, emulsified, unstable sauce.

Ingredients (serves 4)
1 average-sized shallot (about 1 oz. [30 g])
1 ¹/₂ tablespoons (25 ml) dry white wine
2 teaspoons (10 ml) white wine vinegar and/or lemon juice
1 stick (125 g) good quality unsalted butter, very cold and cubed
Salt, white pepper or Cayenne pepper

Peel, wash, and finely dice* the shallots.
Combine the white wine, vinegar, and shallots in a saucepan
(1). Place on low to medium heat and reduce*.
Do not allow the mixture to go completely dry. There should be
2-3 tablespoons of liquid left in the saucepan, and the shallots
will be nice and moist. The alcohol will have evaporated and
much of the acidity is removed.
Add the cubes of butter (2). Whisk in briskly to form the
emulsion (3). Too high a temperature will cause the sauce to
separate so it is best to leave it over a hot water bath at 122°F
(50°C).
Season.
If you wish, strain the sauce through a chinois* or fine-mesh
sieve.

● Chef's notes
*To obtain a nice, airy texture that will coat your dish attractively
without masking it, use an electric blender.
When re-heating the sauce, do not bring it to the boil.
It is best to prepare the sauce at the last minute.
The quality of the butter is all-important, for it determines the
taste of your sauce. For a balance of the salt seasoning, you may
use half unsalted butter and half salted butter.
As with all butter sauces, allow around 1 oz. (25–30 g) butter per
person when calculating the quantities for your guests.*

❙ Recipe idea
Fish terrine with beurre blanc >> p. 283

Melted butter ★

A hot, emulsified, unstable sauce.

Ingredients (serves 4)
1 ¹/₂ tablespoons (25 ml) lemon juice
2 teaspoons (10 ml) water
1 stick (125 g) good quality unsalted butter, cold and cubed
Pinch ground *piment d'Espelette**
Salt

Place the lemon juice and water in a saucepan and reduce* by half.
Whip the cubes of butter in until completely combined.
Season.

● Chef's note
*Even if the sauce is to be served hot (about 130°F or 55°C), make
sure that your butter cubes are well chilled. This will facilitate the
emulsion process.*

● Did you know?
*You can vary this butter with other citrus fruits: use grapefruit,
lime, or orange juice. Reduce* it by half and make an emulsion
with the butter.*

Bisque ★★

This uses crustaceans as a base, and is a thickened sauce. The following recipe is for a crayfish bisque.

Ingredients (serves 8)
1 ¾ lb. (800 g) crayfish shells
2 teaspoons (10 ml) olive oil
1 large onion
2 small shallots (40 g), finely diced*
1 carrot (80 g), finely diced
14 oz. (400 g) chopped tomatoes
3 ½ tablespoons (50 ml) cognac
6 cups (1.5 liters) white wine
6 cups (1.5 liters) fish fumet*
2 cloves garlic
1 bouquet garni*
2 tablespoons or 1 oz. (30 g) tomato paste
¾ cup (125 g) rice flour
¾ cup (200 ml) cream
Table salt, peppercorns

Sauté the shells over high heat in olive oil. They will turn a red-orange color.
Finely dice the onion, shallot, and carrots (make a mirepoix*).
Sweat* the ingredients.
Remove the gut from the crustaceans before you start cooking.
Crush the carcasses.
Add the chopped tomatoes. Deglaze* with cognac and add the white wine.
Reduce* by half and pour in the fish fumet, reserving a little to dilute the rice flour.
Add the garlic, bouquet garni, and tomato paste.
Simmer for 30 minutes, skimming if necessary.
Blend and strain through a chinois*.
Dilute the rice flour in the cold fish fumet you have reserved.
Add it to the crayfish coulis together with the cream. Return to the stove top and bring to the simmer so that it thickens.
Blend again and strain through cheesecloth (muslin).
Adjust the seasoning.

● Did you know?
This bisque has been known since 1651, when it was mentioned in Le Cuisinier François *(The French Cook) by La Varenne, a distinguished chef who authored the first rigorous works on cooking. In 1742, François Marin, who was chef to both Mme de Pompadour and the Marquis de Soubise (who gave his name to the sauce) and also the author of a well-known book on food, published it as a crayfish soup. Today, the bisque is a coulis of crustaceans usually thickened with rice flour.*

Shellfish coulis (or cream) ★★

This is a crustacean fumet* enriched with cream and/or butter.

Ingredients (serves 8)
2 shallots (50 g)
¼ large onion (50 g)
14 oz. (400 g) crustacean shells or whole small crustaceans
3 tablespoons (40 ml) olive oil
Scant ½ cup (100 ml) white wine
4 cups (1 liter) water
1 bouquet garni*
1 slightly heaped tablespoon (20 g) tomato paste
Peppercorns

Peel, wash, and finely slice the vegetables.
Crush the crustacean shells.
Heat the olive oil in a pot. Brown the aromatic base and add the shells.
Pour in the white wine and water. Add the bouquet garni, a few peppercorns, and the tomato paste.
Bring to a boil and simmer for 30 minutes, skimming whenever necessary.
Filter, refresh* over ice, and use within three days.

● Chef's note
All crustacean shells (langoustine, shrimps, crayfish, etc) as well as whole crustaceans, like small crabs, may be used.

❢ Recipe idea
Pike quenelles and crayfish sauce ›› p. 263

Basic savory preparations and sauces

Fresh tomato coulis ★

This is an emulsified, unstable cold sauce.

Ingredients (serves 4)
7 oz. (200 g) fresh ripe tomatoes
2 level teaspoons (10 g) tomato paste (optional)
$^{1}/_{2}$ tablespoon wine vinegar or lemon juice
Fresh herbs (basil, tarragon, chervil, chives)
Salt, freshly ground pepper
3 tablespoons (40 ml) olive oil

Wash the tomatoes and peel them by plunging them in boiling water (see p. 61). If you wish, you may remove the seeds. Process or blend with the tomato paste, vinegar, herbs, salt, and pepper, until the mixture is liquid (1, 2). Use an immersion blender to incorporate the olive oil. Strain through a fine-mesh sieve (3). Cover with plastic wrap and chill.

● Chef's note
This sauce does not remain stable for long—just a few minutes, in fact. It will need to be mixed again just before serving. For best results, make this sauce at the height of the tomato season.

Simple court bouillon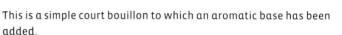

"Court bouillon" literally means "short boil" in French. It must only be simmered briefly with the cooking ingredients. Make sure you have enough liquid to cover all the pieces you are cooking. A simple court bouillon is made by brewing—it is a decoction. It is basically salted water with an acidic ingredient, like white wine, vinegar, or lemon juice. However, it is best not to use an acidic ingredient if you are cooking fish that is not white, such as salmon, because that would whiten it.

Ingredients (for 4 servings)
5 cups (1.25 liters) water
2 cups (0.5 liters) white wine
1 oz. (25 g) kosher salt
Scant ¹/₂ cup (100 ml) vinegar or lemon juice
1 bouquet garni*
5-6 peppercorns

Bring the water to boil with the white wine, kosher salt, and vinegar or lemon juice.
Simmer for 5 minutes and add the bouquet garni and peppercorns. Simmer for a few more minutes. Cool over ice if not using immediately. Keeps, chilled, for 2 days.

● Chef's notes
You may also make a simple court bouillon, from cold, with fish included. Fragile pieces of fish should be tied with twine so that they hold their shape during cooking.
For some shellfish and crustaceans, like shrimp and winkles, try recreating sea water with water and coarse sea salt (1 oz. per 4 cups or 30 g per liter) to use as a cooking base.

Vegetable court bouillon ★

This is a simple court bouillon to which an aromatic base has been added.

Ingredients (for 4 cups or 1 liter)
1 large carrot (3 ¹/₂ oz. or 100 g)
1 large onion (3 ¹/₂ oz. or 100 g)
3 ¹/₂ cups (800ml) water
³/₄ cup (200 ml) white wine
¹/₂ oz. (15 g) kosher salt
1 bouquet garni*
1 teaspoon (5 g) peppercorns

Peel, wash, and finely chop the vegetables.
Bring the water and white wine to the boil with the kosher salt.
Add the onion, and then the carrots.
Simmer for 15 minutes, then add the bouquet garni and the peppercorns. Simmer for a further few minutes.
Chill over an ice bath and use within 2 days.

● Chef's note
Most aromatic vegetables, as well as various kinds of seaweed and whole spices, are a tasty addition to this type of court bouillon.

White stock ★

This is a flavorsome liquid used as a base for many sauces and cooking methods. White stocks may be clear or thickened, and use bones, an aromatic base, and water. The solid ingredients are not browned.

Ingredients (for 4 cups or 1 liter)
1 lb. (500 g) veal, poultry, or game bones
½ carrot (2 oz./50 g)
½ onion (2 oz./50 g)
½ leek , white only (2 oz./50 g)
½ celery stalk (1 oz./30 g)
1 bouquet garni*
2 cloves
6 cups (1.5 liters) water

Slightly crush the bones and blanch* them. Rinse well.
Peel, wash, and cut the vegetables into chunks (1).
Place the bones in a cooking pot and cover with water.
Add the vegetables, bouquet garni, and cloves.
Bring to the boil.
Cook with the lid off, skimming regularly. Cooking time (the time necessary to extract the flavors) will depend on the size of the bones (1 to 3 hours). Here is a rough guide: small poultry bones: roughly 1 hour; chicken: 1 ½ hours; veal: 2 hours; beef: 3 hours.
Strain through a cheesecloth (muslin), skim the fat off, and chill over an ice bath. Chilled, this keeps for a maximum of 2 days.

● Chef's notes
Never season a white stock. If you reduce* it, the concentration of salt will increase.
To thicken it, make a roux liaison (½ cup [50 g] flour for 3 tablespoons plus 1 teaspoon [50 g] butter), or use starch (3 tablespoons cornstarch or 2 tablespoons potato starch [50 g], diluted in cold water).
Freeze-dried stocks or cubes are widely available and can be used to reduce preparation time.
A sauce allemande (literally, German sauce), which is a basic white sauce, comprises a white veal or poultry stock that is thickened and enriched with an aromatic base.

❘ Recipe ideas
Squab fricassee and garden peas à la française ›› p. 347
Rabbit stew with puréed Golden Hubbard squash ›› p. 340

Spiced or creamy court bouillon (*à la nage*) ★★

À la nage means "swimming"; here the main ingredient is served bathed in the liquid, to which a condiment and/or cream has been added. This is a vegetable court bouillon whose aromatic base is served with the main ingredient. Depending on the recipe, fish fumet* and vinegar may also be added.

● Chef's notes
Small pieces of fish and whole shellfish lend themselves particularly well to this court bouillon. The liquid, which is often very spicy, works as a marinade.
To prepare a fish au bleu, pour hot vinegar on very fresh fish to turn the mucus covering the scales a blue color.

● Did you know?
An escabèche is the name of a fish dish in which boiling court bouillon is poured over small fish or fish fillets and then slowly cooled. Escabèche literally means "without a head" (head is cabeza in Spanish; the marinade originated there), as the heads are removed from the fish.

❘ Recipe idea
Mackerel in *escabèche* ›› p. 316

Court bouillon with milk ★

This is used to preserve the natural color of certain white fish, such as turbot, halibut, and brill, or to tone down the intense smoked taste of herring and haddock, for example. Its components are salted water, milk, lemon, and sometimes a bouquet garni*.

Ingredients (for 4 cups or 1 liter)
1 lemon, preferably unsprayed or organic
3 ¼ cups (800 ml) water
¾ cup (200 ml) milk
1 bouquet garni*
½ oz. (15 g) kosher salt

Slice the lemon. Place all the ingredients in a pot to boil.
Chill rapidly over an ice bath, skim, and use within 24-36 hours.

● Chef's note
There is not much milk in this preparation because of the lemon, which causes it to curdle. This court bouillon is particularly good for pieces of large, flat fish such as turbot and halibut (2).

❘ Recipe idea
Turbot poached in cardamom-flavored milk with hollandaise sauce ›› p. 319

1

2

Basic savory preparations and sauces

Brown stock ★★

This flavorsome liquid is used as a base for many sauces and types of cooking. Brown stocks may be clear or thickened. They are made with bones, an aromatic base, and water. The ingredients are browned, unlike the method for a white stock, and this is what makes for a tastier stock.

Ingredients (for 4 cups or 1 liter)
1 lb. (500 g) bones
½ carrot (2 oz./50 g)
½ onion (2 oz./50 g)
½ leek (2 oz./50 g)
4 oz. (100 g) fresh tomato
½ celery stalk (1 oz./30 g)
1 bouquet garni*
2 cloves
6 cups (1.5 liters) water

Crush the bones, or ask your butcher to do so. Brown them in a very hot oven (425°F [220°C]) (1).
Peel, wash, and cut the vegetables into chunks (2).
Place the bones in a large pot and cover with water.
Add the vegetables, bouquet garni, and cloves.
Bring to the boil.
Cook with the lid off, skimming regularly. Cooking time (the time necessary to extract the flavors) will depend on the size of the bones (1 to 3 hours). A rough guide is small poultry bones: 1 hour; chicken: 1 ½ hours; veal: 2 hours; beef: at least 3 hours. Strain through a fine-meshed sieve, remove the fat, and cool down quickly.

● **Chef's note**
Do not confuse the jus* of a roast, made from the juices remaining after cooking, and a brown stock, which uses bones as a base.

● **Did you know?**
Sauce espagnole (basic brown sauce) is a veal stock, thickened and enriched with aromatic ingredients.
Demi-glace is a rich sauce made with sauce espagnole and reduced* by half.
Glace is a clear cooking jus without a liaison (brown stock, reduced court bouillon, fumet*) slowly reduced to a syrupy consistency. Used like this, it is strongly flavored. When cold, it takes on a jelly-like consistency.

Recipe ideas
Boeuf bourguignon with fresh pasta >> p. 363
Veal chops, Normandy-style >> p. 371
Kidneys in mustard sauce >> p. 367

1

2

3

Fumet* ★★ 🎬

This is a clear stock that is used to cook fish. It is also the base for aspic, the *chaud-froid*, and consommé, and can be clarified*. However, it is not recommended for fatty fish like sardines, eel, and herring, and freshwater fish. Some fish are cooked in a fumet with red wine, and this makes a stew called a matelote.

Ingredients (for 4 cups or 1 liter)

1 ¹/₂ lb. (600 g) fish bones
2 small shallots (2 oz./50 g)
¹/₂ large onion (2 oz./50 g)
¹/₂ leek (2 oz./50 g), white only
¹/₂ carrot (2 oz./50 g)
1 oz. (30 g) button mushrooms
1 bouquet garni*
4 cups (1 liter) water
²/₃ cup (150 ml) white wine
Peppercorns

Crush the fish bones. Leave them to soak in cold water until all traces of blood are removed.
Peel, wash, and finely slice the vegetables. Sweat* these gently and add liquid in two stages (see DVD), or just put straight into a large pot with all the other ingredients and bring to the boil (1, 2).
Skim when necessary (3).
Simmer for 25-30 minutes. Do not stir, as this will cloud the liquid.
Strain through a sieve, cool down rapidly, and use within 3 days.

● **Did you know?**
Essences are obtained by reducing liquids, stocks, or infusions to produce a concentrate of flavors.*

Recipe idea
Pollack fillets *bonne femme* >> p. 303

Basic savory preparations and sauces

Boiled vinegar and sugar (*gastrique*) ★

This is the base for a thickened sweet-and-sour sauce obtained by reduction*.

Ingredients (for 1 cup or ¼ liter of sauce)
Scant ½ cup (100 ml) vinegar
Scant ½ cup (80 g) sugar
1 scant cup (200 ml) liquid (juice, water, or stock) to bring the temperature down

Place the vinegar and the sugar in a saucepan (1).
Slowly bring to the boil and reduce until it reaches a syrupy consistency. (This is the stage before it caramelizes.)
Deglaze* with the liquid you have chosen (2) and stir until thoroughly mixed.

● Chef's notes

The liquid you use to reduce the temperature can be as varied as you wish. Try fruit juice, wine, coconut milk, soy sauce, and so on. Substitute honey or maple syrup for the sugar. With its sweet-and-sour taste, sauces that use gastrique show the influence of the cooking of both the English-speaking world and Asia on French cuisine.

❚ Recipe idea
Duckling à l'orange with sautéed potatoes and artichokes ›› p. 333

Marinades

These are flavorful, liquid preparations used to tenderize and enhance food, or, in the case of strong flavors (game and freshwater fish), tone them down. A marinade may also work as a preservative for certain foods. Marinades always include an acidic ingredient that acts on the proteins to tenderize the product. Some or all of the marinade liquid may be used to make sauces or cooking liquids. The food you marinate is always raw, so hygiene must be scrupulous. Check that the storage temperature is appropriately cold, and that the food is covered with plastic wrap or vacuum packed. The length of time a product is marinated depends on its size and type. A marinade will penetrate about ½ in. (1 cm) of a food every 24 hours. Marinades, like stocks, should not be seasoned with salt.

Instant marinade ★

This is used for small pieces, like fish steaks or fillets, steaks, and vegetables, usually before grilling. The base is a flavored oil to which an acidic ingredient like lemon juice is added. The food is left to marinate for 1–2 hours.

Ingredients (to marinate 8 pieces)
1 ½ cups (300 ml) olive oil
½ bunch fresh or dried herbs
1 sprig of thyme
Bay leaf (1 per piece)
2 lemons
Mignonette pepper

Pour half of the oil into a pan. Add the dried or fresh herbs, the thyme, and the bay leaves.
Arrange the pieces to be marinated in the pan and pour over the rest of the olive oil.
Peel the lemons, removing all the white pith, and slice them.
Place the lemon slices over the pieces and sprinkle with mignonette pepper.
Cover with plastic wrap and chill.

Turn the pieces over halfway through the process (allow 1–2 hours total).

● **Chef's note**
To marinate thick pieces, make incisions or prick them with a needle. This will enable the marinade to better penetrate the food and will result in improved flavor.

● **Did you know?**
Fish used to be preserved in a brine called eau marine (marine water) which gave rise to the word "marinade." The aim of the process was not to improve flavor, but merely to help preserve freshness in the days before it was possible to chill food.

Recipe idea
Grilled salmon steaks with braised fennel » p. 308

Raw marinade

This marinade uses wine, coconut milk, or beer, and a raw aromatic base comprising ingredients such as carrots, celery, onions, and seaweed. Add spices to intensify the basic flavors. Marinade the food from between 1 to 3 days.

Ingredients for a raw red wine marinade
(for 8 servings)
¹/₂ carrot (2 oz./50 g)
¹/₂ celery stalk (2 oz./50 g)
¹/₂ fennel bulb (2 oz./50 g)
¹/₂ bunch dried or fresh herbs
A sprig of thyme
Bay leaves (one per piece)
A pinch of peppercorns
6 cups (1.5 liters) red wine
Scant ¹/₂ cup (100 ml) wine vinegar
3 ¹/₂ tablespoons (50 ml) oil

Finely slice the vegetables for the aromatic base.
Place half of them at the bottom of a mixing bowl.
Place the pieces to be marinated over them.
Add the other half of the vegetables, the fresh or dried herbs, thyme, bay leaves, and peppercorns.
Cover with wine and vinegar and drizzle the olive oil over.
Cover with plastic wrap and chill.

● Chef's notes
Depending on your recipe, you may use cognac or Armagnac as well as wine and vinegar.
To make foie gras, soak it in milk to reduce any bitterness and then marinate it in a strong alcohol such as port, cognac, or Armagnac.
You can omit the oil poured over the surface if—when covering the container—you ensure the plastic wrap lies flush with the marinade.

Cooked marinade ★

Cooked marinade contains the same ingredients as raw marinade. Sweat* the aromatic base, add the wine, and simmer for 30 minutes. Cool before using.

Ingredients for a cooked white wine marinade
(for 8 servings)
¹/₂ carrot (2 oz./50 g)
¹/₂ celery stalk (2 oz./50 g)
¹/₂ onion (2 oz./50 g)
3 ¹/₂ tablespoons (50 ml) oil
6 cups (1.5 litres) white wine
Scant ¹/₂ cup (100 ml) wine vinegar
3 ¹/₂ tablespoons (50 ml) cognac or Armagnac
4 garlic cloves (20 g)
¹/₂ bunch dried or fresh herbs
A sprig of thyme
Bay leaves (1 per piece)
Peppercorns

Finely slice the vegetables for the aromatic base.
Sweat them in oil, or brown them just slightly.
Cover them with all the liquid ingredients. Add the garlic, dried or fresh herbs, thyme, bay leaves, and a few peppercorns.
Bring to a simmer and cook for about 30 minutes.
Allow to cool.
Cover with plastic wrap and chill.

● Chef's note
If you are using your marinade as a stock, choose a good-quality wine, as it will determine the final taste.

Mayonnaise ★

A cold, stable emulsified sauce.

Ingredients (serves 4)
1 egg yolk
1 heaped teaspoon (15 g) French mustard*
1 teaspoon (5 ml) wine vinegar
Salt, white pepper or Cayenne pepper
²/₃ cup (150 ml) sunflower seed oil

Combine the egg yolk, mustard, vinegar, salt, and pepper (1).
Pour the oil in gradually, whisking energetically all the while,
(or use an electric beater) (2).
Check that the texture is firm (3), scrape down the sides so that
it forms a compact mass, cover with plastic wrap, and chill.

● Chef's notes
*If your mayonnaise separates (i.e. the emulsion disaggregates),
add a little water, 1 tablespoon maximum, and/or some egg yolk.
Beat together again so that the emulsion re-forms.
Never season with salt when the mayonnaise is ready, as this
might form white spots.
If you add a drop of vinegar when you have finished whipping
the mayonnaise, this will give it a slightly paler color, intensify
the taste a little, and reduce the risk of contamination by
salmonella.
Fresh mayonnaise, covered and chilled, keeps no longer than 48
hours.*

🥄 Recipe idea
Plaice *goujonnettes* with sauce tartare ›› p. 315

Basic savory preparations and sauces

Pesto and *pistou* ★

A cold, unstable emulsified sauce.

Pesto ingredients (serves 4)
3 cloves of new garlic (15 g)
3 tablespoons (25 g) pine nuts
3/4 cup (200 ml) fresh basil leaves
1/4 cup (40 g) finely grated Parmesan cheese
1/3 cup (75 ml) olive oil
Salt, freshly ground pepper

Remove the leaves from the basil. Wash them and dry well.
Remove the shoots from the garlic cloves. Lightly roast the pine
nuts. Crush them all together with a mortar and pestle (1, 2).
Add the basil and Parmesan cheese. Crush again and whisk in
the olive oil (3).
Season with salt and pepper.

● **Did you know?**
Pesto comes from Italy—from Genoa, to be precise.
Pistou is from Provence, and is made of fresh crushed basil with
garlic cloves and olive oil.
Pesto and pistou both work well with pasta.
Both words derive from the Latin "pistare," which means to crush
or pound.

❘ **Recipe idea**
❘ Beef carpaccio, Parmesan, and *pistou* ≫ p. 252

Rouille ★

A cold, stable emulsified sauce.

Ingredients (serves 4)
2 ½ oz. (75 g) mealy potatoes
2–3 garlic cloves (15 g), peeled, shoots removed
1 egg yolk
⅓ cup (75 ml) olive oil
1 ½ tablespoons (25 ml) peanut oil
Saffron, ground or threads
Salt, freshly ground pepper

Boil the potatoes in their jackets. When cooked, peel and mash them, and place them in a mixing bowl.
Crush the garlic cloves and mix with the potatoes.
Mix in the egg yolk (2) and whisk in the oils (3).
Add a little saffron (4) and adjust the seasoning.
Scrape down the sides of the bowl, cover with plastic wrap so it lies flush with the surface, and chill.

● **Chef's note**
This sauce is the perfect accompaniment to fish soup.

● **Did you know?**
The name of the sauce comes from its color (rouille means rust), since it includes orange-yellow saffron.

🍴 **Recipe idea**
Rockfish soup >> p. 268

Basic savory preparations and sauces

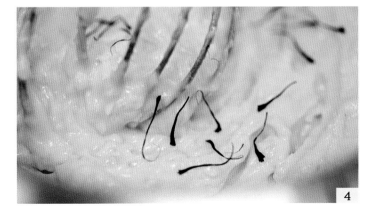

Sauce américaine ★★

This sauce is traditionally made using velvet swimming crabs, but you may also use lobster (which makes a Newburg sauce) or crayfish, which makes a Nantua sauce. It is a thickened sauce.

Ingredients (serves 8)
1 ³/₄ lb. (800 g) small crabs
Scant ¹/₂ cup (100 ml) olive oil
1 large onion (3 ¹/₂ oz./100 g)
3-4 shallots (3 oz./80 g)
1 large carrot (3 ¹/₂ oz./100 g)
7 oz. (200 g) chopped tomatoes
3 tablespoons (40 g) tomato paste
3 ¹/₂ tablespoons (50 ml) cognac
³/₄ cup (200 ml) white wine
6 cups (1.5 liters) fish fumet*
2 garlic cloves
1 bouquet garni*
1 sprig tarragon
1 pinch *piment d'Espelette**
Salt, freshly ground pepper

For the blond (straw-colored) roux (see Velouté, p. 150)
2 tablespoons (1 oz. or 30 g) butter
¹/₃ cup (30 g) flour

Prepare the roux with the butter and flour.
Set aside to cool.
Roughly slice the crabs (1). Heat the olive oil and begin cooking them (2). Finely dice* the onions, shallots, and carrots to make a mirepoix*. Add the vegetables to the pot and sweat* them. Chop up the carcasses into small pieces. Add the chopped tomatoes and tomato paste (3). Deglaze* with Cognac and flambé*. Then add the white wine (4). Reduce* by half and pour in the fish fumet. Add the garlic, bouquet garni, and tarragon leaves. Simmer for 30 minutes, skimming when necessary. Blend in a food processor and strain through a chinois*. Pour the strained liquid over the cooled roux and bring it all to the simmer, stirring all the time so that it thickens (5). Adjust the seasoning and reserve until needed.

● Did you know?
No one quite knows where this sauce originated, despite its name. It is also known as a sauce à l'armoricaine (Armorica is an old Gaulish name for an area including Brittany). However it's likely that it was the invention of Pierre Fraisse, a French cook who had worked in the United States of America before returning to Paris and setting up Peters Restaurant in Paris.

❙ Recipe idea
Monkfish medallions *à l'américaine* and rice pilaf ›› p. 323

Béarnaise sauce ★★★

A hot, stable emulsified sauce.

Ingredients (serves 4)
1 gray shallot
3 tablespoons (40 ml) dry white wine
3 tablespoons (40 ml) tarragon vinegar
1 sprig tarragon
3 egg yolks
$^{1}/_{2}$ cup (120 g) good quality unsalted butter, cubed and softened*
A few chervil sprigs
8 peppercorns, crushed
Fine sea salt

Peel, wash, and finely slice the shallot.
Put the white wine, vinegar, shallots, and some of the tarragon leaves into a saucepan and prepare the reduction* over low heat **(1)**.
Do not reduce until dry; there should be a few tablespoons of liquid left and the shallots will be moist. Most of the acidity will have disappeared.
Allow to cool while the flavors blend.
Add the egg yolks and place the pot over hot water (bain-marie)* or very low heat and whisk until the consistency is nice and thick–it should resemble a sabayon **(2)**.
Add the softened butter, continuing to whisk **(3)**.
Strain through a fine-mesh sieve.
Chop the rest of the tarragon and the chervil. Adjust the seasoning and add the chopped herbs.

● Did you know?
The French term fines herbes* is used for the following herbs only: parsley, chervil, chives, and tarragon. Tarragon has the strongest flavor of the four, with a pronounced aniseed-type taste.

❙ Recipe idea
Grilled rib roast and béarnaise sauce >> p. 356

1

2

3

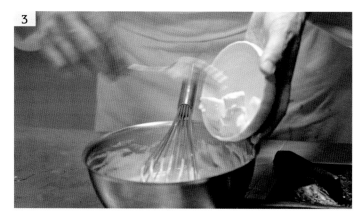

Basic savory preparations and sauces

Hollandaise sauce ★★ 🎬

A hot, stable emulsified sauce.

Ingredients (serves 4)
3 egg yolks
3 teaspoons water
1 stick (120 g) good quality unsalted butter, clarified*
4 teaspoons (20 ml) lemon juice
Table salt
Cayenne pepper or *piment d'Espelette**

Whisk the egg yolks with the water. Place them over a bain-marie* or over very low heat and continue whisking until the mixture is nice and thick. Remove from the heat and whip in the melted butter (2).
Season and add the lemon juice.

● Chef's notes
If your egg yolks become grainy because the mixture is overcooked, add a little water and whip. However, if you have really overcooked the sauce, start again from the beginning.
If the sauce separates into watery liquid and fatty matter, add a small amount of cold water or an ice cube and work into an emulsion again.
Hollandaise sauce, just like béarnaise sauce, cools down rapidly. It is therefore important to make these sauces at the last moment or to keep them warm over a hot water bath.

● Did you know?
The recipe is a tribute to the quality of the dairy products of the Netherlands.

❗ Recipe idea
Turbot poached in cardamom-flavored milk
with hollandaise sauce ›› p. 319

Tartare sauce ★

A cold, stable emulsified sauce.

Ingredients (serves 4)
2 hard-boiled egg yolks
1 tablespoon (15 ml) French mustard*
1 teaspoon (5 ml) wine vinegar
²/₃ cup (150 ml) sunflower seed oil
A few sprigs chives
2 new onions (2 oz./50 g)
Salt, white pepper or Cayenne pepper or *piment d'Espelette**

Prepare a mayonnaise (see p. 143), replacing the raw egg yolk with finely chopped or well crushed hard-boiled yolks.
Finely slice the chives and onions and add them to the sauce.
Season with salt and pepper.
Scrape down the sides of the bowl, cover with plastic wrap flush with the surface, and chill.

🥄 **Recipe idea**
Plaice *goujonnettes* with tartare sauce ›› p. 315

Tomato sauce ★

Recipes for thickened tomato sauce only appeared in cookery books early in the nineteenth century.

Ingredients (serves 8)
3 ¹/₂ oz. (100 g) smoked bacon
3 tablespoons (40 g) butter
1 carrot (3 oz./80 g)
1 onion (3 oz./80 g)
Scant ²/₃ cup (60 g) flour
3 lb. (1.5 kg) ripe tomatoes
2 cloves garlic
1 bouquet garni*
3 tablespoons (40 g) tomato paste (optional)
4 cups (1 liter) water
2 teaspoons (10 g) sugar (optional)
Salt, freshly ground pepper
Special equipment: ovenproof pan

Cut the smoked bacon into small cubes and blanch*.
Peel, wash, and finely dice* the carrots and onions to make a mirepoix*. Sauté the bacon bits in butter in an ovenproof pan and add the diced vegetables.
Preheat the oven to 350°F (180°C).

Allow to brown a little and sprinkle with flour (1). Mix in the flour and place the dish in the oven for a few minutes. (This has the advantage of making the flour digestible without burning the sauce over direct heat.) Remove from the oven and lower the heat to 285°F (140°C).
Wash, peel, seed, and chop the tomatoes and add them to the other ingredients. Remove the shoot from the garlic cloves and crush. Add the garlic, bouquet garni, and tomato paste (2). Pour in the water and season. Cover and cook in the oven for 1 hour. Strain through a sieve or chinois*, check the consistency and the seasoning, adding sugar if necessary.

● **Chef's note**
If serving this sauce plain with pasta, allow 2 cups of sauce for about 10 servings. But this is a basic recipe that can be enriched with flavorings, such as basil or celery, and meat, such as ham.

● **Did you know?**
Tomato sauce is used in many preparations, such as bolognese sauce, with sautéed minced meat, deviled sauce, zingara sauce, tomato chaud-froid, and the hussard, which contains finely sliced onions and shallots, and is deglazed with white wine and covered with a demi-glaze to which tomatoes have been added.*

Velouté ★

A velouté is a cooking liquid (such as a stock or a fumet*) that is thickened with a roux. It has a creamy consistency, and is considered a basic liquid, with fish, poultry, and veal velouté, for example.

Ingredients (for 4 cups or 1 liter)
4 tablespoons (60 g) butter
Scant ²/₃ cup (60 g) flour
4 cups (1 liter) liquid, such as a white stock or fumet
Scant ¹/₂ cup (100 ml) thick crème fraîche (optional)
A pinch of grated nutmeg (optional)
Salt, freshly ground pepper

Make a white roux: melt the butter over low heat. Remove from the heat and add the flour. Mix in well and whisk over very low heat for a few minutes without letting it brown.
Stir in 2 cups (0.5 liter) of the cold cooking liquid. Bring to the boil over high heat, whisking constantly. Pour in the rest of the cooking liquid and the cream and bring to the boil again, stirring constantly. Boil for 2 minutes. Remove from the heat and season.
Transfer to a dish and cover with plastic wrap flush with the surface. This will prevent a skin from forming.

● Chef's notes
If you follow all the steps carefully, whisking well, you should not have any lumps.
If you have a cold roux, use a hot liquid (and vice versa). Use this method if you are making large quantities.

● Did you know?
A blond roux is a white roux that has been cooked just a few minutes longer, until it turns a nice straw color. It is more digestible because the starch in the flour is cooked.

● Some derived sauces
Cardinal sauce: (fish velouté, truffles, lobster coulis); Allemande sauce (ordinary velouté thickened with egg yolks); aurore (chicken velouté with tomatoes); Chivry (chicken velouté with herbs); curry (onions, apples, curry, coconut milk, velouté); normande (sole velouté, mushrooms essence and oyster jus).*

Vinaigrette ★

This is a cold, unstable emulsified sauce, used as a salad dressing.

Ingredients (serves 4)
2 ¹/₂ tablespoons (40 ml) vinegar
¹/₂ cup (125 ml) oil
Salt, freshly ground pepper

Dissolve a little table salt in the vinegar. Grind in the pepper. Whisk the mixture with the oil until it emulsifies.

● Chef's notes
Adding mustard to your vinaigrette will give it a stronger taste and stabilize it too.*
You can vary this basic recipe by using a flavored oil (see p. 155).

● Did you know?
It goes almost without saying that vinegar is the most important ingredient in a vinaigrette. It is produced through the fermentation of wine or other alcohol and contains a minimum of 6 percent acetic acid. In France, wine vinegar is the type most widely used, and it is also used in recipes for deglazing.*
Balsamic vinegar comes from the Modena and Reggio Emilia regions of Italy. The traditional vinegar is produced by cooking/reducing grape juice must, which is then aged in oak casks.*

❘ Recipe ideas
Mixed garden vegetables ›› p. 391
Sesame-coated rabbit liver salad ›› p. 276

Flavored butters

The quality of butter and flavoring you choose will determine the taste of your final ingredient. Bear in mind that butter takes on other tastes and must be carefully stored. Cover it well after each use and return to the refrigerator, where it should be kept at between 35.6°F–39.2°F (2°C–4°C). Once butter has been worked with, it goes rancid more quickly.

Butter

Butter is made from the milk or cream of cow's milk. The minimum fat content of butter is 80 percent. Butter usually contains 18 percent water and 2 percent dry matters, including casein proteins and mineral salts. It should not contain any additives besides salt. France has a number of AOC butters, and the flavor of any particular butter is a result of the fodder given to the cows, their region and breed, and even of the seasons.

The first known written mention of butter goes back to 2500 BCE. It was not a foodstuff that the Romans and Greeks liked much, using it mainly for medicinal purposes (to heal wounds). In the Western world, butter is made from cows' milk, but in Africa and Asia other types of milk may be used.

Until the end of the Middle Ages, butter in Europe was considered to be a poor man's fat. After this period, however, demand for butter as a foodstuff increased. As it climbed the ladder of culinary respectability, the concept of *terroir* gradually came into play. Normandy and Brittany, particularly fertile regions with significant dairy production, are renowned for the quality of their butter. Farm production in France was widespread until the 1960s, when industrial production took over to the detriment of small producers. Today, France is Europe's largest butter-producing country, and has the highest per capita consumption in the world: the average French person consumes just over 17 lb. (8 kg) a year.

If using butter on its own (as a spread), allow about 1 1/2–2 tablespoons (25–30 g) per person. As an ingredient to emulsify a sauce, use much less, 1–2 teaspoons (5–10 g) per person.
Butter may be worked and enriched:
• cold and raw
• cold, incorporating cooked ingredients
• hot

Flavored butters (cold and raw)

Name	Ingredients (for 2 sticks or 250 g butter)
Nut butters (almond, hazelnut, pistachio, etc.)	1 3/4 cup (150 g) ground almonds*, hazelnuts, or pistachios
Anchovy butter	3 1/2 oz. (100 g) anchovies in oil or salt
Beurre d'escargot (snail butter) (see p. 153)	1 chopped shallot (25 g) 1 clove garlic, shoot removed and crushed 2 tablespoons (20 g) chopped parsley Fine sea salt, freshly ground pepper
Maître d'hôtel butter	1 tablespoon (10 g) chopped parsley + 1/4 cup (60 ml) lemon juice Salt, freshly ground pepper
Horseradish butter	2 tablespoons (50 g) shredded horseradish Salt, freshly ground pepper
Smoked salmon butter (and other fish)	3 1/2 oz. (100 g) smoked salmon (or trout, sturgeon, eel, smoked herring) Salt, freshly ground pepper
Mustard* butter	2 heaped tablespoons (80 g) Meaux mustard (with seeds) Table salt, freshly ground pepper
Cheese butters (Roquefort, cream cheeses, etc.)	3–4 oz. (100–125 g) cheese, depending on strength Salt, freshly ground pepper
Sea urchin butter	1 teaspoon (25 g) sea urchin coral + 1 teaspoon (5 ml) lemon juice Salt, freshly ground pepper
Seaweed butter	2 oz. (50 g) fresh nori and/or dulse and/or sea lettuce
Shellfish butter (oyster, cockles, clams, etc.)	3 1/2 oz. (100 g) raw, shelled shellfish with their liquid 1 1/3 tablespoons (20 ml) lemon juice Fine sea salt, freshly ground pepper

Cold flavored butters with cooked ingredients

Name	Ingredients (for 2 sticks or 250 g butter)
Bercy butter	3 small shallots (80 g), finely sliced, reduced with $^{1}/_{3}$ cup (80 ml) dry white wine
	1 teaspoon (5 g) chopped parsley
	3 $^{1}/_{3}$ tablespoons (50 ml) lemon juice
	1 oz. (25 g) poached, diced* spinal marrow of sturgeon
	Salt, freshly ground pepper
Chivry butter	$^{3}/_{4}$ cup (200 g) herbs, blanched* and squeezed to drain
	(salad burnet, chervil, parsley, tarragon, chives)
	2 shallots (50 g), sliced and blanched
	Salt, freshly ground pepper
Shrimp butter	10 oz. (250 g) brown shrimp, poached in salt water and shelled
	Salt, freshly ground pepper
Roe butter	4 $^{1}/_{2}$ oz. (125 g) poached roe (herring, carp, mackerel)
	1 teaspoon (10 g) French mustard*
	Salt, freshly ground pepper
Herb butter (tarragon, parsley, shallot, etc.)	$^{1}/_{3}$ cup or 4 $^{1}/_{2}$ oz. (125 g) tarragon or parsley or shallot, blanched
	and chopped
	Salt, freshly ground pepper
Montpellier butter	Spinach leaves, watercress, parsley, chervil, chives, tarragon,
	shallots ($^{1}/_{6}$ oz. or 5 g of each)
	Blanch and reduce to a paste with:
	Gherkins, capers, anchovy fillets ($^{1}/_{2}$ oz. or 15 g of each)
	1 garlic clove
	1 egg yolk, hard-boiled
	1 egg yolk, raw
	Salt, Cayenne pepper
	Scant $^{1}/_{2}$ cup (100 ml) oil (to facilitate straining)
Paprika butter	3 shallots (80 g), chopped and sweated*
	1 scant teaspoon (4 g) paprika
	Salt, freshly ground pepper
Hôtelier butter (made from maître d'hôtel butter, so no need to add 2 sticks [250 g] uncooked butter)	6 oz. (170 g) maître d'hôtel butter
	4 oz. (125 g) button mushrooms
	1 small shallot (20 g) } dry duxelles
	2 teaspoons (10 g) butter
Marseillaise butter (made from maître d'hôtel butter, so no need to add 2 sticks [250 g] uncooked butter)	6 oz. (170 g) maître d'hôtel butter
	$^{1}/_{4}$ cup or 2 $^{3}/_{4}$ oz. (80 g) chopped, cooked tomato fondue
	3 garlic cloves
	2 pinches (1 g) fennel or anise seeds
Crustacean butter	7 oz. (200 g) cooked crustacean meat
	Salt, freshly ground pepper

Hot prepared butters

Names	Ingredients (for 2 sticks or 250 g butter)
Lobster Butter	$^{1}/_{2}$ lb. (250 g) flesh (head, antenna, appendages) of lobster, plus coral
	Salt, freshly ground pepper
Red Butter (see p. 154)	$^{1}/_{2}$ lb. (250 g) crustacean shells, (crayfish, small crabs, langoustes, etc)
	Salt, freshly ground pepper

Snail butter (*beurre d'escargot*) ★

This is made cold using raw ingredients that are chopped or puréed and incorporated into softened butter*. For this technique, it is advisable to use the blade knife of a food processor.
Allow 1–1 ½ tablespoons (15–20 g) snail butter per person if you are serving individual portions.

Ingredients (serves 8)
2 sticks (250 g) softened butter
1 grey shallot (25 g), chopped
1 clove garlic (4 g), shoot removed, minced
2 tablespoons (20 g) chopped parsley
Salt, freshly ground pepper

Use a rubber spatula to combine all the ingredients, or use a food processor. Check that they are thoroughly mixed.
Scrape down the sides of the bowl, cover with plastic wrap, and chill until needed.

● Chef's note
If you can find butter with salt crystals, such as butter with sel de Guérande, it will give a pleasantly light crunch to your preparation. When keeping the snail butter in the refrigerator or freezer, wrap it in plastic wrap so that it does not absorb any tastes and smells.

● Did you know?
*You should not put aluminum foil in contact with butter, because it oxidizes in the presence of salt and acidic ingredients like lemon juice and vinegar, and imparts its metallic taste.
Snail butter was initially only used with snails, but today it accompanies shellfish, crustaceans, and even frogs.*

Beurre manié ★

Use of this butter will allow you to adjust the creaminess of sauces. Ensure that you cook the preparation sufficiently so that the beurre manié does not give a pasty, grainy texture to them. Another reason for cooking it is to ensure that the flour is digestible.

Ingredients
Equal quantities of softened butter and flour.
Combine the two using a fork until thoroughly blended.

● Chef's note
This liaison butter can be made a few hours ahead of time, and even stored 2–3 days in the refrigerator if completely covered in plastic wrap. It is best to use unsalted butter.

Recipe idea
Soft-boiled eggs on a bed of artichokes with eggplant caviar » p. 392

Shallot butter with red wine (*beurre marchand de vin*) ★

This butter is prepared cold using cooked, cooled, and blended ingredients that are then incorporated into softened butter*. For an even more refined butter, strain it through a sieve.

Ingredients (serves 8)
³/₄ cup (200 ml) red wine
2-3 shallots (80 g), finely sliced
2 sticks (250 g) unsalted butter, softened
Salt, freshly ground pepper

Place the red wine and sliced shallot in a saucepan over low heat.
Reduce* gently until dry.
Allow to cool.
Mix in the softened butter and season (1).
Scrape down the sides of the bowl, cover with plastic wrap, and set to chill until needed.

● Chef's note
The quality of the wine is decisive for the final taste. This sauce comes to us from the Bordeaux region, where it was made using only local red wine.

Red butter (*beurre rouge*) ★★

This is prepared hot. The cooked ingredients infuse slowly in the butter before being blended, strained, and cooled.
This flavored butter is dry, and is mainly used to whip into sauces for crustaceans at the last minute.

Ingredients (serves 8)
2 sticks (250 g) unsalted butter, softened*
10 oz. (300 g) crayfish shells
1 ¹/₃ tablespoons (20 ml) lemon juice
Salt
A little *piment d'Espelette**

Blend all the ingredients together (2).
Place on very low heat–maximum 140°F (60°C)–or over a hot water bath and infuse for 1 hour.
Strain through a fine-mesh sieve, cover with plastic wrap lying flush with the butter. Chill until firm.

● Chef's notes
A flavored butter made using the infusing technique loses some of its delicacy, and the taste of the main ingredient will predominate.

A butter prepared in this way becomes a little dry and hard due to the loss of water and the addition of protein.
If you wish, add other aromatic ingredients while the butter is infusing.

Flavored oils ★

Flavored oils are used for seasoning, hot or cold, as well as to preserve food and cook it (frying, oil fondues, and slow cooking in oil). Select your oil (olive, sunflower seed, grapeseed, etc) according to the use (cooking or seasoning), the taste (neutral or with a pronounced taste), and the consistency you require (fluid or thick). For added taste, immerse one or several aromatic ingredients in the oil or mixture of oils and heat to a maximum of 140°F (60°C) to infuse. This will accelerate the blending of the soluble aromas. Examples: truffle oil, dry or fresh herb oil, lobster shell oil, vanilla oil, chili oil, and cinnamon and star anise oil.

Make sure your oil containers are properly closed and out of the light so that they do not go rancid.

Oils are vegetable products and have many nutritional qualities, contributing to lowering cholesterol levels, prevention of heart disease, thinning the blood, etc.

Variety	Characteristics	Uses
Sweet almond	Delicate flavor with almond taste, clear	Cold seasoning
Peanut	Neutral, clear, multipurpose	Seasoning and cooking
Argan	Strongly flavored, dark red color, musk flavor	Cold seasoning
Hemp	Green, taste of fresh herbs and hay	Cold seasoning
Canola/rapeseed (refined)	Neutral with a slight herbal taste	Cold seasoning
Copra (coconut)	White concentrated oil with very little taste	Seasoning and cooking
Wheat germ	Neutral with a slight seed taste.	Seasoning and cooking, frying
Hazelnut, walnut	Distinctive flavor	Cold seasoning
Olive: may be virgin or extra virgin, depending on the percentage of oleic acid	More or less pronounced green color	Seasoning and cooking
Palm oil (from the fruit pulp)	Solid, red	Seasoning and cooking
Palm kernel (from the kernel of the fruit)	Solid, white	Seasoning and cooking
Grapeseed	Golden green, very little taste	Seasoning and cooking (fondues)
Sesame	Powerful taste, transparent, liquid	Cold seasoning
Soybean oil (most widely consumed in the world)	Neutral with a slight herbal taste, refined	Cold seasoning
Sunflower seed	Neutral, gold	Seasoning and cooking

Basic savory preparations and sauces

Stuffings and forcemeats

A stuffing contains a mixture of ingredients—vegetable, meat, or fish, usually in a combination. It may be mixed to varying degrees of smoothness, cooked, and used to garnish a food. In fact, you can even serve them on their own. Stuffings are used to create a soft texture and combine flavors.

Basic duxelles (mushrooms) ★

Instead of using shallots and onions, you may use one or the other. Lemon juice squeezed over the mushrooms will prevent them from going black; do be careful to use very little so that the mixture does not become too sour.
A duxelles is used as a base for many different dishes. Enrich it with different flavors, such as ham, garlic, or parsley.

Ingredients (serves 8)
2 tablespoons (30 g) butter
1 ¹/₂ shallot (40 g), finely sliced
¹/₂ onion (40 g), finely sliced
¹/₂ lb. (250 g) button mushrooms, chopped
1 teaspoon (5 g) chopped parsley
Salt, freshly ground pepper

Sweat* the shallots and onions in butter. When they are translucent, add the mushrooms and cook, uncovered, until all their water has evaporated.
Season and add the parsley.

● **Chef's note**
Use the basic duxelles for hôtelier butter, stuffed vegetable side dishes, hot oysters, and more.

❡ **Recipe idea**
Rolled Picardy crêpes >> p. 400

Duxelles for stuffing ★

Ingredients (serves 8)
¹/₄ lb. (250 g) dry duxelles (see recipe above right)
3 ¹/₂ tablespoons (50 ml) dry white wine
2 oz. (50 g) glaze* (fish, meat, poultry consommé; prepare ahead of time or buy at specialty stores)
1 thin slice (1 oz. or 25 g) fresh sandwich loaf

Heat the dry duxelles and pour the white wine over. Reduce* over low heat. Add the glaze. Push the bread through a sieve and combine it with the duxelles to bind it.

● **Chef's note**
You can use the duxelles recipe to stuff vegetable side dishes, fish, poultry breasts, and legs.

● **Did you know?**
This mushroom stuffing is mentioned in the cooking treatise Les dons de Comus *(The Blessings of Comus), a book by François Marin published in 1739. It was created by François Pierre de La Varenne, the greatest French chef of the seventeenth century, who developed many master techniques for lavish recipes.*

Mousseline stuffing (cream-based) ★ 🎬

A fine, light, smooth mixture used to stuff meats and fish.

Ingredients (serves 8)
¹/₄ lb. (250 g) fish or meat (poultry, veal, whiting, sole)
1 egg white
Generous ²/₃ cup (180 ml) whipping cream
Salt, pepper or chili pepper

Roughly chop and season the fish or meat (1).
Place it in the food processor with the blade knife (2), process, add the egg white, then process a little further. Transfer to a stainless steel bowl set over an ice bath. Gradually stir the cream in (3). Push the mixture through a sieve (4).
Adjust the seasoning.
Scrape down the sides of the bowl, cover with plastic wrap flush with the mousseline, and chill.

● Chef's notes
Whipping cream is less acidic than crème frâiche or heavy cream.
If your fish has a high water content, reduce the quantity of cream. On the other hand, if you are using meats that are dry, like poultry and rabbit, increase the quantity of cream.
The seasoning will intensify slightly during the cooking process.
Add a personal touch to your stuffing with finely chopped aromatic ingredients (finely diced*, julienned vegetables, vegetable sticks, shrimp salpicon*) or spices. Let your culinary imagination inspire you.

● Did you know?
All the recipes that go under the name of "mousseline" (sauces, creams, and stuffings) designate preparations that are light and airy.
A purée of dried vegetables made using the same technique as this creamy mousseline gives a flan, when made with cream and eggs, or a mousse, when made using only egg whites.
You could put this technique into practice by making a colored terrine with layers of carrots, turnips, and green beans.
Mousseline stuffings are used for paupiettes, timbales, some chartreuses (layered dishes), souffléd or stuffed fish, and pastries with slatted pastry topping.

❙ Recipe idea
Stuffed chicken legs with chestnuts ≫ p. 344

Mousseline stuffing (butter-based) ★

This is a delicate stuffing that is creamy when sliced.

Ingredients (serves 8)
¹/₂ lb. (250 g) fish or meat (poultry, veal, whiting, sole)
2 eggs
1 egg yolk
Generous ³/₄ cup (200 g) unsalted butter, softened*
Salt, pepper or chili pepper

Process the fish or meat with the blade attachment. Push through a sieve.
Add the eggs and the yolk, and then the softened butter.
Blend the ingredients thoroughly.
Season.
Scrape down the sides of the bowl, cover with plastic wrap so that it is flush with the mousseline, and chill.

● Chef's note
The delicacy of the mousseline depends on the meshing of your sieve—the finer the sieve, the finer the mousseline.
Do not work the butter mousseline over ice because it will harden the butter too fast.
This preparation is mainly used for meat and requires slow cooking.
Play on the natural colors of your stuffing—salmon will give a pink hue and anything with chlorophyll will make it green. You can also use natural colorants to accentuate it.

Basic panada stuffing ★★

Panada stuffing uses a paste made with flour, bread, or another starch for thickening. It is particularly suitable for poaching.

Ingredients (serves 8)
¹/₂ lb. (250 g) meat, fish, or crustaceans
2 egg whites
³/₄ cup (200 ml) cream (optional)
1 generous pinch table salt
1 pinch pepper

Panada
¹/₂ cup (125 ml) fumet*, water, or milk
³/₄ stick (¹/₃ cup or 90 g) unsalted butter
1 ¹/₄ cups (125 g) all-purpose flour
4 eggs

Make a panada using the same method as for choux pastry (see p. 20). Bring the liquid and butter to the boil, then pour in the flour. Mix with a spatula over a low heat until it dries out. Remove from the heat and add the eggs, one by one, mixing thoroughly each time. Allow to cool.
Process the meat, fish, or crustaceans in a food processor using the blade knife. Gradually pour in the egg whites, followed by the cold panada.
Adjust the seasoning and push through a sieve.
If necessary, thin your stuffing with cream.

● Did you know?
This recipe is also used to make quenelles (see recipe p. 263).
They are shaped into oval scoops with two spoons and poached.
Quenelles are a typical dish from in and around Lyon.

❘ Recipe idea
Pike quenelles and crayfish sauce >> p. 263

Gratin stuffing (*farce à gratin*) ★

This delicately minced chicken liver can be served on canapés and as an accompaniment for poultry and game birds.

Ingredients
3 ½ oz. (100 g) fatty bacon
10 oz. (300 g) poultry or game bird livers
2 oz. (50 g) shallots, finely sliced
2 tablespoons (30 ml) Cognac
Thyme flowers
Salt, freshly ground pepper

Sauté the fatty bacon so that it renders some of its fat. Clean the livers and remove the nerves. Add them to the pan (1).
When they are half-cooked, i.e. still very pink, add the finely sliced shallots (2) and flambé* with the cognac (3).
Season and scatter with a few thyme flowers.
Process the stuffing and push it through a sieve.
Scrape down the sides of the bowl, cover with plastic wrap flush with the stuffing, and chill.

● Chef's note
Make sure that the livers are browned outside but still pink inside. If they are overdone, your stuffing will be dry and grainy.

● Did you know?
This recipe was traditionally made with the livers of cooked poultry.
Today, it is often spread on canapés to accompany poultry.

▌ Recipe idea
Bay-scented young guinea hen with canapés >> p. 330

Duchess potatoes ★

A dried potato purée, thickened with butter and egg yolks. It is used as a garnish or vegetable stuffing.

Ingredients
1 lb. (500 g) all-rounder potatoes
3 egg yolks
5 1/2 tablespoons (80 g) butter
A pinch of grated nutmeg
Salt, freshly ground pepper

Boil the potatoes in their jackets.
Peel them and purée them in a food mill.
Dry out carefully, if necessary, over low heat. Combine them with the egg yolks and butter.
Season with salt and pepper.

❢ **Recipe ideas**
Lamb medallions with licorice-flavored foamed milk and duchess potatoes >> p. 382

Varieties of potatoes and their uses

As soon as you have peeled your potatoes, cover them in cold water so they do not brown.

Depending on your recipe and the size of your potatoes, some varieties will need rinsing to eliminate their starch (potatoes cocotte, wafers, potato straws, etc), while others will need to maintain their starch to stay firm during cooking (Dauphin, gratin, potatoes Anna, etc.) Do remove all traces of green, which contain a toxic substance (solanine).

Potatoes must be stored away from light and in a well-ventilated place so that they do not begin sprouting. If, despite your precautions, they do, remove the sprout and hollow out the potato a little around the eye.

Variety	Characteristics	Uses
Atlantic, Norwis etc. (Round Whites)	Smooth, thin, light skin with white flesh. Medium in starch level, creamy texture when cooked, hold shape well.	Particularly good for salads, sautéing, roasting, and boiling; generally good all-rounders.
Burbank, Norkotah etc. (Russets)	Netted brown skin, white flesh. High in starch, floury texture when cooked.	Ideal for baking and mashing; generally good all-rounders.
Chieftain, Dakota Rose etc. (Red Potatoes)	Rosy red skin, can have either white, yellow, or even red flesh. Firm, smooth, waxy texture.	Good for salads, roasting, and boiling.
German Butterball, Yukon Gold etc. (Yellow Potatoes)	Golden color. Dense, creamy texture. Mild buttery flavor.	Good for mashing, baking, roasting, and boiling.
Kennebec, White Rose etc. (Long Whites)	Oval-shaped, thin light tan skin. Medium in starch level, firm and creamy texture when cooked.	Excellent for sautéing and boiling; good all-rounders.
Red Thumb, Russian Blue, etc. (Fingerlings)	Narrow elongated shape. Come in a variety of colors, though most have yellow flesh. Firm waxy texture.	Ideal for salads, baking, and boiling.
Anya	Long oval shaped body. Distinctive nutty flavor.	Excellent for salads.
Charlotte	Long oval shape, white skin. Moist texture.	Good for salads, roasting, and boiling.
Desiree	Red skin, light yellow flesh. Medium in starch level.	Ideal for gratins and roasting, also good for chips, baking, boiling, and mashing.
Estima	White to yellow skin, light yellow flesh. Firm texture when cooked, mild taste.	Good for boiling, baking, and mashing.
King Edward	White skin with distinctive pink coloration, creamy colored flesh. Floury texture.	Excellent for gratins, chips, roasting, and mashing, good all-rounder.
Maris Piper	Creamy colored flesh, floury texture, medium in starch level.	Good for chips, baking, boiling, roasting, and mashing.
Rooster	Distinctive red skin, cream flesh. Very versatile.	Ideal for chips, mashing, and roasting.

☐ Common in US ☐ Common in UK

Basic sweet
preparations and sauces

Fruit coulis ★

To make a fruit coulis, you will need to blend ripe fruit and add, if necessary, a little sugar and a squeeze of lemon juice. They are always very quick to prepare, but do not keep for more than a day as they ferment quickly. Here, we'll look at a raspberry coulis.

Ingredients (serves 8)
1 lb. (500 g) raspberries
Juice of 1 lemon
¹/₃ cup (50 g) confectioners' sugar

Wash (see Chef's notes) and prepare the fruit.
Blend it with the lemon juice and sugar (1).
If necessary for your recipe, strain the coulis through a sieve (2).
Cover with plastic wrap and chill.

● Chef's notes
Wash strawberries only after you have hulled them, otherwise they absorb the water. Be especially careful with slightly damaged fruit—dry it quickly so that no water gets in.
Pour in the lemon juice as you blend the fruits to avoid its oxidizing rapidly.
For the tastiest results, choose seasonal fruits when they are at their best (see table, p. 223).
If you find good-quality frozen fruits, they can of course be used at any time.
When making a coulis with a fruit that has thick pulp, like banana, apricot, and peach, we recommend you thin it with a little cold sugar syrup.
However, for a fruit that gives a lot of liquid, you will probably need to add a small quantity of preserves made from the same fruit.
Add a liqueur to enhance the flavor or give it added complexity.
For tomato coulis, see p. 134.

Recipe idea
Iced nougat and raspberry coulis ›› p. 505

Plain printing paste ★★

Printing paste is really nothing more than a cookie paste, colored or plain, on which a sponge cake batter is poured before baking. Create your pattern using an icing comb, a paper cone, or a stencil.

Ingredients
3 ¹/₂ tablespoons (50 g) butter
2 egg whites
¹/₃ cup (50 g) confectioners' sugar
Generous ¹/₂ cup (50 g) cake flour
A few drops of colored extract, such as coffee, or a colorant

Melt the butter and allow it to cool. Whisk the egg whites with the confectioner's sugar. Sift the flour and incorporate it into the mixture.
Pour in the cool melted butter and mix in until quite smooth.
If desired, add the colorant or extract.
Cover with plastic wrap and chill until the butter in the mixture has hardened.
Draw patterns using the paste on a sheet of parchment paper or on a silicone baking sheet.
Place in the freezer for 4-5 minutes, perfectly flat, until the patterns have hardened.
Remove the sheet and cover it with raw cake batter. Bake.
When the sponge cake is baked, remove the parchment paper or silicone sheet. The design will be printed on the base of the sponge which can then be turned upside-down to serve.

1

2

3

Basic sweet preparations and sauces

Chocolate printing paste ★★

Ingredients

3 ¹/₂ tablespoons (50 g) butter
2 egg whites
¹/₃ cup (50 g) confectioners' sugar, sifted
Generous ¹/₃ cup (35 g) all-purpose flour
2 ¹/₃ tablespoons (15 g) cocoa powder, unsweetened
A few drops of colored extract, such as coffee, or a colorant

Melt the butter and allow it to cool. Whisk the egg whites with the confectioners' sugar. Sift the flour with the cocoa powder and incorporate it into the mixture.

Pour in the cool melted butter and the colorant and mix in until thoroughly combined and smooth.

Cover with plastic wrap and chill until the butter in the mixture has hardened.

Use your creativity to draw raised patterns on a sheet of parchment paper or on a silicone baking sheet.

Place in the freezer for 4-5 minutes, perfectly flat, until the patterns have hardened.

Remove the sheet from the freezer and cover it with raw cake batter. Bake in the oven.

When the sponge cake is baked, remove the parchment paper or silicone sheet. The design will be printed on the base of your sponge.

● Chef's notes

You can write using a paper cone, but remember to write backwards because it will be transposed onto the sponge. The most effective method is to make a design on the computer, print it out, and place it below the parchment paper or silicone sheet as a guide.

If you want a more striking design, divide your plain paste into two and color the two halves differently.

Use this batter to make delicate cookies like langues de chat, cigarettes, and tulips, all of which add a sophisticated touch to a dish of ice cream.

Basic sweet preparations and sauces

Caramel sauce ★★

This is caramelized sugar with the cooking process stopped by the addition of cream and/or butter. Add your personal touch to the caramel sauce by adding coffee or vanilla extract, filberts, or whatever else takes your fancy.

Ingredients (serves 8)
²/₃ cup (125 g) granulated sugar
Scant ¹/₂ cup (100 ml) whipping cream, minimum 30 percent butterfat
3 ¹/₂ tablespoons (50 g) butter (salted, if you wish)
Special equipment: candy thermometer

Make a dry caramel: cook the sugar on high heat in a nonstick or copper pan until it becomes a mahogany color–about 350°F (180°C) on a candy thermometer. Remove from the heat.
Slowly pour the cream on to stop the sugar cooking (1). Return the pan to the heat and whisk the caramel smooth.
The texture should be liquid but thick enough to coat the back of a spoon*. Whisk in the butter (2).

● Chef's notes
You can also stop the cooking with the butter, which should be added once the pan is off the heat, and which takes on a light hazelnut flavor. Use unsalted, salted, or butter with salt crystals. Check the color of your caramel by dipping a piece of white parchment paper into it.
Adding fruit juice is another way of halting the cooking process of the caramel.

● Did you know?
Caramel sauce made with salty butter is an excellent accompaniment to crêpes and the sweet specialties of northwest France, like waffles.

Chocolate sauce ★

Chocolate sauce will be thick or runny, depending on how much liquid you add. Serve it on the side or over desserts like profiteroles (see recipe p. 494), ice cream, poached fruits, and tarts, and use it as a suave complement to Bavarian creams and charlottes. The type of chocolate can equally determine the texture of the sauce.

Ingredients (serves 8)
1 cup total (250 ml) milk and/or cream
6 ¹/₂-7 oz. (180 g-200 g) bittersweet chocolate, preferably 64 percent cocoa
Special equipment: candy thermometer

Chop the chocolate. Heat the milk and/or cream over low heat. Do not let the temperature exceed 130°F-140°F (55°C-60°C). Remove the pan from the heat and add the chopped chocolate (1). Mix in with a rubber spatula or whisk (2, 3). Set aside, either over a bain-marie* if you need to keep it warm, or in the refrigerator.

● **Chef's note**
Flavor your chocolate sauce with instant coffee, vanilla extract, spices, honey, or nuts.
If you plan to serve it hot, you may whip in a little butter or add a cooked sugar syrup.

Fruit sauce ★

A fruit sauce differs from a coulis in that it is cooked with a little sugar and lemon juice. Here, we give a recipe for apricot sauce.

Ingredients (serves 8)
1 ½ lb. (650 g) apricots
Scant ½ cup (80 g) sugar
Juice of 1 lemon
1 vanilla bean

Peel the apricots and remove the pits. Cut them into segments and put into a saucepan (1). Slit the vanilla bean lengthways. Stew the apricots gently, with the lid on, together with the sugar, vanilla bean, and lemon juice (or water) until the mixture starts steaming (2). When the apricots are soft, blend them in a food processor and strain (3). Chill if necessary until needed.

● **Chef's notes**
Add a personal touch to your fruit sauce with spices like vanilla, cinnamon, ginger, or others, or fresh herbs like verbena, lemon thyme, or lemon balm.
For a more rustic texture, crush the stewed fruits with a fork.

Syrup ★

This is a liquid preparation with varying degrees of sugar concentration. Depending on the stage of cooking reached, it will be used for specific applications, such as saturating sponge layers, soaking, or making meringues or *pâte à bombe* (see p. 210).

Types of syrup

Syrups are classified by the use for which they are destined.

Syrup	Proportions	Uses
Soaking, poaching	4 cups (1 liter) water 1 $^1/_2$–2 $^2/_3$ cups (300–500 g) sugar Flavoring	Savarins Babas Fruits in syrup
Soaking pastry (punch)	4 cups (1 liter) water 5 $^1/_2$ lb. (2.5 kg) sugar Flavoring	Desserts Sponge cakes Cookies
Candy syrup	4 cups (1 liter) water 5 $^1/_2$ lb. (2.5 kg) sugar Cool the syrup in a closed container to 77°F (25°C), until it feels lukewarm to the touch. Pour the candy syrup over candies or fruit placed on a candy rack. Allow to stand for 16 hours to coat in syrup.	Dried fruit stuffed with marzipan Cake decorations Molded marzipan pieces

Cooking sugar

It is best to use an electronic or candy thermometer for precision. Although less advisable, if you use your fingers be careful not to burn yourself.

Name	Caramel temperatures	Uses
Coated	223°F (106°C)	Pâte de fruit (fruit jellies)
Small thread or small gloss	230°F (110°C)	Florentine cookies
Large thread or large gloss	235°F–239°F (113°C–115°C)	Soft caramels
Soft-ball	244°F (118°C)	Soft fondant/almond paste
Hard-ball	250°F (121°C)	Italian meringue/butter cream/hard fondant
Light or soft crack	275°F –293°F (135°C–145°C)	White nougat/marshmallow
Hard crack	293°F–311°F (145°C–155°C)	Thread stage/poured or pulled sugar/soufflé or blown
Light caramel	329°F (165°C)	Croquembouche, etc./poured or pulled sugar, soufflé, blown sugar
Caramel	350°F (180°C)	Caramel sauce with salted butter
Dark caramel or blackjack	370°F–400°F (190°C–200°C)	Dark caramel or blackjack

Basic ingredients

1 ⅓ cup water (330 ml)
2 lb. (1 kg) sugar cubes

Pour the water into a perfectly clean copper pan or a pot and bring to a simmer.
Add the sugar cubes.
Check the temperature of the syrup with a thermometer, and stop when it reaches the desired temperature for your recipe.

● Chef's notes

If your sugar forms crystals while cooking, add a few drops of lemon juice or vinegar.
Using a copper pan or pot ensures the best heat conduction, and prevents the sugar from forming unwanted crystals.
Do not use high heat—this will darken the sides of the pot or pan.
Use a wet pastry brush to keep the sides of the pan clean.
Sugar may also be cooked without the addition of water. In this case, high heat is required.

Basic sweet preparations and sauces

Sweet cream bases

Pouring custard
(*crème anglaise*) ★★ 🎬

Custard is a sauce that is served cold or warm to accompany a great many desserts. It is also used as a base for a number of more complex recipes, such as Bavarian cream desserts, ice creams, and charlottes.

Ingredients
4 cups (1 liter) milk
1 vanilla bean
10 egg yolks
1 ¼ cup (250 g) granulated sugar

Slit the vanilla bean lengthwise and scrape the seeds out into the milk. Pour the milk into a saucepan and add the vanilla bean. Bring the milk to a simmer. Whisk the egg yolks and sugar vigorously until the mixture becomes pale and thick. When the milk is simmering, remove it from the heat and pour half of it over the beaten egg yolks (1). Combine thoroughly and pour in the remaining milk, mixing again. Return the mixture to the saucepan, straining through a chinois* and bring to the simmer again, stirring constantly, making figure-of-eight patterns with your spoon. While the mixture is cooking, remove it from the heat from time to time so that the yolks do not coagulate. When done, it should coat the back of a spoon* (2), and a line drawn with your finger along the back of the spoon should stay clear. If you have a candy thermometer, the desired temperature is 185°F (85°C). Cover with plastic wrap and allow to cool, preferably over an ice bath.

● Chef's notes
It's essential to cool the custard down rapidly after it is cooked to avoid any risk of bacteria developing.
The custard must not boil. If the temperature is too high, the yolks will coagulate and separate from the milk. This will cause the custard to split. Should this happen, mix it immediately with an immersion blender in a chilled metal bowl.
When the bubbles on the surface of the custard start to disappear during the cooking process, you have an indication that it is practically cooked.

● Did you know?
The traditional flavor for custard is vanilla, but you can enhance it with other flavors of your choice: chocolate, liqueurs, caramel, praline, or orange and lemon zest. In this case, omit the vanilla and add your selected flavor when the custard is cooked.

❙ Recipe ideas
Floating islands with spun caramel ›› p. 463
Opéra ›› p. 480

Butter cream
(with cooked sugar) ★★★

Butter cream is prepared by emulsifying butter on a mixture of egg and cooked sugar (as for a pâte à bombe, see p. 210). There are numerous variations on the basic technique used here, including Genoese sponge and Italian meringue.

Ingredients
1 cup (200 g) sugar
Scant ¹/₃ cup (70 ml) water
2 egg yolks
2 eggs
2 sticks (250 g) unsalted butter, room temperature, cubed
A few drops of flavoring (coffee, rose, bitter almond, caramel, praline, chocolate, etc)

Prepare a sugar syrup and cook until it reaches a temperature of 243°F (117°C). With an electric beater, whisk the eggs and additional yolks until foamy.
Pour the sugar syrup over the eggs, and continue beating for a few minutes to lower the temperature of the mixture.
Incorporate the cubed butter using a whisk (1) or an electric beater (medium speed) (2).
Add your chosen flavoring.

● Chef's notes
For a more delicate taste, prepare the butter cream using only egg yolks (as for a pâte à bombe). For this recipe, you will need 5 egg yolks.
Spread the butter cream onto the cake while it is still soft— approximate temperature 68°F (20°C).

● Did you know?
This is the perfect cream for the traditional French Christmas cake, a Christmas log (buche de Noël), a jelly roll garnished with flavored butter cream that represents the logs we burn in our fireplaces during year-end festivities. Butter cream is also used in the moka cake, created in the mid-nineteenth century. Butter cream was developed shortly before this. Moka is a variety of coffee exported from the port of Moka in the Yemen.

❙ Recipe ideas
Opéra >> p. 480
Chestnut cream Succès and caramelized walnuts >> p. 471

Chantilly cream ★

Chantilly cream fills, garnishes, covers, decorates, and accompanies innumerable pastries, desserts, and ice creams.

Ingredients
2 cups (500 ml) whipping cream, 35 percent fat content, well chilled
Generous $^{1}/_{2}$ cup (75 g) confectioners' sugar
A few drops of natural vanilla extract

Pour the cold cream into a cold mixing bowl or the cold bowl of a food processor (1).
Whisk briskly or beat at medium speed with the whisk of the food processor until the cream begins to thicken (2).
Sift the confectioners' sugar into the cream (3) and then add the vanilla extract.
Whisk the cream briskly for a few moments until it forms stiff peaks.

● Chef's notes
For best results, it is essential that the cream be very cold, or chilled over ice. A minimum butterfat content of 30 percent is required. It is advisable to place the mixing bowl in the refrigerator before you use it. If you are using granulated or caster sugar, make sure it dissolves in the cream. Confectioners' sugar is preferable, however.
Store Chantilly cream no longer than 24 hours in the refrigerator. It is best made at the last moment so that it does not deflate prior to being used.

● Did you know?
The term "Chantilly cream" is reserved for whipped cream with a minimum of 30 percent dairy fat, sucrose, and natural vanilla flavor. Chantilly cream is the ideal cream for pastry chefs. The intense whipping it undergoes increases its volume. It contains between 15 and 20 percent sugar. It is thought to have been created by François Vatel, chef to the Prince of Condé at the Château de Chantilly, just north of Paris, during the reign of Louis XIV.
"Whipped cream" refers to cream that is whipped without sugar or flavoring, and it is a component of other recipes.

Recipe ideas
Tutti-frutti waffles >> p. 464
Iced blackberry vacherin >> p. 498

Chiboust cream ★★

This cream is used with a Saint-Honoré, a grand cake often served on festive occasions. It is a derivation of pastry cream to which gelatin is added, together with Italian meringue.

Ingredients
5 sheets gelatin* (10 g)
2 cups (500 ml) milk
1 vanilla bean
3 eggs, separated
5 egg whites
$^2/_3$ cup (125 g) plus 2 $^2/_3$ cups (500g) sugar
$^1/_3$ cup (2 oz./55 g) cornstarch
A few drops of flavors or extracts of your choice (coffee, rose, bitter almond, caramel, praline, chocolate, etc)
1 pinch salt
Special equipment: candy thermometer

Soak the gelatin sheets in a bowl of very cold water. Slit the vanilla bean lengthwise and scrape the seeds into the milk. Add the vanilla bean to the milk and begin to heat.
Whisk the 3 egg yolks, $^2/_3$ cup (125 g) sugar, and the cornstarch until the mixture is pale and thick.
When the milk begins to simmer, remove it from the heat and pour half of it over the beaten egg yolks. Combine thoroughly. Add flavorings at this stage, unless you are using a liqueur, in which case you should add it when the mixture has cooled.
Pour the egg and milk combination over the rest of the milk and return to the heat. Bring it back to the simmer and leave to simmer for 2 to 3 minutes, whisking continuously.
Remove from the heat. Drain the gelatin sheets, squeezing out all their water, and fold into* the milk-and-egg mixture. Mix thoroughly with a whisk until there are no visible traces of gelatin.
Transfer to a bowl and cover with plastic wrap flush with the cream. Cool until it reaches a temperature of about 60°F (15°C).

Prepare the Italian meringue. Begin by heating $^2/_3$ cup (165 ml) water with the remaining 2 $^2/_3$ cups (500 g) sugar. When the syrup reaches 230°F (110°C), begin beating the 8 egg whites with a pinch of salt in the bowl of your heavy-duty mixer. When the temperature of the cooked sugar reaches 243°F–250°F (117°C–120°C), pour it in a steady stream over the beaten egg whites. Continue to beat the meringue until the mixture is lukewarm. It will be dense and shiny, and will form small firm peaks.
When the pastry cream has cooled but not yet set, mix it to smooth it well. Use a flexible rubber spatula to fold it delicately into the Italian meringue (see p. 49).

● **Chef's notes**
Leave the gelatin leaves to soften completely in very cold water. Squeeze out the excess water before you using. Once you have finished making the cream, add very quickly to your recipe (Saint-Honoré, for example) before it thickens. Chill immediately.
The Italian meringue must be no hotter than lukewarm when it is incorporated into the pastry cream.
With the use of Italian meringue, the risk of contamination is considerably reduced. The meringue has the added advantage of imparting a fine consistency, texture, and shine to your cream.

● **Did you know?**
Chiboust was a pastry chef in Paris, where he set up shop in 1840. He is thought to have created the Gâteau Saint-Honoré as a tribute both to the street where he worked (the still famous rue Saint-Honoré) and to the patron saint of bakers. This delicious cake, made with choux pastry, is garnished with the cream that bears his name.

Recipe idea
Gâteau Saint-Honoré >> p. 451

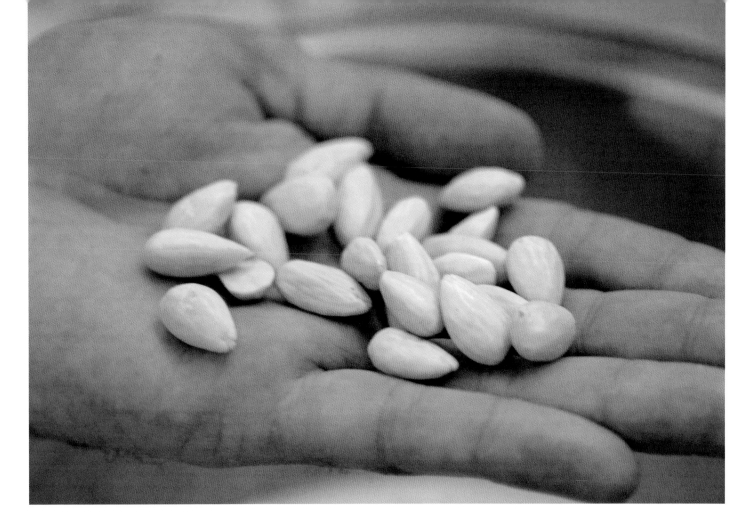

Almond cream ★

This cream is prepared without cooking and uses equal quantities of blanched* ground almonds *(almond meal), eggs, butter, and sugar. Adding flour is optional.
Almond cream is used in many classic French tarts, like the Kings' cake (*galette des rois*), traditionally eaten on Epiphany; the pithiviers, two layers of puff pastry filled with the cream; and the bourdaloue tart, where pears are placed on a bed of almond cream.

Ingredients

7 tablespoons (100 g) unsalted butter, softened*
$^1/_2$ cup (3 $^1/_2$ oz./100 g) granulated sugar
1 generous cup (100 g) blanched ground almonds or almond meal
2 eggs
A few drops of vanilla extract
1 tablespoon (15 ml) rum

Cream the softened butter well with the sugar.
Add the ground almonds, and then the eggs, mixing them in one by one.
Add the flavorings and whisk until smooth.

● **Chef's note**
Almond cream must always be baked in a pastry base.

❙ **Recipe idea**
Apricot tartlets ›› p. 428

Diplomat cream

Diplomat cream is a variation on pastry cream. Gelatin is added to it, and it is enriched with whipped cream. It is used for diplomat pudding (a dessert made with ladyfingers or brioche), mille-feuilles, filled crêpes, and fruit tarts.

Ingredients
5 sheets gelatin* (10 g)
2 cups (500 ml) milk
1 vanilla bean
3 egg yolks
$^2/_3$ cup (125 g) granulated sugar
$^1/_3$ cup (55 g) cornstarch
A few drops of flavor or flavors of your choice (coffee, rose, bitter almond, caramel, praline, chocolate, etc)
3 cups (750 ml) whipping cream, fat content 35 percent

Place the gelatin sheets in a bowl of very cold water to soften. Slit a vanilla bean lengthwise and scrape out the seeds. Place them in the milk, together with the vanilla bean, and bring to a simmer.

Whisk the egg yolks, sugar, and cornstarch briskly together until the mixture thickens and becomes pale.

When the milk is simmering, remove it from the heat and pour half of it over the egg yolk mixture. Whisk together. Incorporate the flavoring, except if you are using a liqueur, which should be added when the mixture is cold.

Pour this back onto the remaining milk, return to the heat, and bring back to the boil. Leave to simmer for 2-3 minutes, whisking constantly.

Remove from the heat. Wring the water out of the gelatin sheets with your hands. Mix the gelatin in with a whisk until the mixture is smooth, with no visible traces of gelatin.

Transfer to a bowl. Cover with plastic wrap flush with the cream. Refresh* to about 60°F (15°C).

Using a stand-alone or hand beater, whip the 3 cups (750 ml) cream until it is the same consistency as a Chantilly cream. When the pastry cream is cold but not yet set, mix it again. Delicately fold* in the cold whipped cream with a rubber spatula.

● Chef's notes
Leave the gelatin leaves to soften completely in very cold water. Squeeze the excess water out with your hands before you use them.

The whipped cream must be firm and smooth.

To fold the pastry cream into the whipped cream, carefully lift it with the spatula so that it does not turn or separate.

If you begin cooking the diplomat cream with boiling milk, it thickens immediately. There is also less risk that it will stick.

If your pastry cream is too hot when you fold in the whipped

cream, it will melt instead of giving an airy dimension to the preparation.

This cream keeps for no longer than 24 hours in the refrigerator, but can be frozen.

When it is ready, add it to your cake or dessert rapidly before it sets, and chill.

● Did you know?
"Light" diplomat cream is a diplomat that does not have gelatin added (and therefore will not set).

▮ Recipe idea
Diplomat-filled mille-feuille >> p. 479

Cream

Name	Characteristics	Fat content	Uses
Clotted cream	Thick, rich, yellow cream, made by heating unpasteurized milk.	Min. 55% (55–60%)	Serve as it is, with scones and jam (English "cream tea"). Also known as Devonshire or Devon cream.
Double cream (UK)	Rich cream that whips easily and holds its shape. A little thicker than heavy cream. Can be over-whipped and become too thick.	48%	For pouring over desserts; in cooking; for whipping. When whipped can be piped or spooned on to desserts and cakes.
Heavy cream (US)	Denser than whipping cream and doubles in volume when whipped; whips well and holds its shape.	36–40%	As above.
Whipping cream	Thickens when whipped but lighter than double/heavy cream (does not whip or hold its shape quite as well). Sometimes contains stabilizers or emulsifiers to help hold shape when whipped.	30–38%	For whipping: toppings, cake fillings, mousses etc.
Crème fraîche	Rich, matured, thickened cream with tangy, nutty flavor.	Min. 30%	Serve with fruit and desserts; for salad dressings and dips; in cooking (sauces, soups, casseroles etc.).
Sour cream	Smooth and tangy cream, made by adding a bacterial culture + incubation until lactose turns to lactic acid.	18–20%	In cooking, particularly sauces and soups; in baking; for dips and dressings.
Light cream (US)	Pouring cream. Does not whip if less than 30%.	18–30%, generally 20%	In coffee; for pouring over desserts; in cooking, soups, sauces, or casseroles (although risk of separation when heated).
Single cream (UK)	Pouring cream. Does not whip or thicken when beaten.	Min. 18%, generally 20%	In coffee; for pouring over desserts; in cooking, in soups, sauces, or casseroles, (although risk of separation when heated).
Half-and-half (US)	Mixture of half cream and half milk. Can't be whipped.	10.5-18%, generally 12%	In coffee, pouring cream (over desserts).

Frangipane cream ★

Frangipane cream comprises half pastry cream and half almond cream.

Ingredients

Pastry cream
1 cup (250 ml) milk
$^1/_2$ vanilla bean
2 egg yolks
$^1/_3$ cup (65 g) granulated sugar
3 $^1/_4$ tablespoons (30 g) cornstarch
A few drops of bitter almond extract or Amaretto

Almond cream
1 generous cup (3 $^1/_2$ oz./100 g) blanched* ground almonds* or almond meal
7 tablespoons (3 $^1/_2$ oz./100 g) unsalted butter, softened*
2 eggs
$^1/_2$ cup (100 g) granulated sugar

Make a pastry cream (see method p. 182) and cool it down rapidly. While it cools, prepare the almond cream (see p. 176). Add the almond extract or Amaretto to soften the pastry cream. Pour in the almond cream and whisk energetically to combine.

● **Did you know?**

Frangipane cream owes its name to the Italian perfumer, Don Cesare Frangipani, who worked in Paris in the seventeenth century. The French term crème frangipane *appears in the 1732 dictionary of Trévoux with its current meaning. Frequent mention of a pastry cream to which almonds have been added are found; a variation called* franchipane *(a pie with almond cream and ground pistachios) is recorded in 1674. There are also records of a pastry cream with broken almond macaroons.*

❗ **Recipe idea**
Kings' cake (*Galette des rois*) ›› p. 445

Ganache ★

Ordinary ganache refers to a mixture of chocolate and cream only. However, there are also buttered ganaches and ganaches with milk. Ganache is used for truffles and in desserts, tarts, and mousses.

Ingredients for ordinary ganache (candies)
1 cup (250 ml) whipping cream
$^1/_2$ lb. (250 g) bittersweet chocolate, minimum 64 percent cocoa mass

Ingredients for buttered ganache (for tarts)
1 scant cup (230 ml) whipping cream (30-35 percent fat content)
$^1/_2$ lb. (250 g) bittersweet chocolate, minimum 64 percent cocoa mass
6 tablespoons (90 g) unsalted butter

Ingredients for ganache with milk (soft)
$^1/_2$ cup (125 ml) whipping cream (30-35 percent fat content)
$^1/_2$ cup (125 ml) milk
$^1/_2$ lb. (250 g) bittersweet chocolate, minimum 64 percent cocoa mass

Bring the cream and/or the milk to the boil.
Chop the chocolate (1). Pour the boiling cream and/or butter over it and whisk until the chocolate has melted.

Do not return to the heat. If using butter, whip it in until the ganache is smooth (2).
Allow the cream to cool, stirring from time to time.
You may flavor it if you wish.

● Chef's notes
To customize your ganache cream, infuse your cream/and or milk with spices or fresh or dried herbs. If you choose to do this, strain it through a chinois* before pouring it over the chopped chocolate.
The higher the proportion of liquid, the softer and more easily the ganache will spread.
The quality of the chocolate (dark, milk, or white) and its percentage of cocoa are decisive in giving your cream its aroma. Flavored pastes, like hazelnut, may also be added.
Unsweetened condensed milk can be substituted for cream.

● Did you know?
Siraudin, a pastry chef in Paris, invented the ganache in 1850.

❙ Recipe ideas
Opéra >> p. 480
Raspberry ganache tart >> p. 460

Mousseline cream ★

As its name indicates, mousseline cream is airy and light, somewhat like a mousse. It is made from pastry cream to which butter has been added. For the Paris-Brest cake, a round choux pastry that represents a bicycle wheel, praline paste is added to pastry cream for the filling. The fraisier, a type of strawberry shortcake, also has a good helping of mousseline cream to cushion the strawberries between two layer of Genoese sponge.

Ingredients
2 cups (500 ml) milk
1 vanilla bean
3 egg yolks
$^2/_3$ cup (125 g) sugar
$^1/_3$ cup (55 g) cornstarch
2 sticks (250 g) unsalted butter

Scrape the seeds of the vanilla bean into the milk. Pour the milk into a saucepan with the bean and bring to a simmer.
In a mixing bowl, whisk the egg yolks with the cornstarch and sugar until the mixture thickens and becomes pale.
When the milk is simmering, remove it from the heat and pour half of it over the egg yolk mixture. Stir well. Pour in the rest of the milk, return to the heat, and bring back to the boil. Allow to simmer for 2-3 minutes, whisking continuously.
Remove from the heat. Whip in half the butter until fully incorporated.
Transfer to a bowl and cover with plastic wrap flush with the cream. Cool rapidly.
Using an electric beater, beat the remaining half of the butter into the cooled pastry cream. Whip at high speed so that the cream expands and becomes airy.

● Chef's notes
When you incorporate the softened butter* at the last stage of the recipe, heat the bowl slightly so that the ingredients blend better.
Add any flavoring right at the end. However, if you are using a flavored paste such as praline paste, work it into the softened butter before you incorporate them both into the cooled pastry cream.
This cream will keep no longer than 24 hours in the refrigerator, but freezes well.
It's particularly important to ensure that the plastic wrap is flush with the cream: since it contains butter, it easily absorbs tastes and smells.
It is the quality of the butter used that is decisive for the delicacy and taste of a mousseline cream.

Pastry cream
(*crème pâtissière*) ★ 🎬

Pastry cream is one of the most widely used creams in French pastry making. It fills éclairs, puff pastries, religieuses, and cream horns, and is a comfortable bed for fruit to nestle into in tarts.

Ingredients
2 cups (500 ml) milk
1 vanilla bean
3 egg yolks
²/₃ cup (125 g) granulated sugar
¹/₃ cup (60 g) cornstarch
A few drops of extract or extracts of your choice (coffee, rose, bitter almond, caramel, chocolate, etc)

Slit the vanilla bean lengthwise and scrape the seeds into the milk (1). Add the vanilla bean to the milk and begin to heat. In a mixing bowl, whisk the egg yolks and sugar briskly until the mixture turns pale and thickens. Add the cornstarch and whisk in (2).
When the milk begins to simmer, remove from the heat and pour half over the thickened egg mixture. Combine thoroughly. Add your chosen flavoring, unless you are using a liqueur, in which case you should add it when the mixture has cooled. Strain the remaining milk through a sieve or chinois*(3) into the egg mixture, return to the heat, and bring back to the boil. Allow to simmer for 2-3 minutes, whisking constantly. Transfer to a bowl. Cover with plastic wrap flush with the cream so that a skin cannot form. Chill or refresh* quickly.

● Chef's notes
If the cream is too liquid: the boiling period was too short, or too little thickener was used. The cream must be thick when removed from the heat.
If pastry cream is cooked with boiling milk, it thickens immediately and the risk of sticking is lessened.
Store this cream for no longer than 24 hours in the refrigerator.

● Did you know?
Pastry cream is a base for many sweet dishes. It is liable to spoil quickly, and is always made as and when needed in pastry shops. Some variations: mousseline cream, diplomat, Chiboust, light, frangipane, and Pont Neuf.

❦ Recipe ideas
Orange liqueur soufflé ›› p. 438
Mixed berry tart ›› p. 446

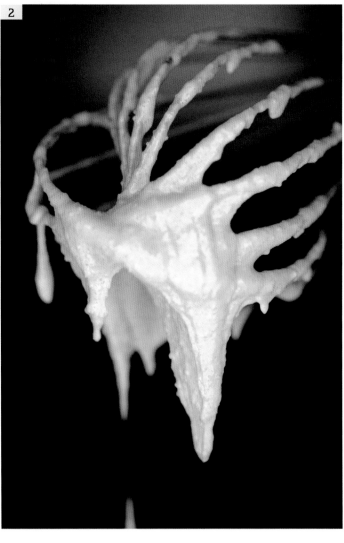

3

Sweet fillings,
molded desserts, and pastry bases

Sweet baked cream ★

This recipe uses milk and eggs. Together, they coagulate when baked and form the filling for sweets such as creamy fruit tarts and the base for flans, and a specialty tart—the Mirabelle plum tart—made in the Alsace region.

Ingredients (for 1 tart)
Scant ¹/₂ cup (100 ml) milk
Scant ¹/₂ cup (100 ml) whipping cream
Vanilla bean
2 eggs
2 egg yolks
3 ¹/₂ tablespoons (40 g) sugar
A little liqueur (optional)

Combine the milk and cream in a saucepan. Slit the vanilla bean lengthwise, scrape the seeds into the milk and cream, and add the bean. Bring to a simmer. Beat the eggs, egg yolks, and sugar, but do not beat so much that the mixture becomes foamy.
Pour the hot liquid over the egg mixture, whisking as you pour, and combine thoroughly (1).
Strain through a fine-mesh sieve or chinois*. Cover with plastic wrap and chill until you need it.

● Chef's notes
Do not use high heat for the milk and cream mixture, as a dark, dry-ish film will form on the surface.
If you are making a tart with fruits that have a high water content, you will probably need to increase the quantity of eggs.

Recipe ideas
Mirabelle plum tart, a specialty of Alsace ›› p. 476
French brioche toast and vanilla-scented stewed rhubarb ›› p. 459

1

Sponge bases and their use

Name	Sponge base	Filling
Christmas log	Jelly roll	Flavored butter cream, preserves, pastry cream, etc.
Hot charlotte	Sandwich loaf	Sautéed fruit
Cold fruit charlotte	Ladyfinger (see p. 188)	Bavarian mousse
Black Forest	Cocoa Genoese sponge	Chantilly cream (see p. 174)
Fraisier (strawberry sponge)	Genoese sponge (see p. 193)	Mousseline cream (see p. 181)
Mascotte	Genoese sponge	Praline butter cream (see p. 173 for butter cream)
Moka	Genoese sponge	Coffee butter cream
Montmorency	Genoese sponge	Cherry butter cream
Baked Alaska	Genoese sponge	Ice cream and meringue
Opéra	Joconde (see p. 194)	Ganache (see p. 180), butter cream (see p. 173)
Diplomat pudding	Ladyfinger	Sweet baked cream (see p. 186)
Singapour	Genoese sponge	Pastry cream (see p. 182), stewed pineapple

Savoy sponge cake ★

This soft sponge owes its attractive golden color to the use of eggs.

Ingredients (serves 8)
4 eggs, separated
²/₃ cup (125 g) granulated sugar
³/₄ cup (2 ¹/₂ oz./65 g) cake flour, plus a little extra for the pan*
4 ¹/₂ tablespoons (45 g) cornstarch
A little butter and flour for greasing
Special equipment: loaf pan or special Savoy sponge pan

Preheat the oven to 325°F–350°F (160°C–170°C). Grease the baking pan and dust it with a smattering of flour. Rap it on the counter to shake off any excess.
Beat the egg yolks with the sugar until the mixture is pale and thick, and forms a ribbon*.
Whisk the egg whites until they form stiff peaks. Fold* carefully into the egg yolk and sugar mixture.
Sift the flour and cornstarch together. Fold gradually into the egg mixture using a rubber spatula.
Fill the baking pan two-thirds full and bake for 30-35 minutes, or until a cake tester comes out clean.

● Chef's notes
Be careful not to overbeat the egg whites as this results in a grainy texture.
The sifted flour and cornstarch may also be added to the beaten egg yolk mixture before being incorporated into the beaten egg whites.

● Did you know?
In French, this type of pastry is known as a biscuit, which literally means "baked twice." This type of baking meant that the pastry would be so dry it could be preserved for lengthy periods, thereby making it useful for food supplies for troops on land or sea. The Savoy biscuit was first made for the ruler of the small kingdom of Savoy in the mid-fourteenth century.

Ladyfingers ★

These are very light, airy sponge biscuits with a crisp crust. They tend to dry out rather easily.

Ingredients (serves 8)
3 eggs, separated, plus 1 egg white
$^1/_2$ cup (100 g) sugar
Generous $^1/_2$ cup (50 g) cake flour
$^1/_3$ cup (50 g) cornstarch
Confectioners' sugar for dusting

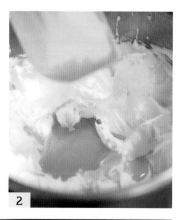

Prepare a French meringue (see p. 49) using 4 egg whites and the sugar.
Combine this with the egg yolks (1, 2).
Sift the flour and the cornstarch directly into the egg mixture (3).
Carefully fold* in using a rubber spatula.
Pipe out the mixture (4), or spoon it onto a silicone baking sheet or parchment paper. Each ladyfinger should be about 3 $^1/_2$-4 in. (8-10 cm) long and $^2/_3$ in. (1.5 cm) wide.
Dust them with confectioners' sugar and allow it to penetrate. Preheat the oven to 400°F (200°C). Sprinkle the ladyfingers again with confectioners' sugar (5) and bake for 10-15 minutes, until pale beige.

● Chef's notes
If you wish, flavor the ladyfingers, or use coloring—or do both. They are delicious alone or with creamy desserts, and you can pair them with sparkling wine or have them with tea or coffee. Pipe them out so that they are all the same size. This will give an even lining for Bavarian cream desserts. However, the ladyfingers should not go all the way to the top of your mold. That way, an attractive layer of your mousse or cream will be visible.

● Did you know?
Ladyfingers are known in French as biscuits à la cuillère, literally, spooned biscuits, and this is how they were made until 1840. Then Antonin Carême, French culinary genius and author of major works on gastronomy, followed by Lasne, a pastry chef, improved the method, using a piping bag. Ladyfingers currently enjoy less popularity than they used to. The pink ladyfinger of Reims, capital of the champagne-producing region, was created specially to be eaten with champagne. It is rectangular, has a vanilla taste, and its shell is particularly crisp. Another member of the "family" is the boudoir, which takes its name from the small salons or boudoirs to which the ladies of the Belle Époque would retire.

❦ Recipe idea
Raspberry charlotte >> p. 456

4

5

Sweet fillings, molded desserts, and pastry bases

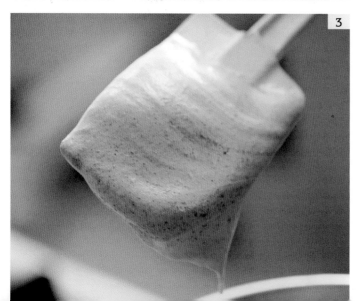

Fruit-based Bavarian cream ★★

This is a fruit purée that is set with gelatin or another jellifying agent. Whipped cream and/or Italian meringue are added.

Ingredients (serves 10)
5 sheets gelatin* (10 g)
14 oz. (400 g) puréed fruit
¼ cup (50 g) granulated sugar
1 ²/₃ cups (400 ml) whipping cream with a fat content of 35 percent
1 scant teaspoon (4 ml) fruit brandy or liqueur

Soak the gelatin sheets in very cold water (1).
Bring the fruit purée and sugar to the boil. Drain the gelatin, wringing out the water with your hands, and add it to the purée (2). Combine thoroughly.
Allow the mixture to cool.
Whip the cream until it forms firm peaks.
When the fruit purée has cooled to about 68°F (20°C), whisk in the fruit brandy or liqueur. Carefully fold* in the whipped cream, little by little, using a rubber spatula (3), taking care not to deflate the mixture.
The Bavarian cream is now ready. Pour it into molds immediately to set and chill.

● **Did you know?**
Strictly speaking, a Bavarian cream uses a custard cream that is set with gelatin and flavored. Some might call the particular recipe given here a fruit mousse.
Add pieces of the same fruit as used in the fruit purée, or another type of fruit, for a variation of textures.

● **Gelatin**
Gelatin is a setting agent of animal origin (pork or beef). Vegetable setting agents made from seaweed are also available. The most widely used type of gelatin in France is available in firm, translucent sheets weighing 1–2 grams. In this book, sheets weighing 2 grams are used.
They must be softened in very cold water for a few minutes and then dissolved in a lukewarm or hot mixture. Gelatin is less effective when combined with acidic fruits like kiwis, pineapple, and raspberries. If using this type of fruit, make sure the purée is boiled right through on its own.

Recipe idea
Raspberry charlotte >> p. 456

Egg-based Bavarian cream ★★

This is a flavored custard cream set with gelatin or other jelling agent. Whipped cream and/or Italian meringue are then added to the mixture.

Ingredients (serves 10)
5 sheets (10 g) gelatin*
2 cups (500 ml) milk
1/2 vanilla bean
5 egg yolks
1/2 cup (100 g) granulated sugar
1 2/3 cups (400 ml) whipping cream, well chilled, with a fat content of 35 percent

Soak the gelatin sheets in very cold water to soften them.
Scrape out the seeds of the 1/2 vanilla bean into the milk. Heat the milk with the vanilla bean in a saucepan over low heat. While it heats, whisk the egg yolks and sugar in a mixing bowl until the mixture becomes thick and pale (ribbon stage*).
When the milk begins simmering, pour half of it over the egg mixture, beating constantly.
Pour the rest of the milk into the mixture. Then return it all to the saucepan and heat until it is thick enough to coat the back of a spoon*. If you have a thermometer, the temperature should be 185°F (85°C).
While it is cooking, remove the pan from the heat from time to time. Too high heat can cause the yolks to coagulate, something that should be avoided here.
Strain the custard through a chinois* or fine-mesh sieve and transfer to a bowl. Wring all the water out of the gelatin sheets and incorporate them thoroughly into the custard mixture.
Cover with plastic wrap and allow to cool, over ice if necessary.
Whip the cold cream until it forms stiff peaks.
When the custard has cooled to room temperature, about 68°F (20°C), whisk it to ensure it is smooth.
Gradually fold* in the whipped cream, very carefully, using a rubber spatula.
The cream is now ready and should be poured into a mold immediately to set.

● Did you know ?
In Carême's authoritative work of 1825, Le Pâtissier royal parisien *(The Royal Parisian Pastrycook and Confectioner) Bavarian creams are referred to as Bavarian cheeses because of both their shape and their origin, the region of Bavaria in Germany.*
Use the same method to make savory Bavarian creams with fish, shellfish, or vegetables. Simply set a liquid such as fish soup or puréed vegetable with gelatin and add whipped cream.

❦ Recipe idea
Mint-chocolate entremets ›› p. 431

Blancmange ★

This is a white, jellied dessert that has traditionally been made with almonds.

Ingredients (serves 8)
5 oz. (150 g) whole, blanched* almonds
3/4 cup (150 g) granulated sugar
3 1/2 tablespoons (50 ml) whipping cream, well-chilled
6 sheets (12 g) gelatin*
A few drops of bitter almond extract

Process the almonds and the sugar until finely ground.
Add half the whipping cream and bring the three ingredients to the boil in a saucepan.
Soak the gelatin sheets in cold water. When they are sufficiently softened, wring out all excess water and incorporate them into the almond-cream mixture. Strain the liquid through a fine-mesh sieve and cool rapidly.
Make sure the remaining cream is still very cold before whipping it. When it forms stiff peaks, fold in the bitter almond extract.
Carefully fold* the whipped cream into the almond mixture.
Pour it into individual ramekins or a serving dish for 8. Chill.

● Chef's notes
Roast the almonds lightly in a hot oven to bring out their flavor.
A fruit coulis is a delightful accompaniment to this blancmange.
You can use coconut instead of all or some of the almonds. You might even substitute other nuts, such as walnuts, hazelnuts, or peanuts.
This blancmange is a variation of the Italian pannacotta.

● Did you know?
Blancmange is known to have been eaten as early as the Middle Ages.

Custard tart

The custard tart is derived from pastry cream made using a ready-made mix.
It is cooked on a pastry base (puff, short, or sweet) and can be divided into the portions you require once it has cooled down.

Ingredients (serves 10)
4 cups (1 liter) milk
5 egg yolks
1 cup (200 g) sugar
3 ¹/₃ oz. (95 g) custard flan mix (buy online or at specialty stores)

Preheat the oven to 350°F-400°F (180°C-200°C).
Heat the milk over medium heat in a saucepan.
Whisk the egg yolks, sugar, and powder briskly in a bowl until the mixture starts to thicken and become pale (ribbon stage*).
When the milk is simmering, pour half of it over the mixture, beating constantly. Ensure it is thoroughly mixed and pour it back over the remaining hot milk until it comes to the boil.
Leave to boil for 2-3 minutes, whisking constantly.
Pour it over the pastry crust of your choice and bake for about 20 minutes, depending on how thick the mixture is. It should be set. Allow to cool.

● **Chef's note**
Check the ingredients of your flan mix and follow the baking instructions.
Alternatively, you may use 1 ¹/₄ cups (125 g) of all-purpose flour or 1 ¹/₄ cups (125 g) of cornstarch instead of custard flan mix.

Genoese sponge ★

This is a simple, light sponge that is used as a base for many desserts and cakes. Genoese sponge may be topped, filled (when cut into layers), and/or soaked in flavored liquid or liqueur.

Ingredients (serves 8)
4 eggs
²/₃ cup (125 g) granulated sugar
1 ¹/₃ cups (125 g) cake flour, plus a little extra for the pan*
A little butter and flour to grease the pan

Preheat the oven to 350°F (180°C).
Whisk the eggs and the sugar together in a round-bottomed mixing bowl over a hot water bath until the mixture reaches the ribbon stage* (1). If you wish, use an electric beater instead. Sift in the flour in stages (2), folding* it in gently each time with a rubber spatula. Work carefully so as not to deflate the batter. Prepare the baking pan, if using: grease it and sprinkle it with flour. Rap the pan to shake off any excess flour (3). Pour the batter into the pan, filling it to three-quarters way up (4). Bake for 15-20 minutes, until well risen and light brown. Test for doneness, remove from the oven, and turn out onto a rack. If you need your Genoese sponge in thin layers, pour the batter onto a large rectangular baking sheet lined with parchment paper or a silicone sheet. Reduce baking time accordingly–it should be a nice golden brown color and the tip of a knife should come out clean.

● Chef's notes
You can add a little melted butter (3 tablespoons or 40 g) into the mixture before baking.
Flavor your sponge with anything you fancy—spices, cocoa powder, or liqueur, for example.

● Did you know?
The Genoese sponge takes its name from the Italian town of Genoa.

Recipe ideas
Passion-fruit and orange mousse ›› p. 441
Baked Alaska ›› p. 502

Sweet fillings, molded desserts, and pastry bases

1

2

3

Joconde sponge ★

This almond-based sponge is light and delicate. It is used for many pastry creations, one of the most notable being the Opéra.

Ingredients (serves 8)
³/₄ cup (140 g) plus ¹/₄ cup (50 g) sugar
1 ²/₃ cups (5 oz., 140 g) blanched* ground almonds* or almond meal
4 eggs plus 4 egg whites
8 tablespoons (45 g) cake flour
1 ³/₄ tablespoons (scant 1 oz., 25 g) butter, melted

Preheat the oven to 350°F (180°C). Sift together ³/₄ cup (140 g) granulated sugar and the ground almonds **(1)**.
Beat this together with the 4 eggs until the mixture reaches the ribbon stage* **(1)**. Fold in the sifted flour, followed by the melted butter.
Beat the 4 egg whites until they form stiff peaks. Add the remaining sugar and beat until the mixture is firm and shiny (it forms a French meringue) **(2, 3)**.
Carefully fold* the French meringue into the egg and butter mixture.
Line a baking sheet with parchment paper and spread the batter over it **(4)**. It should be very thin, about ¹/₅ in. (3-5 mm) thick. Bake for 8-10 minutes.
As soon as it is done, turn it over onto a rack to cool.

● Chef's notes
You can add finely diced pieces of fruit to the batter before baking.*
Use printing paste (p. 164) for decoration. Prepare it as a base for your sponge and you will have an eye-catching dessert casing.

🥄 Recipe ideas
Mint-chocolate entremets ≫ p. 431
Opéra ≫ p. 480

4

Almond macaroons ★★

A round, bite-sized morsel or a cake with a crisp shell and delectably chewy interior. Macaroons come in many varied forms: smooth, crackled, with almond pieces, and the popular Parisian or gerbet macaroons with a filling. This is a delicate recipe where precision is all-important, so you will need to weigh the egg whites.

Ingredients (for 16 large macaroons or 40 small, filled macaroons)

1 ³/₄ cup (5 ¼ oz./150 g) blanched* ground almonds*
1 generous cup (5 ¼ oz./150 g) confectioners' sugar
2 oz. (55 g) egg whites, whipped
³/₄ cup (5 ¼ oz./150 g) sugar
1 ³/₄ oz. (50 g) egg whites, whipped
Special equipment: a candy thermometer

Process the ground almonds and confectioners' sugar finely in a food processor (1). (You may have to sift the mixture, because it is important for the almonds to be very fine.)
Add the 2 oz. (55 g) whipped egg white and stir until the mixture forms a firm paste with the texture of almond paste (2).
Begin cooking the sugar and 3 ¹/₂ tablespoons (50 ml) water to form a syrup. When it reaches a temperature of 243°F-250°F (117°C-121°C) prepare an Italian meringue (see p. 49) using the 1 ³/₄ oz. (50 g) whipped egg white. Whip until cool.
Gradually fold* the Italian meringue into the almond mixture, working carefully (3). Work the mixture until the consistency is somewhat firm but still runny.
Line a baking sheet with parchment paper or use a silicone baking sheet. Spoon the mixture into a piping bag and pipe out your shapes (just under 1 in. [2 cm] diameter for small macaroons, about 2 ¹/₂ in. [6.5 cm] for the larger ones).
Leave them out to dry for about 20 minutes. They will form a light crust.
Ensure that the oven is completely dry (no residual steam from previous use) and pre-heat it to 300°F (150°C). Bake for 8-10 minutes. Remove from the oven and leave to cool. Detach the macaroons from the baking sheet.

● **Chef's note**
You can fill the macaroons with a range of creams, ganaches, and preserves. Use your imagination!

● **Did you know?**
This petit four was imported from Italy by the court of Catherine de' Medici. The name comes from macarone, *which means "fine paste" in the Venetian dialect.*

🍴 **Recipe idea**
Assortment of almond macaroons >> p. 442

1

Chocolate mousse ★

This is a rich, refined chocolate dessert, eaten plain, and not to be used as a layer in another gateau or dessert.

Ingredients (serves 8)
$^1/_2$ lb. (250 g) bittersweet chocolate, 64 percent cocoa mass
$^3/_4$ stick (80 g) butter
3 eggs, separated, plus 3 egg whites
$^1/_2$ cup (100 g) granulated sugar
Special equipment: candy thermometer

Roughly chop the chocolate and dice* the butter. Place in a container over a bain-marie* (1), heated to 122°F (50°C), until melted.
Remove from the heat and stir in the 3 egg yolks until combined. Leave to cool down to about 83°F (28°C).
Stiffly beat the 6 egg whites. Add the sugar and beat until firm and shiny (see French meringue p. 49).
Carefully fold* the meringue and chocolate mixtures together using a rubber spatula. Make sure you do not deflate the egg whites (2).
Spoon into a serving dish and leave to set for at least 1 hour.

2

● **Chef's note**
It's best to eat this mousse soon after it has been prepared, preferably on the same day.

● **Did you know?**
To assemble layered desserts, a pâte à bombe is frequently used. Italian meringue and whipped cream are added to a ganache.

❙ **Recipe idea**
Mint-chocolate entremets >> p. 431

Fruit mousse ★★ 🎬

This light mousse is used to prepare many fruit desserts, and is often combined with a sponge layer.

Ingredients (serves 12)
7 sheets (14 g) gelatin*
1 lb. 2 oz. (500 g) puréed fruit
10 egg whites
³/₄ cup (150 g) granulated sugar
2 cups (500 ml) water
2 cups (500 ml) whipping cream, 30 percent fat content
A few drops of fruit brandy or liqueur, depending on the fruit

Soak the gelatin sheets in very cold water to soften them.
Bring the fruit purée to the boil. Wring the water from the gelatin and incorporate the sheets into the purée with a whisk until completely dissolved.
Allow to cool.
Make an Italian meringue using the egg whites, the sugar, and water (see p. 49). Alternatively, if using an electric beater or mixer, you may incorporate the sugar directly into the eggs, without any water (see DVD).
In a separate bowl, whip the cream until it forms stiff peaks. When the fruit purée has cooled to 68°F (20°C), whisk in the fruit brandy if using.
When the Italian meringue has cooled, gradually and carefully fold* it in to the fruit purée using a rubber spatula (1). Then carefully fold in the whipped cream until all the ingredients are blended (2).
Chill for 1-1 ¹/₂ hours to allow it to set.

● Chef's notes
If you use other gelling agents such as agar-agar, made from seaweed, make sure you change the quantities accordingly and follow the instructions carefully.
For the best taste experience, use fruits that are in season.
It is far quicker to add only whipped cream to a fruit purée with a gelling agent, but the taste will not be comparable.
You can try making a dessert with different fruit mousses. You can layer them, insert one into another, or use one to line the others.

🍴 Recipe idea
Passion-fruit and orange mousse ›› p. 441

Sweet fillings, molded desserts, and pastry bases

Sweet fillings, molded desserts, and pastry bases

Genoa loaf cake ★

This is considered to be a heavy cake. Ground almonds* are the main ingredient, and it is eaten on its own or used to make petit fours and as a base for certain desserts.

Ingredients (serves 8)
2 whole eggs plus 3 eggs, separated
1 ¹/₂ cups (125 g) ground almonds
²/₃ cup (125 g) granulated sugar
Flavoring, such as vanilla or orange blossom water
³/₄ cup (75 g) all-purpose flour
5 ¹/₄ tablespoons (75 g) unsalted butter, melted until brown* and cooled

Preheat the oven to 350°F (170°C).
Whisk the 2 whole eggs together with the 3 egg yolks, the ground almonds, sugar, and flavoring until the mixture is light and foamy. Sift the flour and blend it in.
Whisk the 3 egg whites until they form stiff peaks. Fold* them in to the batter.
Pour in the cooled melted brown butter and stir until combined.
Butter the cake pan* and dust it with flour. Pour the batter in–it should be no higher than two-thirds of the way up the sides of the pan. Bake for 30 to 40 minutes, until a cake tester comes out dry and the edges start to pull away from the sides.
Turn out to a rack and allow to cool upside down. This cake is eaten when cooled.

● Chef's notes
There are many variations on this recipe. Choose yours depending on the taste you are looking for and the use to which you will put it (coffee cake, petit-four base, etc).

● Did you know?
Chiboust, the nineteenth-century pastry chef who created the cream that bears his name (see p. 170), made a variant of the Genoa loaf cake known as the Ambroisie.

Rice pudding ★

Round grains of rice are cooked in milk, flavored with vanilla, and thickened, if you wish, with egg yolk.

Ingredients (serves 6)
²/₃ cup (5 oz./140 g) Arborio or other round-grain rice
4 cups (1 liter) milk
1 vanilla bean
1 pinch fine salt
3 egg yolks
²/₃ cup (125 g) granulated sugar
Special equipment: an ovenproof pot with a lid

Preheat the oven to 325°F (160°C).
Rinse the rice.
Begin cooking it in cold water. As soon as it starts to boil, remove the pot from the heat and refresh* the rice under cold running water.
Drain well.
Scrape out the seeds from the vanilla bean into the milk and bring to the boil (with the whole vanilla bean).
Pour in the rice and cover with a lid.
Bake the rice for a good hour.
Test for doneness by squeezing the rice between your fingers; the grains should be tender.
Beat the egg yolks with the sugar until the mixture become thick and pale (ribbon stage*).
Pour the thickening mixture into the rice and combine. Return to the stove and bring back to a simmer.
Transfer to a serving dish and allow to cool.

● Chef's notes
Give a silky touch to your rice pudding by adding a little whipped cream when it has cooled.
The advantage of round-grain rice is that it absorbs a great deal of liquid when cooked.

❙ Recipe idea
Cinnamon-scented rice pudding >> p. 469

Semolina pudding ★

Semolina pudding is prepared in milk and flavored with vanilla. If you wish, you may bind it with egg yolks.

Ingredients (serves 8)
4 cups (800 ml) milk
1 vanilla bean
1 scant cup (5 oz./140 g) fine semolina
1 scant cup (180 g) sugar

Slit the vanilla bean lengthwise and scrape the seeds into the milk. Place the bean with the milk in a saucepan and bring to the simmer.
Pour the semolina into the simmering milk and turn the heat down to low.
Simmer gently for 7–10 minutes, whisking constantly.
When this is done, add the sugar and mix.
Transfer to individual ramekins or a serving dish. Cover with plastic wrap so that it is in direct contact with the pudding. Leave to cool.

● Chef's notes
Vary the quantity of semolina depending on how creamy a texture you want.
Fine corn semolina (polenta) can also be used. The proportions are identical.
Plump up a handful of raisins and add them to the pudding.

Almond rock cakes (*rochers*) ★

Rocher means "rock," and these petit fours take their name from their irregular shape. They can also be made with shredded coconut, ground almonds*, chocolate or hazelnuts.

Ingredients (for about 25 rochers)
3 egg whites
1 cup (200 g) sugar
2 ²/₃ cups (7 oz./200 g) shredded coconut

Preheat the oven to 200°F (90°C). Line a baking tray with parchment paper or a silicone baking sheet.
Beat the egg whites and the sugar in the bowl of a heavy-duty mixer over a bain-marie* (1) heated to about 122°F-131°F (50°C-55°C). Do not let the mixture get too hot (test with your finger). Remove from the bain-marie and continue to beat on the mixer for 5 minutes on medium speed until you have a firm Swiss meringue texture (see p. 50) (2).
Add the shredded coconut (3) and combine with a spatula.
Pipe or spoon heaps of the mixture onto the sheet (4).
Bake for about 1 hour until the cakes are well browned. Leave to stand.

Sweet fillings, molded desserts, and pastry bases

Hot soufflé
(pastry-cream base) ★ ★ ★

This light, hot dessert rises significantly when baked, thanks to the beaten egg whites.

Ingredients (serves 8)
Pastry cream base
2 cups (500 ml) milk
1 vanilla bean
$^2/_3$ cup (125 g) sugar
4 egg yolks
$^1/_3$ cup (60 g) cornstarch
$^1/_4$ cup (60 ml) of a liqueur or fruit brandy of your choice
6 egg whites plus 2 whole eggs, separated
1 pinch salt
$^1/_3$ cup (60 g) sugar

For the soufflé mold
2 tablespoons (30 g) unsalted butter, melted
2 $^1/_2$ tablespoons (1 oz./30 g) sugar

Prepare a pastry cream (see p. 182).
Slit the vanilla bean lengthwise and scrape the seeds into the milk. Place the vanilla bean, seeds, and milk in a saucepan and place over medium heat.
Beat the egg yolks, sugar, and cornstarch until the mixture becomes thick and turns a pale color (ribbon stage*).
When the milk begins to simmer, pour half of it over the egg yolk mixture and combine thoroughly.
Pour this mixture back onto the remaining milk and return to the heat. Bring back to a simmer. Simmer for 2-3 minutes, whisking constantly.
Transfer to a bowl, cover with plastic wrap, and cool rapidly.
Use a pastry brush to grease the ramekins or soufflé mold (1), making upward strokes as this will help the soufflé rise.
Sprinkle the mold or ramekins with sugar, coating them evenly.
Turn the ramekins upside down and give them a rap on the counter to remove any excess sugar (2).
Add the liqueur or brandy to the pastry cream.
Setting aside the 2 egg yolks, beat the 8 egg whites stiffly with the pinch of salt. Add the sugar and beat until the mixture is firm and shiny.
Place a baking tray in the oven and preheat to 400°F (200°C).
Add the 2 egg yolks to the pastry cream.
Use a rubber spatula to gently fold* the beaten egg whites into the pastry cream, taking care not to deflate the mixture.
Fill the molds or ramekins to the top and smooth the surface.
Press your thumb lightly around the rim of the mold to create a "moat." This will help the soufflés to rise evenly.

1

2

Place them on the hot baking tray and bake for about 20 minutes, depending on the size. Your soufflés should have a nice golden brown crust, and the inside must remain light and airy.
Serve immediately.

● Chef's notes
Some recipes call for ladyfingers soaked in liqueur, coffee, etc., to be placed horizontally in the center of the soufflé.
Beat the egg whites at the last minute, just before you are ready to put the dishes in the oven.
It's essential to serve a soufflé as soon as it comes out of the oven, for it falls very quickly.

❙ Recipe idea
Orange liqueur soufflé >> p. 438

Hot fruit soufflé ★ ★ ★

This light, hot dessert can be made with a range of fruit purées.

Ingredients (serves 8)
2 cups (390 g) sugar
$^1/_2$ cup (125 ml) water
6 egg whites
1 pinch of salt
$^3/_4$ lb. (350 g) puréed fruit

For the soufflé mold
2 tablespoons (30 g) unsalted butter, melted
2 $^1/_2$ tablespoons (1 oz./30 g) sugar
Special equipment: a candy thermometer

Grease the soufflé mold (or ramekins) with butter, using a pastry brush and making upward strokes to help your soufflé rise. Sprinkle it with sugar, ensuring that the coating is evenly distributed. Turn the dish upside down and give it a little rap to shake off excess sugar.
Prepare an Italian meringue (see p. 49). Place the water and sugar in a saucepan and bring to the boil. When the syrup reaches 230°F (110°C), begin beating the egg whites with the pinch of salt in the bowl of a mixer.
Place a baking tray in the oven and preheat to 400°F (200°C). When the syrup reaches 243°F-250°F (117°C-120°C) and the egg whites form firm peaks, pour the syrup in. Continue beating until the mixture has cooled down. It will be dense and shiny, and form lots of small peaks.
Gently fold* in the fruit purée (1).
Fill the soufflé mold (or ramekins) to the top (2) and smooth the surface. Press your thumb lightly around the rim of the mold to create a "moat." This will help the soufflés to rise evenly.
Place the mold or ramekins on the hot baking tray and bake for about 20 minutes, depending on the size of your soufflés.
They are done when the top is nice and yellow, but the inside is still soft.
Serve immediately.

Sweet fillings, molded desserts, and pastry bases

Succès ★

This is a meringue batter that uses blanched*8 ground almonds*. It is used as a base that can be garnished with toppings, creams, etc.

Ingredients (serves 10)
5 egg whites
²/₃ cup (125 g) sugar, divided
¹/₃ cup (25 g) cake flour
1 ¹/₂ cups (125 g) ground almonds

Preheat the oven to 400°F (200°C).
Beat the egg whites until they form firm peaks. Add 1 generous tablespoon (15 g) sugar and beat until shiny.
Sift the remaining sugar, flour, and ground almonds together.
Pour into the beaten egg whites and fold* in carefully so that the mixture does not deflate.
Spoon into a piping bag immediately and pipe out onto a baking sheet. A close whirl pattern is the one most frequently used in French pastry making.
Bake for 8-10 minutes, depending on the size and shape.
Transfer immediately to a rack to cool.

● **Chef's notes**
Small, broken bits of macaroon added to the batter will give your pastry a delightful crunch.
The Succès bases may be prepared ahead of time, cut up if need be, and even frozen.
Use a plain tip to pipe out your spirals.

● **Did you know?**
The Succès is a pastry comprising two disks of almond meringue filled with a praline butter cream (just like the small, filled macaroons).
The Dacquoise is a meringue specialty from the town of Dax in the southwest of France. It contains ground hazelnuts instead of ground almonds.
A Japonais simply contains less sugar.
A Progrès uses half ground almonds and half ground hazelnuts.

🍴 **Recipe idea**
Chestnut cream Succès and caramelized walnuts ›› p. 471

Almond tuiles ★

A crisp, delicate round almond cookie traditionally served as ⟨...⟩ four with coffee. The French word *tuile* means "tile."

Ingredients (for about 30 tuiles)
3 egg whites
²/₃ cup (125 g) sugar
Scant ¹/₃ cup (25 g) cake flour
2 teaspoons (10 g) butter, melted
1 teaspoon (5 ml) vanilla extract
¹/₂ cup (2 oz./60 g) sliced blanched* almonds
Special equipment: rolling pins or bottles to drape the cookies over

Preheat the oven to 350°F (180°C).
Whisk the egg whites (1, 2). Add all the other ingredients except the sliced almonds.
Chill for about 20 minutes.
Drop the batter in teaspoonfuls onto a baking sheet (silicone or parchment paper), smoothing them out with the back of a spoon until thin and about 2 in. (5 cm) in diameter (3).
Scatter the sliced almonds over the cookies.
Bake until they are a golden color, 5-8 minutes.
Remove them from the baking sheet and drape them immediately over a rolling pin so that they take on a curved shape. Allow to cool.

● **Chef's note**
The mixture spreads, so leave enough space between your cookies when you prepare your baking sheets.

● **Did you know?**
There are many variations on this recipe. One of the finest is the lace tuile. It resembles open lace work and is particularly crisp. This requires ¹/₃ cup (80 g) butter, melted; ¹/₂ cup (100 g) sugar; 4 ¹/₂ tablespoons (50 ml) orange juice; 3 ¹/₂ oz. (100 g) chopped almonds; ¹/₃ cup (1 oz./30 g) flour; and 1 ¹/₃ tablespoons (20 ml) Cointreau or other orange liqueur.

🍴 **Recipe idea**
Assorted tuiles ›› p. 483

Ice creams, sorbets,
and iced desserts

Some people will say it's not worth making your own: save yourself the effort and buy your ice cream at your favorite specialty store. But there's nothing quite like homemade ice cream, nothing quite so festive and gratifying. Even without an ice-cream maker, you can achieve astonishingly good results. And if you do have an ice-cream maker, well, your desserts will be just that much better.

Although ice cream is widely appreciated today, it is by no means a recent invention. At the court of Alexander the Great, in 350 BCE, cooks prepared mixtures of fruit and filtered juice, sweetened with honey, that they froze by burying the container in the snow. Marco Polo is said to have brought the method of cooling foods without ice from Asia to Europe, introducing water ices to Italy. From there, Catherine de' Medici brought iced desserts to the French court. A seventeenth-century chef actually discovered how to make ices using milk, cream, and eggs, but it was only in the late eighteenth century that such desserts became popular .

The range of flavors eaten today—fruit, flowers, and spices—keeps widening. There are more and more reasons to invite ice creams to our tables.

Upside-down apple cake, in France known as a *tarte Tatin*, with its traditional scoop of vanilla ice cream, has inspired many other imaginative pairings. One could serve a melon sorbet to accompany cured ham, a dill and lemon sorbet with marinated salmon, and even a sweet wine sorbet with foie gras.

There are two types of ice cream:
• churned iced preparations
• unchurned iced preparations
Ice cream is best when served at a temperature between 9°F–14°F (-10°C–13°C), and so must be taken out of the freezer a few minutes before you serve it.

Churned iced preparations

Churned preparations are recipes that require chilling accompanied by a paddle movement—preferably using an ice-cream maker.

These fall into three categories:
• sorbets
• egg-rich ice creams (custard-based)
• iced creams

Ice-cream professionals juggle with their recipes in the manner of chemists, using specific ingredients like stabilizers, atomized glucose, and inverted sugar.

Here we merely give you a few recipes without delving into the complexities of the ice-cream making profession.

No stabilizers are required here, and our recipes are meant for immediate consumption, to be enjoyed at home within twenty-four hours.

Sugar is all-important in ice cream making; it has a key role in giving the right texture. Its antifreezing properties prevent ice cream from becoming excessively hard. The same is true of alcohol, which will considerably soften your iced desserts.

Sorbet ★

Sorbets are iced preparations made with water, sugar, and fruit or wine or liqueur.

Ingredients (for strawberry sorbet)
1 ¼ cup (250 g) granulated sugar
Scant ½ cup (100 ml) water
1 ½ lb. (650 g) pureed strawberries

Prepare a syrup of cooked sugar (see p. 169) and leave it to cool to room temperature. Add the puréed fruit. Chill for 4-6 hours and transfer to an ice-cream maker.

❚ **Recipe idea**
❚ Iced blackberry *vacherin* >> p. 498

Custard-based ice cream ★

Ingredients (for vanilla ice cream)
1 vanilla bean
1 ²/₃ cups (400 ml) full fat milk
Scant ½ cup (100 ml) whipping cream, 35 percent fat content
6 egg yolks
½ cup (100 g) sugar

Slit the vanilla bean lengthwise. Bring the milk and cream to the boil with the vanilla bean.
Beat the yolks with the sugar in a mixing bowl until they are thick and pale (ribbon stage*).
Pour the milk and cream mixture over the egg yolks, beating constantly, then return all the liquid to the saucepan.
Heat as you would to make a custard (see p. 172) to a temperature of 185°F (85°C).
Cool rapidly over ice and then transfer to an ice-cream maker for 2 ½-3 hours.

❚ **Recipe ideas**
❚ Baked Alaska >> p. 502
❚ Rum and raisin profiteroles >> p. 494

Egg-enriched ice cream ★

This type of ice cream has a high egg-yolk content, and is often made with milk.

Ingredients (for coffee ice cream)
4 cups (1 liter) full cream milk
Scant ½ cup (100 ml) whipping cream, 35 percent fat content
3 tablespoons (10 g) instant coffee
10 egg yolks (this should weigh 7 ½ oz./200 g)
1 ½ cup (300 g) granulated sugar

Combine the milk with the cream and the coffee, making sure the coffee granules are dissolved. Use the ingredients to make a custard (see p. 172). When the mixture has reached 185°F (85°C), remove from the heat and cool. Chill for 4-6 hours in the refrigerator and transfer to an ice-cream maker.

● **Chef's note**
For a more authentic coffee taste, infuse roughly chopped roasted coffee beans in the milk. However, it is instant coffee that will give the coffee color.

Unchurned iced desserts

Iced parfait ★

The parfait is made using a pâte à bombe (see following recipe) to which lightly whipped, unsweetened cream is added.

Ingredients for a fruit parfait (serves 10)
10 egg yolks (these should weigh 7 ½ oz. or 200 g)
3 ¼ lb. (7 cups plus 1 scant cup or 1.5 kg) granulated sugar
3 ½ tablespoons (50 ml) water
3 cups (750 ml) whipping cream, whipped
8 oz. (250 g) fruit pulp

To make a fruit parfait, simmer the egg yolks and sugar over a hot water bath (poaching, see pâte à bombe recipe on this page) to a temperature of 185°F (85°C).
Whisk the mixture until it cools down. Carefully incorporate the whipped cream and the fruit pulp.

Ingredients for a milk-based iced parfait (serves 8)
1 cup (250ml) milk
8 egg yolks (these should weigh 5 ½ oz. or 160 g)
1 ¼ cup (250 g) granulated sugar
1 ¾ cups (425 ml) whipping cream, whipped

Use the recipe for custard on p. 172, but simmer the ingredients over a hot water bath, which will take slightly longer. Allow to cool before carefully incorporating the whipped cream.

❚ Recipe ideas
Iced nougat and raspberry coulis ›› p. 505
Iced hazelnut parfait ›› p. 496

Pâte à bombe ★

It is useful to master the technique for pâte à bombe. Here, we give you two methods, both of which involve cooking the egg yolks.

With cooked sugar
Prepare a sugar syrup and heat it to 244°F-250°F (118°C-121°C). Beat the egg yolks. Pour the syrup over the egg yolks, beating constantly. Continue whisking until the mixture has cooled down completely.

Poaching
Place the egg yolks and sugar in a bowl and beat together. Place the bowl over a hot water bath, stirring, until the yolks start to coagulate at the edges. The mixture will have reached a temperature of 131°F (55°C). Remove from heat. Whisk energetically until the mixture reaches the ribbon stage* (see the method for Genoese sponge p. 193) and it cools down.

● **Chef's notes**
The pâte à bombe mixture is not the same thing as a bombe glacée! A bombe glacée is a domed iced dessert. For the pâte à bombe mixture, whipped cream or Chantilly cream (sweetened) is added.

Iced mousse ★★

Milk-based iced mousse is made of custard and whipped cream. You may also add an Italian meringue.
Fruit mousse comprises puréed fruit to which meringue and whipped cream are added.

Ingredients for iced raspberry mousse (serves 8)
1 lb. (500 g) raspberry pulp
1 cup (250 ml) whipping cream, whipped
To make 1 ¼ lb. (550 g) Italian meringue
5 egg whites (these should weigh 5 oz. or 150 g)
1 ½ cups (11 oz./300 g) granulated sugar
Scant ½ cup (100 ml) water

Prepare an Italian meringue (see method p. 49). Add the fruit pulp to it. Delicately fold in* the whipped cream.
Freeze until set.

Soufflé ★

A soufflé is basically a parfait to which Italian meringue has been added. It has the same shape as a hot soufflé, which is a pastry dessert.

Ingredients for iced soufflé with liqueur (serves 10)
10 egg yolks (these should weigh 7 oz./200 g)
³/₄ cup (150 g) granulated sugar
2 ¹/₂ tablespoons (50 ml) water
3 cups (750 ml) whipping cream, whipped
4-5 tablespoons (60-75 ml) liqueur

Italian meringue
2 egg whites (these should weigh 2 oz./60 g)
²/₃ cup (120 g) granulated sugar
2 tablespoons plus 2 teaspoons (40 ml) water

Prepare a pâte à bombe with cooked sugar (see p. 210).
Make up the Italian meringue (see p. 49 for method).
Flavor your whipped cream with the liqueur of your choice and delicately fold* it into the mixture.

● **Did you know?**
In the soufflé family of desserts, there is another category that uses fruits: iced fruit soufflés. These use a mixture of fruit pulp or fruit juice, Italian meringue, and whipped cream. Fruit macerated in alcohol, candied fruit, or dried fruit may also be added.

🥄 **Recipe idea**
Iced banana soufflé ≫ p. 501

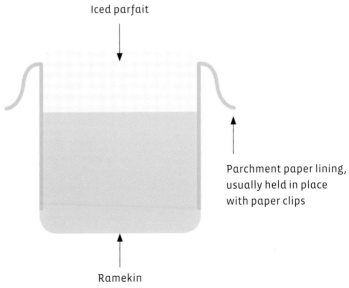

Iced parfait

Parchment paper lining, usually held in place with paper clips

Ramekin

Other iced dishes

Iced *vacherin*
An iced *vacherin* comprises a meringue base or shell that holds several flavors of ice cream and/or sorbets, covered by a smothering of Chantilly cream–usually vanilla, but other flavorings that pair with the ice cream inside may be used.

Iced "logs"
This is an iced version of the log cake, traditionally served in France for Christmas–it resembles a log of wood. Various types of sponge base hold ice creams and/or sorbets. Today, ice-cream makers prepare their logs using an imaginative range of shapes, decorations, and flavors.

Ice cream profiteroles
Small choux or puff pastries are filled with ice cream and topped with a hot or cold sauce or coulis. Profiteroles are most popularly to be found on menus teamed with vanilla ice cream and hot chocolate sauce, sometimes with Chantilly cream as well.

Iced charlotte
Like the pastry version of a charlotte, the iced charlotte is lined with ladyfingers and filled with ice cream, sorbet, or an

unchurned iced dessert, such as a parfait, soufflé, and mousse. Chantilly cream can add a delicious decorative touch.

Baked Alaska
A soaked sponge (usually a Genoese sponge) is the base for an ice cream, sorbet, or iced dessert. This is covered all over in meringue and browned, either in the oven or using a caramelizing blow torch. Sometimes, the Baked Alaska is flambéed* just before serving. In French it is known as a Norwegian omelet.

Iced citrus fruit (*fruits givrés*)
Lemons and oranges are hollowed out and left whole and their flesh is used to make a sorbet or ice cream that then fills the skin. Other flavors may be added when the dessert is assembled.

Plombières
This name refers to an egg-based ice cream or ordinary ice cream made with vanilla or kirsch. Candied fruits soaked in syrup or kirsch are added to this, as is almond milk or almonds.

Sundaes

Name	What's in it?	The story behind it
Peach Melba	2 scoops of vanilla ice cream	The illustrious Auguste Escoffier was working at the London Savoy in 1893 when he created this dessert for the Australian opera singer Nelly Melba.
	Whole peaches poached in vanilla syrup	
	Redcurrant jelly	
	Chantilly cream	
	Sliced, toasted almonds	
Colonel	Lemon sorbet	
	Vodka	
Poire Belle-Hélène	2 scoops of vanilla ice cream	This dessert was created around 1864 in homage to Offenbach's popular comic opera, *La Belle Hélène*.
	Pear halves poached in syrup	
	Warm chocolate sauce	
	Chantilly cream	
	Sliced, toasted almonds	
Banana split	A split banana	
	3 scoops of ice cream, preferably vanilla or chocolate	
	Chocolate sauce or fruit coulis	
	Chantilly cream	
Café liégeois	2 scoops of soft coffee ice cream made with a coffee infusion	An iced version of the Belgian coffee drink.
	Chantilly cream	
Dame blanche	2 scoops of vanilla or almond milk ice cream	This dessert probably takes its name from a successful opera by the French composer Boieldieu, published in 1825. The name means "white lady."
	Chocolate sauce	

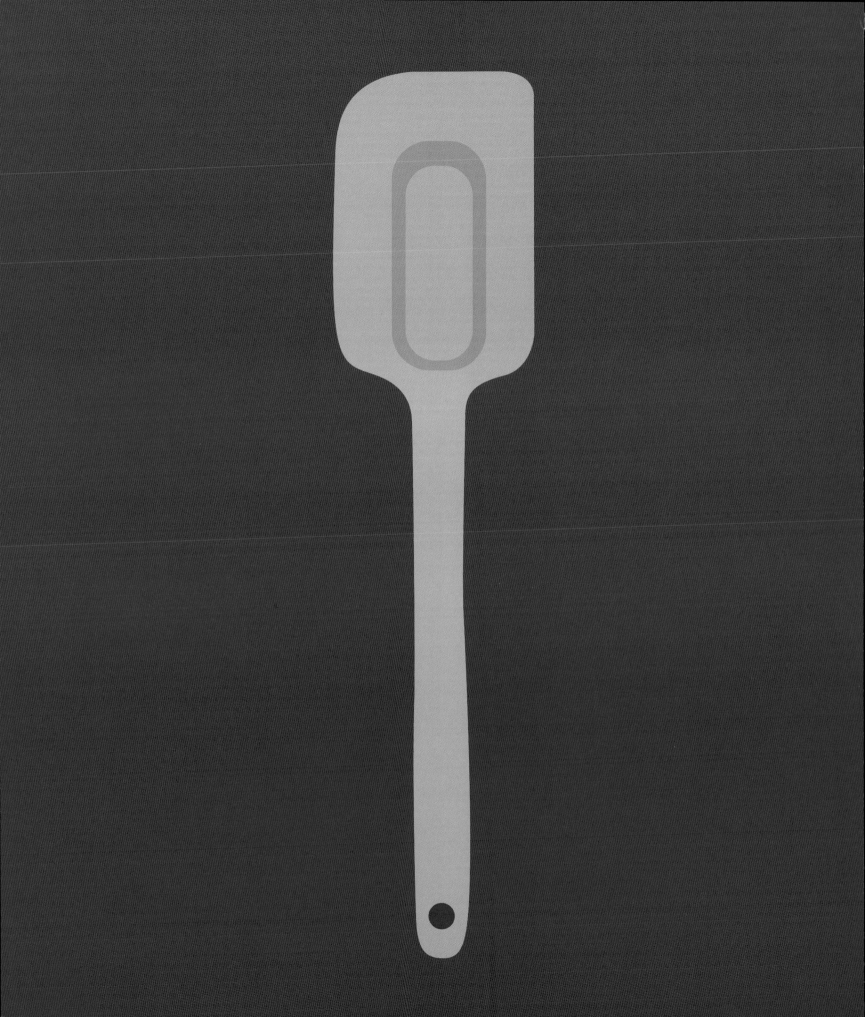

Practical
Guide

Dessert mold

Dariole mold

Tart ring

Tart ring

Dessert mold

Dessert mold

Oyster knife

Canelle knife

Vegetable peeler

Scoop or melon baller

Turning knife

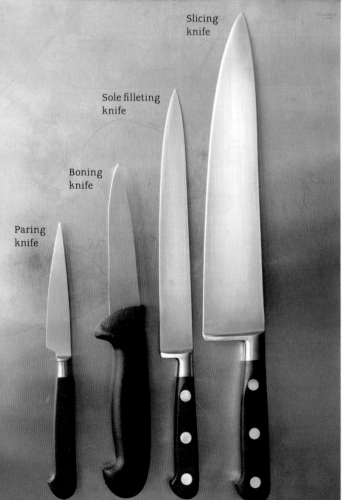

Slicing knife

Sole filleting knife

Boning knife

Paring knife

Sauté pan

Chinois

Mandolin vegetable slicer

Flexible rubber spatula

Tip for piping bag

Basic Equipment

Chinois
A conical perforated metal sieve that is used to strain thicker sauces.

Dutch Oven
A large pot with a tight-fitting lid, ideal for stews as it can be used both on the stove top and in the oven.

Fine-Mesh Sieve or Strainer
For smooth sauces, mousselines, and coulis.

Flexible Rubber Spatula
Indispensable for mixing two or more ingredients gently, scooping, scraping, and spreading.

Grill Pan
This will allow you to grill meat, sear it in attractive patterns, and ensure that it does not cook in its own fat.

Heavy-Duty Stand-Alone Mixer
Ideal for kneading dough, preparing Italian meringue, or generally preparing recipes in larger quantities.

High-Sided Sauté Pan
Preferably with an ovenproof lid and handle so that you can finish cooking in the oven.

Ice-Cream Maker
This will enable you to make sorbets and ice creams by churning and freezing your preparations to well below freezing point.

Mandolin, also known as a Japanese mandolin
To make attractive, paper-thin slices.

Mixing Bowls
Two types of mixing bowls are useful, the flat-bottomed kind that serves most purposes, and the round-bottomed kind for whisking egg whites and cream and preparing your own mayonnaise. The latter is shaped so that a whisk can reach right to the lowest levels of the liquid.

Plastic Scraper
This unpretentious, half-moon-shaped tool will ensure that every last little bit of batter is scraped out of the mixing bowl.

Siphon
A device that uses a gas cartridge to foam the liquid placed inside it.

Stock Pot
A high-sided pot for slow evaporation used to prepare stocks and soups.

Whisks
There are two types of whisks, a balloon whisk for egg whites, short and rounded, and a sauce whisk, longer with more rigid wires.

Because precision is important:

Scales and measuring utensils
An electric scale is useful, particularly if you have one that switches between the metric and imperial systems. Measuring jugs, cups, and spoons will ensure your volumes are accurate.

Thermometers
A meat or an instant-read thermometer to check on the progress of roasts and ensure that terrines do not overcook. A candy thermometer, essential if preparing an Italian meringue to incorporate into a dessert. If it has a sufficiently large range, you may use it for both dairy and fat.
A fat thermometer will come in handy for deep frying.

Meat Cuts

Beef

USA

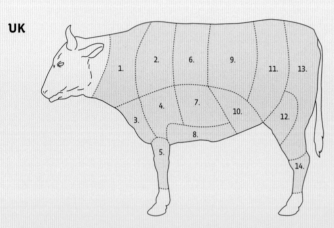

1. Chuck 2. Rib 3. Brisket 4. Shank 5. Plate 6. Flank 7. Short Loin 8. Sirloin
9. Tenderloin 10. Top Sirloin 11. Bottom Sirloin 12. Round

Lamb

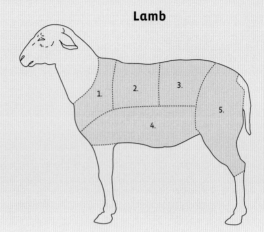

1. Shoulder 2. Rack 3. Loin 4. Foreshank and Breast 5. Leg

UK

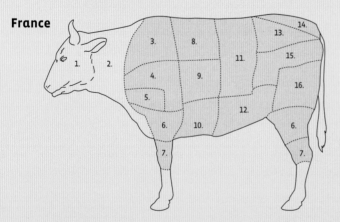

1. Neck 2. Chuck and Blade 3. Clod 4. Thick Rib 5. Shin 6. Fore Rib 7. Thin Rib
8. Brisket 9. Sirloin 10. Thin Flank 11. Rump 12. Thick Flank
13. Topside and Silverside 14. Leg

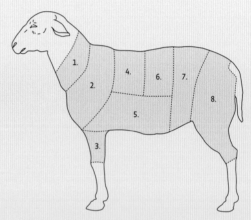

1. Scrag 2. Shoulder 3. Shank 4. Best end of neck
5. Breast 6. Loin 7. Chump 8. Leg

France

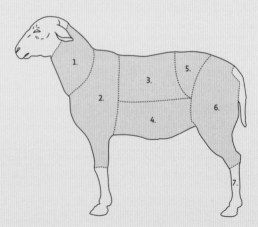

1. Joue 2. Collier 3. Paleron 4. Macreuse 5. Veine grasse 6. Gîte 7. Crosse
8. Côtes couvertes 9. Plat de côtes 10. Poitrine 11. Filet et aloyau
12. Flanchet 13. Culotte 14. Rumsteck 15. Tranche 16. Gîte à la noix

1. Collet 2. Épaule 3. Carré 4. Poitrine 5. Selle 6. Gigot 7. Pieds

Pork

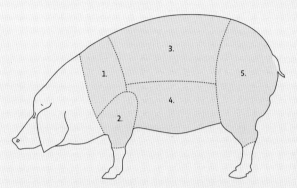

1. Shoulder Butt 2. Picnic Shoulder 3. Loin 4. Spare Ribs/Belly 5. Ham

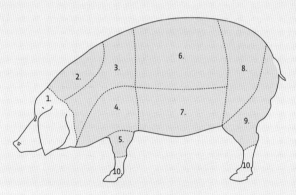

1. Head 2. Spare Rib 3. Blade 4. Hand 5. Hock 6. Loin 7. Belly
8. Chump 9. Leg 10. Trotters

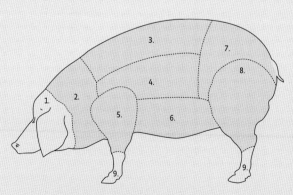

1. Tête 2. Collier 3. Carré 4. Travers 5. Épaule 6. Poitrine
7. Filet 8. Jambon 9. Pieds

Veal

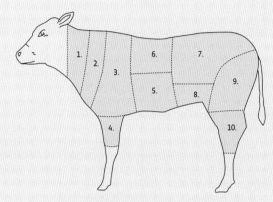

1. Neck 2. Chuck 3. Shoulder 4. Fore Shank 5. Breast 6. Ribs
7. Loin 8. Flank 9. Leg 10. Hind Shank

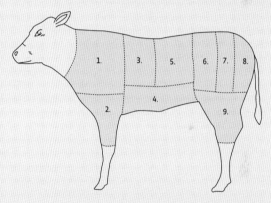

1. Shoulder 2. Fore Shank 3. Best End 4. Breast 5. Loin 6. Rump
7. Silverside 8. Topside 9. Hind Shank

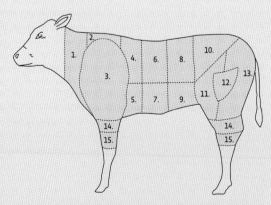

1. Collier 2. Côtes découvertes 3. Épaule 4. Côtes secondes 5. Poitrine
6. Côtes premières 7. Tendron 8. Longe 9. Flanchet 10. Quasi
11. Noix patissière 12. Noix 13. Sous-noix 14. Jarret 15. Crosse

Heirloom Vegetables

1. Sunchoke or
   Jerusalem artichoke
2. Parsnip
3. Oriental radish
4. Crosne, Japanese
   or Chinese artichoke
5. White radish
6. Black salsify, scorzonera,
   or black oyster plant
7. Swede or rutabaga,
   also known as Swedish,
   yellow, Canadian,
   or Russian turnip

AOC and AOP (Appellation d'Origine Contrôlée/Protégée)

Appellation d'Origine Contrôlée (AOC)

The AOC, which means controlled designation of origin, is the French certification awarded by the governmental body L'Institut National des Appellations d'Origine (INAO) to certain regional agricultural products such as wines, cheeses, butters, and honey. All AOC products must adhere to clearly defined and strict standards, and be produced in a particular, traditional way, with ingredients from classified producers, within the region that holds the AOC status. These products are usually identified by a seal printed on the label, as with wines, or, in the case of cheese, on the rind.

Appellation d'Origine Protégée (AOP)

The European Union introduced a system of protected designation of origin in 1992, for products that are produced, processed, and prepared in a certain geographical area using a certified and recognized method. It is an extension of the French AOC and is designed to protect locally produced butters, cheeses, and other agricultural products within the EU member states. The AOP is also expanding globally and at present it is recognized by more than 180 countries.

Cheeses

The first cheese to be given AOC status was Roquefort, in 1925; today, more than forty cheeses bear the AOC stamp. The list below categorizes cheeses according to the source of the milk used to make them. Most are made from cows' milk, as are the majority of cheeses in the world; however, many are produced using milk from goats and sheep, the most famous example probably being Roquefort, produced using ewe's milk.

Cheeses made from cows' milk: Abondance; Beaufort; Bleu d'Auvergne; Bleu de Gex Haut Hura; Bleu des Causses; Bleu du Vercors Sassenage; Brie de Meaux; Brie de Melun; Camembert de Normandie; Cantal; Chaource; Comté; Epoisses; Fourme d'Ambert; Fourme de Montbrison; Gruyère AOC; Laguiole; Langres; Livarot; Maroilles; Mont d'Or; Morbier; Muenster; Neufchâtel; Pont-l'Evêque; Reblochon; Saint-Nectaire; Salers; Tome des Bauges

Cheeses made from goats' milk: Banon; Brocciu; Chabichou du Poitou; Chavignol; Chevrotin; Mâconnais AOC; Pélardon; Picodon; Pouligny-Saint-Pierre; Rigotte de Condrieu AOC; Rocamadour; Sainte-Maure de Touraine; Selle-sur-Cher; Valençay

Cheeses made from ewes' milk: Brocciu; Ossau-Iraty; Roquefort

Other Regional (AOC) Products

Moules de bouchot de la baie du Mont-Saint-Michel (Bouchot mussels from the bay of the Mont-Saint-Michel)
These mussels, produced in the bay of the Mont-Saint-Michel, were awarded the Appellation d'Origine Controlée– the first seafood to be awarded the French label. The moules de bouchot are the most sought-after mussels in France, mainly due to their medium size and distinctly firm, orange-yellow flesh. They are grown on wooden pillars, or *bouchots*, which means they are underwater at high tide, yet exposed to the sea air when the water recedes, giving them their distinctive flavor.

Lentilles vertes du Puy (Green Puy lentils)
These lentils have been grown in the Auvergne region since Roman times, an area of volcanic soil free from fertilizer, which gives them their unique, nutty, and mineral-rich flavor. The climate of this area–a lack of humidity and plenty of sunshine due to the volcanic deposits and surrounding mountains–contributes to their unique texture, as the lentils are able to dry on the plants before being harvested. As a result, these Puy lentils have less starch than others and are not as mushy. They were awarded their Appellation in 1996.

Volaille de Bresse (Bresse poultry)
This is the only poultry to carry the AOC quality label. Bresse poultry is renowned for its quality of meat and unbeatable flavor, and is raised according to traditional local methods, remaining completely separate from any form of industrialization.

Piment d'Espelette (Ezpeletako Biperra)
The beloved chili pepper of the Basque region, the Espelette chili has become not only a culinary, but a cultural icon in this area, where it has gained controlled-name status. It has been grown in the small town of Espelette since the sixteenth century, and is noted for having a robust peppery and slightly smoked flavor.

Cocos de Paimpol (Breton semi-dried beans)
These beans originate from a seed brought back to the Paimpol region in 1928 by a sailor. They were marketed in 1948 and obtained the AOC in 1998. The pods are yellow, with purplish veins, and the beans are white and round.

Fruit Seasons

Type of Fruit	Southern Hemisphere Season	Northern Hemisphere Season
Apricot	November–March	May–September
Avocado	August–December	February–June
Banana	January–December	January–December
Blackberry (Mulberry)	November–February	May–August
Blackcurrant	December	June–August
Blood Orange	November–May	December–March
Blueberry (Bilberry)	November–March	May–September
Cape Gooseberry	September–November	June–July
Cherry	October–February	June–August
Chestnut	March–April	November–January
Clementine	February–September	November–January
Coconut	October–December	Not usually grown
Cranberry	Not usually grown	October–February
Elder	July–September	September–November
Fig	December–May	June–September
Grape	December–May	September–October
Grapefruit	September–November	September–November
Guava	September–February	November–March
Kiwi	November–May	January–August
Kumquat	September–January	November–March
Lemon	All year round	January–March
Lime	March–September	September–December
Lychee	December–February	April–June
Mango	September–January	March–September
Melon	All year round	July–October
Orange	March–November	January–March
Papaya	All year round	Not usually grown
Passion fruit	February–July	July–March
Peach	December–February	June–August/September
Pear	March–November	September–January
Persimmon (Sharon Fruit)	February–June	September–December
Pineapple	All year round	March–July
Plum	November–May	May–October
Pomegranate	March–May	October–January
Quince	December–May	October–December
Raspberry	November–February	June–September
Redcurrant	December	July–August
Rhubarb	November–February	January–May
Star Fruit (Carambola)	June–August	July–September
Strawberry	October–March	June–August
Tangerine	May–November	October–April
Tomato	March–July	June–September
Watermelon	December–March	August–October

Berries

Raspberry

Blackberry (mulberry)

Strawberry

Blueberry (bilberry)

Redcurrant

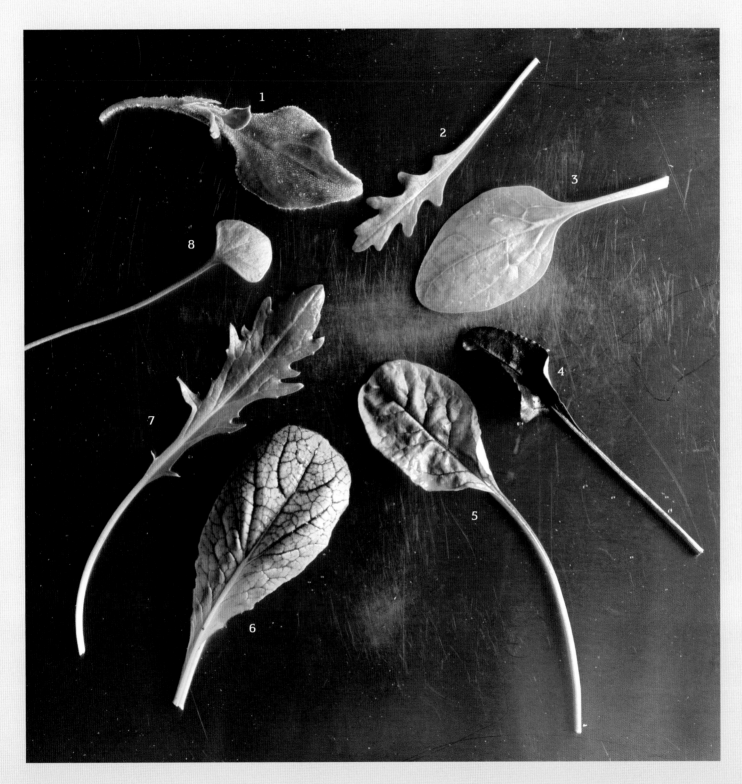

Salad Greens

1. Tetragonia or New Zealand ice plant or spinach (*Cryophytum cristallinum*)

2. Arugula (rocket)
3. Baby spinach
4. Beet leaf
5. Young Swiss chard

6. Miniature Japanese mustard
7. Mizuna
8. Purslane

Herbs

1. Chives
2. Rosemary
3. Mint
4. Basil
5. Frizzy-leaf (curly-leaf) parsley
6. Dill
7. Chervil
8. Bay leaf
9. Flat-leaf parsley
10. Tarragon
11. Thyme

1. Roquefort de Baragnaude
2. Comté (ripened 18 months)
3. Ossau-Iraty (Napoléon)
4. Saint-Nicolas
5. Camembert de Normandie
6. Crottin de Chavignol
7. Boulette d'Avesnes
8. Sainte-Maure-de-Touraine
9. Saint-Nectaire
10. Mâconnais sec
11. Époisses

French Cheese

Cheese, with bread and wine, symbolizes the gastronomy of France. The country produces some three hundred widely diverse varieties, and all of the regions and many small villages have their own unique specialty.

A slice of history

The word for cheese in French is *fromage*; its etymology is both Latin and Greek. *Forma* in Latin and *formos* in Greek both refer to a cheese mold. Dairy products were molded into shapes, and the origin of the word is still seen in the numerous regional cheese products that bear the name fourme.

Cheese-making goes back some 12,000 years, to the time when livestock farming began. Around 60 CE, Pliny the Elder mentioned what was certainly the forerunner to the eponymous hard cheese of the Cantal when describing the cheeses of the Arvernes and Gabales tribes of Gaul, much appreciated in Rome. Around 800 CE, monks began developing the first Roquefort (blue) cheeses and strong Muenster cheeses.

What exactly is cheese?

Cheese is made by coagulating milk or other dairy products, such as cream, draining it in a mold, and then–in some cases–ripening. In French, these cheeses are known as *affinés*, and the professional whose task it is to bring cheese to maturity is known as an *affineur*. France counts a number of master specialists: *maîtres affineurs*.

Cheeses are categorized according to several criteria, one of which is their fat content:
· "Triple creams" contain at least 75 percent fat
· "Double creams" contain between 60 and 75 percent fat;
· "Fatty cheese" contains from 50 to 60 percent fat;
· "Light cheese," to which no sugar has been added, contains from 20 to 30 percent fat;
· "Low fat cheese" contains less than 20 percent fat.

Farmhouse cheeses (*fromages fermiers*) must be made only from the milk produced at their farm of origin. The label "*au lait cru*," made with unpasteurized milk, is used for cheeses made from milk that has not been heated to above 104°F (40°C).

The eight types of cheese

Fresh cheeses

Fresh soft cheeses are made by coagulation with lactic ferments. They are not ripened and have a high water content–between 60 and 80 percent. Salt may be added to them, or they may be enriched with crème fraîche.
Examples: fromage blanc, literally "white cheese," a soft cheese often sold in pots or jars that may be eaten as a dessert with sugar and fruit; brousse, made of ewe's milk, and fresh cheese spreads with herbs.

Soft cheeses with downy rind

These cheeses are generally not kneaded, and are never cooked. As they ripen, they are covered with a bacteria culture, giving them a more or less velvety appearance.
Examples: Camembert from Normandy, Brie from Meaux, and the rich Chaource made in the area between Champagne and Burgundy.

Soft cheeses with washed rind

These cheeses are washed in salted water that sometimes has colorant added to it. The wax of annatto seeds, for example, imparts an orange color to the rind.
Examples: Muenster (eastern France), Maroilles (northern France), Livarot (Normandy). Interestingly, all these cheeses were first developed in monasteries.

Veined cheeses

The curds are first cut up into small crumbs and then injected with culture before being shaped. As they ripen, blue-gray veins develop within the cavities, imparting a strong flavor to the cheese that can even be slightly piquant.
Examples: Roquefort, Vercors-Sassenage blue, Gex blue.

Pressed cheeses

These cheeses are ripened over a lengthy period. When the curds are cut, they are drained and then pressed. Finally, they are ripened. The texture of such cheeses is firm but not hard; in fact, they are also known as semi-hard cheeses.
Examples: Cantal, Saint-Nectaire, Reblochon, Tomme de Savoie.

Pressed and cooked cheeses

Such cheeses undergo a similar process to that of pressed cheeses, but the curds are heated for nearly an hour when they are cut and stirred. Maximum water content is drained from the curds by strong pressure to ensure that the cheese keeps well, so the resulting cheese is fairly dry.
Examples: Beaufort, Comté, Gruyère.

Processed cheeses

Such cheeses are made from pressed cheeses (semi-hard) and from pressed and cooked cheeses (hard). Flavors are often added to processed cheeses.
Examples: Cancoillote, walnut cheese, "La vache qui rit" (The Laughing Cow) cheese spread.

Goat milk cheeses

Cheeses made from goat's milk are fresh or soft. They are often rolled in ash and may have a downy rind.
Examples: Sainte-Maure de Touraine, Crottin de Chavignol, Picodon de la Drôme.

Conversion Tables

These conversion tables are meant as a guide and show the approximate equivalents. Exact conversions from metric to imperial measures do not generally give very convenient working quantities, and so the imperial measures in the recipes have often been rounded off into workable units. When making the recipes in this book, use either imperial or metric measurements (rather than a combination of the two) for best results.

Liquid Measures (Volume)		
Cup/tbsp/tsp	Metric	Imperial
2 tbsp	30 ml	1 fl. oz.
4 tbsp	60 ml	2 fl. oz.
Scant ½ cup	100 ml	3 fl. oz.
Generous ½ cup	150 ml	5 fl. oz. (¼ pint)
Scant cup	215 ml	7 fl. oz.
1 cup	240 ml	8 fl. oz. (½ pint)
Generous cup	300 ml	10 fl. oz.
2 cups	475 ml	1 pint
3 cups	700 ml	1 ½ pint
3 ½ cups	830 ml	1 ¾ pint
4 cups	1 l	2 pints

Dry Measures (Weight)	
Metric	Imperial
15 g	½ oz.
20 g	¾ oz.
30 g	1 oz.
45 g	1 ½ oz.
60 g	2 oz.
70 g	2 ½ oz.
85 g	3 oz.
100 g	3 ½ oz.
120 g	4 oz.
130 g	4 ½ oz.
140 g	5 oz.
170 g	6 oz.
200 g	7 oz.
215 g	7 ½ oz.
230 g	8 oz.
255 g	9 oz.
340 g	12 oz.
455 g	1 lb.
680 g	1 lb. 8 oz.
900 g	2 lb.

Measurement Conversion Guide

Fluid (Volume)									
	Teaspoons	Tablespoons	Fluid Ounces	¼ Cups	½ Cups	Cups	Fluid Pints	Milliliters	Liters
1 Teaspoon	1	0.33	0.16	0.083	0.0416	0.0208	0.010416	5	0.005
1 Tablespoon	3	1	0.5	0.25	0.125	0.0625	0.03125	15	0.015
1 Fluid Ounce	6	2	1	0.5	0.25	0.125	0.0625	29.56	0.030
¼ Cup	12	4	2	1	0.5	0.25	0.125	59.125	0.059
½ Cup	24	8	4	2	1	0.5	0.25	118.25	0.118
1 Cup	48	16	8	4	2	1	0.5	236	0.236
1 Fluid Pint	96	32	16	8	4	2	1	473	0.473
1 Milliliter	0.2	0.6	0.3	0.15	0.008	0.004	0.002	1	0.001
1 Liter	203	68	34	17	8.5	4.2	2.113	1000	1

Mass (Weight)				
	Ounces	Pounds	Grams	Kilograms
1 Ounce	1	0.0625	28.35	0.28
1 Pound	16	1	454	0.454
1 Gram	0.035	0.002	1	0.001
1 Kilogram	35.2	2.2	1000	1

Conversions for Common Ingredients

The conversion of volume and weight varies somewhat depending on the ingredient; this table provides weight equivalents for some commonly-used ingredients.

Ingredient	1 tsp	1 tbsp	1 cup	1 stick (butter)
Flour	$^1/_{13}$ oz. (2 g)	$^1/_5$ oz. (6 g)	3 ½ oz. (100g)	
Sugar	$^1/_7$ oz. (4 g)	$^1/_{25}$ oz. (12 g)	7 oz. (195g)	
Brown Sugar	$^1/_7$ oz. (4 g)	½ oz. (13 g)	7 oz. (200g)	
Confectioners' (Icing) sugar	$^1/_{10}$ oz. (3 g)	½ oz. (8 g)	5 oz. (130g)	
Ground almonds	$^1/_{14}$ oz. (2 g)	$^1/_5$ oz. (5 g)	3 oz. (85g)	
Sultanas/Raisins	$^1/_{10}$ oz. (3 g)	½ oz. (9 g)	5 ½ oz. (155g)	
Uncooked rice	$^1/_5$ oz. (4.5 g)	½ oz. (13 g)	7 ½ oz. (215g)	
Baking Powder	$^1/_7$ oz. (4 g)	½ oz. (12 g)		
Salt	$^1/_5$ oz. (5 g)	½ oz. (15 g)		
Oil	$^1/_5$ fl. oz. (5 ml)	½ fl. oz. (15 ml)	8 fl. oz. (240 ml)	
Butter	$^1/_5$ oz. (5g)	½ oz. (15g)	8 oz. (230g)	4 oz. (125g)

Temperature

This table provides approximate temperature conversions between degrees Fahrenheit, degrees Celsius, and Gas marks, to correspond with oven settings.

Temperature °F	240	265	290	310	335	355	380	400	425	450	470
Temperature °C	115	130	140	155	170	180	195	200	220	230	245
Gas Mark	¼	½	1	2	3	4	5	6	7	8	9

Some useful temperatures

Room temperature: Approximately 68°F (20°C)
Optimal temperature for yeast dough to rise: 82°F (28°C)
Custard temperature (for pasteurization): 189°F (87°C)
Syrup (final temperature for Italian meringue): 244°F- 250°F (118°C-121°C)

Mushrooms

Mushrooms belong to the group of organisms known as Fungi. The numerous species have no chlorophyll and produce no flowers. They grow in the fields and in forests, and some are cultivated. With their high water content, they are low in calories. The mushrooms most commonly consumed in France are the button mushroom–which in French is known as a Paris mushroom–porcini (cèpes or *Boletus edulis*), chanterelles, morels, and the prized black truffle.

A word of caution

Only eat mushrooms if you are certain that they are edible. Morels should not be eaten raw. Even if you have some knowledge about mushroom gathering already, double-check with an expert on your harvest if you have the slightest doubt.

Storing mushrooms

Most mushrooms can be kept for a few days in the refrigerator, wrapped in a slightly damp, clean cloth. Mushrooms of various species can be bought all year round; if they are not fresh, they will be available dried, canned, or frozen.

How to use mushrooms

Cook or eat raw (except morels), on their own or as a side dish. Marinate them to serve them in salads, fill their caps, incorporate them in sauces, prepare soups with them.

● Chef's tips

Remove the sandy base and any imperfections. Avoid washing them because they absorb water very easily; it is preferable to brush them with a dry brush.
Most mushrooms are cut using a knife; the exceptions are the oyster mushroom (Pleurotus ostreatus) and the black trumpet, which must be torn or shredded using your hands.
Season mushrooms with salt only after cooking so that they do not render too much water.

● Did you know?

The black truffle that comes from Périgord (Tuber melanosporum), a region in southwest France, is the most prized in France. Truffles are subterranean fungi that grow beneath certain trees, notably the oak. With their distinctive, heady aroma, they are much appreciated by chefs; the flavor of truly fine truffles is so powerful that a little goes a long way. This is fortunate, as they are one of the most expensive foodstuffs in the world, partly because of the labor required to find them, and partly because of their scarcity. Black truffles can be bought fresh (they will keep for five to six days), canned, jarred, whole, puréed, and in the form of juice (jus), and their full aroma enjoyed by sprinkling shavings on scrambled eggs, omelets, mashed potatoes, and risotto.

Fats and Oils

◆ **Melting Point**
■ **Maximum Temperature**
● **Smoke Point**

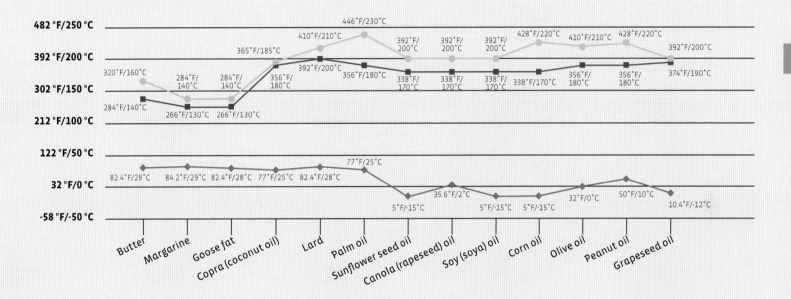

Type	Used for
Butter	Cooking
Margarine	Cooking
Goose fat	Cooking
Copra (coconut oil)	Cooking
Lard	Cooking
Palm oil	Cooking
Sunflower seed oil	Cooking/Seasoning
Canola (rapeseed) oil	Seasoning
Soy (soya) oil	Seasoning
Corn oil	Cooking/Seasoning
Olive oil	Cooking/Seasoning
Peanut oil	Cooking/Seasoning
Grapeseed oil	Cooking/Seasoning

Curry powder

Green pepper

Cayenne pepper

Saffron threads

Star
anise

Green cardamom

Coriander seeds

Cinnamon

Black peppercorns

Dried pink pepper berries

Paprika

White pepper

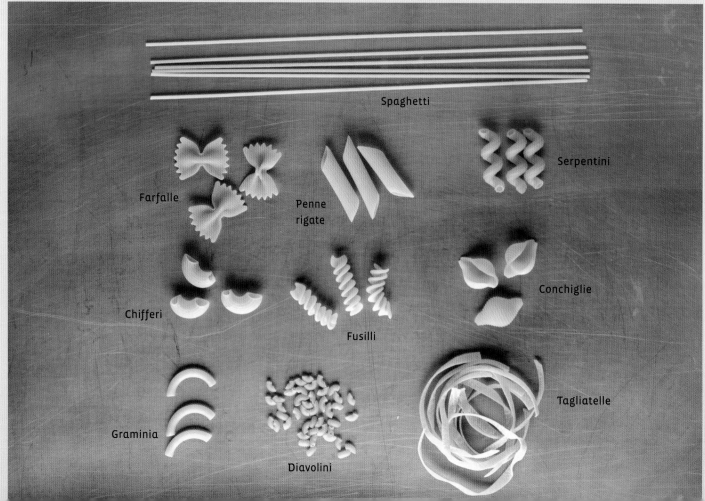

Spaghetti

Serpentini

Farfalle

Penne
rigate

Chifferi

Conchiglie

Fusilli

Graminia

Tagliatelle

Diavolini

Corn

Spelt

Husked oatmeal

Round-grained rice

Whole wheat

Quinoa

Long-grain Basmati rice

Semi-wholewheat long grain rice

Dried red beans

Green Puy lentils

Broad beans

Split peas

Brown lentils

Chickpeas

Lingot beans

Red lentils

Glossary

Bain-marie (or hot water bath)

If you have a double boiler, you can easily melt chocolate and make delicate sauces in it without fear of burning. If not, just place a smaller pan or container over a larger one half filled with hot water (obviously it should not be filled enough to risk bubbling over into your preparation). Depending on the recipe, this water may or may not have to simmer. A bain-marie may also be used to keep food warm. Certain recipes here specify the temperature of the bain-marie if it has to be lower than simmering, so a thermometer may come in handy.

Bake blind

This refers to baking a pastry crust before it is filled, and is required for shells that will be garnished with a filling that will not go into the oven, and for those that require a longer baking time than their filling, which would otherwise be soaked if filled with wet ingredients.
To bake blind, prick the pastry all over with a fork and leave to rest. Then line it with parchment paper or heat-resistant plastic wrap and fill with dried beans or pie weights to keep it from rising. Remove them, with the paper, a few minutes before baking time is up, so that the pastry can turn an even golden color.

Baste

Basting involves using a spoon or pastry brush to cover food with liquid, melted butter, or fat, generally to prevent it from drying out.

Beurre noisette

See Browned butter.

Blanch

This is a term that has two different meanings in cookery:
- placing a food in cold water and then bringing it to a boil. This is done to remove excess salt (salted bacon, for example); some starch (potatoes); soften the outer skin of pulses; and eliminate impurities (in meat, perhaps).
- plunging a vegetable in boiling water for as little as a few seconds or no longer than a few minutes to remove its acridity (spinach) or reduce its volume (lettuce), as well as to prepare vegetables for freezing.

Browned butter *(beurre noisette)*

To brown butter, gently heat it until golden brown. The milk proteins and sugar in the whey will caramelize, thus giving beurre noisette its particular hazelnut aroma.

Brunoise

See Dice (vegetables, fruit, etc.) *and* Fine cubes, p. 62.

Chinois

See Basic Equipment, p. 217.

Clarify/clarification

To clarify butter, melt it slowly, either in a bain-marie or microwave oven, so that most of its water content evaporates. The milk solids will sink to the bottom and the gold-colored liquid will remain at the top. Skim off the foam from the top and then pour the clear butter off to use for your cooking. Without the milk solids, the clarified butter now has a higher smoke point (350°F/180°C), thereby facilitating cooking.
Note that when "clarified butter" is listed as an ingredient, the weight in grams is given after clarification, i.e., with about 20 percent water removed.
To clarify a liquid is to rid it of its impurities. A commonly used method involves the addition of egg whites, which attract particles floating in the liquid. The liquid is simmered, thus bringing the egg white with the impurities to the surface, cooled, and then strained, so that the egg white with the residue remains in the sieve or cheesecloth.
Simple clarification may also be achieved just by straining the liquid through cheesecloth.
To clarify, or separate, an egg means to separate the white from the yolk.

Coat the back of a spoon

See Sauce consistency.

Cream of tartar

Cream of tartar serves three purposes: it is an ingredient in baking powder; it stabilizes beaten egg whites, and prevents sugar from crystallizing.

Deglaze

An instruction to deglaze a pan means dissolving the congealed solids at the bottom of the pan by adding a liquid and then scraping and stirring to combine liquids and solids. This should generally be done over high heat and the liquid brought to a boil. It is then used as part of the sauce of the dish.

Dice (vegetables, fruit, etc.)

Many recipes call for finely diced vegetables, particularly aromatics and garnishes. The sizes required are variable, depending on the purpose or the delicacy of the dish.
A **brunoise** calls for extremely finely diced ingredients: approximately $1/10$ in. (2-3 mm) cubes.
A **salpicon** requires slightly larger dice, approximately $1/5$ in. (5 mm) cubes.
The size of cubes for a **mirepoix** depends on the cooking time, and ranges from $1/5$ to $2/5$ inch (5-10 mm), depending on whether it is for a stock or a sauce.

It is important to dice all ingredients to the same size; they will cook more evenly, and if used as a garnish, uniformly small cubes will make for a more attractive presentation.

Dress (poultry, fish)
This is the preparation of these foods prior to cooking. Poultry must be plucked, gutted, and often trussed. Fish must have fins trimmed and be gutted. It is usually scaled before being washed.

Flambé
This means pouring an alcoholic beverage (often cognac or liqueur) over a food and then setting a flame to it. The process intensifies the flavor of the dish and is often recommended when the juices in a pan are required to make a sauce. It is also a rather spectacular way to serve certain desserts. To flambé, warm brandy or liqueur in a deep dish, pour it over the hot food, and ignite using a long match set to the edge of the pan holding the food. Be careful, of course, not to lean over the dish. Allow to cook until all the flames have burned out.

Fold in (egg whites and cream)
Many recipes call for stiffly beaten egg whites or cream. Beating such ingredients means that they have incorporated a great deal of air, and this is what will help a cake or soufflé rise, and give it a light, airy texture. To incorporate whisked ingredients into the batter, chocolate, etc., proceed carefully so that you do not deflate all those minute bubbles you or your electric beater have worked so hard to create. Use a flexible rubber spatula to mix in the whisked ingredient, turning the bowl as you work, and take care not to apply pressure to the sides of the bowl.
Beaten egg whites are always incorporated into the heavier mixture, usually in several stages.
The same is true for whipped cream, but cream may only be folded into other cold ingredients. Note that cream whips up best when well chilled; if you can, place the bowl in the refrigerator prior to whipping so that it, too, is cold. Stop folding in as soon as the color of the batter or other mixture is even throughout.
By extension, delicate "folding in" is required for fragile ingredients that must be combined with a sturdier mixture.

Fumet
A clear stock used to cook fish. *See* Fumet, p. 139.

Glaze
A glaze is the highly concentrated reduction with a syrupy consistency that results from boiling down a fish, meat, or poultry stock. Glazing literally means giving a shine to a food. There are many ways to glaze different types of food. Vegetables: these may be turned (*see* p. 65) and then cooked with a little sugar and butter. When the cooking liquid has evaporated, the vegetables are coated in the sugar and butter. You may leave them with a clear glaze or cook them further, leaving them with a light or dark coating.

Meat: when cooked meat has sauce poured over it, it is left under the broiler until a shiny film forms. Cold fish and terrines may be glazed with aspic, which is not only decorative but also provides a protective casing.
Pastries and cakes: covering the top (and in some cases, the sides) of a tart with a fondant icing, water icing, chocolate, sugar syrup, fruit glaze, etc. Some pastries (for example, the Kings' cake (galette des rois), p. 445) may also be glazed by dusting them with confectioners' sugar or basting with sugar syrup as soon as you remove them from the oven, and then returning them very briefly to the oven.

Jus
In addition to the meaning of "juice," this term refers to a gravy prepared with the pan juices, usually of a meat dish, diluted with stock or water and then boiled until all the flavors have melded into the stock. Truffle *jus*, available in cans, will add a striking note to your dishes.

Knead
Kneading dough by hand involves flattening down the ingredients using your palm and pushing it away from you. The procedure smooths the dough (if no fat has been incorporated), and blends the ingredients smoothly to give it the right texture.

Mirepoix
See Dice (vegetables, fruit, etc.).

Offal
The edible internal parts of an animal, as well as some external parts and extremities, are known as offal (variety meats). These include the liver, kidneys, sweetbreads, and brain. The edible internal parts of poultry are known as giblets.

Pans (cake or loaf), preparation for baking
To ensure that cakes do not stick to the pan, brush them with a little melted butter, making sure the pan is thoroughly coated. Allow the butter to harden (if you are in a hurry, place it in the refrigerator for a few moments) and then sprinkle a little flour into the pan. Shake it round so that it adheres to the entire surface of the cooled butter, turn the pan upside down, and give it a rap to remove any excess. You should have no more than a fine film of flour when this is done.
To prepare molds for recipes such as charlottes, the recipe may call for the pan to be lined with sponge, ladyfingers, and so on. Pack your lining ingredients as tightly as possible, unless otherwise specified, so that you have an even, attractive external surface for your finished result.

Reduce/reductions
Reducing liquids is an all-important stage in sauce preparation and involves boiling down a liquid to concentrate its taste. It is

best to season with salt when the reduction is ready to serve to avoid the risk of a too-high salt concentration. If reducing a sauce that has shallots in it, such as a beurre blanc, do be careful not to reduce so much that all the liquid evaporates.

Refresh (cooked food)
To refresh, or cool food down rapidly, prepare a large bowl with cold water and ice cubes, and place your sauce, purée, etc in a smaller bowl over this.
To stop the cooking process of vegetables and pasta, cool down briefly under running water. This will prevent them from softening further and, in the case of vegetables, help maintain their color.

Ribbon stage
When you beat egg yolks and sugar together, the final result will be a pale yellow color and will have reached what is known as the ribbon stage. This means that it is sufficiently thick that when a little of the mixture is lifted with the whisk or beater, it slowly flows back down into the bowl in a ribbon shape.

Salpicon
See Dice (vegetables, fruit, etc.).

Sauce consistency (coating the back of a spoon)
This traditional test for the desired thickness of a sauce works if one is using a wooden spoon. The spoon is dipped into the mixture so that it is thoroughly coated in the sauce. When you draw a line with your finger across the back of it, the sauce stays in place, instead of filling the gap. However, in the modern kitchen it is far more reliable and hygienic
to test the temperature of the sauce using a thermometer.
A custard, for example, should reach a temperature of 185°F (85°C).

Sear (Seal)
To sear meat, poultry, or fish means to begin the cooking process at high temperature in fat without necessarily browning it. This method is required for dishes in sauces that are not browned.

Softened butter
This is butter brought to a temperature of close to 86°F (30°C), when it takes on a creamy consistency that makes it easier to incorporate with other ingredients and/or mold it.

Sous vide
The sous vide or "vacuum packing" technique involves, as its English name implies, preparing food in sealed, vacuum-packed plastic. The method allows the cook complete control of time and temperature. Its benefits include meat remaining tender and moist, and fish not overcooking. *See* Grilling, p. 102.

Sweat (vegetables, fruit, etc.)
When it is important for vegetables, aromatic ingredients, or fruit not to change color, they must be cooked briefly, often until just translucent (for onions and shallots) and slightly softened. They will exude their own liquid in the process.

Truss
To truss poultry is to tie it up with trussing twine so that the wings and thighs stay in place. If the technique is well mastered, the twine is hardly visible. Trussing facilitates roasting and carving. The twine is removed when the bird is ready to serve.

Typical French products and aromatics

Bouquet garni
A French bouquet garni traditionally comprises the following aromatic plants: a bay leaf, a sprig of thyme (preferably fresh), two sprigs of parsley (preferably the more flavorful flat-leaf variety), one green leek leaf (about 5 in./12-15 cm), and optionally, a celery stalk of the same length as the leek leaf. These are all tied together so that they are easily removed just before serving, or whenever called for by your recipe. A bouquet garni of this size will flavor a dish of 4-6 servings.
This form of the bouquet garni goes back to the mid-seventeenth century, a time when culinary enthusiasm for exotic spices was waning, and was invented by the Breton Pierre de Lune, a disciple of La Varenne.

Caul
Caul or caul fat is the fat-laced membrane surrounding the stomach of animals. Pig's caul is frequently used to secure ingredients that would otherwise come apart during cooking, such as pâtés, stuffed cabbage leaves, and some sausage meats.

Fines herbes
This combination of aromatic herbs that includes parsley, chives, tarragon, and chervil is used to flavor sauces, omelets, cream cheeses, and other dishes. The mixture should be added just prior to serving as it loses its flavor rapidly.

Five-pepper mix
This attractive blend contains black, green, gray, and white peppercorns, and Jamaican pepper, also known as allspice.

Four-spice mix
This classic French blend contains ground black pepper, nutmeg, ginger, and cloves, and is frequently used in meat and poultry dishes.

Ground almonds

Sweet almonds are a staple in French pastry-making. Whether whole, sliced, chopped, or ground, they tend to be used blanched. To make your own almond meal, place blanched almonds (skins removed) in a food processor or blender and process until thoroughly ground. Fine grinding is essential for a delicate recipe such as macaroons (*see* p. 442). Almond paste, not to be confused with marzipan, is made with ground almonds and sugar in proportions that depend on their usage.

Hard cider

Cidre in France is the bubbly drink produced from fermented apple juice, principally in the regions of Brittany and Normandy, where it features in local cuisine. Like champagne, it is available both "sweet," with a minimum alcoholic content of 3 percent, and "dry," with a minimum of 5–5.5 percent alcohol. Regulations concerning cider production date back to Emperor Charlemagne's time.

Herbes de Provence

An assortment of dried herbs native to the region of Provence, this blend includes rosemary, thyme, fennel seeds, marjoram, and savory.

Mustards

A condiment firmly entrenched in French cooking traditions, it is made from the seeds of a herbaceous plant and sold in the form of a paste. Dijon mustard contains verjuice, wine must, or white wine, and powdered brown or black mustard seeds. *Moutarde à l'ancienne*, mustard in the old style that generally comes from Meaux, contains roughly crushed seeds. French mustards tend to be very tangy; they are a component of many sauces and dressings, and are used to coat poultry and meat for cooking.

Piment d'Espelette

The only native French chili pepper is grown exclusively in the village of Espelette and nine other villages in the Basque region in southwest France. Its relatively low grade on the Scoville chili heat scale means it adds piquancy rather than fire. It is sold ground or in paste form. *See* AOC p. 230.

A few words on technique

Precision

French chefs, pastry chefs in particular, work with scientific precision, carefully weighing each ingredient to achieve their spectacular results. Scales are also a basic tool in many French home kitchens. The quantities here have been converted to cups and spoons, with sticks for solid butter, and although every effort has been made to achieve as much accuracy as possible, this inevitably results in a little rounding up or down, sometimes to avoid awkward amounts. For the more straightforward recipes,

small differences will not significantly change the end result. However, it is preferable, if possible, to weigh your ingredients (*see* Basic Equipment, p. 217) and check cooking and baking temperatures with a thermometer. Do not mix imperial measurements and metric in the same recipe.

From stove top to oven

Cooking over gas is practical as it provides high heat very rapidly; however, it is difficult to control with precision, and cooks only from below. This is why it is sometimes advisable to continue cooking the contents of a pot or pan in the oven; the temperature there can be more finely controlled and the heat is more evenly distributed

Using gelatin sheets

Gelatin in transparent sheets (or leaves) weighing precisely 2 grams is the form used in France, and we have opted to maintain this for the recipes given in this book. Gelatin sheets are available for purchase online or at specialty stores.

To use, soak them in a bowl of very cold water (unless otherwise specified), completely covered, until they are softened and very pliable, about 10 to 15 minutes. When they are ready for use, remove them from the water and squeeze out all the liquid with your hands. The texture will be rubbery but they will not break. Dissolve them in the quantity of warm liquid specified by your recipe, ensuring that there are no visible traces left. Follow the directions of the recipe for setting times. Gelatin is animal-derived; should you decide to use a plant-based setting agent (agar-agar is made from seaweed), carefully follow the directions for jelling quantities and times.

Cooking with chocolate

Chocolate comes in many forms. Couverture chocolate has long been used by professionals but is increasingly available to the general public; its high cocoa butter content (between 35 percent and 50 percent), not to be confused with its cocoa liquor content, makes it eminently suitable for baking and desserts as it melts smoothly. Couverture chocolate is available as bittersweet, semisweet (both with varying percentages of cocoa liquor), milk, and white chocolate.

Unsweetened or baking chocolate consists of 100 percent chocolate liquor.

In France, the percentage of chocolate liquor is stipulated on the label, hence chefs' requirements on their recipes depending on just how chocolaty they wish the result to be.

Cocoa powder is made by extracting most of the cocoa butter from the pure chocolate liquor.

Chocolate scorches easily, and scorching ruins its taste. This is why it is important to melt it gradually, preferably over a hot water bath. When it is combined with another ingredient, it should still be warm. If the other ingredient is also heated, check that both are at a similar temperature.

Recipes

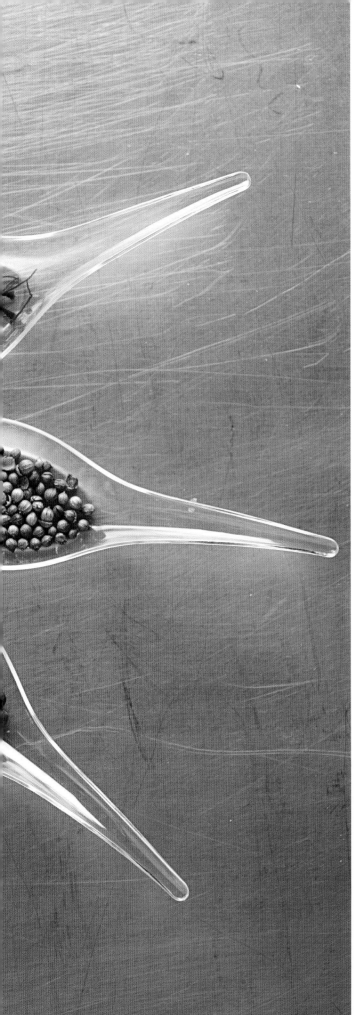

Some words of advice

Read the recipe from start to finish before you begin cooking. This will ensure that:

• you understand all the culinary terms (those marked with an asterisk are explained in the glossary);
• you have all the necessary equipment and can preheat if required;
• you can ask your butcher or fish seller to make certain preliminary preparations;
• if there are several stages or components to the recipe, or there are lengthy cooking procedures, you can clarify order of approach and timings. Gauge what you can make ahead and what will need to be done at the last minute for an optimal result.
Equally important:
• Make sure you have a well-stocked pantry with a wide range of basic groceries, such as oils, condiments, and various types of flour. If at the last minute you realize that something is missing, you'll have a substitute.
• Select your recipes according to the seasons. Using products that are in season is a guarantee of a better tasting result.

● **Cleanliness and food safety**
• Hands and cooking utensils must be spotlessly clean.
• Store raw and cooked food carefully. Practically all cooked foods must be covered in plastic wrap so that their smells do not permeate the refrigerator.
• Do check the best-before/expiration dates on food packaging.

● **A note on using these recipes**
• Unless otherwise specified, the oils given in the lists of ingredients are neutral. Use canola, sunflower seed, grapeseed, or peanut oil interchangeably; their fluidity and cooking temperatures are practically identical.
• Eggs in the recipes refer to hens' eggs with an average weight of 2 oz. (55–57 g), "large" in the USA and Canada, "medium" in the UK.
• Each oven has its own quirks, and this is why certain recipes indicate a range of temperatures. You will need to decide, based on past experience, whether your oven should be set at the lower or higher temperature given in the recipes.

● **And always remember:**
• A recipe involves subtle alchemy and calls for a handful of technique, a generous pinch of creativity, a goodly hint of practicality, and the merest *soupçon* of daring imagination.

Appetizers

Anne-Sophie Pic
presents her recipe

For this book, I have selected an appetizer using as its main ingredients a vintage Gouda from Holland called Reypenaer VSOP, and black truffles. It comprises a hot soufflé with a melting truffled core and shredded vegetables with black truffle. I chose the soufflé because it is a classic of French cuisine and involves an interesting technique. My aim was to update it by varying its textures: the molten center is spiced up with a very creamy Gouda. I simply love to combine truffles and cheese. Since I work in France's major truffle-producing area, truffles are essential to my cuisine and a source of endless inspiration.

Appetizers always reflect the seasons. In winter, I like to create tasty, creamy appetizers, and in summer, they are fresher, with more piquancy. It is the appetizer that sets the tone and tempo of the meal, so it requires both lightness and precision, though it also allows a great freedom of expression. I can add original notes and pay attention to the appearance; I always find the visual side of my work fascinating.

Reypenaer VSOP vintage Gouda and black truffle soufflé, with a truffled molten center

Soufflé mixture

Prepare a béchamel sauce using the flour, salted butter, and milk. When it begins to boil, remove from the heat. Transfer to a mixing bowl and allow to cool to 150°F (65°C). Season the egg yolks with the cumin and nutmeg and incorporate into the béchamel.

To prepare the molds and inserts

Chill the molds. Using a pastry brush, grease them with some clarified butter. Be careful to make regular strokes from bottom to top as this facilitates the rising of the soufflés. Return to the refrigerator. When the butter has set, repeat the operation. After you have buttered them a third time, coat them with the fine breadcrumbs. Turn the molds upside down and rap them to remove any excess.

Chill the inserts just as you have done for the molds. Grease them on the outside with clarified butter from top to bottom, taking care not to leave any fingerprints on the butter. Wrap the inserts in parchment paper, which will stick to the butter. The paper should be hardly higher than the insert and should adhere well, without any creases. Then butter the parchment paper, working from top to bottom in the direction the soufflés will rise.

Creamed Gouda

Heat the milk and Gouda together. Blend and strain through a fine-mesh sieve. Chill until needed.

Gouda foam

Prepare a sabayon (see basic techniques p. 50) with the 2 oz. (55 g) egg yolks and truffle juice. Gradually add the scant 1/2 cup (100 g) melted butter, and then 1 1/2 oz. (40 g) strained, creamed Gouda. Adjust the seasoning. Pour into a siphon and keep in an oven preheated to 130°F (56°C).

To bake the soufflés

Pour the soufflé mixture into a round-bottomed mixing bowl. Add the grated Gouda and combine. Do not overmix.

Remove the four molds and inserts from the refrigerator. Place the inserts in the center of each mold, being careful not to touch them directly, and ensure that the buttered parchment paper is placed with the butter strokes upward (so that the soufflé will rise). Preheat the oven to 400°F (200°C).

In another mixing bowl, beat the egg whites until they form very soft peaks. Add the 1/2 teaspoon (2.5 ml) cream of tartar and continue whisking. When they are firm, add the potato starch. Fold* the beaten egg whites into the remaining creamed Gouda mixture, turning the bowl as you fold in carefully so as not to break the air bubbles.

When the mixture is thoroughly combined, spoon it into a piping bag. Fill the molds almost to the top. Make sure there is no direct contact between your fingers and the containers. Bake for 11 minutes.

Assembly and presentation

Remove the soufflés from the oven and immediately and very carefully take out the inserts. Fill the cavity to the top with the gouda foam from the siphon. Carefully garnish with truffle slices and serve immediately.

Serves 4

Preparation time: 45 minutes
Cooking time: 11 minutes

Ingredients

Soufflé mixture
1 3/4 oz. (9 tablespoons or 50 g) cake flour
1 3/4 oz. (3 1/2 tablespoons or 50 g) salted butter
2 cups (500 ml) milk
5 eggs, separated, plus 3 egg whites
1 pinch cumin
1 pinch grated nutmeg
3 1/2 oz. (100 g) grated Gouda cheese
1/2 teaspoon (2.5 ml) cream of tartar*
1 teaspoon (5 ml) potato starch

Creamed Gouda
2 1/2 tablespoons (40 ml) milk
2 oz. (60 g) Gouda, finely diced*

Gouda foam
2 oz. (55 g) egg yolks
2 tablespoons (30 ml) truffle juice
scant 1/2 cup (100 g) melted butter
2 tablespoons (30 g) clarified butter*, for greasing molds
3/4 oz. (2 1/2 tablespoons or 20 g) extremely finely ground breadcrumbs (packaged breadcrumbs possible)

1/7 oz. (4 g) black truffles, for garnish
Sea salt
Special equipment: a siphon, 4 inserts, 4 small soufflé molds

Scandinavian canapés ★

Ingredients

²/₃ cup (160 ml) thick cream
8 slices smoked salmon
A little grated nutmeg
A little five-pepper mix*
Juice of 1 lemon
1 tablespoon (15 ml) salmon roe; ¹/₂ red onion,
sliced in fine rings; ¹/₄ bunch dill; for garnish
Fleur de sel, freshly ground pepper
Optional: a few sprigs of chives

Blinis

1 ¹/₄ cups (125 g) all-purpose flour
2 eggs, separated
1 cup (250 ml) milk
6 tablespoons butter, clarified*, or ¹/₃ cup (80 g)
clarified butter
1 pinch fine salt

Serves 8

Preparation time: 40 minutes
Cooking time: 10 minutes

To prepare the blinis, sift the flour with the salt and make a well. Pour the egg yolks in and dilute with the milk, whisking constantly.
Beat the egg whites until they form stiff peaks and fold* them gently into the mixture.
Grease a small crêpe pan or crêpe maker with the clarified butter and pour out the batter to a thickness of about ¹/₅ in. (4-5 mm). Turn them over when they begin to color.
Beat the thick cream with a whisk or electric beater until it forms peaks. Season with salt and pepper.
Cut out the salmon slices to the same size as the blinis (use a cookie cutter or glass) and place a piece of salmon on each blini. Season with lemon juice and freshly ground pepper.
Top with some whipped cream and garnish with the salmon roe, a thin slice of onion, and a sprig of dill.
If you wish, tie each canapé with chives to make an easy-to-eat little "parcel."

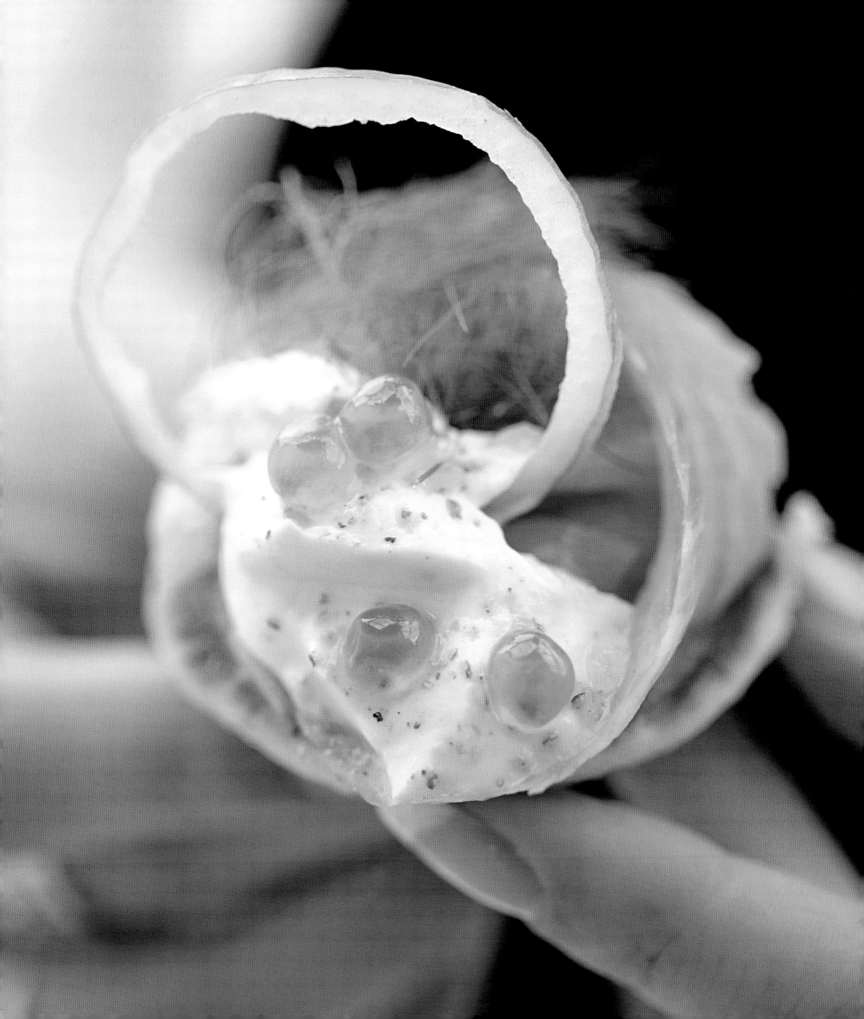

Ingredients

1 lb. (480 g) tuna fillet
1 small pinch *piment d'Espelette**
Juice of 1 lemon
2 heaped tablespoons (40 g) tomato paste
1 ½ oz. (40 g) fresh horseradish,
for garnish
A few sprigs of chervil, for garnish
Table salt

Tuna rillettes with horseradish ★

Serves 6
Preparation time: 30 minutes

Trim the tuna and remove the bones.
Process the tuna with the seasonings and lemon juice in the bowl of a
food processor using the blade attachment. Add a dash of tomato paste to
heighten the color.
Arrange the tuna rillettes on canapés or in cocktail spoons, garnished with a
few shreds of horseradish and a chervil leaf.

● Chef's notes
*Lemon juice or vinegar is essential because the acidity slows down the
development of germs.
Other oily fish like salmon, sardines, and mackerel work well with the rillette
recipe.*

● Did you know?
*Rillettes were traditionally made with pork or goose. Contemporary cuisine
takes tried and tested preparations and transforms them with quite different
ingredients.*

Beef carpaccio, Parmesan, and *pistou* ★

Serves 4
Preparation time: 30 minutes
Chilling time: 30 minutes

Prepare the *pistou*. Crush the garlic cloves with the basil leaves using
a pestle and mortar.
Drizzle the olive oil in as you crush and then thin with the lemon juice.

Trim the fillet of beef and remove all sinews. Cut into very thin slices and
arrange them attractively on a serving platter, as regularly as possible.
Use a pastry brush to dab the beef here and there with the *pistou*.
Chill for 30 minutes.

Scatter with the Parmesan shavings and fleur de sel. Give a few turns of the
pepper mill.
Garnish with basil leaves.
Allow between 30 minutes and two hours for the flavor of the *pistou* to meld
into the meat. Basil loses some of its taste and smell after two hours and
becomes slightly bitter.

Technique
Pesto and *pistou* >> p. 144

Ingredients
10 oz. (300 g) beef fillet
$^1/_2$ cup (2 oz./35 g) Parmesan cheese,
in shavings
A few leaves of basil, for garnish
4 pinches fleur de sel
Freshly ground pepper

Pistou
4 garlic cloves, peeled, shoots removed
$^1/_2$ bunch basil
3 $^1/_2$ tablespoons (50 ml) olive oil
Juice of 1 lemon

Ingredients

2 lb. (1 kg) mussels
2 shallots
A few sprigs flat-leaf parsley
6 tablespoons (90 g) unsalted butter
Scant $^1/_2$ cup (100 ml) dry white wine
$^1/_3$ cup (80 ml) thick cream
2 teaspoons (10 g) curry powder
Freshly ground pepper

Mussel mouclade ★

Serves 4
Preparation time: 30 minutes
Cooking time: 30 minutes

Scrape off the dirt from the mussels and remove the beards. Finely slice the shallots and chop the parsley. Sweat* the shallots in 3 $^1/_2$ tablespoons (50 g) butter and then pour in the white wine.
Add the mussels and half the chopped parsley.
Cover and cook over high heat, stirring regularly.
Check that all the mussels are open, discarding any that aren't, and transfer them to a dish with a slotted spoon.
Filter the cooking liquid to remove any traces of sand.
Reduce* it by half. Add the thick cream and reduce further, until it is thick enough to coat the back of a spoon*. Whisk in the remaining butter.
Sprinkle half the curry powder into the sauce and leave it to infuse. Season with pepper.
Serve the mussels on the half shell (remove one half of each shell) and arrange them all in a serving dish or in soup plates.
Sprinkle the remaining the parsley over the dishes, and pour over the hot sauce. Sprinkle with the remaining curry powder.

● **Chef's note**
Use the finest mussels you can find for this tasty regional dish.
Allow about $^1/_2$ lb. (250 g) of mussels per person for an appetizer.

● **Did you know?**
The mouclade is a specialty of the Poitou-Charentes region, but other coastal regions have their own variations.

 Techniques
Marinière » p. 104

Hot oyster gratin ★ ★

Serves 6
Preparation time: 45 minutes
Cooking time: 25 minutes

Open the oysters (see p. 72) and remove them from their shells, keeping their water.
Over high heat, bring them to a simmer in their water. Allow to simmer for no longer than 2–3 seconds. Remove immediately and leave to cool, preferably in a bowl on a stainless steel surface.
Carefully clean the hollow shells and poach them in boiling water to sterilize them.
Prepare the vegetable julienne. Peel and wash the carrots and the celery root (celeriac). Slit the leek whites in two and wash.
Cut the three vegetables into fine julienne strips (see p. 59).
Braise each one, separately if possible, in 4 tablespoons (60 g) butter with 4 1/2 tablespoons (50 ml) water. This will preserve the taste of each one.
Season with salt and pepper.

To make the sauce, set the oven to "broil." Place the egg yolks and the sparkling wine in a high-sided pan and whisk before placing on low heat or over a bain-marie*. Continue whisking over the low heat until the mixture becomes foamy (a sabayon or *zabaglione* texture).
Remove from the heat and whisk in the remaining 1 stick (4 1/2 oz./120 g) cubed butter. Season with salt and cayenne pepper.
Stir the fish velouté into the sabayon mixture.

Cover heat-resistant plates with a layer of kosher salt. Place 3 oyster shells on each plate.
Arrange the julienned vegetables in the shells, and then place 2 oysters in each one.
Drizzle the sauce over and place under the broiler for a few minutes.
Serve immediately.

● Chef's notes
Use medium-sized oysters for this recipe if you can.
The velouté in this recipe gives creaminess and stability to the sabayon when it is broiled.

Techniques
Opening oysters and shellfish ›› p. 72
Julienne strips ›› p. 59
Sabayon (*zabaglione*) ›› p. 50

Ingredients
3 dozen medium-sized hollow oysters
Equal quantities of the following vegetables
1 large carrot (5 oz./150 g)
1 large slice celeriac or celery root (5 oz./150 g)
1 leek, white only (5 oz./150 g)
4 tablespoons (60 g) unsalted butter for the vegetables
1 stick (120 g) unsalted butter, cubed, for the sauce
4 egg yolks
Scant 1/4 cup (50 ml) dry white sparkling wine
3/4 cup (200 ml) fish velouté (see p. 150)
Cayenne pepper
1/2 lb. (250 g) kosher salt, for garnish
Fine sea salt, freshly ground pepper

Ingredients

1 $^1/_2$ cups (5 oz./150 g) button mushrooms

2 tablespoons (30 g) plus 4 tablespoons (60 g)
clarified butter*

15 eggs

$^1/_2$ bunch chives, snipped, for garnish

Fine sea salt, freshly ground pepper

Rolled mushroom omelet

Serves 6

Preparation time: 30 minutes

Cooking time: 10 minutes

Wipe the mushrooms with a damp cloth, or brush with a dry brush (see p. 232), and cut them into quarters.

Melt 2 tablespoons (30 g) butter over high heat and, when it is sizzling, sauté the mushrooms. Season with salt and pepper.

Break the eggs into a mixing bowl. Season and beat, using a whisk or a fork. Grease a nonstick pan with most of the remaining butter (set aside a little to clarify and brush over the omelet) and heat it. When it is hot, pour the eggs in and cook over high heat, constantly folding over the coagulated edges towards the center as the omelet cooks. It must be creamy and the omelet must not brown. Add some of the quartered button mushrooms.

Tilt the pan downward holding the handle upward. Roll the omelet over itself, from top to bottom, with a fork.

Give it a nice gloss with a little clarified butter.

Arrange the remaining mushrooms on the serving dish and scatter with snipped chives.

● Chef's notes

Contrary to popular belief, a good omelet is barely browned or golden. A pale color is a guarantee that the texture will be just right.

Use a mixture of fresh, frozen, and canned mushrooms if you wish.

Techniques

Quartering button mushrooms ›› p. 58

Omelet (rolled) ›› p. 46

Rabbit terrine with pistachios and exotic fruit chutney ★★

Serves 6

Preparation time: 1 hour 30 minutes
Cooking time: 30 minutes

Best made a day ahead, or a minimum of 12 hours.

Preheat the oven to 275°F (140°C).
Trim the rabbit by removing the transparent membrane and all sinews.
Take about 2 oz. (50 g) each of rabbit and pork meat, and cut it into cubes or strips.
Grind the remaining meat and season it with the salt and pepper.
Combine the chopped meats, whole pistachio nuts, cognac, egg, and flour.
Wrap the mixture in caul and fill the terrine mold. Press down often to remove any air pockets. Arrange the 3 bay leaves on top.
Cook for 30-40 minutes with the thermometer inserted into the center until the core temperature reaches 160°F (68-70°C).
As soon as you remove the terrine from the oven, pour the aspic over it to prevent it from drying out. It will soften the texture and give it an attractive shine. Allow to chill for a minimum of 10 hours before serving.
Prepare the chutney.
Dice* the pineapple and mango into very small (1/5 in. or 5 mm) cubes.
Prepare a light caramel with the orange juice and sugar (see pp. 168-69).
Add the diced fruit as soon as the caramel reaches the desired color to stop the cooking.
Leave to stew for a few minutes and then cool.
Cut the terrine into slices of about 3 oz. (70-90 g) each.
Serve with the chutney, a green salad, and sliced country bread.

● Chef's notes

This recipe works very well with almost all white meats.
Rabbit meat is lean and the terrine would be dry without the fattier pork cut.
As a general rule, allow 1 heaped teaspoon of salt and six turns of the pepper mill per pound (15 g of salt and 2 g of pepper per kilo) of meat used to prepare a terrine.
The terrine will keep—well wrapped in plastic or in an airtight container, and chilled—for up to 4 days.

● Did you know?

Traditionally, charcuterie (from the French chair cuite, cooked meat), comprised only pork products, with sausages, cured meats, and pâtés and terrines, but the range has widened to include other meats. A plate of charcuterie products is a typical light dish served at cafés and restaurants throughout France.

Techniques
Mincing meat >> p. 83
Preparing terrines >> p. 90
Caramel >> p. 169

Ingredients

14 oz. (400 g) rabbit meat
5 oz. (150 g) fatty pork cut, such as blade shoulder (US) or spare rib (UK)
1 oz. (25 g) whole pistachios
1 1/3 tablespoons (20 ml) cognac
1 egg
1/3 cup (1 oz./30 g) flour
2 oz. (60 g) caul fat*
3 bay leaves
Scant 1/2 cup (100 ml) clear aspic, prepared using a mix
1 heaped teaspoon (7 g) fine sea salt
6 turns of the pepper mill (1 g)

Chutney
1/4 pineapple
1/2 mango
1/3 cup (60 g) sugar
Juice of 1 orange
Special equipment: a meat thermometer

Ingredients

¹/₂ lb. (250 g) pike fillets
3 eggs plus 1 egg white
²/₃ cup (150 ml) whipping cream
1 cup (250 ml) water
6 tablespoons (90 g) butter
1 ¹/₂ cups (130 g) flour
A few sprigs flat-leaf parsley, for garnish
Fine sea salt, freshly ground pepper

Crayfish Sauce
1 ¹/₂ tablespoons (25 g) butter
¹/₄ cup (25 g) flour
1 onion
1 shallot
¹/₂ carrot
2 ¹/₂ tablespoons (40 ml) olive oil
¹/₂ lb. (250 g) crayfish
1 tomato (3 ¹/₂ oz./100 g)
2 tablespoons (1 oz./30 g) tomato paste
2 ¹/₂ tablespoons (40 ml) cognac
Scant ¹/₂ cup (100 ml) white wine
2 cups (500 ml) water
Bouquet garni*
Fine sea salt, freshly ground pepper

Pike quenelles and crayfish sauce ★★

Serves 8
Preparation time: 1 hour 15 minutes
Cooking time: 45 minutes

Prepare the finely ground pike forcemeat, which is the base for the quenelles. Process the fish using the blade attachment of a food processor. Add the egg white and mix in.
Strain through a fine-mesh sieve. Transfer to a stainless steel bowl and place over an ice bath. Gradually stir in the cream.
Season with salt and pepper, scraping down the sides. Cover with plastic wrap flush with the forcemeat so no skin forms on the surface. Chill.
Bring the water to boil with the butter. When the mixture comes to the boil, pour in the flour. Lower the heat and stir with a spatula to dry out the moisture. Remove from the heat, and stir in the three eggs, one by one. Incorporate this mixture into the minced pike.

Bring a pot of salted water to the boil.
Use two soup spoons to form oval quenelles and drop them into the boiling water. Leave to boil for 4-5 minutes, then remove and drain.

For the crayfish sauce, prepare a blond roux with the butter and flour (see p. 150).
Allow to cool.
Dice* the onion, shallot, and carrot to make a mirepoix*. Place the olive oil in a pan over high heat and sear* the crayfish. Add the diced vegetables and allow to sweat*.
Chop the shells and the tomato. Add the shells, chopped tomato and tomato paste to the crayfish pan.
Deglaze* with the cognac and add the white wine.
Reduce* by half, then pour in the water.
Add the bouquet garni. Simmer for 30 minutes, skimming the surface from time to time.
Blend the mixture and strain through a chinois*. Be careful when blending the crayfish shells, particularly if using an immersion blender–it is best to crush them with a knife before you blend them to avoid splashes and decrease wear on the blade.
Pour it over the cooled blond roux and bring all the liquid to the boil so that it thickens.
Adjust the seasoning and set aside.

Arrange the quenelles in a serving dish or in soup plates and drizzle with sauce. Scatter chopped parsley over for garnish.

● **Chef's note**
This is a very tasty dish if you get the seasoning right, so do be sure that both quenelles and sauce are properly seasoned.

Techniques
Basic panada stuffing >> p. 158
Blond (straw-colored) roux >> p. 150

Terrine of foie gras ★★

Serves 6

Preparation time: 1 hour
Chilling time: 12 hours
Marinating time: 2 hours
Cooking time: 15-25 minutes

This should preferably be made a day ahead of serving.

Remove the veins from the foie gras lobes (see p. 80).
Place them in a deep dish and cover with milk. Cover the dish with plastic wrap and chill for 12 hours. This procedure is advisable as it removes some of the bitterness and makes any traces of blood paler.
Drain well, dabbing the lobes to remove excess moisture.
Combine the salt, sugar, and freshly ground pepper. The right seasoning at this stage is essential, so do pay attention to quantities–too little and your foie gras will be somewhat bland. Sprinkle the seasoning all over the foie gras. Return to a dish and pour in the Armagnac. Cover with plastic wrap and leave to soak for 2 hours, either in the refrigerator or at room temperature.
Preheat the oven to 175°F (85°C).
Place the foie gras in a terrine, pressing down to eliminate pockets of air. Cook for 15-25 minutes, depending on the size and type of your terrine. The core temperature must not exceed 135°F (57°C). Allow to cool for at least 4-5 hours.

To serve:
Slice the brioche sandwich loaf and toast. Keep the toast warm under a clean napkin. Slice the foie gras and sprinkle with crystals of fleur de sel and freshly ground pepper.

● Chef's notes
Duck foie gras is easier to find than goose. It is also smaller, weighing on average 1 lb (500 g), and its taste is slightly more pronounced. When buying, choose foie gras without reddish or greenish spots.

● Did you know?
Foie gras terrine is considered a great delicacy and is traditionally served at meals during the festive season, accompanied by a fine sweet white wine, such as Sauternes.

Technique
Deveining a foie gras >> p. 80

Ingredients
1 lb. (500 g) raw foie gras, whole lobes
2 cups (500 ml) full cream milk
1 slightly heaped teaspoon (6 g) fine sea salt
$^1/_2$ teaspoon (2 g) granulated sugar
At least 6 turns of the pepper mill (1 g)
3 $^1/_3$ tablespoons (50 ml) Armagnac
1 loaf of brioche sandwich loaf
Fleur de sel, freshly ground pepper
Special equipment: a terrine that fits the foie gras snugly and a meat thermometer

Ingredients

2 eggs
2 tablespoons (30 ml) oil
2 ¼ cups (220 g) flour
½ bunch flat-leaf parsley
2 shallots
3 ½ tablespoons (50 g) butter
2 dozen snails (de-shelled)
A few sprigs of chervil for garnish
Fine sea salt, freshly ground pepper

Creamed garlic
5 oz. (150 g) garlic cloves, peeled,
shoots removed
¾ cup (200 ml) milk
¾ cup (200 ml) cream
1 scant tablespoon (10 g) potato starch
Fine sea salt, freshly ground pepper

Snail ravioli and garlic cream ★★

Serves 8
Preparation time: 50 minutes
Resting time: 45 minutes
Cooking time: 15 minutes

Prepare the pasta dough (see p. 15). Beat the eggs with the oil and salt.
Sift the flour and make a well in the center. Pour the egg mixture in and combine, working quickly so that the dough does not become too elastic. Shape it into a ball and chill, covered, for 30-45 minutes.
Roll it out roughly using a rolling pin and then work it through the pasta maker to make a fine sheet.
Cut out twenty-four disks with a cookie cutter.
Chop the flat-leaf parsley and finely slice the shallots.
Heat the butter until it turns hazelnut brown (*beurre noisette**).
Sauté the snails in the butter, and then add the parsley and shallots.
Season with salt and pepper.
Place a snail on each dough circle.
Fold over to form a half-circle, pinching around the edges to seal the dough.
Bring some salted water to the boil.
Place the ravioli in the boiling water for 3 minutes.
Drain carefully and serve immediately.
If you prepare the ravioli ahead of time, keep them well chilled and reheat briefly in the creamed garlic.

Prepare the creamed garlic.
Blanch* the garlic cloves in cold milk, bringing it all to the boil. Discard the milk and repeat the procedure once more.
Combine the cream, the potato starch, and the seasoning, and heat. Add the garlic and reduce*, stirring constantly until the garlic cloves are soft.
Blend in a food processor.
Serve in soup plates, miniature pots, or ramekins, and garnish with a few sprigs of chervil.

● Chef's note

Add an extra touch by flavoring or coloring (or both) your pasta dough. Try spices, vegetable colorants, or cuttlefish ink.

 Technique
Pasta dough ›› p. 15

Rockfish soup ★★

Serves 8

Preparation time: 55 minutes
Cooking time: 50 minutes

Prepare and trim the fish and rinse them under cold water. You may leave them in the sink with the tap running until the water is perfectly clear while you prepare your vegetables.
Cut the fish into chunks.
Dice* the aromatic vegetables (onions, carrots, leeks, tomatoes, celery, and fennel) finely to make a mirepoix*. Sweat* them in olive oil or butter.
Add the chunks of fish. Pour in 8 cups (2 liters) of water and the white wine.
Add the bouquet garni, garlic, tomato paste, and saffron and bring to the boil.
Boil over high heat for 30-40 minutes, skimming when necessary.
Remove the bouquet garni. Blend the soup with an immersion blender or in a food processor and then process it through a food mill. (This will take care of any fish bones, while leaving the soup relatively thick.) Adjust the seasoning.

Prepare the accompanying garnishes: slices of bread or croutons dabbed with olive oil, toasted and rubbed with a garlic clove (shoot removed); grated cheese, and rouille sauce.
Serve in a soup tureen or individual bowls.

● Chef's notes

Professionals fillet the fish instead of slicing it. If you opt for this technique, prepare a fumet* to cook the fish. This method will take longer, but there will be no solid residue from the fish bones.
If you add the fish fillets to the soup, it makes an excellent main course.

● Did you know?

From north to south, France offers many different types of fish soup.

Techniques

Rouille sauce ›› p. 145
Cutting chunks ›› p. 69

Ingredients

4 lb. (2 kg) fish such as red gurnard, scorpion fish, weever fish, and conger or sea eel
1 large or 2 medium onions (7 oz./200 g)
1 large carrot (7 oz./200 g)
1 leek (5 oz./150 g), white only
4 tomatoes (10 oz./300 g)
½ celery stalk (3 ½ oz./100 g)
½ fennel bulb. (3 ½ oz./100 g)
Scant ½ cup (100 ml) olive oil or butter
1 ¼ cups (300 ml) dry white wine
1 bouquet garni*
2 oz. (60 g) garlic cloves
3 tablespoons (50 g) tomato paste
8 threads saffron
½ French baguette
5 oz. (150 g) grated Gruyère cheese
7 oz. (200 g) rouille sauce (see recipe p. 145)
Fine sea salt, freshly ground pepper

Ingredients

Shortcrust pastry

2 ½ cups (250 g) all-purpose flour
1 egg yolk
1 stick (125 g) butter
Fine sea salt

¾ cup (200 ml) milk
¾ cup (200 ml) cream
2 eggs plus 1 egg yolk
A little grated nutmeg
7 oz. (200 g) bacon
4 oz. (120 g) grated Gruyère cheese
or similar
Fine sea salt, freshly ground pepper

Quiche Lorraine ★

Serves 8
Preparation time: 40 minutes
Baking time: 30 minutes

Prepare the shortcrust pastry (see p. 12). Sift the flour and salt together.
Make a well in the center and incorporate the egg yolk, cubed butter,
and 3 ⅓ tablespoons (50 ml) water.
Work rapidly with your fingertips to combine the ingredients so that the
dough does not become elastic. Form it into a ball.
Press it down with the palm of your hand so that it is smooth.
Chill for 30 minutes, covered in plastic wrap.
Roll out the dough very thinly, to a thickness of about ¹/₁₀ in. (3 mm). Drape
it over a rolling pin and transfer it to a tart dish. Trim the edges, making a
decorative border.

Combine the milk, cream, eggs, egg yolk, and nutmeg together well, but
make sure the mixture does not become foamy. Season with salt and pepper.
Strain through a chinois*, cover with plastic wrap, and chill.

Remove the hard rind from the bacon and dice* it into small pieces.
Place the diced bacon bits in a pot with cold water and blanch* them. Allow to
boil briefly and drain well.

Preheat the oven to 350°F (180°C).
Arrange the bacon pieces on the tart base. Fill the base with the egg mixture.
Spread out the grated Gruyère cheese over the mixture. Bake immediately
for 25-30 minutes, until the top just starts to brown and the base is done.
It's best to cut the quiche at the table and to serve it warm.

● **Chef's note**
Quiches can be made a day ahead.

● **Did you know?**
*There are many variations on this recipe, which may call for vegetables, meat,
or fish.*

Techniques
Shortcrust pastry ›› p. 12
Savory cream mixture for baking ›› p. 130

Sweetbread vol-au-vents with cider and apples ★★★

Serves 8
Preparation time: 55 minutes
Cooking time: 2 hours 10 minutes

Place the sweetbreads in cold water and bring to the boil to blanch* them.
Allow to boil for 5 minutes.
Remove the white membrane.

Preheat the oven to 350-400°F (180-200°C)
Finely dice* the aromatic vegetables (carrots, onions, and leeks) to make a mirepoix*.
Allow the sweetbreads to color lightly in a pan, making sure that all sides are evenly done. Remove the sweetbreads and clean the pan of excess fat.
Sweat* the aromatic vegetables and the bouquet garni, and then cover with the cider. Turn the heat to high and reduce* the liquid by half. Return the sweetbreads to the pan and pour in enough thickened brown veal stock to half cover the sweetbreads.
Place the pan in the oven for 1 hour with the lid on. Turn the sweetbreads over after 30 minutes.

Make the sauce:
Remove the sweetbreads from the pan and tent under aluminum foil to keep them warm.
Skim the fat from the braising liquid.
Return the pot to the stove top and turn the heat to high. Reduce the braising liquid until it is thick enough to coat the back of a spoon*.
Strain through cheesecloth or a very fine-mesh sieve. Adjust the seasoning.

Pick the leaves off the cabbage and wash them. Roll them up and cut them into a chiffonade (see p. 56). Braise in butter with the seasoning.
Scoop out small balls from the apples (see p. 60). Sauté the apple balls in hot butter. Flambé* them with the calvados and sprinkle with a little sugar.
Set aside.
Preheat the oven to 350°F (180°C).
Cut out sixteen rounds of puff pastry, each with a diameter of about 3-3 1/2 in. (8-9 cm).
Using a smaller pastry cutter with a diameter of about 2-2 1/2 in. (5-6 cm), cut out disks from the center of eight of the pastry rounds to make the tops of your vol-au-vents.
Place the eight large disks on a baking tray and baste* them with the beaten egg. Place the disks with the cut-out directly over them and baste these with the egg.
Bake the puff pastry disks for 20 minutes. Then bake the smaller tops, which will be ready in less time.
Dice the sweetbreads and combine the cubes with the apple scoops.
Place the cabbage at the bottom of each vol-au-vent and then fill with the sweetbread and apple scoop mixture. Drizzle with the braising stock.

Ingredients
1 3/4 lb. (800 g) sweetbreads
1/2 small carrot (1 1/2 oz./40 g)
1/2 onion
1/2 small leek (1 oz./30 g), white only
1 bouquet garni*
2/3 cup (150 ml) hard cider*
3/4 cup (200 ml) brown veal stock, bound
10 oz. (300 g) Savoy cabbage
2 generous tablespoons (35 g) unsalted butter
2 apples (7 oz./200 g)
2 teaspoons (10 ml) calvados or other apple brandy
1 1/2 tablespoons (20 g) sugar
1/2 lb. (250 g) puff pastry (see recipe p. 16)
1 egg, beaten
Fine sea salt, freshly ground pepper
Special equipment: an ovenproof sauté pan with lid

● **Chef's note**
Vary the fillings: try sautéed mushrooms, fruit, or heirloom vegetables.

Techniques
Brown stock ›› p. 117
Shredding (chiffonade) ›› p. 56
Scooping ›› p. 60
Puff pastry ›› p. 16

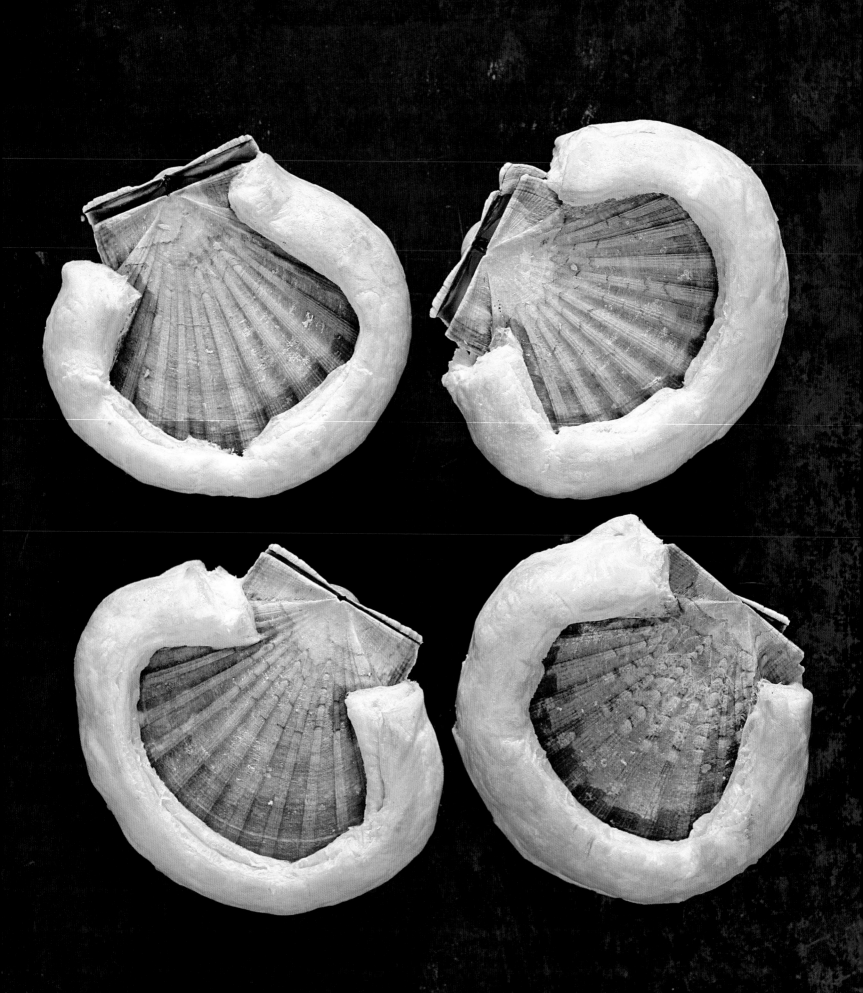

Ingredients

18 scallops in their shells
1 ¹/₂ leeks (7 oz./200 g), white part only
1 ¹/₂ large carrots (7 oz./200 g)
3 tablespoons (40 g) butter
2 oz. (60 g) canned salicornia (samphire)
(buy online or at specialty stores)
7 oz. (200 g) strips of leftover puff pastry
1 egg, beaten
¹/₂ lb. (250 g) kosher salt
Fine sea salt, freshly ground pepper

Velouté
1 shallot
¹/₂ leek (80 g) , white part only
1 ¹/₂ tablespoons (20 g) butter plus 1 ¹/₂ tablespoons
(20 g) butter
1 lb. (500 g) fish bones
²/₃ cup (150 ml) dry white wine
1 bouquet garni*
¹/₄ cup (20 g) flour
Scant ¹/₂ cup (100 ml) thick cream
Fine sea salt, freshly ground pepper

Luted scallops on a bed of gently cooked vegetables ★ ★

Serves 6
Preparation time: 45 minutes
Cooking time: 45 minutes

Open the shells (see p. 73). Scrub the scallops and the beards. Wash several times, particularly the beards, to rid them of all sand.
Wash six shells and place them in hot water for a few minutes.

Prepare the velouté (see p. 150).
Chop the shallot and finely slice the leek.
Sweat* them in 1 ¹/₂ tablespoons (20 g) butter. Add the scallop beards and the fish bones.
Pour in the white wine and reduce* by half.
Pour in ³/₄ cup (200 ml) water and add the bouquet garni.
Simmer for 30 minutes, skimming whenever necessary.
Strain the liquid through a chinois*. Reduce it until you have 1 cup (250 ml) of fumet*.
Thicken with a roux (see p. 150) made with 1 ¹/₂ tablespoons (20 g) butter and ¹/₄ cup (20 g) flour, add the cream, and season.

Slit the white of the leek lengthwise and wash well.
Peel and wash the carrots. Slice them to make julienne strips (see p. 59).
Gently stew the julienne strips (see p. 98) in butter and season. Add the salicornia (samphire).

Preheat the oven to 350°F (180°C).
Spread the softened vegetables out in the shells.
Place three scallops in each shell, slicing the larger ones if necessary,
add 2 tablespoons of the velouté, and close.
Cut out strips of leftover puff pastry 8 in. × 1 ¹/₄ in. (20 cm × 3 cm).
Baste* both sides of the strips with beaten egg and apply tightly to seal the shells.
Prepare small heaps of kosher salt on a baking sheet.
Place the scallop shells on the heaps of salt, ensuring that they are perfectly horizontal–apply a little pressure if necessary–so that they stay sealed.
Cook for about 10 minutes.
Arrange them on flat plates. Your guests will cut open the pastry seal themselves to savor the aromas.

● **Chef's notes**
Make this dish when scallops are at the height of their season.
The coral can also be added to the scallop.

 Techniques
Opening scallops ›› p. 73
Velouté ›› p. 150
Julienne strips ›› p. 59
Gentle stewing ›› p. 98
Luting ›› p. 103

Sesame-coated rabbit liver salad ★

Serves 4

Preparation time: 40 minutes
Cooking time: 10 minutes

Trim the rabbit livers and season them with salt and pepper. Coat them in sesame seeds.

Wash the green salad leaves, checking that there are no traces of sand and no wilted leaves. Dry well. Chop the nuts roughly and add them to the leaves.

Dissolve a little fine sea salt in the vinegar and season with the freshly ground pepper. Drizzle in the oil, whisking constantly.

Pour the clarified butter into a skillet and sauté the rabbit livers over high heat. Brown them, but do not overcook: they should be slightly pink inside.

Form little mounds with the salad leaves and arrange the warm livers over them.

Drizzle with the vinaigrette.

● Chef's notes

Use the idea for this recipe as a base for variations with smoked duck breast, vegetable sticks, croutons, and more.

Rabbit liver is more delicate than chicken liver, and has a slightly sweet note.

Technique
Vinaigrette ›› p. 150

Ingredients

11 oz. (320 g) rabbit livers
$^1/_4$ cup (1 $^1/_2$ oz./40 g) sesame seeds
1 large sachet (for 4) mesclun (including, for example, Batavia lettuce hearts, oak leaf lettuce, raddichio, and lamb's lettuce)
$^1/_3$ cup (1 $^1/_2$ oz./40 g) walnuts
1 $^1/_3$ tablespoons (20 ml) aged wine vinegar
3 tablespoons (40 ml) oil
2 tablespoons (30 g) clarified butter*
Fine sea salt, freshly ground pepper

Cheese straws ★

Serves 8

Preparation time: 35 minutes
Cooking time: 45 minutes

Prepare a Mornay sauce. Make a white roux with the butter and flour (see method p. 150). Add half of the cold milk and the grated nutmeg. Bring to the boil over high heat, whisking constantly. Pour in the remaining milk and bring back to the boil. Season.
Remove from the heat and add the egg yolks, combining well. Stir in the grated Gruyère cheese.
Cover with plastic wrap flush with the surface so that a skin does not form. Chill.

Preheat the oven to 375°F (190°C).
Roll out the puff pastry in a rectangle $1/10$ in. (3 mm) thick.
Spread the chilled Mornay sauce evenly over it. Sprinkle with grated, chopped Gruyère cheese.
Cut out thin strips measuring 5 $1/2$ in. × 1 $1/2$ in. (14 cm × 4 cm). Allow 2 straws per person.
Bake for 25-30 minutes and serve immediately.

Techniques

Puff pastry ≫ p. 16
Mornay sauce ≫ p. 131

Ingredients

14 oz. (400 g) puff pastry (see recipe p. 16)
7 oz. (200 g) Gruyère cheese, grated and then finely chopped (for a better texture)

Mornay sauce
2 tablespoons (30 g) butter
$1/3$ cup (1 oz./30 g) flour
1 $1/4$ cups (300 ml) milk
A little grated nutmeg
2 egg yolks
1 $1/2$ oz. ($1/3$ cup/40 g) grated Gruyère cheese
Fine sea salt, freshly ground pepper

Ingredients

5 ¹/₂ oz. (160 g) button mushrooms
1 ¹/₃ tablespoons (20 g) butter
4 oz. (120 g) smoked bacon
3 ¹/₂ oz. (100 g) grated Gruyère cheese
Fine sea salt, freshly ground pepper

Choux pastry

1 ³/₄ cups (180 g) flour
²/₃ cup (150 ml) water
²/₃ cup (150 ml) milk
7 tablespoons (100 g) unsalted butter
4 eggs
Fine sea salt, freshly ground pepper

Béchamel sauce

1 tablespoon (15 g) butter
2 ¹/₂ tablespoons (15 g) flour
1 cup (250 ml) milk
A little grated nutmeg
Fine sea salt, freshly ground pepper

Mushroom *gougères* ★ ★

Serves 8
Preparation time: 40 minutes
Cooking time: 50 minutes

Prepare the choux pastry (see method p. 20). Sift the flour. In a pot, bring the water, milk, salt, and cubed butter to the boil. Remove from the heat and add the flour all at once. Return to the heat and stir vigorously with a spatula to dry out the mixture. Transfer it to a bowl. When it is tepid, incorporate the eggs, one by one, mixing them in with the spatula. Season with pepper.

To make the béchamel (see p. 131), prepare a white roux with the butter and flour. Add half of the cold milk and the grated nutmeg. Bring to the boil over high heat, whisking constantly. Pour in the other half of the milk and bring back to the boil. Remove from the heat and season.

Clean the mushrooms and cut them into julienne strips. Sauté them in sizzling butter and season them.
Remove the rind from the bacon and dice* it finely.

Preheat the oven to 375°F (190°C). Lightly butter a baking sheet. Make sure there is no steam in the oven from previous use–the oven must be perfectly dry to bake the choux pastry.
Combine the choux pastry, the béchamel sauce, the mushrooms, bacon bits, and Gruyère. Spoon the mixture into a piping bag without a nozzle. The hole should have a diameter of just under ¹/₂ in. (1 cm).
Pipe out the mixture onto the baking sheet to form a crown shape. To make the task easier, trace out a circle on a piece of parchment paper.
Pipe out the first circle. Just inside that circle, and touching it, pipe out a second circle of mixture. Pipe out a third circle just above them that overlaps the two others.

Bake for 25-30 minutes. As soon as it is done, place it on a round serving dish and cut slices as they are required.
Alternatively, prepare individual *gougères* in buttered ramekins and reduce the cooking time accordingly. Be careful to fill the ramekins no more than two-thirds full as this mixture will rise.

● **Did you know?**
This recipe highlights the versatility of choux pastry, also used to make the cheese gougères that accompany wine-tasting in Burgundy.

Techniques
Choux pastry » p. 20
Béchamel sauce » p. 131
Julienned strips » p. 59

Provençal-flavored sardine *tartes fines* ★ ★

Serves 8

Preparation time: 1 hour 45 minutes
Resting time: 1 hour
Marinating time: 1 hour
Cooking time: 45 minutes

Prepare the puff pastry (see p. 16).
Sift the flour and salt together and make a well in the center. Add the water.
Work rapidly to combine the ingredients into a smooth dough, the *détrempe*,
which is the base for your puff pastry, and chill for about 20 minutes.
Bring the butter to the same consistency as the dough mixture (see details
on p. 16). Now roll out the dough mixture to form a cross shape, leaving the
center–where you will place the butter–about ¹/₅ in. or 5 mm thicker than the
four other parts. Place the butter in the center of the dough and wrap it with
the four other sections so that it is completely enclosed.
Roll out the dough to form a rectangle whose length is three times greater
than its width. Fold it in three, rotate it a quarter-turn and repeat the
procedure five times–a total of six–chilling it for 20 minutes after you have
rolled it out and folded twice.
Preheat the oven to 350°F (180°C).
Cut out eight ovals about 5 ¹/₂ in. (14-15 cm) long. Prick them with a fork and
bake for 15 minutes.

Peel the tomatoes (see p. 61).
Cut them in two, between the stem and the incision you have made.
Squeeze the halves in the palm of your hand to eliminate the seeds and dice*
the flesh. Finely chop the shallot and sweat* it in the olive oil.
Add the diced tomatoes.
Remove the shoot from the garlic cloves and chop them. Add the cloves with
the herbes de Provence* to the tomatoes.
Allow the mixture to stew gently over low heat for 30 minutes.
Season with salt and pepper.
Clean and fillet the sardines (see p. 70). Season the fillets with fleur de sel and
ground pepper. Marinate them in the olive oil, lemon juice, and herbes de
Provence for 1 hour in the refrigerator.
Spread the chopped tomatoes over the puff pastry ovals.
Drain the sardine fillets and arrange them over the chopped tomatoes.
Garnish with a lemon wedge.

Techniques
Puff pastry ≫ p. 16
Peeling using hot water ≫ p. 61
Filleting a fish (two round, flat fillets) ≫ p. 70

Ingredients
8 fresh sardines
3 tablespoons (40 ml) olive oil
Juice of 1 lemon
1 teaspoon herbes de Provence
1 lemon, for garnish
Fleur de sel, freshly ground pepper

Puff pastry
3 cups (300 g) flour
Generous ¹/₂ cup (130 ml) water
7 ¹/₂ oz. (200 g) puff pastry margarine
or 1 ³/₄ sticks (200 g) butter
1 teaspoon (5 g) salt

Chopped tomatoes
1 ³/₄ lb. (800 g) tomatoes (about eight)
1 shallot
3 tablespoons (40 ml) olive oil
2 garlic cloves
1 teaspoon herbes de Provence
Fine sea salt, freshly ground pepper

Ingredients

10 oz. (300 g) whiting fillets
10 oz. (300 g) salmon fillets
2 egg whites
1 1/2 cups (350 ml) whipping cream
Pinch of ground turmeric
1 1/3 tablespoons (20 g) butter
1 lemon, for garnish
Fine sea salt, freshly ground white pepper

Beurre blanc

2 shallots
Scant 1/2 cup (100 ml) white wine
7 tablespoons (100 g) salted butter,
well chilled and cubed

Fish terrine with beurre blanc ★ ★

Serves 8

Preparation time: 50 minutes
Cooking time: 50 minutes

Prepare the forcemeats of the two fish separately (see p. 157). Remember to use half the ingredients (egg white, cream, and butter) for the whiting and the other half for the salmon.

Process the fish fillets using the blade attachment of a food processor and strain the mixture through a fine-mesh sieve. Return it to the bowl of the food processor with the egg white and pulse very briefly (so that no air bubbles form) to incorporate it.

Transfer to a stainless steel bowl over an ice bath. Gradually mix in the cream and then season. Add a pinch of ground turmeric to the salmon mixture to heighten its orangey color.

Preheat the oven to 250°F (120°C).

Butter a terrine and layer the two mixtures. You may make either two or four layers altogether. Cook for about 40 minutes; the terrine is done when the tip of a knife comes out clean.

Prepare the beurre blanc (see p. 132). Finely chop the shallot and place in a small saucepan. Pour in the white wine and reduce* over low heat until there is very little liquid left.

Whisk in the cold cubed butter.

Arrange the terrine on flat plates. Place a slice of hot terrine on each plate and surround it with a ribbon of beurre blanc.

Decorate it with a canelled lemon slice.

Techniques

Mousseline stuffing (cream-based) >> p. 157
Beurre blanc >> p. 132
Canelling >> p. 54

Fish

Gérald Passédat
presents his recipe

With the sea lapping three of France's long coasts, it is only natural that fish plays a primordial role in our culinary heritage, and our deep-rooted traditions of cooking fish—fish soups, in particular—certainly owe a great deal to geography. Each port, no matter its size, has a worthy variation on the theme, so we can sample a bouillabaisse at one, a cotriade at another, and a matelote elsewhere. I have adopted the Mediterranean as my own. It is vital to me, providing me with not only peace and tranquility, but the fish of its coastlines and its depths. I share much with the fishermen who work it and respect it, and with them, I endeavor to protect it, supporting those who practice long-line fishing. I marvel when I discover humble, often long-forgotten fish such as the dentex, the prosaically named axillary sea bream, whose French name literally means "lovely eyes," and ocean catfish or sea bass, whose flavors are heightened by a light cuisine. Their rich textures and their wide range of flavors mean that I can give free rein to my imagination. Nature offers itself up to us on condition that we respect it, and I pick from my marine garden to serve dishes every day with the conviction that I am a mere link in a chain whose origin starts in the depths.

Sea bass, as Lucie Passédat liked it

To prepare
Remove the scales of the fish, gut it, and wash it. Prepare the fillets, removing the bones. Set them aside to use for the fish fumet*. Slice the two fillets to make four equal servings of 5 $^1/_2$ oz. (160 g). Make shallow, regular incisions in the skin.

Fish fumet
Prepare the aromatic garnish. Wash, peel, and chop the shallot, carrot, and leek half. Prepare the bouquet garni.
Crush the fish bones and sauté them with the olive oil. Add the garnish and pour in the water. Cook for 20 minutes, strain through a chinois*, and set aside. You should have 4 $^3/_4$ cups (1.2 liters) clear fumet; keep 4 cups (1 liter) for Lucie's base and the remainder to cook the fish.

Lucie's base
Place 4 cups fish fumet in a pot with the chopped tomatoes, tomato paste, sugar, and coriander seeds and reduce* by half. Strain through a chinois and set aside. This is the base.

While it is reducing, prepare the lemon zest of one lemon: dice* it into a fine brunoise*, blanch* it 3 times, and refresh*. Set the diced zest aside.

Peel four vine tomatoes and dice them to make a brunoise. Prepare the leaves of the basil and cilantro (fresh coriander). Wash and chop the leaves. Squeeze the other two lemons.
Prepare the four truffle shavings and cut them into round disks with a small pastry cutter. Dice the trimmings into a brunoise. Set aside.
Peel the cucumber and use a mandolin or peeler to cut the tagliatelle-shaped strips from the flesh. Do the same with the zucchini skin. Work carefully so that they are all nicely shaped and the same size.
Blanch them and refresh. Line a pan with parchment paper and arrange the vegetable tagliatelle on it, alternating seven zucchini skins with six cucumber strips.
Brush a stainless steel ovenproof dish with clarified butter and season it with salt and pepper.
Arrange the slices of green tomato and sea bass fillets in the dish, and season with the wild fennel seeds, olive oil, Camargue salt and mignonette pepper. Pour the reserved fish fumet over and cook for 12 minutes in a steam oven at 140°F (60°C), or use a steam cooker. When done, allow it to rest.

Finish and present
Take Lucie's base and add the chopped cilantro (coriander) and basil, diced lemon zest, tomato cubes, truffle brunoise, olive oil, juice of two lemons, and the truffle *jus*. Adjust the seasoning with salt and pepper. Re-heat slightly but do not allow to boil.
Place the vegetable tagliatelle on the cooked fish. Reheat slightly over steam. Take four truffle shavings, brush them with olive oil, and season them with salt and pepper. Reheat them in the oven at 300°F (150°C) and then place them carefully on the fish pieces just before serving.
Pour the base into soup plates, place the fish in this, drizzle the vegetable tagliatelle and base with a little olive oil. Sprinkle with a little Camargue salt or fleur de sel.

Serves 4
Preparation time: 2 hours
Cooking time: 40 minutes

Ingredients
1 sea bass weighing 3 lb. 5 oz. (1.5 kg)
3 lemons
4 ripe vine tomatoes
2 stalks (20 g) basil
2 stalks (20 g) cilantro (coriander)
1 truffle weighing $^2/_3$ oz. (20 g)
1 cucumber
2 zucchini
3 tablespoons (50 ml) clarified butter*
1 green tomato
2 pinches (2 g) wild fennel seeds
Olive oil
Mignonette pepper
Fleur de sel (preferably from Camargue)
Scant $^1/_2$ cup (100 ml) truffle *jus*

Fish fumet
Bones of the sea bass
1 cup (250 ml) olive oil
6 cups (1.5 liters) water
1 shallot
1 carrot
$^1/_2$ leek
1 bouquet garni*

Lucie's base
14 oz. (400 g) tomatoes (fresh off the stalk or beefsteak tomato, "coeur de boeuf" if possible)
1 teaspoon (5 ml) tomato paste
$^1/_2$ teaspoon (2.5 g) sugar
1 teaspoon (8 g) coriander seeds

Dogfish stew in red wine with Brussels sprouts, a specialty of the Gironde region ★★

Serves 8
Preparation time: 1 hour 10 minutes
Marinating time: 3 hours minimum
Cooking time: 50 minutes

Slice the dogfish into eight equal portions. Make a few incisions on the back so that the pieces do not curl up during cooking.

Prepare the marinade (see basic technique p. 142).
Peel and wash the vegetables and slice them finely.
Place half the vegetables at the bottom of a baking dish and arrange the pieces of fish over them.
Then put in the other half of the vegetables with the dried and fresh herbs and peppercorns.
Cover with the wine and cognac.
Cover the dish with plastic wrap and chill for at least 3 hours.
Drain the fish pieces over a bowl, and strain the marinade through a chinois*. Use it to make a fumet* (see p. 139).
Rinse the fish bones well and sweat* them together with the chopped shallot in butter. Pour in the wine and the marinade and add the bouquet garni.
Cook over high heat for 30 minutes, skimming when necessary.

Preheat the oven to 325°F-350°F (160°C-170°C).
In another pan, sauté the bacon bits without adding any fat. (At this point, if you have not marinated the fish, coat it in flour to add taste to the dish and thicken the sauce.)
Quarter the mushrooms (see p. 58) and add them to sweat briefly.
Flambé* the ingredients with the cognac and then pour in the fumet.
Add the fish pieces and bouquet garni, cover with a lid, and cook in the oven for 20-25 minutes.
Remove the fish pieces and the bouquet garni. Reduce* the cooking liquid by half over medium heat.
Thicken the liquid with beurre manié (see p. 153) and adjust the seasoning.

Make the croutons: rub slices of toasted sandwich loaf with garlic.

Remove the outer leaves of the Brussels sprouts, wash, and boil them.
Refresh* immediately under cold water. Coat the Brussels sprouts with a knob of butter and season them.

Arrange the slices of dogfish in soup plates and pour the sauce over. Scatter the croutons in the plates.

● Chef's notes
You can begin marinating the dogfish a day ahead.
Eel and lamprey are equally good with this recipe.

Ingredients
3 ½ lb. (1.6 kg) dogfish
4 oz. (120 g) bacon bits
Scant ⅔ cup (60 g) flour (optional)
10 oz. (300 g) button mushrooms
3 tablespoons (40 ml) cognac
1 bouquet garni*
1 oz. (30 g) beurre manié (see p. 153: 1 tablespoon [15 g] butter, 2 ½ tablespoons [15 g] flour)
8 slices sandwich loaf
4 garlic cloves
2 lb. 4 oz. (1 kg) Brussels sprouts
1 tablespoon (15 g) butter
Fine salt, freshly ground pepper

Marinade
1 shallot
2 oz. (60 g) garlic chives or 1 large white onion
4 garlic cloves
1 small carrot (2 oz./60 g)
1 bouquet garni*
1 bunch of assorted fresh herbs, such as flat-leaf parsley, chives, thyme, and summer savory
½ teaspoon (2 g) peppercorns
4 cups (1 liter) red wine
Scant ½ cup (100 ml) cognac

Fumet
1 shallot
4 tablespoons (60 g) butter
1 lb. 5 oz. (600 g) fish bones
1 bouquet garni

● Did you know?
The Bordeaux region enjoys a rich variety of fish, both sea and fresh water, as well as fish that migrate up river, such as the unappealingly named dogfish that goes under a number of euphemisms (rock salmon, for example). Its flesh withstands relatively longer cooking times and goes well with a robust wine—Bordeaux red is of course ideal.

Techniques
Raw marinade ›› p. 142
Fumet ›› p. 139
Quartering button mushrooms ›› p. 58
Beurre manié ›› p. 153

Ingredients

6 trout weighing about $^{1}/_{2}$ lb. (250 g) each
1 cup (100 g) flour
$^{1}/_{3}$ cup (80 g) clarified butter*
4 tablespoons (60 g) salted butter
1 cup (4 oz./100 g) sliced almonds
Juice of 1 lemon
$^{1}/_{2}$ bunch parsley, chopped
Fine salt, freshly ground pepper
Special equipment: oval frying pan

Trout with almonds ★

Serves 6

Preparation time: 25 minutes
Cooking time: 20 minutes

Dress* the trout and dry them well, dabbing up all excess moisture with paper towel.
Spread out the flour in a conveniently sized flat dish and season it. Dip the trout in to coat. Shake lightly to remove any excess flour.
Heat an oval non-stick pan with the clarified butter over low to medium heat. Place the trout in the pan and gently brown them. Turn over and brown lightly on the other side. Check for doneness (the flesh should come away easily from the bone) and, if necessary place them in the oven at 325°F–350°F (160°C-170°C) for a few minutes to complete cooking.
Remove the skin.
Melt some butter in a small pan until it is brown (*beurre noisette**). Gently sauté the sliced almonds in the butter and deglaze* with the lemon juice.
Arrange the trout on a large, flat serving platter, heads to the left.
Drizzle with the butter-almond mixture and scatter with chopped parsley.

 Technique
Sauté meunière ›› p. 121

Aniseed-flambéed* sea bream ★

Serves 4

Preparation time: 20 minutes
Cooking time: 25 minutes

Prepare the sea bream: remove the fins and scales, and gut them.
Preheat the oven to 325°F (160°C). Grease a baking tray.
Chop the dill and crush the star anise. Combine with salt and pepper. Fill the sea bream with this mixture.
Arrange the sea bream on the baking tray. Use a brush to coat them with oil and season them with salt and pepper.
Cook for 20-25 minutes.
Just before serving, flambé them with a generous dose of pastis.
Cut the sea bream, making sure you remove all the bones.
Serve nice and hot with a beurre blanc sauce (see p.132) or a hollandaise sauce (see p. 148).

● Chef's note

Rice flavored with turmeric or sautéed potatoes make good sides for this fish dish.

Technique
Roasting ›› p. 118

Ingredients

2 gilthead sea bream (*Sparus aurata*) weighing about 1 ¹/₂ lb. (700 g) each
6 sprigs dill
4 star anise
A little olive oil
Scant ¹/₂ cup pastis (the French aniseed-flavored aperitif, similar to raki and ouzo)
Fine salt, freshly ground pepper

Ingredients

2 whole whiting
14 oz. (400 g) fresh cod
1 turnip (5 oz./140 g)
2 carrots (5 oz./140 g)
2 small zucchini (5 oz./140 g)
3 tablespoons (40 ml) olive oil
1 egg white
6 sprigs dill
3 ½ tablespoons (45 ml) fish glaze* (reduced* fish fumet*)
¼ cup (50 ml) Noilly Prat (white vermouth)
Fleur de sel
Fine salt, freshly ground pepper

Fish papillotes with vegetable scoops ★★

Serves 4

Preparation time: 45 minutes
Cooking time: 25 minutes

Trim and fillet the whiting and the cod (see p. 60).
Remove the bones and cut portions weighing about 3 oz. (80 g) each.
Wash the vegetables. Peel the turnips and carrots. Leave the zucchini unpeeled.
Using a small scoop, prepare the vegetable balls (see p. 60), keeping the three vegetables separate.
Rinse to remove any residue.
Braise the vegetables (separately) in a little olive oil and just enough water to half cover them. Season with salt and pepper.
Preheat the oven to 325°F (160°C).
Lightly whisk the egg whites with a pinch of salt using a fork.
Cut out parchment paper rectangles measuring 14 × 10 inches (35 × 25 cm). Fold in half lengthwise.
Place two fish fillets, one of each kind, in the center of the bottom half of parchment paper and season with salt and pepper.
Arrange a few sprigs of dill over the fillets and drizzle with the fish glaze and Noilly Prat.
Now arrange a few of the vegetables scoops over the fillets, setting aside the rest to serve separately.
Using a pastry brush, wet the edge of the parchment paper with the egg white.
Fold the paper over and make a small fold at the edges. Keep in place with paper clips.
Place the papillotes on a baking tray and cook for 8-10 minutes.
Place each papillote on a plate and serve with a dish of the remaining vegetable scoops. Pass around some fleur de sel for each guest to sprinkle.

● Chef's notes

Most fish fillets can be prepared in papillotes.
The vegetables can also be cut into julienne strips, diced, or finely sliced.*

Techniques

Filleting a fish (two round, flat fillets) ≫ p. 70
Fruit and vegetable scoops ≫ p. 60
Gentle stewing ≫ p. 98
Cooking en papillote ≫ p. 105

Brandade: puréed salt cod with mashed potatoes ★

Serves 6
Preparation time: 35 minutes
Soaking time: 48 hours
Cooking time: 40 minutes

Soak the cod in cold water or milk for 48 hours to remove some of the salt. Drain the pieces of fish and poach them with the bouquet garni in boiling water for 1-2 minutes. Repeat as many times as you need to remove the excess salt, so taste as you proceed.
When the cod is ready, remove the skin and bones and flake it.
Brush the potatoes with a vegetable brush and place them in a pot of cold water to bring to the boil. Cook for about 35 minutes. Peel them and press them through a vegetable mill.
Chop the garlic cloves. Add to the mashed potatoes with the remaining ingredients (milk, butter, grated nutmeg, ground coriander, and freshly ground pepper).
Using a spatula, vigorously stir the cod with the olive oil until it reaches a light texture. Thin with the cream and incorporate the mashed potatoes. Adjust the seasoning.

● **Chef's note**
If you wish, serve this as a gratin. Either prepare individual portions in ramekins or serve in a large dish, accompanied by a salad or vegetables.

● **Did you know?**
The brandade—puréed salt cod, cream or milk, and olive oil—is a typical dish of the southern French regions of Languedoc and Provence, with regional variations that may include garlic or not. Antoine Augustin Parmentier (1737–1813) was the man responsible for promoting the potato in France; it was intended to complement cereal production, which was more likely to suffer in difficult climatic conditions. He had soup kitchens opened in Paris where potato soup was served, and had an all-potato meal prepared for Benjamin Franklin. A number of dishes in which potatoes play a key role bear his name.

Ingredients
2 lb. (900 g) salted cod
1 bouquet garni*
$1/4$ cup (60 ml) olive oil
2 tablespoons (30 ml) whipping cream
Freshly ground pepper

Mashed potatoes
$1 1/2$ lb. (800 g) potatoes
2 garlic cloves, peeled, shoots removed
Scant $2/3$ cup (150 ml) milk
3 tablespoons (40 g) unsalted butter
A little grated nutmeg
1 pinch ground coriander
Freshly ground pepper

Ingredients

2 lb. (1 kg) pike perch fillets

2 ¹/₂-3 tablespoons (40 g) clarified butter*

1 lb. (500 g) assorted grains, such as barley, quinoa, wheat, and oats

2 ¹/₂ tablespoons (40 g) butter

2 cups (500 ml) meat stock, broth, or juice

Fine salt, freshly ground pepper

Roasted pike perch with meat *jus**

Serves 6

Preparation time: 15 minutes

Cooking time: 20 minutes

Preheat the oven to 325°F (160°C).

Prepare fillets weighing about 5 oz. (140-160 g) each.

Butter a roasting tray. Place the fillets on the tray and drizzle the clarified butter over. Season with salt and pepper.

Poach the assortment of grains using the shallow poaching method as indicated on page 108. Add a knob of butter when they are done and season.

Reduce* the meat *jus* until it coats the back of a spoon*.

Spoon a layer of grains on each plate and place the pike perch fillets on the top.

Serve the sauce from a bowl.

Technique

Shallow poaching (cold start) for vegetables, grains, fish, etc. >> p. 108

Ingredients

12 langoustines
1 pineapple
18 scallops
Scant $1/2$ cup (100 g) clarified butter*
5 $1/2$ tablespoons (80 g) butter, softened*
4 sprigs of tarragon
Five-pepper mix*
10 oz. (300 g) quinoa
1 onion, chopped
Fleur de sel, freshly ground pepper

Langoustine and pineapple skewers ★

Serves 6

Preparation time: 40 minutes
Cooking time: 35 minutes

Shell the langoustines, leaving the heads on.
Peel the pineapple and cut it into large cubes.
Skewer two langoustines and three scallops, alternating them with
pineapple cubes onto each of your six skewers. Set aside some pineapple
cubes for garnish.
Season with salt and pepper.
Sauté them in clarified butter over high heat.
Combine the softened butter with the tarragon, setting aside a few leaves
for garnish. Season with fleur de sel and the five-pepper mixture.
Prepare the quinoa with the chopped onion using the shallow poaching
technique on p. 108. When it is ready, mix in the tarragon-flavored butter.
Prepare small domes of quinoa and arrange a skewer with a few pineapple
cubes attractively scattered on each plate.
Garnish with tarragon leaves.

Techniques
Shelling crustaceans ›› p. 67
Shallow poaching (cold start) for vegetables, grains, fish, etc. ›› p. 108

Sea bass in a salt crust ★

Serves 8

Preparation time: 25 minutes
Resting time: 15 minutes
Cooking time: 20 minutes

Ingredients
1 sea bass weighing about 1 ³/₄ lb. (800 g)
Aromatic ingredients, such as dill, thyme, or olive oil
¹/₂ lb. (250 g) kosher salt
1 cup (3 oz./100 g) flour
1 egg, beaten, plus 3 egg whites
Freshly ground pepper

Remove the scales and fins of the fish and gut it. If you wish, remove the head.
Season the cavity with pepper and add other aromatic ingredients if you wish.
Combine the kosher salt with the flour. Make a well in the center.
Lightly beat the three egg whites with a fork. Incorporate them into the flour-salt mixture to make a smooth paste. Leave to rest for 15 minutes.
Preheat the oven to 350°F (180°C). Using a rolling pin, roll the paste out to a thickness of about ¹/₅ in. (4 mm). Make sure the paste is long and wide enough to roll around the fish, and seal the edges with a little water or egg white.
When you have wrapped the fish, baste* the paste with the whole egg.
Cook for 17-20 minutes until the crust turns a light golden color.
Serve immediately. Break the crust at the table and carefully take out the flesh of the fish.

● **Chef's notes**

Use one of any number of sauces to accompany this dish. Even a simple squeeze of lemon juice enhances it wonderfully.
Do not leave the fish for more than 15 minutes in the crust before you cook it, because it will absorb some of the salt.
Try to find line-caught sea bass as it is not damaged when it is fished and you will be supporting sustainable fishing methods.

● **Did you know?**

Cooking in salt is a technique that originated in ancient China. This method retains the moisture of fish, poultry, and even meat as it cooks. Because the crust is hermetic, all seasoning permeates the food; the crust (pure coarse or kosher salt, or a paste as in this recipe) creates a kiln effect, speeding up the cooking process. Cracking open a salt crust at a dinner table makes for a dramatic effect.

 Technique
Cooking in a crust >> p. 99

Ingredients

1 whole pollack weighing about 3 ¹/₂ lb. (1.5 kg)
1 shallot
4 oz. (120 g) button mushrooms
5-6 sprigs parsley
1 tablespoon (15 g) plus 3 tablespoons (40 g) butter
1 bouquet garni*
²/₃ cup (150 ml) thick cream

Fumet

About 14 oz. (400 g) fish bones
¹/₂ small leek (40 g), white only
1 shallot
¹/₂ onion
²/₃ cup (150 ml) white wine
1 bouquet garni
¹/₂ teaspoon (2 g) peppercorns

Techniques

Filleting fish (two round, flat fillets) ›› p. 70
Fumet ›› p. 139
Simple slicing ›› p. 55
Shallow poaching (cold start) ›› p. 108

Pollack fillets *bonne femme* ★ ★

Serves 6
Preparation time: 45 minutes
Cooking time: 50 minutes

Fillet the pollack and remove the skin. Keep the central bone to use for the fumet*.
Cut six portions weighing about 5-6 oz. (160 g) each.
Prepare the aromatic base: chop the shallot, slice the button mushrooms, and chop the parsley.

Prepare the fumet (see p. 139).
Crush the central bone as well as the other bones, and soak them in cold water to remove any traces of blood.
Peel, wash, and finely slice the vegetables (leek, shallot, and onion).
Place all the ingredients in a large pot with 1 cup (250 ml) water and bring to the boil, skimming when necessary.
Simmer lightly for 25-30 minutes, but do not stir as this would make the fumet cloudy.
Strain through a chinois* and chill over an ice bath.

Preheat the oven to 250°F (120°C).
Butter the bottom of a flameproof cooking dish or tray with 1 tablespoon (15 g) butter. Arrange the aromatic base in the dish (shallot, button mushrooms, and parsley).
Place the fish fillets over the aromatic base and pour in just enough fumet and white wine to half cover the ingredients. Add the bouquet garni.
Bring to the simmer over heat and cover with parchment paper (see DVD for method).
Cook in the oven for a few minutes.
Remove the fish and keep it warm.
Turn the oven to "broil."
To make the sauce, reduce* the cooking liquid by 90 percent.
Incorporate the cream and reduce again until thick enough to coat the back of a spoon*.
Whip in the remaining butter.
Arrange the pollack fillets in a buttered serving dish and pour over the sauce.
Reheat the dish in the oven briefly.

● Chef's notes
To gain time, use a good-quality dried fumet mix instead of making it yourself from scratch.
This dish is traditionally served with rice pilaf (see p. 323).

● Did you know?
Bonne femme *literally means "good wife," and refers to dishes that are cooked simply, as one would eat them at an everyday family meal.*

Steamed fillets of bib (pouting) in a green robe ★

Serves 4
Preparation time: 35 minutes
Cooking time: 30 minutes

Wash the lettuce leaves. Blanch* the larger leaves very briefly—no more than a few seconds—in boiling water. Refresh* immediately under very cold water and dry carefully and thoroughly.

Remove the bones from the fish fillets. Season them and wrap them in the lettuce leaves.

Steam them (use a steam cooker or steam oven if you have one) for 8-12 minutes.

Cook the basmati rice in boiling water according to instructions. Refresh briefly under cold water, add a knob of butter, and season with salt.

Cut the red cabbage into quarters. Remove the heart and shred the leaves finely.

Melt the 3 tablespoons (40 g) butter in a sauté pan. Add the red cabbage. Deglaze* with the red wine vinegar. Add the water, cover with the lid, and leave to braise for about 20 minutes. Season.

Brush the fish fillets in their wrapping with the clarified butter to give them a nice gloss.

Arrange the braised red cabbage in a serving dish or in the plates. Center the fish fillets and sprinkle them with fleur de sel.

● **Chef's note**
This recipe will work for most types of fish fillets.

Techniques
Steaming ›› p. 123
Cooking in a crust ›› p. 99
Deep poaching (hot start) ›› p. 106
Gentle stewing ›› p. 98

Ingredients
1 lettuce
1 lb. (500 g) bib (pouting) fillets
7 oz. (200 g) Basmati rice
3 tablespoons (45 g) butter, plus a little for the rice
1/2 red cabbage
2 tablespoons (30 ml) red wine vinegar
Scant 1/2 cup (100 ml) water
2 tablespoons (30 g) clarified butter*
Fleur de sel
Fine salt, freshly ground pepper

Ingredients

1 lb. (500 g) conger (sea eel)
2 red gurnets (gurnards)
1 ¹/₂ lb. (800 g) John Dory
7 oz. (200 g) crustaceans of your choice

¹/₂ long loaf of country or sourdough bread

Stock

¹/₂ large onion
¹/₂ leek (50 g), white only
10 oz. (300 g) tomatoes
4 garlic cloves
3 green crabs
Scant ¹/₄ cup (50 ml) olive oil
1 bouquet garni*
2 pinches (2 g) ground saffron, or 8 filaments
Zest of ¹/₂ dried orange
Fine salt, freshly ground pepper

Rouille

5 oz. (150 g) mealy potatoes
4 garlic cloves, peeled, shoots removed
2 egg yolks
²/₃ cup (150 ml) olive oil
Scant ¹/₂ cup (100 ml) sunflower seed oil
1 pinch (1 g) ground saffron or 4 filaments
Fine salt, freshly ground pepper

Bouillabaisse ★ ★ ★

Serves 8
Preparation time: 1 hour
Cooking time: 1 hour 10 minutes

Prepare and trim the fish. Fillet them and remove all the bones, setting them aside with the heads for the stock. Reserve the fillets in the refrigerator. You may either shell the crustaceans or leave them whole.

Prepare the stock: peel, wash, and dice* the onion to make a mirepoix*. Slit the leek white lengthwise in two, wash it thoroughly, and slice it finely.
Peel the tomatoes and remove the seeds, and remove the shoots from the garlic cloves.
Cut the small crabs into halves.
Heat a little olive oil in a low-sided pot and put in all the ingredients. Leave them to sweat* briefly, then pour in 8 cups (2 liters) cold water. Bring to the boil and simmer for 45 minutes over medium heat.
Filter and season with salt and pepper. Place in the refrigerator until needed.

Prepare the rouille (see p. 145). Boil the potatoes in their jackets, then peel and press through a vegetable mill.
Crush the garlic cloves.
Mix in the egg yolks, one by one, and whisk in the oils. It is best to use a combination of a neutral oil with olive oil added for the taste. Add the saffron and adjust the seasoning.

Place the fish fillets and shellfish in the cold stock. Bring rapidly to the boil and lower the temperature after a few moments.
Prepare the croutons: slice the bread and toast it.
Serve the bouillabaisse in a soup tureen or in individual soup plates, with the rouille and croutons in separate dishes.

● **Chef's note**
Boil potatoes in the stock as a tasty side dish.

● **Did you know?**
Along the coast from Marseille to Toulon, restaurants and fishermen are proud of their beautifully colored soup, which they vary with the catch of the day.

Techniques
Filleting a fish (two round, flat fillets) ≫ p. 70
Peeling using hot water ≫ p. 61
Rouille ≫ p. 145

Grilled salmon steaks
with braised fennel ★ ★

Serves 6

Preparation time: 35 minutes
Marinating time: 2 hours
Cooking time: 1 hour 40 minutes

Remove the fins and scales from the salmon and gut it. Cut six steaks weighing about 7 oz. (200 g) each.
Prepare the instant marinade (see p. 141). Peel the lemon, removing all the white pith, and slice it.
Place the olive oil, aromatic ingredients, and lemon slices in a tray. Place the salmon steaks in the tray and marinate in the refrigerator for 2 hours, turning them every 30 minutes.

Preheat the oven to 300°F (150°C).
Cut the fennel bulbs in halves and remove the hearts. Blanch* in boiling water for a few minutes and refresh*.
Dice* the carrot and onion to make a mirepoix*. Sweat* the mirepoix in the butter in a roasting pan over low heat. Place the fennel halves in the pan. Pour over the white veal stock and add the bouquet garni.
Cover with parchment paper. Cook in the oven for 1 hour 15 minutes, turning the fennel halves over after about 35-40 minutes. You will need to have the oven at the same temperature to finish cooking the salmon steaks, so don't turn it off.
Remove the fennel from its braising liquid.
Strain the liquid through a chinois* and reduce* over low heat until the consistency is thick. Return the fennel halves to the roasting pan to keep them warm.
Heat the grill pan and oil it. Place the salmon steaks at an angle so that the final pattern will be diamond shaped. Sear* to make a diamond pattern on both sides. Place the salmon steaks on a baking tray and finish cooking them for 10-15 minutes in the oven.
Serve individually or in a large dish.

● Chef's note

Use tuna, sardines, or other fatty fish for this recipe.

Techniques

Instant marinade ›› p. 141
Braising vegetables ›› p. 96
Grilling ›› p. 102

Ingredients

1 whole salmon weighing about 2 lb. 10 oz. (1.2 kg)
3 fennel bulbs
$^1/_2$ carrot (50 g)
$^1/_2$ large onion
3 tablespoons (40 g) butter
4 cups (1 liter) white veal stock
(use a mix or see recipe p. 136)
1 bouquet garni*
$^1/_4$ cup (60 ml) oil
Fine salt, freshly ground pepper

Instant marinade
1 lemon
$^3/_4$ cup (200 ml) olive oil
A few sprigs of thyme
6 bay leaves
Five-pepper mix*

Ingredients

12 large langoustines
4 tablespoons (60 g) clarified butter*
1 celery branch (10 oz./300 g), for the batons
3 tablespoons (40 g) butter
A few sprigs of tarragon, for garnish
Fine salt, freshly ground pepper

Sauce

1 shallot, minced
1 small piece (1 ¹/₂ oz./40 g) celery stalk, diced*
A few sprigs of tarragon, leaves chopped
2 tablespoons (30 ml) cognac
²/₃ cup (150 ml) thick cream
Fine sea salt, freshly ground pepper

Tarragon-scented langoustines ★

Serves 4

Preparation time: 40 minutes
Cooking time: 35 minutes

Slice the langoustine into pieces comprising two segments. Break the claws in half and reserve the heads for the sauce. Heat a pan with the clarified butter and sauté the segments and claws. Season with salt and pepper.

Prepare the sauce. Remove the segments and claws from the pan and replace them with the heads. Sauté them for a few minutes and add the chopped shallot and diced celery. Flambé* with cognac. Pour in the cream and add the chopped tarragon.
Reduce* by half and strain through a fine-meshed conical sieve. Season.

Remove the tough outer fibers from the celery branch and cut it into batons about ¹/₅ in. (5 mm wide) and 2 in. (5-6 cm) long.
Stew them for a few minutes in the butter and ¹/₄ cup (50 ml) water. They should retain some of their crunch.
Arrange the langoustine pieces in soup plates and pour the sauce over them. Arrange the celery sticks attractively in rows at the side. Garnish with tarragon leaves.

● Chef's note

You can also make this recipe with lobster.

Techniques

Cutting into batons ›› p. 62
Cutting fish and shellfish into chunks ›› p. 69

Bacon-wrapped braised monkfish ★ ★

Serves 6

Preparation time: 35 minutes
Cooking time: 45 minutes

Prepare the monkfish: remove the skin, membranes, and violet-colored parts of the tail (see p. 67).
Preheat the oven to 275°F (140°C).
Bard the fish with the bacon slices and tie with twine.
Peel, wash, and finely dice* the vegetables to make a mirepoix*.
Lightly color the monkfish in a sauté pan.
Add the diced vegetables and pour in the fumet*. Add the bouquet garni.
Cover with the lid and cook in the oven for 20-30 minutes, depending on the size of the monkfish.
Remove the fish and keep it warm.

To make the sauce, reduce* the cooking liquid, add the cream, and reduce until thick. Whip in the butter.
Adjust the seasoning.

Remove the twine from the fish. Serve either whole or cut in individual portions. Pour over the sauce.

● Chef's note
It's important to have equal weights of the vegetables for the mirepoix.

Techniques
Filleting monkfish ≫ p. 67
Tying a roast ≫ p. 81

Ingredients
3 ¹/₂ lb. (1.5 kg) monkfish
12 slices bacon
¹/₂ carrot (1 ¹/₂ oz./40 g)
¹/₄-¹/₃ leek (1 ¹/₂ oz./40 g), white part only
¹/₃-¹/₂ celery stalk (1 ¹/₂ oz./40 g)
3 cups (750 ml) fumet (see p. 139)
1 bouquet garni

Sauce
²/₃ cup (150 ml) thick cream
3 ¹/₂ tablespoons (50 g) butter
Fine salt, freshly ground pepper

Special equipment:
ovenproof sauté pan with lid

Ingredients

6 fillets of John Dory
4 tablespoons (60 g) clarified butter*
3 lb. 5 oz. (1.5 kg) potatoes
2 tablespoons (30 g) kosher salt
A little dried seaweed, soaked, for garnish
1 lemon, for garnish
Fine salt, freshly ground pepper

Sauce
2 shallots
A little dried seaweed, soaked
Juice of 2 lemons
$^1/_4$ cup (60 ml) thick cream
1 stick (120 g) butter, cubed
Piment d'Espelette*
Fine salt
1 pinch sugar (optional)

Sautéed fillets of John Dory
with seaweed ★ ★

Serves 6
Preparation time: 40 minutes
Cooking time: 45 minutes

Preheat the oven to 325°F (160°C).
Season the fish fillets.
Heat a pan with the clarified butter and sauté them until lightly browned.
It will probably be necessary to finish cooking them in the oven for just
a few minutes.
Prepare the sauce. Finely chop the shallots. Chop the seaweed.
Place the shallots, the seaweed, and the lemon juice in a small pan. Reduce*
to a quarter of the original quantity.
Stir in the cream and whisk in the butter.
Season with salt and piment d'Espelette. If the sauce is too bitter because
of the seaweed, add a pinch of sugar.

Cut the potatoes into small oval shapes and put them in a pot. Cover them
with cold water and add the kosher salt. Bring to the boil and simmer for
about 20 minutes. Check for doneness with the blade of a small sharp knife.
The potato should fall apart immediately.
Arrange the fish fillets, potatoes, and sauce on a serving dish or on
individual plates. Garnish with seaweed and/or sliced lemon.

● **Chef's note**
If your seaweed is preserved in salt, blanch* it briefly in boiling water and
refresh* immediately in ice water.

Technique
Sautéeing ›› p. 121

Ingredients

3 plaice, weighing 1 1/4 lb. (600 g) each
3 eggs
Scant 1/2 cup (100 ml) oil plus oil for frying
3/4 cup (80 g) flour
1 cup (120 g) breadcrumbs
1 lemon, for garnish
Fine salt, freshly ground pepper

Sauce tartare

Yolks of 2 hard-boiled eggs
1 tablespoon (15 ml) French mustard*
1 teaspoon (5 ml) wine vinegar
3/4 cup (200 ml) sunflower seed oil
A few sprigs of chives
1 onion (3 oz./80 g)
1 pinch Cayenne pepper
Salt

Plaice *goujonnettes* with tartare sauce ★ ★

Serves 6
Preparation time: 45 minutes
Cooking time: 5 minutes

Remove the fins from the plaice and prepare the fillets (see p. 71). Remove the skin.
Wash and dab carefully to dry.
Cut the fillets into strips (see p. 70). Season with salt and pepper.
Beat the eggs with the oil. Prepare the fish strips for frying: dip first in the flour, then in the egg-oil mixture, and lastly in the breadcrumbs.

Prepare the sauce tartare (see p. 149). Make a mayonnaise, using hard-boiled egg yolks instead of raw egg yolks. Add the snipped chives and finely chopped onions. Season with salt and Cayenne pepper.

Pour just under 1/2 in. (1 cm) oil into a frying pan and heat. When it is hot, begin frying the first batch of strips (*goujonnettes*) for 1-2 minutes. Drain on paper towel. Filter the oil and repeat for the next batch.

Arrange the fried plaice on a serving dish or flat plates with a few lemon wedges. Serve the sauce tartare on the side.

● Chef's note
You can also use this recipe to prepare sole goujonnettes.

Techniques
Filleting fish (four flat fillets) ›› p. 71
Cutting strips (*goujonnettes*) ›› p. 70
Sauce tartare ›› p. 149
Crumbed sauté technique ›› p. 122

Mackerel in *escabèche* ★

Serves 6
Preparation time: 40 minutes
Cooking time: 15 minutes

Fillet the mackerel and remove the bones.
Roll them up and secure them with toothpicks or small wooden skewers.
Arrange them side-by-side in a deep pan.

Prepare the vegetable court-bouillon (see p. 135).
Bring the 2 cups (500 ml) of water and the wine to the boil.
Finely dice* the mushrooms (brunoise* size) and slice the lemon.
Add the peas, beans, baby carrots, and baby onions to the liquid. Simmer for 3-4 minutes.
Add the lemon slices, finely diced mushroom, bay leaves, peppercorns, and salt.
Bring to the boil again. As soon as it begins boiling, pour the liquid over the mackerel fillets.
Allow to cool gradually.

Place the mackerel fillets in soup plates and pour over the cold court-bouillon. Arrange the vegetables attractively around the fillets.

● Chef's notes
It's essential to have a court bouillon with a fine taste. There are many variations possible, depending on the herbs and vegetables available. You may also add a little seaweed to your court bouillon.

Techniques
Filleting fish (two round, flat fillets) ›› p. 70
Vegetable court bouillon ›› p. 135

Ingredients
6 mackerel
1 cup (250 ml) dry white wine
2 cups (500 ml) water
2 oz. (60 g) button mushrooms
1 unsprayed or organic lemon
2 oz. (60 g) peas
2 oz. (60g) French green beans
12 baby carrots
2 oz. (60 g) baby onions
2 bay leaves
$^3/_4$ teaspoon (2 g) peppercorns
Fine sea salt

Ingredients

3 $^1/_2$ lb. (1.5 kg) turbot
1 unsprayed or organic lemon
6 cups (1.5 liters) full cream milk
2 cups (500 ml) water
30 green cardamom seeds
2 tablespoon (30 g) kosher salt
$^3/_4$ teaspoon (2 g) peppercorns
1 lemon, for garnish
A few sprigs of dill, for garnish

Hollandaise sauce
$^1/_2$ cup (5 oz./140 g) clarified butter*
4 egg yolks
1 $^1/_3$ tablespoons (20 ml) water
Juice of 1 lemon
1 small pinch Cayenne pepper
Fine salt

Turbot poached in cardamom-flavored milk with hollandaise sauce ★★

Serves 6
Preparation time: 25 minutes
Cooking time: 35 minutes

Cut the turbot into chunks (see p. 69).
Slice the lemon.
Prepare the court bouillon. Bring the milk and water to the boil in a pot with the lemon slices, cardamom seeds, kosher salt, and peppercorns. Simmer for 2-3 minutes.
Strain through a fine-mesh sieve and refresh* over ice.
Place the pieces of turbot in a sauté pan. Cover with the court-bouillon and, over low heat, bring slowly to a temperature of 160°F (70°C). If you don't have a thermometer, turn off the heat as soon as the liquid begins to simmer. Leave for a few minutes and bring to the simmer again.
Maintain the liquid at this temperature for 12-15 minutes and turn off the heat.

Prepare the hollandaise sauce (see p. 148).
Heat the clarified butter.
Whisk the egg yolks with the water. Then put them in a bain-marie* or over very low heat and whisk until the consistency is that of a thick sabayon.
Whisk in the hot clarified butter. Season and stir in the lemon juice.

Remove the dark and white skin from the turbot pieces, as well as the central bone. Arrange the pieces in plates.
Drizzle the hollandaise sauce over some of the fish.
Garnish with the lemon segments (see p. 60), sprigs of dill, and the remaining cardamom seeds.

● Chef's notes
Other flat fish are suitable for this type of cooking, but they must be thick. Examples are halibut, flounder, and brill.
Substitute other aromatic ingredients, such as green tea, rosemary, and spices in the court-bouillon.

Techniques
Cutting fish and shellfish chunks ›› p. 69
Hollandaise sauce ›› p. 148
Citrus segments ›› p. 60

Sole meunière and potatoes cocotte ★★

Serves 4
Preparation time: 40 minutes
Cooking time: 30 minutes

Begin by preparing the garnish: chop the parsley and cut the lemon segments.
Remove the fins and scales from the soles.
Make an incision at the head and pull off the dark skin from the top side. (The other side does not need to have its skin removed.)
Wash, peel, and rinse the potatoes.
Cut them into oval shapes about 2 inches (5 cm) long.
Place them in a pan and cover with cold water.
Bring to the boil and leave to simmer for 2 minutes.
Drain them, but do not refresh*. Melt half the salted butter in a pan big enough to hold the potatoes in one layer and sauté them.
Dab the soles with paper towel to dry them. Season them with salt and dip them in the flour.
Shake gently to remove any excess.
Pour the clarified butter into an oval (or large) frying pan and heat over medium heat. Place the soles in the pan, white skin side downward. Leave them to brown gently.
Turn over and cook the other side in the same way. While they cook, brown the other half of the salted butter in a small pan.
Remove the fish from pan and spoon over the lemon juice and browned butter.
Place the soles on large flat plates. Sprinkle with chopped parsley and garnish with the lemon segments. Arrange the potatoes cocotte around.

● Chef's note
Purists do not remove any skin at all before cooking. They take it off afterwards so that the flesh of the sole is not soaked in butter.

Techniques
Citrus segments ≫ p. 60
Sauté meunière ≫ p. 121

Ingredients
4 soles
2 lb. (900 g) potatoes
2 ³/₄ tablespoons (40 g) plus 2 ³/₄ tablespoons (40 g) salted butter
¹/₂ cup (50 g) flour
4 tablespoons (60 g) clarified butter*
Juice of 1 lemon
1 lemon, in segments, for garnish (see p. 60)
A few sprigs of parsley, for garnish
Fine salt

Ingredients

1 monkfish tail weighing about 2 $^1/_2$ lb. (1.2 kg)
1 onion, for the rice
5 $^1/_2$ tablespoons (80 g) butter, for the rice
10 oz. (300 g) long-grained rice (tip: measure the rice in a cup. You will need 1 $^1/_2$ times the volume of liquid to cook it)
Bouquet garni*
Scant $^1/_4$ cup (50 ml) olive oil
Zest of 1 unsprayed or organic lemon, for garnish
A few sprigs of tarragon, for garnish
Fine salt, freshly ground pepper

Sauce américaine
6 small crabs
3 tablespoons (40 ml) olive oil
$^1/_2$ onion
$^1/_2$ shallot
$^1/_2$ carrot (1 $^1/_2$ oz./40 g)
$^1/_2$ tomato (20 g/$^2/_3$ oz.)
1 $^1/_2$ tablespoons (20 g) tomato paste
1 $^1/_3$ tablespoons (20 ml) cognac
Scant $^1/_2$ cup (100 ml) white wine
1 $^1/_4$ cup (300 ml) fish fumet*
2 garlic cloves, peeled, shoots removed
1 bouquet garni
A few sprigs of tarragon

For the roux
1 $^3/_4$ tablespoons (1 oz./25 g) butter
$^1/_4$ cup (25 g) flour

Techniques
Preparing monkfish ›› p. 67
Cutting medallions ›› p. 68
Sauce américaine ›› p. 146
Blond roux ›› p. 150
Shallow poaching (cold start) ›› p. 108

Monkfish medallions *à l'américaine* and rice pilaf ★★

Serves 6
Preparation time: 45 minutes
Cooking time: 50 minutes

Prepare the monkfish tail for cooking (see p. 67). Cut the fillets along the central bone.
Cut out six medallions (see p. 67) and flatten them slightly. Cover them in plastic wrap and chill.

Prepare the sauce américaine (see p. 146). Finely dice* the onion, shallot, and carrot to make a mirepoix*.
Cut the small crabs in halves. Sauté them over high heat in hot olive oil.
Turn down the heat. Add the mirepoix and sweat*.
Pour in the chopped tomato and add the tomato paste.
Flambé* with cognac, then add the white wine.
Reduce* by half and pour in the fish fumet.
Add the garlic cloves, the bouquet garni, and the whole tarragon leaves.
Simmer for 30 minutes, skimming when necessary.
Blend, with the shells, and strain through a very fine mesh sieve.
Prepare a cold blond roux (see p. 150) with the butter and flour. Pour the strained liquid over this and bring it all to the boil to thicken it.
Adjust the seasoning and set aside over a hot bain-marie*.

Preheat the oven to 250°F (120°C).
Peel, wash, and chop the onion. Sweat it in the 5 $^1/_2$ tablespoons (80 g) butter in an ovenproof pot.
Add the rice and cook until it is translucent.
Pour in 1 $^1/_2$ times the volume of cold water or fumet. Add the bouquet garni and season.
Bring to a simmer and cover with a lid of parchment paper (see DVD).
Place in the preheated oven to cook for 15-20 minutes. Test for doneness: all the liquid will have been absorbed and the rice should be the right texture.
Fluff the rice with a fork before serving.

Heat the olive oil in a sauté pan over medium heat. Season the monkfish medallions and cook without browning them.
Arrange them on individual plates or in a serving dish. Pour the sauce over. Garnish with grated lemon zest and chopped tarragon.

● **Chef's note**
Be careful to cook monkfish very briefly as it dries out quickly and becomes rubbery.

● **Did you know?**
If you use other crustaceans to prepare a sauce américaine, *it is given the name "crustacean sauce."*

Tagliatelle with fresh
and smoked salmon ★

Serves 6

Preparation time: 25 minutes
Cooking time: 15 minutes

Cook the tagliatelle in a large pot of boiling salted water and refresh* under cold water immediately.
Drizzle in a litle of the olive oil and mix through so that the tagliatelle do not stick.
Dice* both the fresh and smoked salmon, keeping them separate.
Sauté the cubes of fresh salmon in the remaining olive oil. Season and drain on paper towel.
Heat the tomato sauce.
Carefully combine all the ingredients.
Serve in a large dish or individual soup plates, topped with a leaf of basil.

Techniques

Deep poaching (hot start) >> p. 106
Tomato sauce >> p. 149

Ingredients

$^3/_4$ lb. (360 g) tagliatelle
1 tablespoon (20 g) kosher salt
$^1/_4$ cup (65 ml) olive oil
$^1/_2$ lb. (250 g) fresh salmon
7 oz. (200 g) piece smoked salmon
1 cup (250 ml) tomato sauce with basil
(see recipe p. 139)
A few sprigs of basil for garnish
Fine sea salt, freshly ground pepper

Ingredients

4 skate wings, skinned
$^1/_3$ cup (80 ml) olive oil
16 anchovy fillets in oil
16 pitted black olives
Juice of 1 lemon
1 lemon, sliced, for garnish
A handful of chopped parsley, for garnish
Fine sea salt, freshly ground pepper

Shredded skate wing with olives and anchovies ★★

Serves 4
Preparation time: 35 minutes
Cooking time: 20 minutes

Prepare the garnish: chop the parsley and slice one lemon.
Heat the olive oil in the sauté pan. Season the skate wings. When the oil is hot, cook each side of the wings, being careful not to burn them, and baste* them regularly with the oil.
To check for doneness, lift up the flesh next to the central bone. If it is quite white, then the fish is ready to eat. Remove it and keep warm.
Thread the anchovy fillets through the pitted olives and sauté them lightly. Deglaze* with the lemon juice.
Remove the fish from the wings and arrange it on plates. Pour the sauce from the pan over the shredded skate wings. Scatter with chopped parsley and garnish with slices of lemon.

● **Chef's note**
Skate is a fragile, cartilaginous fish that does not keep well. When buying skate, make sure that it is extremely fresh. If it still has its skin, it should be covered in a viscous substance. If the skin has been removed, smell it: there should be no odor at all.

Poultry

Jean-François Piège

presents his recipe

Lebanon is a country I know a little, and one I like to recreate in my cooking, suggesting its colors, the hustle and bustle of its markets, lingering moments over mezze, and early evening drinks that extend into the small hours.

When I think of Lebanon, the bright red of its plump, juicy tomatoes, the thin round breads hot out of the bakers' ovens, the generosity of its herbs, the abundant bunches of parsley, and all the flavors of the Mediterranean, lemons, olives, toasted sesame seeds ... and garlic—the essence of Lebanese cuisine—all come to mind.

The recipe I give here is an interpretation of shish taouk, a bouquet of flavor and freshness. It must be prepared ahead of time, but the simple generosity it conveys makes it well worth the effort. Serve it with arak, an aniseed-flavored liqueur, or a red Lebanese wine.

Free-range marinated chicken in pita, Lebanese-style

A day (or 12 hours) ahead

Marinate the chicken fillets. Mix together all the ingredients for the spice mix.Chop the flat-leaf parsley and slice the red onion finely.

Cut the tomatoes into quarters, remove the seeds, and cut them into strips.

Cut the chicken fillets into fine strips, ¼ in. (5 mm) wide.

Sprinkle the bottom of a dish with a third of the spice mix, place the chicken pieces on it, ensuring they are flat, scatter over half the onions, tomatoes, parsley, and another third of the spice mix. Repeat the procedure with the rest of the ingredients. Pour over the lemon juice and 4 tablespoons (60 ml) olive oil. Cover with plastic wrap and chill for at least 12 hours.

A day (or 12 hours) ahead
Chickpea purée (hummus)

Soak the chickpeas in water overnight or for 12 hours. Slice the shallot and drain the chickpeas. In a large pot with a little olive oil, sweat* the sliced shallot. Add the chickpeas to the pot. Pour in water to just under double the volume of the chickpeas. Add the unpeeled garlic cloves and the parsley stalks, and simmer for about 1 hour. Drain the chickpeas, reserving some of the liquid, and remove the parsley stalks and garlic cloves.

Place the chickpeas into the bowl of a food processor with a little of the cooking liquid. Add the juice of 1 lemon, a little sherry vinegar, and 3 tablespoons (45 ml) olive oil. Process for 5 minutes, adding more cooking liquid if necessary to obtain a soft texture. Transfer to a bowl and cover with plastic wrap flush with the surface of the purée.

To serve (or 12 hours later)
Prepare the pita bread

Remove the chicken fillets from the marinade, scraping off all the onions, tomatoes, and other ingredients. Season them with salt and grill rapidly on both sides, on a grill or in a very hot skillet without any fat. Drain the garnish ingredients and season with salt and freshly ground pepper. Set aside.

Preheat the oven to 400°F (200°C). Open the pitas. Combine the tomato paste and chopped garlic and spread the mixture inside the pitas. Spoon the chicken pieces, together with the marinade ingredients, into the pitas. Roll them up and place them on a baking dish. Cook for 4–5 minutes.

Tomato salad with sumac vinaigrette

Cut the two tomatoes into quarters. Set aside twenty large leaves of parsley and chop the rest. Make a vinaigrette with the sumac, lemon juice, and olive oil. Season the tomato quarters with salt and freshly ground pepper, and leave them to marinate. Scatter with chopped parsley and snipped young spring onions.

To assemble

On a flat plate, arrange an oval scoop of chickpea purée and some tomato quarters. Top the chickpea purée with a parsley leaf. Drizzle some marinade attractively round the plate. When the pitas are nice and crisp, cut them in two at an angle and arrange them on the plate.

Serves 4
Preparation time: 45 minutes
Marinating time: 12 hours or overnight
Cooking time: 1 hour 20 minutes

Ingredients

4 free-range chicken fillets
½ bunch flat-leaf parsley
1 red onion
2 tomatoes, fresh off the stalk
Juice of 1 lemon
4 tablespoons (60 ml) olive oil
4 pita breads
4 tablespoons (50 g) tomato paste
1 clove garlic, chopped
Salt, freshly ground pepper

Lebanese spice mix

1 tablespoon (10 g) cumin seeds, crushed
1 tablespoon (10 g) fennel seeds, crushed,
1 tablespoon (10 g) ground star anise
2 tablespoons (20 g) sumac
2 tablespoons (20 g) ground *piment d'Espelette**
1 tablespoon (10 g) thyme flowers, crushed
⅓ cup or 1 oz. (30 g) freshly shredded coconut
2 tablespoons (20 g) white sesame seeds, toasted

Chickpea purée (hummus)

14 oz. (400 g) dry chickpeas
1 long shallot
4 tablespoons (60 ml) olive oil
2 garlic cloves, unpeeled
1 bunch flat-leaf parsley, stalks only
Juice of 1 lemon
A little sherry vinegar
Salt, freshly ground pepper

Tomato salad with sumac vinaigrette

2 tomatoes, fresh off the stalk, or other tasty tomatoes
½ bunch flat-leaf parsley
1 generous pinch (2 g) sumac
Juice of 1 lemon
3 tablespoons (45 ml) olive oil
1 bunch young spring onions
Salt, freshly ground pepper

Bay-scented young guinea hen with canapés ★★

Serves 4

Preparation time: 40 minutes
Cooking time: 50 minutes

Dress* the young guinea hen and slip the bay leaves under its skin (see p. 76). Season the cavity with salt and pepper.

Preheat the oven to 350°F (180°C). Lightly grease a roasting pan with a little butter and place the guinea hen on it. Melt 1 $^1/_3$ tablespoons (20 g) butter and pour it over. Season the outside of the bird. Cook it for 15 minutes, then lower the temperature to 325°F (160°C) and cook for a further 20 minutes.

Hollow out the center of the sandwich loaf, leaving a border of $^3/_4$ in. (1.5 cm) all round. Fry the hollowed-out loaf in oil until it is light brown and drain on paper towel.

Prepare the stuffing (see p. 159). Dice* the bacon and remove the veins of the livers. Chop the shallot.

Sauté the bacon and liver on high heat, ensuring that the livers remain pink inside. Add the chopped shallots and flambé* with cognac.

Process the mixture, push through a fine-mesh sieve, and season with salt and pepper.

Boil the green beans in salted water. Lower the oven temperature to 300°F (150°C).

Melt the remaining butter. Make eight bundles with the beans, wrap a slice of bacon round each one, and pour the butter over them. Season with salt and pepper. Place the bundles on a roasting pan and cover them with aluminum foil. Heat the beans for 10-12 minutes. Fill the hollowed-out sandwich loaf with the stuffing and cut into thick slices to make the canapes. Place the guinea hen over the canapés, and arrange the bundles of green beans around it.

● Did you know?

Guinea fowl originated on the African continent; references to the bird on the tables of France are found from the Renaissance onward. Rabelais mentions them in Pantagruel. *The meat is more delicate and has less fat than that of chicken.*

Techniques
Encrusting poultry >> p. 76
Gratin stuffing >> p. 159
Roasting >> p. 118

Ingredients

1 young guinea hen
6 bay leaves
4 tablespoons (60 g) butter, divided
1 whole sandwich loaf (150 g)
A little oil for frying
1 lb. (500 g) green beans, prepared for boiling
8 thin rashers of bacon
Fine sea salt, freshly ground pepper

Gratin stuffing

3 oz. (80 g) cured bacon slab
4 $^1/_2$ oz. (120 g) chicken livers
1 shallot
2 teaspoons (10 ml) cognac
Fine sea salt, freshly ground pepper

Ingredients

1 duckling
3 ¹/₂ oz. (100 g) bard
3 tablespoons (40 ml) oil
1 ¹/₂ lb. (600 g) potatoes
2 tablespoons (30 g) plus 2 tablespoons (30 g)
clarified butter*
3 artichokes
Juice of 1 lemon
¹/₂ cup (50 g) flour
A few sprigs of flat-leaf parsley
1 orange, for garnish
Fine sea salt, freshly ground pepper

Sauce

2 unsprayed or organic oranges
Scant ¹/₂ cup (100 ml) wine vinegar
¹/₃ cup (70 g) sugar
2 teaspoons (10 ml) Cointreau or other
orange liqueur
1 ¹/₄ cups (300 ml) thickened brown veal stock
(made with a mix, or use recipe p. 138)
Fine sea salt, freshly ground pepper

Duckling à l'orange with sautéed potatoes and artichokes ★★

Serves 4
Preparation time: 1 hour 45 minutes
Cooking time: 1 hour 15 minutes

Preheat the oven to 325°F (160°C).
Dress* the duckling and season the cavity with salt and pepper. Truss* it (see p. 82).
Drizzle a little oil into an ovenproof pot and color the duckling all round. Season the outside of the duckling with salt and bard it. Tie with twine to keep the bard in place.
Put a tight-fitting lid on the pot and cook for about 1 hour 15 minutes in the oven.
Prepare the sauce. Cut fine julienne strips in the orange zest (see p. 59) and blanch* them three times.
Prepare a *gastrique* (see p. 140). Place the vinegar and the sugar in a saucepan.
Slowly bring to the boil and reduce* until it reaches a syrupy consistency. (This is the stage before it caramelizes.)
Deglaze* with the Cointreau and then add the juice of the oranges. Reduce again, and add the thickened brown veal stock and julienned orange zest. Season with salt and pepper.
Wash, peel, and rinse the potatoes. Cut them into cubes, sauté them in clarified butter, and season with salt.
Turn the artichokes (see p. 65). Squeeze lemon juice over them and cook them in a *blanc* (see Deep poaching method, p. 106). Cut them into cubes, sauté them in clarified butter, and season with salt.
Combine the two vegetables and scatter chopped parsley over them.
Cut the duck fillets into two or three thin strips, and cut the thighs into two pieces.
Arrange two or three thin strips and a piece of thigh on each plate and pour over the sauce.
Add the sautéed vegetables and garnish with orange slices and segments (see p. 60).

● **Chef's note**
Duck pairs marvelously with sweet-and-sour sauces, particularly those with a fruit base, such as peach, pineapple, and cherry.

Techniques
Dressing and trussing poultry ›› p. 82
Boiled vinegar and sugar (*gastrique*) ›› p. 140
Turning vegetables ›› p. 65
Deep poaching (hot start), preparing a *blanc* ›› p. 106
Citrus segments ›› p. 60

Quail stew and potatoes

à la boulangère ★★

Serves 6

Preparation time: 50 minutes
Cooking time: 1 hour

Preheat the oven to 375°F (190°C).

Dress* the quails and season the insides with salt and pepper. Truss* them (see p. 82). Drizzle a little oil over them, and a little more into an ovenproof sauté pan. Cook the quails for 8-10 minutes until they are lightly browned. At this stage, though, they should be barely cooked–carefully check the color of the juice, which should still be red, with the tip of a very fine knife.

Cut each quail in two along the backbone–each piece will have a leg, a wing, and a breast. Reserve the carcass for the sauce.

Drizzle a few drops of cognac over the quails and keep them warm.

Prepare the sauce. Finely chop the shallots. Crush the quail carcasses and return them to the same sauté pan in which you browned them briefly. Add the chopped shallots and sweat* them. Deglaze* with the red wine, add the bouquet garni and peppercorns, and reduce* by three-quarters. Heat the stock, pour it in, and bring back to the boil for a few minutes. Strain through a chinois* and whisk in the butter. Adjust the seasoning.

Wash, peel, and rinse the potatoes. Slice them into very thin disks ($^1/_{10}$ in./2 mm), and rinse once more to remove some of the starch.

Peel and wash the onions. Slice them thinly and sauté them in clarified butter until they are golden. Sauté the thin potato slices in clarified butter in another sauté pan.

Preheat the oven to 325°F (160°C).

Butter an ovenproof gratin dish and arrange the sliced potatoes and onions in alternate layers, seasoning as you go. Begin and end with a layer of potatoes. Pour in the white stock and cook for about 30 minutes.

Pour the sauce over the quail pieces in a sauté pan and finish cooking them over low heat (as you would a stew). Allow about 15 minutes for the thighs, and about 10 minutes for the wings, so put the wings in 5 minutes after the thighs.

Arrange a bed of potatoes *à la boulangère* on each plate, place two quail halves on it, and drizzle the sauce over.

● Chef's note

Cooking in two stages—roasting and then stewing—is a method typically used for small game birds. They contain little fat, and it is a method that prevents them from drying out.

● Did you know?

A dish called à la boulangère *(in the style of the baker's wife) was traditionally cooked in the baker's oven, after the bread baking was finished for the day and the oven had begun cooling.*

Techniques

Dressing and trussing poultry ›› p. 82
Game stew ›› p. 119

Ingredients

6 quails
2 tablespoons oil
A few drops of cognac
2 lb. (900 g) potatoes
3 large onions
7 tablespoons (100 g) butter,
clarified*, divided
1 $^1/_4$ cups (300 ml) thickened white poultry stock
Fine sea salt, freshly ground pepper

Sauce

2 shallots
1 $^1/_4$ cups (300 ml) red wine
1 bouquet garni*
6-8 peppercorns
1 scant cup (200 ml) thickened veal stock
(use a mix or see recipe p. 138)
3 tablespoons (40 g) butter, cubed
Fine sea salt, freshly ground pepper

Ingredients

6 turkey scaloppine (*escalopes*)

$^1/_2$ cup (50 g) flour

2 eggs

3 tablespoons (40 ml) oil, plus a little for frying

1 scant cup (100 g) ready-made breadcrumbs

2 tablespoons (30 g) butter

1 cup (250 ml) thickened brown veal stock
(an instant mix or see recipe p. 138)

A few sprigs of parsley, chopped, for garnish

1 lemon, for garnish

Fine sea salt, freshly ground pepper

Sautéed potatoes (without parboiling)

2 lb. 7 oz. (1.2 kg) potatoes

3 tablespoons (40 ml) oil

3 tablespoons (40 g) butter

Fine sea salt, freshly ground pepper

Crumbed turkey scaloppine with sautéed potatoes ★ ★ ★

Serves 6

Preparation time: 35 minutes

Cooking time: 20 minutes

Flatten the scaloppine (*escalopes*) evenly and trim them (see p. 86). Season them with salt and pepper.
Dust them with flour and then tap them lightly to remove any excess. Beat the two eggs with the oil.
Dip the scaloppine in the egg-oil mixture and then coat them in breadcrumbs. It is important not to leave them like this for more than 30 minutes before cooking.

Wash, peel, and rinse the potatoes.
Using a mandolin, slice them into very thin disks ($^1/_{10}$ in./2 mm). Rinse them under water and dry well with paper towel to remove any moisture.
Heat a non-stick pan with the oil and butter. Place a single layer of potato slices in the pan and cook them until they turn a hazelnut color. Turn them over and leave until they are the same color on the other side. Remove them from the pan, place on paper towel, and season. Repeat the procedure with successive layers of sliced potatoes until they are all done. Keep them warm.

Heat a nonstick pan with oil and butter over medium heat. Place the breaded scaloppine in the pan and cook until they are browned. Turn them over and cook until the same color. If they are not cooked through (test with the tip of a knife), finish them in the oven at 325°F (160°F) for a few minutes. Deglaze* the pan with the veal stock. Arrange the scaloppine in a serving dish or individual plates. Arrange the sautéed potato slices in concentric circles and sprinkle them with chopped parsley. Serve lemon wedges with the scaloppine, and pass round the sauce separately.

● Chef's note

It's best to cook the scaloppine as soon as you have breaded them, otherwise the crumbs become sticky.

Techniques

Preparing scaloppine >> p. 86

Crumbed sauté technique >> p. 122

Duck confit and potatoes sarladaises ★

Serves 6
Preparation time: 25 minutes
Marinating time: 12 hours, minimum
Cooking time: 1 hour 45 minutes

A day ahead
Remove the pin-feathers from the duck thighs (cylindrical, tough feather case) and any remaining feathers. Make superficial incisions in the skin. Trim the tips of the bones so that the meat can retract more easily during cooking. Leave in brine for at least 24 hours, minimum overnight.

To prepare
Rinse the duck thighs. Place a grilling rack at the bottom of a large pot and place the duck thighs on it. Cover the thighs with the fat and aromatic ingredients. Leave the garlic cloves unpeeled. Bring slowly to a simmer, and leave to cook for between 1 hour 30 and 1 hour 45 minutes.
Wash, peel, and rinse the potatoes. Use a mandolin to cut $1/10$-in. (2-mm) thick slices. Sauté them directly, without parboiling, in the duck fat until golden. Preheat the oven to 325°F (160°C). Combine the potatoes and the chopped parsley and garlic mixture. Add the truffle bits and season with salt and pepper.
Place the potatoes in a deep ovenproof dish, cover, and cook for about 30 minutes.
Serve the duck confit and sarladaises potatoes in separate dishes.

● Chef's notes
Filter the duck fat and reuse it next time you make a confit. Alternatively, use it to cook vegetables such as potatoes or Jerusalem artichokes.
Make brine by combining water with coarse sea salt (1 oz. salt per 4 cups water, 30 g per liter).

● Did you know?
Duck and duck fat are typical ingredients in the cooking of the Périgord region. A dish cooked à la sarladaise is prepared with duck or goose fat, and the name comes from the town of Sarlat, the capital of the Black Périgord region.

Technique
Slow cooking in oil or fat ›› p. 97

Ingredients
6 duck thighs
3 lb. (1.5 kg) duck or goose fat
(buy at specialty stores or online)
6 cloves pink garlic, unpeeled
2 bay leaves
8 peppercorns

Potatoes sarladaises
2 lb. 7 oz. (1.2 kg) potatoes
3 1/2 oz. (100 g) duck fat
1/2 bunch flat-leaf parsley
1/6 oz. (3 g) truffle bits
1 clove garlic
Fine sea salt, freshly ground pepper

Ingredients

4 chicken scaloppine *(escalopes)*
1 scant teaspoon (2 g) curry powder
2 tablespoons (30 g) butter
1 large onion
Scant $^1/_2$ cup (100 ml) soy cream
Fine sea salt, freshly ground pepper

Sautéed zucchini

2 zucchini (courgettes)
2 tablespoons (30 ml) olive oil
A few thyme flowers
Fine sea salt, freshly ground pepper

Sliced chicken curry

Serves 4
Preparation time: 25 minutes
Cooking time: 30 minutes

Cut the flattened chicken breasts into thin strips.
Season them with salt and pepper and sprinkle with curry powder.
Sauté the strips in half the butter in a sauté pan. Remove the chicken and keep it warm.
Chop the large onion and sweat* it in the remaining butter, then deglaze* with soy cream. Reduce* the liquid until thick. Adjust the seasoning and return the chicken to the pan.
Wash and canelle the zucchini (courgettes) (see p. 54).
Cut them into slices about $^1/_{10}$-$^1/_8$ in. (2-3 mm) thick. Heat the olive oil in a nonstick pan and sauté the slices, until just lightly browned.
Season and scatter with thyme flowers.
Arrange in individual plates or serving dishes.

Technique
Canelling >> p. 54

Rabbit stew with puréed
Golden Hubbard squash ★ ★

Serves 6
Preparation time: 45 minutes
Cooking time: 1 hour 10 minutes

Cut the raw rabbit into pieces (see p. 77). Season them with salt and pepper.
Melt the butter in an ovenproof pot or dish and lightly brown the rabbit
pieces over low heat.
Place them on a rack.

Preheat the oven to 350°F (170°C).
Thinly slice the mushrooms, chop the shallot, and snip the chives. Sauté
the mushrooms in the same pan in which you cooked the rabbit. Add the
chopped shallot and chives. Flambé* with cognac and deglaze* with the
white wine. Add the cream, the white stock, and the bouquet garni.
Return the rabbit pieces to the pot and cook for 1 hour with the lid on.
Remove the pieces from the pot. Strain the cooking liquid through a chinois*
and reduce* over low heat until thick enough to coat the back of a spoon*.
Season the sauce and return the rabbit pieces to the pan.

Peel and rinse the vegetables for the squash puree. Cut them into large
cubes. Place them in a pot, add the cold milk and a little grated nutmeg
and bring to the simmer. When the vegetables are tender, drain them and
process. Dry the purée out over low heat, stirring constantly so that it does
not burn. Stir in the butter and season with salt and pepper.

Cut the leek into julienne strips (see p. 59). Fry them in the oil and season
with salt.
Cook the All Blue potatoes in water, peel them, and slice finely.
Arrange the puréed squash in a circle on each plate and place a piece of
rabbit in the center. Drizzle with sauce. Place a small bunch of fried leek
white on top and garnish with a few slices of All Blue potatoes.

● **Chef's note**
*Try other vegetables, alone or in combination, to vary your purées. Broccoli,
carrots, and mushrooms are some ideas to start with.*

Techniques
Jointing rabbit >> p. 77
Julienne strips >> p. 59

Ingredients
1 rabbit
3 tablespoons (40 g) butter
5 oz. (150 g) button mushrooms
1 shallot
A few sprigs of chives
1 ½ tablespoons (20 ml) cognac
⅔ cup (150 ml) white wine
Scant ½ cup (100 ml) thick cream
2 cups (500 ml) thickened white chicken stock (use
an instant mix or see recipe p. 136)
1 bouquet garni*
2 small leeks (150 g), white part only, for garnish
A little oil for frying
3 ½ oz. (100 g) All Blue potatoes, for garnish
Fine sea salt, freshly ground pepper

Puréed Golden Hubbard squash
1 ¾ lb. (800 g) Golden Hubbard squash or
Hokkaido Orange
3 carrots (7 oz./200 g)
10 oz. (300 g) potatoes
4 cups (1 liter) milk
A little grated nutmeg
4 tablespoons (60 g) butter
Fine sea salt, freshly ground pepper

Ingredients

4 duck fillets
2 unsprayed or organic limes, sliced
2 ½ tablespoons (50 g) runny honey
1 ½ lb. (600 g) zucchini (courgettes)
Scant ¼ cup (50 ml) oil
A few sprigs of thyme
Fine sea salt, freshly ground pepper

Sauce
2 tablespoons (40 g) honey
Juice of 1 lime
Scant ¼ cup (50 ml) soy sauce
Freshly ground pepper

Lime- and honey-scented duck fillets on a bed of zucchini ★

Serves 4
Preparation time: 35 minutes
Cooking time: 30 minutes

Preheat the oven to 375°F (190°C).
Remove all visible nerves as well as the pin-feathers (cylindrical, tough feather case) from the duck fillets. Grill briefly skin-side down, making a diamond pattern, and season with salt and pepper.
On the other side, make small incisions ⅕ in. (5 mm) deep in which to slip the half-slices of lime.
Drizzle the honey and grind some pepper over each piece of duck.

Wash the zucchini and canelle them (see p. 54).
Slice them thinly (about ⅙ in. or 3 mm). Sauté them in oil and season with salt and pepper. Keep warm.

Heat another sauté pan without any fat. When it is really hot, place the duck fillets in it, skin side down. Leave to brown over medium heat. When the skin is browned, transfer the fillets to the oven. Cook for 7-10 minutes, until the desired doneness.

Prepare the sauce. Place the honey and lime juice in a small saucepan and reduce* until it reaches a thick consistency.
Deglaze* with the soy sauce and season with pepper.

Arrange the zucchini slices in a circle and scatter with thyme. Place the duck fillet in the middle and drizzle with sauce.

● **Chef's notes**
Duck breast is best when pink, rare even.
Although a wide range of honeys are available, with correspondingly varied tastes, a multi-floral honey is best for cooking.

● **Did you know?**
The description "magret" is used only for the breast of a duck fattened for its foie gras.

 Technique
Canelling >> p. 54

Stuffed chicken legs with chestnuts ★★

Serves 8
Preparation time: 1 hour 10 minutes
Cooking time: 45 minutes

Cut each chicken into four pieces (two wings and two thighs).
Remove the small fillet from the wings and cut off the tips of the wing bones.
Remove the thigh bone and the drumstick bone, being careful not to cut
the meat (see p. 77). Set aside 1/2 lb (250 g) of the chicken meat to use for the
stuffing.
Season this meat with salt and pepper.
Prepare the mousseline stuffing (see p. 157). Place the seasoned meat in the
bowl of a food processor and with the blade attachment grind it finely. Add
the egg white and process for a few more seconds.
Push the stuffing through a sieve.
Transfer it to a stainless steel bowl over a bowl of ice water. Gradually stir in
the cream.
Fill the wings and thighs with the stuffing. Fold over the meat to form nice
plump thighs, and roll them in caul. If necessary, tie with kitchen twine.

Preheat the oven to 350°F (170°C).
Finely dice* the shallots and celery to make a mirepoix*.
Melt 3 tablespoons (50 g) butter in a pot or sauté pan and brown the chicken
pieces. Remove from the heat and add the diced shallots and celery. Add a
few sage leaves. Put the chicken pieces back into the pot. Cover the pot or
pan and cook for about 35 minutes in the oven until the chicken is cooked
through.
Transfer the chicken pieces to another dish. Reduce* the cooking liquid and
strain it through a chinois*. Season it and return the chicken pieces to the
pot.
Prepare a pot of boiling water. Make one incision on the rounded side of each
chestnut. When the water is boiling, add the chestnuts and boil them for
3 minutes. Remove the skin while they are still hot, taking care not to burn
yourself.
Melt the 4 tablespoons (60 g) of butter over the chestnuts and coat them.
Season just before serving. Place in a serving dish or on individual plates.
Drizzle the sauce over the chicken pieces and surround them with chestnuts.
Garnish with edible marigolds and sage leaves, or other seasonal flowers.

● Chef's notes
*Fall is chestnut season. Fall is also the season for other fruits and vegetables
that make excellent side dishes for this recipe, like pears, apples, stewed leeks,
and cabbage. Try roasting the chestnuts on a wood fire—this will give them a
lovely color and impart a slight grilled taste to them.*

Techniques
Cutting up raw, dressed* poultry >> p. 77
Stuffing a chicken leg >> p. 89
Mousseline stuffing (cream-based) >> p. 157

Ingredients
2 free-range or organically raised chickens,
around 2 1/2 lb. (1 kg) each
10 oz. (300 g) caul*
3 tablespoons (50 g) butter, to sauté the chicken
2 shallots
2 celery stalks (100 g)
5 sage leaves
3 1/2 lb. (1.6 kg) chestnuts
4 tablespoons (60 g) butter, for the chestnuts
8 marigolds, fresh or dried
Fine sea salt, freshly ground pepper

Mousseline stuffing
1 egg white
1 scant cup (200 ml) whipping cream
Fine sea salt, freshly ground pepper

Ingredients

3 squab (pigeons)
1 large onion
1 large leek (100 g), white part only
7 tablespoons (100 g) butter, divided (to sear* the squab, glaze* the onions, and stew the lettuce)
3 cups (750 ml) thickened white chicken stock (use an instant mix or see recipe p. 136)
Scant ¹/₂ cup (100 ml) thick cream
2 lb. (1 kg) garden peas
3-4 new onions (4 ¹/₂ oz./120 g)
1 ¹/₂ tablespoons (20 g) sugar
1 lettuce
Fine sea salt, freshly ground pepper

Squab fricassee and garden peas
à la française ★ ★

Serves 6
Preparation time: 50 minutes
Cooking time: 45 minutes

Cut the squab in half. Bone each half partially, removing most of the superficial bones, and season with salt and pepper.
Peel, wash, and finely chop the large onion. Slit the leek white in two lengthwise and cut into fine slices (*à la paysanne*).

Preheat the oven to 350°F (170°C).
Sear the squab halves in a pot with half of the butter, ensuring that they do not brown.
Add the chopped onion and sliced leek white, and sweat* with the lid on.
Cover the contents of the pot with the chicken stock, and place in the oven, still with the lid on, for 30-35 minutes.
Remove the squab pieces.
Reduce* the cooking liquid until it is thick. Add the thick cream (spoon a little hot liquid into the cold cream, mix, and then put it all into the pot) and reduce again until the sauce coats the back of a spoon.
Strain through a chinois*, season with salt and pepper, and return to the pot.
Return the squab pieces to the pot to keep them warm.

Prepare a pot of salted boiling water and boil the peas.
Glaze* the new onions with 1 ¹/₃ tablespoons (20 g) butter and the sugar (see p. 101).
Shred the lettuce (make a chiffonade–see p. 56) and braise it in 2 tablespoons (30 g) butter and a scant ¹/₄ cup (50 ml) water.
Combine the garden peas, onions, and shredded lettuce in a sauté pan.
Season with salt and pepper.
Serve the fricassee in a casserole dish, surrounded by the vegetables.

● **Chef's note**
This recipe may be used with most types of poultry.

● **Did you know ?**
Until the French Revolution, only the nobility enjoyed squabs. Today, they are still considered to be a refined dish for special occasions. La Varenne (1618–1678) wrote a recipe for squab with peas (it included lettuce and bacon bits) that is still found on French tables.

Techniques
Simple slicing (*émincer à la paysanne*) ›› p. 55
Brown braising ›› p. 94
Glazing vegetables ›› p. 101
Shredding (chiffonade) ›› p. 56

Grilled cockerel and *diable* sauce ★ ★

Serves 4

Preparation time: 1 hour
Cooking time: 50 minutes

Preheat the oven to 350°F (170°C).
Cut the cockerels in two, lengthwise, along the backbone. Remove the bones from the ribcage, the wishbone, and the cartilage attached to it.
Heat a ridged grill pan.
Brush the skin of the cockerel with oil, and grill the pieces on the pan, making a diamond pattern with the ridges, skin side first, and then flesh side. Place them on a baking tray.
Baste* the skin with mustard using a pastry brush, and sprinkle with breadcrumbs. Cook the cockerels for 25-30 minutes. (You will need to have the oven at the same temperature to broil the vegetables afterward.)

Wash, peel, and rinse the potatoes. Cut them into wafers (see p. 63) using a mandolin. Rinse twice and dry thoroughly, dabbing with paper towel to remove any excess moisture.

Peel the garlic, remove the shoots, and chop. Wash the tomatoes, remove the stems, and cut them in half. Season them with salt and pepper, and then with the herbes de Provence and chopped garlic. Drizzle a little oil and place 1 bay leaf on each piece. Arrange them on a roasting pan. Rinse the mushrooms and dry them well. Baste them with oil and grill them, cap side down. Remove the stems and place the caps in the roasting pan with the tomatoes. Season the vegetables with salt and pepper.

Prepare the *diable* sauce. Peel and wash the shallots and chop them. In a small saucepan, place the shallot, mignonette pepper, vinegar, and dry white wine.
Reduce* slowly, over low heat, until almost dry. Pour in the veal stock and add the chopped tarragon leaves.

Place the vegetables in the oven and cook for 10-15 minutes, until softened.
Fry the potato wafers and drain well.
Cut the cockerel pieces in two and serve one wing and one thigh to each person. Serve the vegetables and the sauce separately.

● Chef's note

Use this recipe for other types of poultry, whole or in pieces.

Techniques
Wafers » p. 63
Grilling » p. 102

Ingredients

2 cockerel (young cock of about 1 lb./500 g)
Scant 1/3 cup (70 ml) oil
2 1/2 tablespoons (40 g) French mustard*
1/2 cup (60 g) packaged breadcrumbs
3 tablespoons (40 ml) oil
1 1/2 lb. (600 g) potatoes
4 cloves garlic
2 tomatoes
A little herbes de Provence*
4 bay leaves
4 button mushrooms
Fine sea salt, freshly ground pepper

Diable sauce
2 shallots
1 teaspoon (2 g) mignonette pepper
3 1/2 tablespoons (50 ml) red wine vinegar
3 1/2 tablespoons (50 ml) dry white wine
1 cup (250 ml) thickened brown veal stock (use an instant mix or see recipe p. 138).
A few sprigs of tarragon, leaves chopped

Ingredients

6 chicken breasts

3 tablespoons (40 g) butter, to sauté the chicken

2 cups (500 ml) vegetable broth

2 tablespoons (20 g) cornstarch *or* 1 ¹/₂ tablespoons (20 g) butter, to thicken the sauce (optional)

2 bunches of baby vegetables, such as carrots, zucchini (courgettes), fennel, onions

2 tablespoons (30 g) butter, clarified*, for the vegetables

Fine sea salt, freshly ground pepper

Chicken breasts with baby vegetables ★

Serves 6

Preparation time: 30 minutes

Cooking time: 35 minutes

Preheat the oven to 350°F (170°C).

Trim the skins of the breasts and make incisions in the skin. Season with salt and pepper. Sauté them, skin side down, in the butter, using an ovenproof pan or skillet. Pour the vegetable broth over the chicken pieces. Finish the cooking in the oven. This will take 25-30 minutes. Remove the chicken breasts from the pan and reduce* the cooking liquid to one quarter of its volume. Use a little butter or starch to thicken it. (Whisk in 1 ¹/₂ tablespoons (20 g) butter, or dilute 2 tablespoons (20 g) cornstarch in a little liquid before pouring it into the liquid. Bring to the boil and remove from the heat.)

Adjust the seasoning.

Cook the vegetables separately in a pot of salted boiling water.

To remove the thin skin of the carrots when they are cooked, simply press them downward with your fingers.

Give the vegetables a nice gloss by brushing them with the clarified butter.

Cut the breasts into thin strips. Arrange the chicken pieces in the plates with the baby vegetables in attractive rows.

● Chef's note

Baby vegetables are best left slightly crunchy, so don't over-boil them. If you use this boiling method, you can also marinate them afterward.

Meats

Régis Marcon
presents his recipe

In Auvergne, my region, meat used to be cooked in a broth with hay. Mountain hay in particular is very flavorful—it is packed with sweet-smelling grasses and flowers, especially spignel, an aromatic plant that grows wild in pastures. And naturally, it is organic. A method my mother used to cook rabbit by coating it in wild thyme gave me the idea of preparing lamb in a hay-scented crust. I serve the lamb in a juice infused with a little hay, and use what is known as *épice au loup* (literally, the wolf's spice), a ground mixture of garlic, dried orange peel, ginger, juniper, and black pepper, in homage to the wonderful Suzanne Robaglia who, in 1935, published *Margaridou*, far more than just a cookery book, on the traditional recipes of Auvergne.

Lamb cooked in a spignel-scented hay crust, épice au loup, and seasonal vegetables

To prepare
Trim and season the leg of lamb. Brown it all round over high heat and set it aside. Prepare your seasonal vegetables. Boil them separately in the white chicken stock.

To make the *jus*
Heat the lamb *jus* with a little hay. Leave to infuse, then strain through a chinois* and season.

Method
Roll out the bread dough and cover it with the remaining hay. Place the leg of lamb in the center and wrap the dough around it. Cook at 400°F (200°C) for about 45 minutes.

To finish
Melt the butter with the pork belly and glaze* the cooked vegetables in the mixture.

To serve
Cut open the hay crust and remove the leg of lamb to slice it. Place a slice on each plate and arrange the vegetables attractively around it. Drizzle with sauce.

Serve the spice mixture separately.

Serves 4
Preparation time: 35 minutes
Cooking time: 1 hour

Ingredients
1 leg of milk-fed lamb
1 1/2 lb. (650 g) of your choice of seasonal vegetables
4 1/4 pints (2 liters) white chicken stock
1 2/3 cups (400 ml) prepared lamb *jus** (make ahead or buy at specialty stores)
1 handful of spignel-scented hay
2 lb. 4 oz. (1 kg) of herb-scented bread dough
3 tablespoons (40 g) butter
4 slices of rolled pork belly
Épice au loup (ground juniper, ginger, dried garlic, dried orange peel, black pepper)
Salt, pepper

Grilled rib roast and béarnaise sauce ★★

Serves 8

Preparation time: 30 minutes
Cooking time: 25 minutes

Trim the ribs and tie them with twine so that they maintain their shape.
Make sure the rack of your barbecue is clean and begin heating it, or heat a
ridged grill pan.
Lightly oil the beef and sear* each side, making a diamond pattern. Leave
it to cook until it reaches the desired degree of doneness. If you prefer your
meat well done, finish cooking it in a hot oven, heated to 350°F (180°C), for a
few minutes.
When it is done, sprinkle with fleur de sel and mignonette pepper.
Wrap it well in aluminum foil and leave to rest in a warm place.

Prepare the béarnaise sauce (see p. 147). Peel, wash, and finely chop the
shallots.
Pour the white wine, vinegar, shallots, and a little tarragon into a saucepan
and prepare the reduction* over low heat. While the sauce reduces, melt the
clarified butter and keep it warm.
Do not reduce until dry; there should be a few tablespoons of liquid left and
the shallots will be moist. Most of the acidity will have disappeared.
Add the egg yolks to the reduction with 5 tablespoons (75 ml) water. Place
the pot over hot water (bain-marie*) or very low heat and whisk until the
consistency is nice and thick–it should resemble a sabayon (see p. 50).
Pour in the warm melted butter gradually, continuing to whisk. Add the salt.
Strain through a fine-mesh sieve and serve immediately.

Cut the beef, parallel to the bone, into strips. Place them in a serving dish
so that the guests can immediately see which portion is done to their taste.
Serve the sauce separately, in a sauce dish.

● Chef's notes

*Potatoes or green vegetables are the classic, and still much appreciated, side
dishes for this cut of beef.*
*Bear in mind that the resting time for the beef is the same as the time you
will need to make the sauce; get all your ingredients and equipment ready
beforehand.*

Technique
Grilling ›› p. 102
Béarnaise sauce ›› p. 147

Ingredients
2 double-cut rib steaks (prime beef)
about 2 lb. (1 kg) each
3 tablespoons (40 ml) oil, for cooking
1 teaspoon (4 g) fleur de sel
1 teaspoon (2 g) mignonette pepper

Béarnaise sauce
2 shallots
Scant ½ cup (100 ml) dry white wine
Scant ¼ cup (50 ml) wine vinegar
A few sprigs of tarragon
2 sticks (220 g) unsalted butter, clarified*
5 egg yolks
1 teaspoon (2 g) mignonette pepper
Fine salt

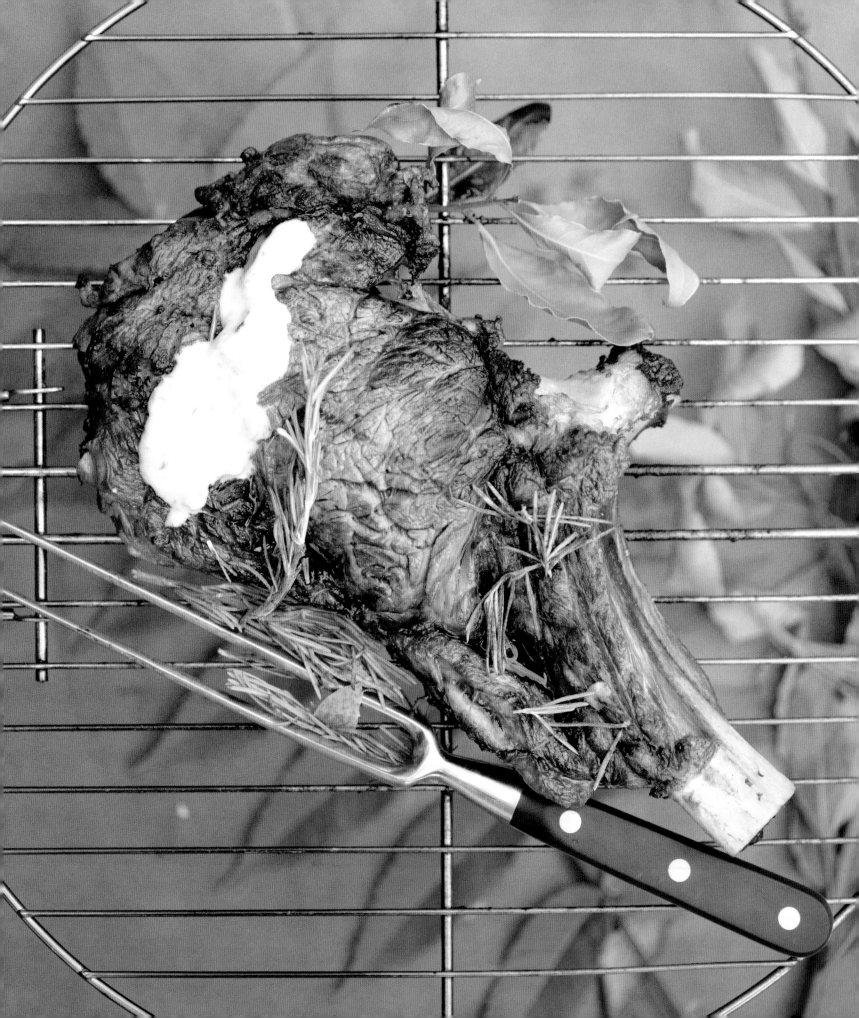

Ingredients
1 shoulder of lamb
3 cloves garlic, unpeeled
3 ½ tablespoons (50 ml) olive oil
Salt, freshly ground pepper

Vegetable tian
2 large onions
2 tomatoes
1 zucchini (courgette)
1 eggplant (aubergine)
3 ½ tablespoons (50 ml) olive oil
A scattering of herbes de Provence*
A few sprigs of basil
Salt, freshly ground pepper

Pistou
4 garlic cloves, peeled, shoots removed
½ bunch basil
3 ½ tablespoons (50 ml) olive oil
Juice of 1 lemon

Provençal shoulder of lamb and vegetable *tian* ★ ★

Serves 5
Preparation time: 50 minutes
Cooking time: 55 minutes

Preheat the oven to 425°F (220°C).
Bone the shoulder (see p. 78).
Prepare the *pistou*. Crush the garlic cloves with the basil leaves using a pestle and mortar. Drizzle the olive oil in as you crush and then thin with the lemon juice.
Brush the cavity with the *pistou* (see p. 144) and season with salt and pepper. Roll the shoulder up and tie with twine (see p. 81). Baste* it with oil and season with salt and pepper. Cook for 10 minutes, then lower the temperature to 350°F (170°C). Add the garlic cloves and cook for a further 15 minutes.
Remove the lamb from the baking dish, wrap it in aluminum foil, and keep warm. You will need to have the oven at the same temperature for the vegetable *tian*.

Peel and wash the onions and wash all other the vegetables. Cut them into disks ¹/₁₀ in. (2-3 mm) thick (see p. 56).
Oil a baking dish. Arrange the vegetable slices–tomatoes, zucchini, onions, and eggplant–vertically in rows. It's best to alternate all the vegetables in each row, rather than placing one vegetable in each row.
Scatter with herbes de Provence, tuck in a few sprigs of basil, drizzle over a little olive oil, and season with salt and pepper.
Cook the vegetables for 30 minutes until soft, allowing them to stew a little in their own liquid.

Heat the plates before serving and cut up the meat as it is required.

● Chef's note
Try to select vegetables that are the same diameter. This will make it easier to put your tian *together and your presentation will be just that much more attractive.*

● Did you know?
A tian *is a Provençal earthenware baking dish used to make gratins. It has given its name to this assortment of typically southern vegetables, cooked to a confit texture, that accompany the lamb flavored with olive oil and basil, other typical ingredients of the region.*

Techniques
Boning a Shoulder of Lamb >> p. 78
Cutting round slices >> p. 56

Medallions of veal, green lentils, and horn of plenty mushrooms ★★

Serves 6
Preparation time: 35 minutes
Cooking time: 40 minutes

Cut twelve thin round medallions of veal, about $1/3$ in. (1 cm) thick. Season them with salt and pepper.

Peel and wash the carrot and the onion, and remove the shoots from the garlic cloves. Chop the vegetables into thick sticks so that you can remove them from the lentils before serving if you wish; if you intend to serve them with the lentils, chop them finely.
Place the lentils in a pot and pour in twice their volume of cold water (see poaching method p. 109). Add the aromatic garnish (carrot, onion, garlic, bay leaves, cloves, and smoked bacon) and bring to the boil. Leave to simmer gently until cooked, about 15 minutes.

Brush the horn of plenty mushrooms, wash them if necessary, and cut them in half lengthwise. Sauté them half of the butter and then add them to the lentils. Remove the piece of bacon and season the lentils.

Heat a sauté pan. Melt the remaining butter and place the veal medallions in to brown on both sides. Check for doneness and transfer to a rack, keeping them warm.

Make the sauce: chop the shallots and sweat* them in the same sauté pan. Flambé* them with the cognac. Add the veal stock, and whip in the butter. Season with salt and pepper.
Spoon servings of lentils in soup plates and arrange the veal medallions on top. Pour the sauce over.

● Chef's note
You can replace medallions of veal with loin chops.

Techniques
Cutting medallions and noisettes ›› p. 91
Shallow poaching (cold start) ›› p. 108

Ingredients
2 lb. (900 g) veal fillet (filets mignons or chops)
$1/4$ carrot
1 large onion
2 garlic cloves
14 oz. (400 g) green lentils,
if possible *lentilles vertes du Puy AOC*
2 bay leaves
2 cloves
$1 1/2$ oz. (40 g) slab smoked bacon
2 oz. (60 g) horn of plenty
or black trumpet mushrooms
5 tablespoons (70 g) butter
Salt, freshly ground pepper

Sauce
2 shallots
$1 1/3$ tablespoons (20 ml) cognac
1 cup (250 ml) brown veal stock
3 tablespoons (40 g) butter, cubed
Salt, freshly ground pepper

Ingredients

3 ½ lb. (1.6 kg) stewing beef

4 cups (1 liter) red Burgundy wine

½ carrot

1 large onion

¼ cup (60 ml) oil

6 cups (1.5 liters) thickened brown veal stock (use an instant mix or see recipe p. 138)

1 bouquet garni*

3 garlic cloves, peeled, shoots removed

5 oz. (150 g) slab bacon

3 ⅓ tablespoons (50 g) butter

7 oz. (200 g) button mushrooms

5 oz. (150 g) new onions

1 ½ tablespoons (20 g) sugar

Salt, freshly ground pepper

Fresh pasta

2 ½ cups (220 g) cake flour

2 eggs, beaten

1 ½ tablespoons (20 ml) oil

1 teaspoon (5 g) table salt

Boeuf bourguignon with fresh pasta ★★

Serves 8

Preparation time: 40 minutes

Resting and drying time: 12 hours (for pasta dough)

Cooking time: 2 hours 45 minutes

A day ahead

Prepare the fresh pasta (see p. 15).

Sift the flour. Beat the eggs and combine with the oil and salt. Make a well in the center and pour in the liquid ingredients. Rapidly knead* the ingredients so that they form a ball. Do not overwork or else the dough will become too elastic.

Chill for 30 to 45 minutes.

Roughly spread the dough out using a pastry roller, then process it through a pasta maker. Use the pasta maker to cut out tagliatelle (p. 15: images 5, 6). Allow the pasta to dry for several hours before using it.

To prepare the main dish

Pour the wine into a pot and reduce* it by half over high heat. While it is simmering, peel and wash the carrot piece and the onion. Dice* them to make a mirepoix*. Oil a sauté pan and, over high heat, brown the meat. Add the diced carrot and onion.

Lower the heat and sweat* the vegetables. When they have softened, pour in the reduced red wine and veal stock. Add the bouquet garni and garlic cloves. Bring to a simmer and cover with the lid. Now you may either leave it on low heat, or cook in the oven at 325°F (160°C), for 2 ½ hours.

Cut the bacon into lardons, making sure you leave no rind or cartilage. Place them in a pot of cold water to blanch* them. When they are done, lightly butter a pan to sauté them.

Wash the mushrooms, pat them dry immediately, and quarter them (see p. 58). Place a knob of butter in a pan and sauté the mushrooms over high heat until all their liquid evaporates. When they are done, season them with salt and freshly ground pepper.

Glaze* the baby onions with the sugar until brown (see p. 101).

Cook the pasta in a large pot of boiling salted water.

Remove the pieces of beef from the pot. Strain the sauce through a chinois* and reduce it if there is too much or if it is thin.

Season the sauce and return the meat to the pot with the mushrooms, onions, and lardons.

Serve in a large serving dish or individual soup plates.

● Chef's notes

Cooking this dish in the oven is preferable to cooking it over the stove top as the heat will be more evenly distributed.

Boeuf bourguignon is excellent when reheated a day later.

Techniques

Pasta dough ›› p. 15

Quartering button mushrooms ›› p. 58

Glazing vegetables ›› p. 101

Roast veal with balsamic reduction ★ ★

Serves 8

Preparation time: 35 minutes
Cooking time: 1 hour 55 minutes

Preheat the oven to 350°F (180°C). Trim the veal roast and tie it with twine.
Place it in a large pot or Dutch oven and pour over the clarified butter. Season
with salt and pepper. Place over low heat and brown lightly. Deglaze* with
balsamic vinegar.
Place the pot in the oven and cook for 1 hour 45 minutes, turning the roast
over every 20 minutes.
Wash, peel, and rinse the carrots. Turn them (see p. 65) to make oblong
shapes 2 in. (5 cm) long.
Place the carrots in a pot and cover with water. Add 4 tablespoons (60 g)
butter, a little salt, and the sugar.
Cover with a parchment paper lid (see DVD for technique) and bring to the
boil.
When all the water has evaporated (by now, the carrots should be easy to
cut), coat them in the butter and sugar mixture by whirling them in the pot.
Place the dried plums and red wine in a saucepan. Slowly bring to a simmer
and remove from the heat.
When the veal roast is done, remove it from the pot and cover it with
aluminum foil to keep it warm.
Remove the fat from the cooking liquid and whip in the remaining
4 tablespoons (60 g) butter.
Adjust the seasoning. Slice the meat, arrange it in a dish, and pour the sauce
over. Surround the sliced veal with carrots and dried plums.

Techniques
Turning vegetables ›› p. 65
Glazing vegetables ›› p. 101

Ingredients
3 ½ lb. (1.6 kg) boneless veal roast
3 tablespoons (40 g) butter, clarified*
⅔ cup (150 ml) balsamic vinegar
4 lb. (1.8 kg) carrots
¼ cup (2 ¼ oz./60 g) plus ¼ cup (2 ¼ oz./60 g) butter
3 ½ tablespoons (40 g) sugar
7 oz. (200 g) dried plums (prunes)
Scant ½ cup (100 ml) red wine
Salt, freshly ground pepper
Special equipment: a large ovenproof pot or Dutch oven

Ingredients

4 lb. (2 kg) boned shoulder
of lamb
1 large onion
3 garlic cloves
3 ¹/₃ tablespoons (50 ml) oil
Scant ²/₃ cup (60 g) flour
Scant ¹/₂ cup (100 ml) white wine
3 tablespoons (40 g) tomato paste
1 bouquet garni*
Salt, freshly ground pepper

Sautéed turnips
3 lb. (1.5 kg) turnips
4 tablespoons (60 g) butter
3 ¹/₂ tablespoons (40 g) sugar
Salt

Lamb stew with turnips (*navarin*) ★ ★

Serves 8
Preparation time: 35 minutes
Cooking time: 1 hour 25 minutes

Preheat the oven to 350°F (180°C).
Trim the lamb and cut it into 2-2 ¹/₂ oz. (60-70 g) pieces.
Dice* the large onion to mirepoix* size.
Peel, wash, and crush the garlic cloves.
Heat a low-sided pan over high heat and pour in the oil. Brown the pieces of lamb evenly all over.
Tip the pan to the side to remove the fat, holding the lid to retain the lamb. (Cool the fat before discarding it.)
Add the diced onion and leave it to sweat* with the lid on.
When it is translucent, sprinkle the flour over. Place the pot in the oven for 5 minutes (this will cook the starch). Pour in the white wine, and add enough water to just cover the meat. Then add the tomato paste, bouquet garni, and garlic, and season with salt and pepper.
Cover with the lid and cook for 1 hour 15 minutes.

Peel and wash the turnips, and cut them into quarters.
Gently stew them with butter, sugar, salt, and a little water for 7-8 minutes.
Check for doneness with the tip of a knife, which should slide in easily.

Skim the surface of the lamb stew and remove the fat when you take the pot out of the oven. Remove the bouquet garni.
Serve the meat and turnips separately.

● **Chef's note**
The turnip quarters will be considerably tastier if you use the cooking liquid from the meat instead of water.

 Technique
Gentle stewing >> p. 98

Ingredients

2 veal kidneys
2 tablespoons (30 g) butter, clarified*
1 tablespoon (20 ml) red port
Scant ¼ cup (50 ml) thick cream
Scant ½ cup (100 ml) thickened brown veal stock
(use an instant mix or see recipe p. 138)
1 scant tablespoon (20 g) *moutarde à l'ancienne,*
French mustard* with crushed brown mustard
seeds (from specialty stores or online)
Salt, freshly ground pepper

Kidneys in mustard sauce ★

Serves 5

Preparation time: 35 minutes
Cooking time: 15 minutes

Remove the fine membrane from the kidneys (see p. 88).
Cut them in half and remove the nerves. Separate the lobes, cutting them
into pieces of about 1 oz. (25-30 g) each.
Pour the clarified butter into a sauté pan and heat over high heat. Brown the
kidney lobes, making sure that they do not dry out–they should remain pink
inside. Transfer them to a rack to let their juices drip out. Season with salt
and pepper. Discard the fat from the pan.
Deglaze* with port and reduce* by half. Add the cream, followed by the
thickened veal stock.
Stir in the mustard but do not allow the sauce to boil, or else it will separate.
Adjust the seasoning.
Arrange the kidneys in a serving dish and pour the sauce over them.

● Chef's notes

*Rice, sautéed potatoes, or vegetable flans make excellent side dishes to eat
with kidneys.*
Veal kidneys are considered to have the finest taste of all types of kidney.
*They should always be served pink, with a little drop of clear juice appearing in
the center, or else they become rubbery.*

Technique
Preparing kidneys >> p. 88

Roasted rack of lamb
and garden vegetables ★ ★

Serves 8
Preparation time: 50 minutes
Cooking time: 30 minutes

Preheat the oven to 425°F (220°C).
Trim the racks and remove the backbones (see p. 83).
Make small, shallow incisions in the fine membrane that covers the racks.
Tie them with kitchen twine.
Oil a roasting pan and place the racks on it. Baste* them with oil and season
with salt and pepper. Cook for 10 minutes at 425°F (220°C), and then turn the
temperature down to 350°F (170°C) to cook for a further 10 minutes.
Remove the racks from the pan and tent them under aluminum foil. Keep
them warm, and set aside the pan. Discard the fat.

Peel and wash the carrot and the large onion. Dice* them finely to make a
brunoise*. Place the roasting pan over medium heat to caramelize the juices
from the lamb.
Add the finely diced vegetables, and sweat* over low heat.
Deglaze* with the white wine and reduce* by half. Add the bouquet garni
and pour in the scant cup water or clear stock. Reduce by half again. Strain
through a chinois* and season.

Prepare the garden vegetables. Peel and wash the carrots and turnips.
Cut them into little sticks 1/5 in. × 1 1/4 in. (5 mm × 30 mm).
Cook the carrots, turnips, peas, and beans separately in boiling salted water.
As soon as they are done, cool them briefly under cold running water and
dry on paper towel.
Cut the beans so that they are they same length as the carrot and turnip
sticks. Gently heat all the vegetables together with butter.

Cut the racks, allowing two chops per person.
Serve on flat plates with the garden vegetables, and pour over the hot sauce.

● **Chef's note**
Your butcher will be able to dress* the racks of lamb for you if you prefer.

Techniques
Preparing a rack >> p. 83
Cutting into batons (*jardinière*) >> p. 62

Ingredients
2 racks of lamb with 8 chops in each
3 tablespoons (40 ml) oil for cooking
1/2 carrot
1/2 large onion
Scant 1/2 cup (100 ml) white wine
1 bouquet garni*
1 scant cup (200 ml) water or
clear stock
Salt, freshly ground pepper

Garden vegetables
4 carrots (14 oz./400g)
4 turnips (14 oz./400 g)
10 oz. (300 g) shelled peas
10 oz. (300 g) green beans
4 tablespoons (60 g) butter
Salt, freshly ground pepper

Ingredients

6 veal chops
1 ¼ sticks (5 oz./140 g) unsalted butter
1 ¾ lb. (800 g) green beans
12 rashers bacon
Salt, freshly ground pepper

Sauce
5 oz. (150 g) button mushrooms
2 shallots
1 tablespoon (15 ml) calvados or other
apple brandy
Scant ½ cup (100 ml) hard cider*
½ cup (120 ml) thick crème fraîche
Scant cup (200 ml) thickened brown veal
stock (use an instant mix or see recipe p. 138)
Salt, freshly ground pepper

Veal chops, Normandy-style ★

Serves 6

Preparation time: 30 minutes
Cooking time: 35 minutes

Trim the chops and cut off the tips of the bones. Make a small incision on the nerve on the outside (curved side) so that the meat does not shrink during cooking.
Season the chops with salt and pepper.
If you like your veal chops well done, you will need to finish cooking them in the oven. In this case, preheat it to 350°F (180°F).
Begin heating 7 tablespoons (100 g) unsalted butter in a sauté pan. When it is sizzling, place the chops in the pan over low heat and brown gently on both sides, spooning the butter frequently over the meat as it cooks. Check for doneness and, if necessary, place the chops in the oven for a few minutes. Remove from the oven as soon as they are done to your liking, cover with aluminum foil, and keep warm.

Discard some of the fat from the sauté pan.
Finely slice the mushrooms and chop the shallots. Sauté the mushrooms until brown. Add the shallots and cook until translucent. Flambé* the contents of the pan with calvados (apple jack brandy) and deglaze* with the hard cider. Reduce* to a quarter of the original quantity. Stir in the thick cream.
Pour in the veal stock and reduce again until the sauce is thick. Whip it well and season with salt and pepper.
Ensure that your oven is at 300°F (150°C) so that you can heat your beans at the last moment.
Prepare a pot of salted boiling water and cook the green beans. Refresh* them briefly under cold running water and pat dry to remove all moisture. Arrange the green beans in bundles and wrap each one with a thin rasher of bacon.
Butter a roasting pan and arrange the bundles of beans on it. Brush them with a little butter to give them a nice gloss and season them.
Ten minutes before you are ready to serve, place the beans in the oven to reheat them. Arrange the chops and bundles of beans on the plates and drizzle with mushroom sauce.

● Did you know?

Normandy is a fertile region in northwestern France, famous for its dairy products, including cream and butter, and apples, from which wonderful hard cider and calvados are made. This dish showcases the best of the produce.

● Chef's note

The secret to getting the veal chops just right is to cook them in hot butter without allowing them to burn.

 Technique
Preparing chops » p. 85

Fillet of beef in a brioche crust ★ ★ ★

Serves 6

Preparation time: 45 minutes
Resting time: 1 hour 55 minutes
Cooking time: 30 minutes

Prepare the brioche dough (see p. 24).
Dilute the yeast in 2 tablespoons (30 ml) of water at room temperature. Sift the flour onto a flat surface and make a well in the center. Sprinkle the salt and sugar outside the well so that they do not come into direct contact with the yeast.
Beat the eggs and incorporate them into the mixture using a rubber scraper. Knead* the dough energetically to give it elasticity. You may use the hook attachment of an electric beater to do this. If you opt for the electric beater, use medium speed for about 10 minutes. Then knead in the butter at room temperature until it is completely incorporated and the dough is smooth, and place the dough in a mixing bowl (p. 24: image 3).
Cover with plastic wrap (otherwise an unwanted crust will form) and leave to rise for 30 to 40 minutes at a temperature of 77°F-82°F (25°C-28°C) with a bowl of water. When the dough has doubled in volume, remove from the bowl and turn out onto a lightly floured surface. Flatten it and fold into three. Shape into a ball and chill until it hardens, about 45 minutes.

Trim and season the beef. Brown it lightly over high heat in the oil.
Place it on a rack to allow it to drain.
Combine all the ingredients for the herbed crust (breadcrumbs, parsley, chervil, and olive oil) and season them with salt and pepper.
Take the brioche pastry out of the refrigerator and roll it out into a rectangle about 1/10-1/8 in. (3-4 mm) thick.
Spread the herbed crust over the brioche pastry, place the piece of beef in the middle, and roll it up. If you have any leftover pieces of pastry, use them to make decorative pieces.
Leave to rise for 30 minutes at 82.5°F-86°F (28°C-30°C). The brioche dough should almost double in volume.
Preheat the oven to 375°F (190°C), ensuring there is no residual steam in the oven.
Beat the egg and baste* the pastry with it. Cook for about 30 minutes, depending on how well done you like your beef. When you remove it from the oven, brush the brioche pastry with a little clarified butter and serve whole.

● Chef's notes

Instead of the herbed crust, try a dry mushroom duxelles (see p. 156).
Sugar is included in the brioche recipe to ensure the dough begins rising; it will not impart a sweet taste to your dish.

Techniques

Brioche ›› p. 24
Cooking in a crust ›› p. 99

Ingredients

2 lb. (900 g) tenderloin or fillet of beef
3 tablespoons (40 ml) oil for cooking
Generous 2/3 cup (100 g) packaged breadcrumbs
5 sprigs flat-leaf parsley
6 sprigs chervil
3 1/2 tablespoons (50 ml) olive oil
1 egg
2 tablespoons (30 g) butter, clarified*
Salt, freshly ground pepper

Brioche dough

1/6 oz./1/3 cake (5 g) fresh (compressed) yeast
2 1/4 cups (220 g) flour
1 generous tablespoon (15 g) sugar
2 eggs
7 1/2 tablespoons (110 g) unsalted butter, room temperature
Salt

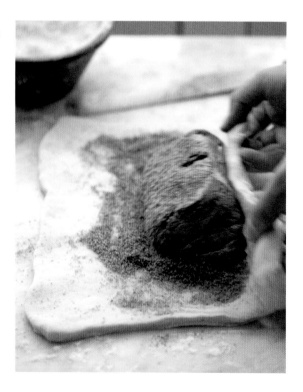

Slow-cooked caramelized pork ★

Serves 6
Preparation time: 15 minutes
Cooking time: 1 hour 15 minutes

Preheat the oven to 350°F (170°C).
Brown the pork in a pot with the clarified butter and sugar. Season it with salt and freshly ground pepper. Cover with the lid and cook for 1 hour 15 minutes.
Slice the meat and pour over the sauce from the pot.
Serve this dish with tagliatelle or potatoes in their jackets.

● **Did you know?**
Since the time of the Gallic tribes, pork has been widely eaten in France in many forms, with new recipes constantly being created. Spiced vegetables, such as cumin-flavored carrots, make an excellent side dish here.

Ingredients
2 ½ lb. (1.2 kg) top of pork shoulder butt (US)
or top of spare rib (UK)
3 tablespoons (40 g) butter, clarified*
3 ½ tablespoons (40 g) sugar
Salt, freshly ground pepper

Ingredients

4 lb. (1.8 kg) veal shoulder
1 tablespoon (20 g) kosher salt
1 large onion
3 cloves
1 large green leek leaf
1 stalk celery
1 bouquet garni*
5 peppercorns
¹/₂ cup (125 ml) thick cream

For the roux

4 tablespoons (60 g) butter
Scant ²/₃ cup (60 g) flour
(You may need slightly more or less, depending on the final volume of your cooking liquid.)

Veal stew (*blanquette*) ★

Serves 8

Preparation time: 25 minutes
Cooking time: 1 hour 30 minutes

Trim the veal and cut it into pieces weighing about 2-2 ¹/₂ oz. (60-70 g).
Place them in cold water in a pot and bring to the boil to blanch*. Remove as soon as the water begins to boil.
Discard the cooking liquid.
Place the pieces of veal in a clean pot, cover with water, and add the kosher salt.
Peel and wash the onion. Cut it in half and stud it with the cloves.
Add the aromatic ingredients (onion, leek, celery stalk, bouquet garni, and peppercorns) to the meat.
Slowly bring to a simmer.
Leave to cook for 2-2 ¹/₂ hours, skimming when necessary. Remove the meat from the cooking liquid and strain the liquid through a fine-mesh sieve, if possible into a large measuring jug so that you can calculate how much roux you will need (see below). Discard the aromatic ingredients.

Prepare a white roux with the butter and flour. For every 4 cups (1 liter) of cooking liquid, you should have 2 oz. (55 g) of roux, i.e. 1 oz. butter for 1 oz. or ¹/₄ cup (27.5 g) flour. Combine the butter and flour without heating. Pour half of the cooking liquid over the roux, whisking as you pour. Add the remaining cooking liquid, still whisking. Stir in the thick cream. When the cream and the liquid are thoroughly combined, pour this mixture back into the cooking liquid with the roux and stir in until heated, without bring to the boil.
Transfer the veal stew to a large serving dish and serve with vegetables and rice.

● **Did you know?**

Another classic of French cuisine, the recipe for blanquette de veau *has remained practically unchanged since the eighteenth century. The secret lies in mastering the liaison (thickening) of its sauce.*

 Technique
Deep poaching (cold start) » p. 113

Ingredients

1 ½ lb. (700 g) *cocos de Paimpol, AOC*, white haricot beans
1 leg of lamb, about 4 ½ lb. (2 kg), allow 7-9 oz. (200-250 g) per person, with shrinkage
3 ½ tablespoons (50 g) butter
¾ cup (200 ml) hard cider*
1 onion
½ carrot (2 oz./60 g)
2 cloves
½ leek greens
3 tomatoes
1 bouquet garni*
15 peppercorns
Salt, freshly ground pepper
Special equipment: a Dutch oven or flameproof dish with a tight-fitting lid.

Braised leg of lamb, Breton-style ★

Serves 10
Preparation time: 40 minutes
Soaking time: 12 hours
Cooking time: 1 hour 20 minutes

A day ahead, shell the beans and leave them to soak in cold water.
Preheat the oven to 350°F (170°C).
Prepare the lamb for cooking.
Trim it and remove the pelvic bone (see p. 84). Remove the fine membrane, tie it with twine, and season with salt and pepper.
Melt the butter in a pot and brown the lamb all over. Pour over the hard cider, cover with the lid, and transfer the pot to the oven. Cook for 30 minutes, or longer, depending on how pink you like it.
Peel and wash the onion and half-carrot, and cut in half lengthwise. Push the cloves into the base of each onion half (as shown in the photo below).
Wash the leek greens and tie them together.
Peel the tomatoes, remove the seeds, and dice* the flesh.
Place the dry beans in a large pot and cover them with cold water.
Add the aromatic vegetables, the bouquet garni, and the peppercorns.
Bring to the boil and simmer over low heat for at least 1 hour, adding extra boiling water if necessary. They should be completely softened, almost stewed. Drain the beans, remove the bouquet garni, and season with salt and pepper.
Slice the leg of lamb when you serve it. Pour the cooking liquid over the sliced meat and accompany with the coco beans, served separately in a vegetable dish.

● **Chef's note**
A light, green salad is a welcome accompaniment to this dish.

● **Did you know?**
Inland Brittany, like Normandy, is an apple-producing region, and excellent hard cider is made there. This recipe brings together two of its many star products, its manually harvested semi-dry coco de Paimpol *bean, and its popular cider.*

Techniques
Preparing a leg of lamb ›› p. 84
Brown braising ›› p. 94
Peeling using hot water ›› p. 61

Pot-au-feu ★

Serves 8

Preparation time: 35 minutes
Cooking time: 2 hours 30 hours

Trim the meat, leaving each piece whole.
Prepare the aromatic ingredients. Peel and wash the onion and carrot. Wash the leek green. Cut the vegetables in two and push the cloves into the onions near the base (see photo on previous page).
Place the pieces of meat in a large pot, cover with cold water, and bring to the boil. Remove the meat immediately and transfer the pieces to another pot. Cover them with cold water. Add all the aromatic ingredients and put in the kosher salt. Bring to the boil, turn down the heat, and simmer for 2 $1/2$ hours. Thirty minutes before the time is up, add the marrow bones.
Remove the aromatic ingredients and adjust the seasoning.

Wash, peel, and rinse the potatoes and carrots. Wash the zucchini. Shape the vegetables into regular oval "egg" shapes weighing about 2-2 $1/2$ oz. (50-60 g) per piece.
Take 4 cups (1 liter) of the cooking liquid and cook the vegetables in it separately for just the time required for each.
Serve the vegetables with the meat, and the broth in a tureen or vegetable dish. Accompany with fleur de sel and French mustard in small dishes.

● Chef's notes

Use other types of meat besides beef, like pork and veal. You may even try fresh, cured, or smoked meats. If you opt for this kind of variation, don't cook the meats together. Choose your vegetables according to the seasons.
Every European country has its own version of this boiled dish. The pot-au-feu, the hearty winter meal par excellence, is a one-pot dish comprising of broth, meat, and vegetables; and leftover meat may be eaten cold, reheated, or minced to make a pie.

Technique
Deep poaching (cold start) >> p. 113

Ingredients
1 lb. (500 g) beef ribs (US) or fore/thin ribs (UK)
2 lb. (1 kg) beef chuck (US) or chuck and blade (UK)
1 tablespoon (20 g) kosher salt
1 $1/4$ lb. (600 g) marrow bones
1 $1/4$ lb. (600 g) potatoes
1 $1/4$ lb. (600 g) carrots
1 lb (400 g) zucchini (courgettes)
Fleur de sel
French mustard*

Aromatic ingredients
1 large onion
1 carrot
Green leaf of 1 leek
2 cloves
1 bouquet garni*
6-8 peppercorns

Ingredients

¹/₂ lb (250 g) whole fresh foie gras
4 beef tournedos (medallions)
4 teaspoons (20 ml) grapeseed oil
Salt, freshly ground pepper

Sauce
Scant ¹/₂ cup (100 ml) sweet white wine
Scant ¹/₂ cup (100 ml) thickened brown
veal stock (use an instant mix or see recipe p. 138)
¹/₅ oz. (5 g) black truffle bits
1 ¹/₂ tablespoons (20 g) butter, cubed
Salt, freshly ground pepper

Beef tournedos with foie gras ★

Serves 4
Preparation time: 20 minutes
Cooking time: 25 minutes

Cut the foie gras into slices less than ¹/₂ in. (1 cm) thick. Season them with salt and pepper.
Sauté the tournedos in oil until it is cooked to your liking, and season with salt and pepper.
Transfer to a rack and keep warm.
Heat a non-stick pan without adding any fat to it. When it is hot, sauté the slices of foie gras. When they have reached the desired degree of doneness, place them on paper towel to drain.
Prepare the sauce. Discard the fat from the sauté pan and deglaze* with white wine. Reduce* the liquid by half and pour in the veal stock.
Add the truffle bits and whisk in the butter. Adjust the seasoning.
Place each tournedos on a plate and top with a slice of foie gras. Drizzle the sauce attractively around the meat.

● Chef's notes
Any number of side dishes, from the simplest to the most elaborate, go well with this dish.
This is a simple recipe for a gastronomic treat with a decidedly southwestern French influence.

● Did you know?
The story goes that Gioacchino Antonio Rossini (1792–1868), composer, fine musician, and true gourmet, who spent many years in Paris, had a variation on this dish created for him by the chef of one of his favorite restaurants. When it is served with a generous slice of truffle, it is known as Tournedos Rossini.

Techniques
Cutting medallions and noisettes ≫ p. 91
Sautéing ≫ p. 121

Lamb medallions with licorice-flavored foamed milk and duchess potatoes ★ ★

Serves 6
Preparation time: 50 minutes
Cooking time: 1 hour 30 minutes

Remove all the bones from the racks of lamb (see p. 91) to prepare the filets mignons, or ask your butcher to prepare them for you.
Remove the outer membrane.
Season them on both the flesh side and the fatty side, and roll the belly flap over the filets. Tie every 1 ¼ in. (3 cm) to keep the meat in place as it cooks. Cut between every round of string to create regular medallions that will cook evenly (see p. 83). Allow 3 medallions per person.

Prepare the sauce. Soak the sheets of gelatin in cold water. Slowly bring the milk to a simmer with the licorice sticks. Leave to infuse for at least 1 hour at about 120°F-140°F (50°C-60°C). If you don't have a thermometer, leave it over a hot water bath that is below simmering point. Drain the gelatin, squeezing it between your fingers to eliminate the water, and mix it into the milk until no traces are visible. Strain the milk through a chinois*.

Prepare the duchess potatoes (see p. 161).
Brush and wash the potatoes. Boil them in their jackets for about 30 minutes. Peel them and purée them through a food mill. Place the puréed potatoes in a sauté pan and, stirring with a spatula, dry them out over low heat for a few minutes.
Remove from the heat and add the egg yolks and 5 ½ tablespoons (80 g) cubed butter. Season with salt and pepper.
Spoon the potato mixture into a piping bag fitted with a star tip to create decorative mounds of potato mixture on parchment paper.

Heat a sauté pan. Add the remaining butter and, when it begins sizzling, place the lamb medallions in it to cook. Brown both sides until the meat reaches the desired degree of doneness.
Transfer the medallions to a rack and keep them warm. Preheat the oven to 400°F (200°C) to reheat the duchess potatoes before serving.
Deglaze* the pan juices with the licorice-flavored milk, and allow to reduce* over low heat.
Strain through a chinois and season with salt and pepper. Place the duchess potatoes in the oven for 5 minutes.
Stand the medallions on the plates on their sides. Whisk the sauce until it is foamy, pour it over the meat, and serve with the duchess potatoes.

● Chef's note
Licorice-flavored milk may be used to braise a leg of lamb or to cook the vegetables served as a side dish. The method of infusing an aromatic ingredient in milk can be used with many varied aromatics.

Techniques
Preparing a rack >> p. 83
Cutting medallions and noisettes >> p. 91
Duchess potatoes >> p. 161

Ingredients
2 racks of lamb with 6 chops each
2 lb. (1 kg) potatoes
3 egg yolks
1 stick (4 ½ oz./120 g) butter, divided
Salt, freshly ground pepper

Sauce
2 leaves gelatin* (4 g)
2 cups (½ liter) whole (full-cream) milk
2 licorice sticks
Salt, freshly ground pepper

Vegetables

Alain Passard
presents his recipe

I want to make vegetables the equivalent of wines; they should have their own *grand cru* labels. The idea of talking about a carrot as one talks about a sauvignon grape variety is one I find particularly appealing. In culinary terms, the vegetable is first and foremost a product of the four seasons—marked differences in the range of flavors available are detectable with every change. The vegetable also constitutes a true source of inspiration, each one with its particular texture, skin, color, and design. Believe it or not, the curve of an eggplant can become an invaluable starting point when a recipe is created.

We have three vegetable gardens, each one with its own *terroir*: sandy earth in the Sarthe, a region southwest of Paris; clay in the Eure in Normandy; and alluvial deposits in the Bay of Mont Saint-Michel. These three quite different types of soil have led us to think about just what a vegetable needs for optimum growth, and we plant specific seeds according to what the soils can best support. The Eure is perfect territory for bulbs like new garlic, red and yellow onions, and gray shallots. In the Sarthe, we have our carrots, asparagus, and leeks, and in the microclimate of the Bay of Mont Saint-Michel, we cultivate our aromatic plants. After a tasting session, we choose the best produce.

Harlequin vegetable platter

Prepare the vegetables
Wash and peel the vegetables. Cook in boiling water in separate pots: the yellow and orange carrots ; the round and golden turnips ; the broccoli; and the green cabbage– each with 2–3 tablespoons of butter. Cook the three types of radishes with 4 tablespoons of butter. Set aside a total of 1 ²/₃ cups (400 ml) of the cooking liquid, taken from each of the pots.

Semolina
Place the semolina and olive oil in a saucepan. Heat together, whisking as you incorporate 20 fl. oz. (2 ¹/₂ cups or 600 ml) hot water. Set aside.

Onion sauce
Peel the onions, slice them finely, and sauté them in a pan with the salted butter and 1 ²/₃ cups (400 ml) water. Be careful not to brown them, but cook until they reach a *confit* texture. (see p. 97). When they are done, process them with the whipping cream, strain through a chinois*, and adjust the seasoning with fleur de sel.

Eggplant caviar
Place the eggplants on a baking tray and broil at 425°F (220°C) for 20 minutes, turning regularly, to scorch the skin. When they are done, peel them, and chop the flesh, incorporating the hazelnut oil, chopped ginger, four-spice mixture, and fleur de sel. Transfer to a bowl.

To assemble
Cut each vegetable into pieces. Place them together in a sauté pan with the currants, the vegetable cooking liquid, 4 tablespoons (60 g) salted butter, and a few drops of lemon juice. Heat it all together, swirling the pan so that all the vegetables are glazed*. Arrange them on four plates. Flavor the semolina with the argan oil and fleur de sel. Place two oval scoops of eggplant caviar on each plate and sprinkle some of the semolina over the vegetables, dotting the onion sauce attractively around.

Serves 4
Preparation time: 40 minutes
Cooking time: 50 minutes

Ingredients
4 yellow carrots
4 orange carrots
2 round turnips
2 golden turnips
4 green cabbage leaves
A few broccoli florets
2 black radishes
4 green radishes
4 red radishes
¹/₂ lb. (220 g) salted butter
36 currants
Juice of 1 lemon

Semolina
7 oz. (200 g) extra-fine semolina
4 drizzles of olive oil
2 teaspoons argan oil
4 pinches fleur de sel

Onion sauce
4 sweet Cévennes onions, or other sweet onions
1 stick (120 g) salted butter
1 ²/₃ cups (400 ml) whipping cream
Fleur de sel

Eggplant caviar
4 eggplants, weighing 3 ¹/₂ oz. (100 g) each
4 teaspoons hazelnut oil
2 teaspoons fresh chopped ginger
4 pinches four-spice mixture*
4 pinches fleur de sel

Gnocchi, Florentine-style ★★

Serves 8
Preparation time: 55 minutes
Cooking time: 40 minutes

Remove the stems of the spinach leaves and wash them well. Chop the garlic cloves. Prepare a *beurre noisette** (butter that is melted until brown) with garlic and sauté the spinach in it. Leave to cook over low heat for 5 minutes and then season.

To make the gnocchi, prepare a choux pastry (see p. 20).
Sift the flour. Bring to the boil 1 cup (250 ml) water, the cubed butter, salt, and ground white pepper. Remove from the heat and add all the sifted flour at once. Return the saucepan to the heat and dry the batter by stirring energetically with a spatula until the moisture has evaporated.
Transfer the choux batter to a bowl and leave to cool. Mix in the eggs one by one, using a spatula to stir them in until completely incorporated.
Bring about 4 ¹/₂ pints (2 liters) salted water to the boil. Spoon the choux pastry into a piping bag with a plain, medium-sized tip.
Pipe small cylinder shapes into the boiling water, cutting them off with a paring knife. Simmer for 4-5 minutes. Remove from the water and strain.

Prepare the béchamel sauce (see p. 131). Make a white roux with the butter and flour.
Pour over half the cold milk and add the grated nutmeg. Bring the mixture to the boil over high heat, stirring constantly with your whisk. Pour in the remaining milk, bring to the boil again, and season.
Cover with plastic wrap flush with the surface to prevent a skin from forming.

Preheat the oven to 425°F (220°C).
Spread a little béchamel sauce at the bottom of an ovenproof dish. Arrange the spinach over it, and then the gnocchi. Cover with béchamel sauce. Scatter with grated Gruyère cheese and bake until brown and crisp on top, about 15-20 minutes.

● **Chef's note**
If you can, use fresh spinach rather than frozen for a far better taste.

Techniques
Choux pastry >> p. 20
Béchamel sauce >> p. 131

Ingredients
1 ¹/₂ lb. (650 g) fresh spinach
3 garlic cloves, peeled, shoots removed
3 ¹/₂ tablespoons (50 g) salted butter
1 ¹/₄ cups (120 g) grated Gruyère cheese
Freshly ground pepper

Choux pastry
6 tablespoons (90 g) butter, cubed
1 ²/₃ cups (150 g) flour
3 eggs
Salt, ground white pepper

Béchamel sauce
4 tablespoons (60 g) butter
Scant ²/₃ cup (60 g) flour
4 cups (1 liter) milk
A little grated nutmeg
Salt, freshly ground pepper

Ingredients

1 orange bell pepper (150 g)
1 large carrot (150 g)
6 violet asparagus spears
7 oz. (200 g) button mushrooms
10 pink radishes
2 lettuce hearts
A few sprigs of chervil, for garnish
A few sprigs of chives, for garnish

Vinaigrette

Scant ¹/₄ cup (50 ml) vinegar
²/₃ cup (150 ml) oil
Salt, freshly ground pepper

Mixed garden vegetables ★

Serves 6
Preparation time: 30 minutes

Wash the vegetables. Peel the bell pepper, either with a vegetable peeler or by roasting in a hot oven and removing the charred skin (see p. 61). Peel the carrot. Finely slice the asparagus, button mushrooms, and pink radishes lengthwise.
Remove the stem of the bell pepper. Cut it into quarters, remove the seeds and all the white ribs, and slice it finely. Cut the carrot into fine julienne strips. Remove the leaves of the lettuce hearts and wash them.
Dissolve a little salt in the vinegar and season with pepper. Whisk in the olive oil.
Arrange the vegetables attractively and garnish with chervil and chives. Drizzle the vinaigrette over at the last moment.

● Chef's note
This garden salad will vary with the seasons; what's essential is to use the freshest produce. Make it more interesting by using different types of oil and vinegar; the juxtaposition of varied colors will whet your appetite!

Techniques
Julienne strips >> p. 59
Vinaigrette >> p. 150

Soft-boiled eggs on a bed of artichokes with eggplant caviar ★★

Serves 6
Preparation time: 1 hour
Cooking time: 45 minutes

Prepare a pot of boiling water. Pour in the vinegar and immediately place the eggs gently in the pot. Leave to simmer for 4 $\frac{1}{2}$ to 5 minutes. Cool under running water immediately. Remove the shells.
Turn the artichokes (see p. 65). Break the stems and remove the leaves using a knife with a short, rigid blade (a boning knife).
Trim the bottoms neatly so that there are no traces of green left, as these parts taste very bitter. Shave off the top a short distance (under 1 inch or a couple of centimeters) from the bottom at the level of the fuzzy choke. Squeeze lemon juice over the entire artichoke bottom so that it doesn't go black. You may also tie a slice of lemon to the bottom (stem end) during cooking.
Keep the prepared artichokes in water with lemon juice until you are ready to cook them.
Prepare a *blanc* (see p. 106). Bring 6 cups (1.5 liters) water to boil with the juice of 1 lemon, kosher salt, and oil. Dilute the flour in cold water and pour into the boiling liquid. Simmer until it thickens–it will make a light velouté. Place the artichokes in the *blanc* and cook for 10 minutes. Refresh* as soon as they are done.
Prepare the eggplant caviar. Preheat the oven to 350°F (170°C).
Wash the eggplant and cut it in half lengthwise. Make fairly deep incisions in the flesh. Season with salt and pepper and scatter with herbes de Provence.
Drizzle a little oil into a roasting pan. Place the eggplant halves in the pan, drizzle them with a little olive oil, and cook for 25-30 minutes.
Scoop out the eggplant flesh. Chop it and adjust the seasoning.
To make the sauce, chop the shallots and place them in a small pot with the red wine. Reduce* over medium heat until practically dry. Add the thickened brown veal stock. Whip in the butter and season.
Fill the artichoke bottoms with the eggplant caviar and top with a soft-boiled egg. Pour over the red wine sauce and garnish with a small sprig of rosemary on the side.

● **Chef's notes**
The success of this dish depends on how you cook the egg and the choice of your wine, which should be slightly tannic and not acidic. You can enjoy it cold or hot. If you are going to eat it hot, prepare the eggs last or reheat them by dipping them for a few moments in a pot of salted boiling water.

Techniques
Soft-boiled eggs (*oeufs mollets*) ›› p. 40
Turning vegetables ›› p. 65
Deep poaching (hot start) ›› p. 106

Ingredients
6 eggs
3 tablespoons (40 ml) vinegar
3 large green artichokes
2 lemons
2 $\frac{1}{2}$ teaspoons (15 g) kosher salt
1 tablespoon (15 ml) oil
$\frac{1}{3}$ cup (1 oz./30 g) flour
6 sprigs rosemary, for garnish

Eggplant caviar
1 large eggplant (aubergine) (10 oz./300 g)
Herbes de Provence*
Scant $\frac{1}{4}$ cup (50 ml) olive oil
Salt, freshly ground pepper

Red wine sauce
1 $\frac{1}{4}$ cups (300 ml) red wine
2 shallots
1 scant cup (200 ml) thickened brown veal stock
(instant mix or see recipe p. 138)
2 tablespoons (30 g) butter, cubed
Fine sea salt, freshly ground pepper

Ingredients
6 tomatoes
2 celery stalks (180 g)
1 red bell pepper (180 g)
3 small violet artichokes
4 new onions
$1/2$ lb. (240 g) canned tuna in brine
5 pink radishes
2 eggs
18 black olives, for garnish
12 salted anchovy fillets, for garnish
A few sprigs of basil, for garnish

Vinaigrette
2 tablespoons (30 ml) wine vinegar
5 tablespoons (25 ml) olive oil
Salt, freshly ground pepper

Salad Niçoise ★

Serves 6
Preparation time: 35 minutes
Cooking time: 12 minutes

Finely slice the vegetables, choosing the cut you prefer (for example slices, quarters, or sticks).
Drain and flake the tuna.
Finely slice the pink radishes.
Prepare the hard-boiled eggs (see p. 39). Remove the shells and cut them into quarters.

Prepare the vinaigrette. Dissolve a little salt in the vinegar, add pepper, and whisk in the olive oil.

Arrange the vegetables and tuna attractively in a large salad dish or serving platter. Add the garnish (olives, anchovy fillets, and basil). Drizzle with the vinaigrette just before serving.

● **Chef's note**
You can rub the salad dish with a garlic clove for extra taste.

● **Did you know?**
This refreshing yet satisfying salad contains the best of what the Mediterranean city of Nice and its surroundings have to offer, hence its name. The exact ingredients of this dish have been the subject of much debate, the use of lettuce and potatoes being the most controversial.

Techniques
Hard-boiled eggs >> p. 39
Vinaigrette >> p. 150

Creamed lettuce soup (*velouté Choisy*) ★

Serves 8
Preparation time: 35 minutes
Cooking time: 40 minutes

Remove and discard the hearts of two of the lettuces and blanch* the leaves whole. Peel, wash, and cut the leek whites.
Sweat* the leek white in the butter. Add the flour and stir with a spatula.
Pour in the veal stock and bring the liquid to the boil, stirring constantly.
Add the blanched lettuce leaves.
Cook for 30-45 minutes, until the lettuce is cooked.
Process or blend and strain through a chinois*.
Combine the cream and egg yolks and mix into the strained soup in a mixing bowl to thicken it. Season with salt and pepper.
Cut the half lettuce into a chiffonade. Sweat the chiffonade briefly in the butter. Add it to the velouté.
Cut the bread into small cubes (less than 1/2 in./1 cm). Fry them in a pan and drain on paper towel.
Pour the soup into a soup plate or tureen. Garnish with a nice sprig of chervil and a few croutons.

● Chef's note
Use this recipe with other vegetables, such as broccoli, cauliflower, and zucchini (courgette).

● Did you know?
Any dish that bears the name "Choisy" contains lettuce as its predominant ingredient. A Choisy omelet is filled with creamed shredded lettuce, while a Sole Choisy is garnished with julienned lettuce.

Technique
Shredding (chiffonade) ≫ p. 56

Ingredients
2 1/2 lettuces
2 leek whites (200 g)
5 1/2 tablespoons (80 g) butter, for the leeks
Generous 3/4 cup (80 g) flour
9 cups (2 1/4 liters) clear white veal stock
2/3 cup (150 ml) thick cream
2 egg yolks
2 tablespoons (30 g) butter for the lettuce chiffonade
8 slices sandwich loaf
Oil for frying
A few sprigs chervil, for garnish
Salt, freshly ground pepper

Ingredients

1 ¼ lb. (600 g) large onions
3 tablespoons (50 g) butter
10 cups (2 liters) clear white stock
(ready-to-use mix or recipe p. 136)
1 bouquet garni*
16 slices of baguette, toasted to
make croutons
5 oz. (140 g) grated Gruyère cheese
Kosher salt to taste
Fine salt, freshly ground pepper

Onion soup ★

Serves 8

Preparation time: 10 minutes
Cooking time: 1 hour

Peel, wash, and slice the onions.
Sweat* them in butter.
Add the light white stock, the bouquet garni, and the kosher salt.
Simmer for 45 minutes to 1 hour.
Adjust the seasoning.
Set your oven to "broil."
Pour the broth into individual ovenproof bowls.
Place two croutons in each bowl of soup and sprinkle with the grated cheese.
Place in the oven until a gratin crust forms on top.

● Chef's note

It's the quality of the clear stock that will determine the final taste of the soup. Adding a slice of bacon when you begin cooking will bring a pleasant rustic taste to your dish.

Techniques

Cutting round slices ›› p. 56
White stock ›› p. 136

Rolled Picardy crêpes ★

Serves 8

Preparation time: 1 hour
Cooking time: 1 hours

Prepare the crêpe batter (see p. 18).
Sift the flour and salt into a mixing bowl. Crack the eggs one by one into the mixture and whisk briskly with a little of the milk.
Incorporate the remaining milk, beating energetically until the batter is smooth and fluid.
Strain through a fine-mesh sieve. Melt the butter until it browns* to a hazelnut color.
Mix it into the batter with the snipped chives and chill for about 30 minutes.
Heat a skillet over high heat. Drizzle a little oil in and cook the crêpes one by one, turning them when they begin to brown at the edges.

Prepare the mushroom duxelles (see p. 156).
Chop the button mushrooms, the shallots, and the onion. Melt the
3 ½ tablespoons of butter and sweat* the chopped shallot and onion.
Add the button mushrooms and cook, lid off, until all the liquid has evaporated. Season with salt and pepper and add the chopped parsley.
Finely dice* the ham.
Prepare the béchamel sauce (see p. 131) using the butter and flour to make a white roux.
Add 2 cups (500 ml) milk and the grated nutmeg.
Bring the mixture to boil over high heat, whisking constantly.
Pour in the remaining milk, bring to the boil again, and season.
Transfer to a bowl and cover with plastic wrap flush with the surface. This will prevent a skin from forming.

Preheat the oven to 425°F (220°C).
Place the mushroom preparation, the diced ham, and a little of the béchamel sauce in a mixing bowl and combine. Adjust the seasoning.
Spread the crêpes out and butter them with the remaining butter. Fill them with the mushroom and ham mixture and roll up. Arrange them in a shallow ovenproof dish. Pour over the béchamel sauce and scatter the grated cheese on top.
Bake for 15-20 minutes.

● Chef's note

The traditional filling for rolled crêpes uses mushrooms and ham, but feel free to add whatever ingredients you would like to use.

Techniques
Crêpe batter >> p. 18
Duxelles >> p. 156
Béchamel sauce >> p. 131

Ingredients

3 ½ tablespoons (50 g) butter plus 1 ½ tablespoons
(20 g) to butter crepes before filling
¾ lb. (350 g) button mushrooms
1 shallot (50 g)
1 onion (80 g)
1 ½ tablespoons (20 g) parsley, chopped
½ lb. (250 g) ham
4 oz. (120 g) grated Gruyère cheese
Salt, freshly ground pepper

Crêpe batter
2 ¾ cups (250 g) cake or all-purpose flour
3 eggs
2 cups (500 ml) low-fat (semi-skimmed) milk,
room temperature
5 ½ tablespoons (80 g) butter
10 sprigs of chives, snipped
1 pinch of salt
Oil for the skillet

Béchamel sauce
4 tablespoons (60 g) butter
⅔ cup (60 g) flour
4 cups (1 liter) milk
A little grated nutmeg
Salt, freshly ground pepper

Ingredients
10 eggs
3 tablespoons (40 g) butter
3 tablespoons (40 ml) whipping cream
Salt, freshly ground pepper

Ratatouille
$^1/_2$ eggplant (aubergine) (3 oz./100 g)
1 medium-sized zucchini (courgette) (3 oz./100 g)
1 large onion
1 small red bell pepper (3 oz./100 g)
2 garlic cloves, peeled, shoots removed
3 oz. (100 g) tomatoes
3 tablespoons (40 ml) olive oil
A sprinkling of herbes de Provence*
A pinch of ground *piment d'Espelette**

Scrambled eggs and a mini-ratatouille ★

Serves 4
Preparation time: 35 minutes
Cooking time: 30 minutes

Wash all the vegetables. Keeping them separate, dice* the eggplant, zucchini, large onion, and red bell peppers finely to make $^1/_5$ in. (5 mm) cubes.
Chop the garlic cloves.
Peel the tomatoes, remove the seeds, and chop them (see p. 55). If you wish, reserve the skins to fry for garnish.
Combine all the ingredients in a pot, add the oil and the herbes de Provence, and leave to simmer on very low heat for about 30 minutes. Season with salt and *piment d'Espelette*.
Prepare the scrambled eggs (see p. 42).
Break the eggs into a round-bottomed mixing bowl. Season and beat them with a fork or a whisk.
Melt half of the butter in the pan over low heat. Pour the eggs into the hot pan. Stir constantly with a spatula or wooden spoon. The final texture should be creamy. Remove from the heat and stir in the remaining butter, and/or cream. Keep warm at a temperature of 122°F (50°C) maximum.
Serve in a dish or on individual plates.

● **Chef's note**
The mini-ratatouille may be prepared a day ahead, or several hours before serving.

Techniques
Peeling in hot water ≫ p. 61
Chopping tomatoes ≫ p. 55
Scrambled eggs ≫ p. 42

Cheese

Xavier Thuret
presents his recipe

Cheese came into being when humankind felt the need to preserve milk, the divine drink that is also known as "white gold" because it is the first nourishment of life. The cheese maker's art is akin to that of the alchemist: he solidifies milk using the action of an acid, rennet in particular. This seemingly simple process has given rise to the diversity of cheeses we find on our cheese platters. The personality of a cheese stems first and foremost from its type of milk: cow, goat, sheep, or buffalo. What these animals feed on depends on what we call *terroir*, which varies from the plains to the mountains, from the pastures of Normandy, to the Alps, and the plateaus of the Larzac. France has an unrivaled range of this fine foodstuff. The specialist *affineurs*, ripeners, take the milk and transform it into a signature product, giving it creaminess, elasticity, suavity, and aromas that may be fruity, toasty, animal, or strong. Tasting cheese is an experience to be shared, a moment of pure conviviality. But what will make it a truly sublime event is the wine— preferably a white wine. Don't ever forget: cheese doesn't like water! Cheese is part of France's gastronomic heritage and is an essential element in many dishes. It works wonders in binding ingredients, and its flavorful generosity constantly inspires new culinary creations.

Beet nougat with Baragnaudes Roquefort chips

Balsamic vinegar jelly
Soften four sheets of gelatin in water at room temperature. Pour the vinegar into a small saucepan and warm it. When the gelatin sheets have softened, squeeze them out and incorporate them into the vinegar, allowing them to dissolve completely. Pour the mixture into a terrine and chill.

Beet purée
Cook the beets if using raw beets, and peel them. Peel the precooked beets if that is what you have. Place them in the blender and process until completely smooth. Finely dice* the Roquefort. Mix the pine nuts, pistachios, and cubed Roquefort into the puréed beets. Season with salt and freshly ground pepper. Soften the eight remaining sheets of gelatin in a bowl of water. Slightly heat the scant 1/2 cup (100 ml) hazelnut oil. Dissolve the softened gelatin sheets in the warm oil, and then incorporate the mixture into the beet puree.
When the balsamic vinegar jelly has completely set in the terrine, pour the rest of the mixture over it. Chill for at least 3–4 hours.

To assemble
Dip a knife into warm water and cut nice, thick slices of terrine.
Serve with oak leaf salad seasoned with hazelnut oil and scattered with a few slightly crushed nuts and dried fruit.

Serves 4
Preparation time: 20 minutes
Chilling time: 3–4 hours

Ingredients
10 oz. (300 g) raw beets, cooked and peeled,
or precooked beets if available
7 oz. (200 g) Roquefort Baragnaudes, or other good
strong blue cheese
1 oz. (30 g) pine nuts
1 oz. (30 g) shelled pistachios
8 sheets gelatin* (16 g)
Scant 1/2 cup (100 ml) hazelnut oil
Fine sea salt
Freshly ground pepper

Balsamic jelly
4 sheets gelatin (8 g)
1/2 cup (120 ml) balsamic vinegar

Brie fritters with spicy stewed black cherries ★

Serves 10
Preparation time: 25 minutes
Cooking time: 35 minutes

Remove the stems and pits of the black cherries. Place them in a pot with the sugar and spices and cover with water. Leave to stew gently until practically all the water has evaporated.
Allow to cool.

Prepare a batter for frying (see p. 23).
Sift the flour into a mixing bowl and add the salt. Break the whole eggs one by one, and whisk them in to the dry ingredients. Incorporate the oil.
Pour in the liquid (milk or beer) and whisk until the mixture is smooth.
Stiffly beat the egg whites.
Gently fold* in the beaten egg whites using a flexible rubber spatula.

Cut the Brie into fairly large cubes, just under 1 in. (2 cm). Heat an oil bath to 325°F (160°C). Dip the Brie cubes in the batter, ensuring that they are evenly coated, and place in the oil bath.
When they are lightly golden to brown all over, remove them from the oil with a slotted spoon and place on paper towel to drain.
Serve immediately with the spicy stewed black cherries.

Technique
Batter for frying >> p. 23

Ingredients
2 cups (200 g) all-purpose flour
1 teaspoon (5 g) table salt
2 whole eggs plus 3 egg whites
1 $^{1}/_{3}$ tablespoons (20 ml) sunflower seed oil
$^{3}/_{4}$ cup (200 ml) milk or beer
2 lb. 4 oz. (1 kg) Brie cheese
Oil for frying

Spicy stewed black cherries
7 oz. (200 g) black cherries
$^{3}/_{4}$ cup (150 g) sugar
8 star anise
2 heaped tablespoons (10 g) cinnamon
1 vanilla bean, slit lengthways
1 teaspoon (5 g) ground ginger

Ingredients

3 teaspoons (10 g) pink peppercorns
4 sheets brick pastry (or 8 sheets filo)
8 baguette croutons
$^1/_3$ cup (80 ml) olive oil
1 log of fresh goat milk cheese, preferably coated with ash
Scant $^1/_3$ cup (100 g) acacia honey
8 sprigs fresh rosemary
8 sprigs chives
Freshly ground pepper

Hot goat cheese in crisp pouches with rosemary honey and toasted pink peppercorns ★

Serves 8
Preparation time: 25 minutes
Baking time: 15 minutes

Toast the pink peppercorns in the oven. Leave them to cool, then rub them between your hands to remove some of the skin.
Crush roughly and set aside.

Preheat the oven to 325°F (160°C).
Cut the sheets of brick (or filo) pastry in half. (Note that brick pastry is sold in disks. Filo pastry is more fragile and should be doubled, though you will still need to cut them in half.) In the center of each piece of pastry, place a crouton of fresh baguette and drizzle it with a little olive oil.
Place a piece of goat milk cheese less than $^1/_2$ in. (1 cm) thick on each crouton. Brush some acacia honey over it and top with a small sprig of rosemary. Season with freshly ground pepper. Fold the pastry upward and make small pouch shapes, holding them together with a toothpick.
Bake for about 10 minutes, until the pastry is a nice, even golden color.
When you remove them from the oven, take out the toothpick and make a knot with a chive sprig so that it looks like a little pouch.
Serve hot, accompanied by a salad.

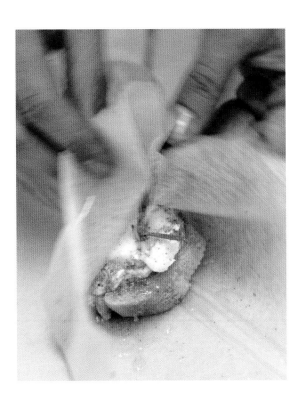

Lyonnaise cream cheese with *fines herbes* *
(*cervelle de canut*) ★

Serves 8
Preparation time: 40 minutes
Draining time: overnight (optional)

Drain the *faisselle* cream cheese, overnight if possible.
Peel the shallot and chop it finely. Finely snip the chives and chop the chervil.
Combine the shallot and herbs with the drained cream cheese using a spatula. Add the white wine and/or vinegar, salt, and pepper and mix again.
Whip the chilled cream stiffly and carefully fold* it into the cream cheese mixture.
Garnish the top with finely snipped chives. Chill until serving–it should be very cold.
Accompany with breads with dried fruit or seeds, or crudités.

● Did you know?
This is a specialty of the region of Lyon, a city where silk weaving was a major industry. The dish takes its name from the canuts, silk workers who rose up against their working conditions in the nineteenth century. It literally means "silk workers' brains"!
Faisselle actually means a cheese strainer, but it now refers to a type of fresh, unsalted cheese packed with its own strainer for the whey to drain out. It is popular in France served with fruit coulis as a dessert, and works equally well with savory ingredients. To make this recipe, you may use any light cream cheese, and even fresh goat milk cheese.

Ingredients
3 lb. (1.5 kg) *faisselle* cheese
1 shallot
1 bunch (20 g) chives, plus a few extra sprigs for garnish
A few sprigs (10 g) chervil
Scant ¼ cup (50 ml) dry white wine (optional)
2 teaspoons (10 ml) white vinegar, flavored if you wish (tarragon, for example)
1 cup (250 ml) whipping cream, 35 percent fat content, well chilled
Salt, pepper

Ingredients

1 large loaf of country bread
1 garlic clove, peeled, shoot removed
1 lb. (500 g) Beaufort cheese
14 oz. (400 g) Comté or Appenzell cheese
10 oz. (300 g) tome de Savoie (hard cheese from the Savoy region) or Emmental
2 tablespoons (20 g) cornstarch
2 tablespoons (30 ml) kirsch
2 ¼ cups (600 ml) young white wine (Swiss Fendant, French Apremont, etc)
A little grated nutmeg
Freshly ground pepper
Special equipment: fondue pot

Cheese fondue (*fondue savoyarde*) ★

Serves 8
Preparation time: 30 minutes
Cooking time: 25 minutes

Cut the bread into bite-size cubes and leave them out to dry.
Rub the inside of the fondue pot with a garlic clove.
Dice* the cheese. If you want to save time, you may grate it in the food processor. Dilute the cornstarch in the kirsch.
Slowly heat the white wine. When it begins to simmer, gradually add the cheese cubes, stirring with a wooden spoon to mix them well. When all the cheese has melted, incorporate the cornstarch and kirsch mixture. First spoon a little hot cheese into the liquid, mix thoroughly, then pour this into the fondue mixture.
Season with pepper and grate in a little nutmeg.
Place the pot on the burner in the center of the table (if possible, use an electric burner or a spirit burner). Give the guests fondue forks so that they can swirl their bread cubes in the fondue mix.

● Chef's notes
Flambé the wine before stirring in the cheese cubes.
If these particular cheeses are not available, substitute half Gruyère, half Emmental.

Roquefort and caramelized
pear *tartes fines* ★★

Serves 8
Preparation time: 50 minutes
Resting time: 1 hour 20 minutes
Cooking time: 15 minutes

Prepare the puff pastry (see p. 16).

Sift the flour and add the salt. Pour the water into the flour and stir with your fingers to combine. Blend the ingredients together rapidly until thoroughly mixed. You should have a smooth paste, known as the *détrempe*. Form it into a ball, and chill, covered, for about 20 minutes.

Check that the butter has the identical consistency of the dough mixture. Beat it, if necessary, between two sheets of parchment paper, with your rolling pin. This enables it to be incorporated more easily into the dough, and gives it a longer rectangular shape.

Now roll out the dough mixture to form a cross shape, leaving the center—where you will place the butter—thicker (about 1/3 in./8 mm) than the four other parts. The butter should fit over this part of the dough.

Place the butter in the center of the dough (p. 16: image 1) and fold over each of the four parts of the cross. The final result will look like the back of an envelope.

Lightly dust a cool working counter with flour (use as little as possible each time, so that the pastry does not become too hard). Roll out the dough (called a *paton*) to form a rectangle whose length is three times greater than its width (p. 16: 2).

Fold this into three, starting at each end (three layers) (p. 16: 3). Rotate the folded dough a quarter turn and roll out again to form the same shape as previously, a rectangle three times its width. Repeat the folding operation. Cover with plastic wrap and chill again for about 20 minutes.

Repeat this procedure—rolling out and folding—five more times (a total of six times), chilling for 20 minutes between each stage.

Roll out the pastry very thinly and cut out eight 6-in. (15-cm) diameter circles.

Prepare a syrup with the water and the sugar. Allow the syrup to cool. (It will be poured over the pastry, so it should not soften or melt the butter it contains.)

Preheat the oven to 350°F (180°C).

Leave the pears unpeeled. Cut them in half, squeezing a little lemon juice over so that they don't go brown, then cut the halves into fans.

Place the cut pears on the pastry disks. Baste* the tops of the tarts with the cooled syrup. Crumble the Roquefort cheese over the tarts and bake for about 15 minutes, until the cheese has melted and the pastry is a nice golden brown.

Garnish with the walnuts.

Techniques
Puff pastry ›› p. 16
Syrup ›› p. 168

Ingredients
4 Conference or other firm winter pears
Juice of 1 lemon
1/2 cup (125 ml) water
2/3 cup (125 g) sugar
1 1/2 lb. (640 g) Roquefort
8 walnuts

Puff pastry
2 3/4 cups (250 g) cake flour
1 teaspoon (5 g) salt
1/2 cup (125 ml) water
1 1/2 sticks (185 g) unsalted butter

Ingredients

1 lb. (500 g) Comté cheese (alternatively, Gruyère or Emmental)

32 green grapes

32 red grapes

Comté and grape skewers ★

Serves 8

Preparation time: 10 minutes

Take 16 wooden skewers and alternate the fruit and cheese in the following order: 1 green grape, 1 cheese cube, 1 red grape, 1 cheese cube, and so on.

● **Chef's notes**

Use small skewers to serve this at buffet meals.

Try various other types of cheese, and pair them with seasonal fruits for a tasty mix. Berries also work well.

A strong contrast in flavors, for example a mild cheese with a tangy fruit, makes an interesting variation. Alternately, try a mild fruit with a tangy cheese.

Mushroom caps stuffed with cream cheese ★

Serves 8

Preparation time: 40 minutes, + 20 minutes marinating
Cooking time: 5 minutes

Prepare an instant marinade (see p. 141).
Pour half of the oil into a pan. Add the dried or fresh herbs, the thyme, and the bay leaves.
Arrange the mushroom caps in the pan and pour over the rest of the olive oil.
Peel the lemon, removing all the white pith, and slice it. Place the lemon slices in the marinade and sprinkle with mignonette pepper.
Cover with plastic wrap and chill for 10 minutes. Turn the mushroom caps over and return to the refrigerator, covered, for another 10 minutes.

Snip the chives and finely chop the dill. Add the herbs and the garlic immediately to the cream cheese and chill.
Remove the mushroom caps from the marinade and grill the tops, making a diamond pattern when you sear* them.
Spoon the cream cheese-herb mixture into the hollow of the mushroom caps.
Sprinkle with a few grains of fleur de sel and serve.

Techniques
Instant marinade >> p. 141
Grilling >> p. 102

Ingredients
8 caps of large white button mushrooms
6 garlic cloves, peeled shoots removed
$^{1}/_{2}$ bunch chives
3 dill sprigs
1 lb. 5 oz. (600 g) *faisselle* (see p. 412)
(alternatively, unsalted ricotta,
Philadelphia, or other fresh cheese with
a high water content)
Fleur de sel, freshly ground pepper

Marinade
Scant $^{1}/_{2}$ cup (125 ml) olive oil
2 sprigs thyme
2 bay leaves
$^{1}/_{4}$ bunch parsley
1 lemon
1 tablespoon (20 g) mignonette pepper

Ingredients

1 baguette
$^1/_3$ cup (80 ml) olive oil
10 garlic cloves, peeled, shoots removed
1 Mont d'Or cheese
2 $^1/_2$ cups (600 ml) vin jaune (this wine is sold exclusively in 620 ml bottles)
Freshly ground pepper

Baked Mont d'Or and yellow wine ★

Serves 8

Preparation time: 15 minutes
Cooking time: 35 minutes

Preheat the oven to 300°C-325°F (150°C-160°C).
Prepare some croutons: cut the bread, drizzle with olive oil, and grill in the oven until light brown.
Rub the croutons with the garlic and set aside.
Cut a hole into the center of the Mont d'Or, reserving the top, and pour in the amount of yellow wine you desire, no less than a scant $^1/_2$ cup (100 ml). Press the pieces of garlic into the cheese. Cover the central hole with the reserved piece of cheese. Place the cheese in its box, wrap the box in aluminum foil, and bake for about 35 minutes.
Remove as soon as it is melted to your liking.
Give a few grinds of the pepper mill and serve immediately, to eat with spoons and croutons.

● Did you know?

The Mont d'Or cheese is a specialty of the Jura region in eastern France, and takes its name from the highest mountain there. It is sold in a box made of spruce. Highly prized yellow wine, vin jaune, is produced in the same region from the Savagnin grape, and is aged for a requisite time of six years and three months, during which time it acquires its characteristic yellow color.

Desserts

Yves Thuriès
presents his recipe

Pastry tasting has literally become a voyage of discovery. In its modern-day form, it allows food lovers a three-in-one treat, for less time and at less cost. This is why, in pastry making and cuisine, tasting plates have come into being. Three recipes, three different products, and three different flavors, all in one plate and part of the same course. A seven-course menu gives the client the opportunity to taste twenty-one different recipes. This technique, when completely mastered, simplifies the preparation and the plating in both the kitchen and the restaurant. Food stylists, all impassioned food lovers themselves, work in close collaboration with the great chefs. They too have the know-how to adapt their creations to all types of restaurant service. Pastry chefs, today more than ever before in history, work hand in hand with designers—invaluable allies—to create the elements of a tasting plate (here, in a trilogy). These tasting plates convey the essence of what a pastry chef can do. The aim is to seduce an epicurean public, sensitive to nuances even when pressed for time. What we have here is a new style of pastry and cuisine, service and menus *à la française* for all those who, today, aspire to create the gastronomy of tomorrow.

Sweet trilogy on a tasting plate

I. Spiced cream and crisp rolled wafers

Method
Bring the milk to the boil, add the spices, and leave to infuse for about 15 minutes. Strain and prepare a custard (see method p. 172) with the egg yolks and sugar using the spiced milk. Remove from the heat and incorporate the gelatin. Pour the cream into small bowls and chill to set.

Crisp wafer tubes
Melt the couverture chocolate in a bain-marie*. Add the praline paste and then the feuillantine. Roll out the mixture very finely (1/10 in./2 mm) between two sheets of parchment paper. Cut out rectangles and roll them up to form cylinders. Leave them to crystallize.

Finish and assemble the first component
Arrange the rolled wafer tubes over the spiced cream and garnish with a sprig of fresh mint.

Serves 10
Preparation time: 45 minutes
Cooking time: 45 minutes
Freezing time: 3-4 hours

Ingredients (I)
Spiced cream
3/4 cup (200 g) milk
1 star anise
1 cinnamon stick
3 cloves
1 vanilla bean, slit lengthwise and scraped
2 egg yolks (50 g)
1/4 cup (50 g) sugar
1 1/2 sheets gelatin* (1.5 g), soaked and drained
1 sprig of mint, for garnish

Crisp wafer tubes
2 2/3 oz. (75 g) dark couverture chocolate, 64 percent cocoa*
2 oz. (50 g) praline paste (50 percent hazelnut, 50 percent sugar; buy online or at specialty stores)
2 oz. (60 g) feuillantine (from professional suppliers), or fine, crushed wafers

II. Lemon-scented wild strawberry gratin and apricot coulis

Soufflé cream
Lemon-scented pastry cream (first stage of soufflé cream)
Bring the lemon juice to boil with the whipping cream. Whisk the egg yolks with the sugar and flour together until the mixture is thick and pale. Pour the hot lemon cream over, whisking constantly. Return the mixture to the heat and bring to a fast boil for a few minutes, continuing to whisk. Remove from the heat and incorporate the gelatin.

Italian meringue (second stage of soufflé cream) (see method p. 49)
Cook the sugar with a scant $^2/_3$ cup (150 ml) water and bring it to a temperature of 250°F (120°C). In the meanwhile, begin beating the egg whites. Pour the syrup over the beaten egg whites.

Method
Immediately begin to incorporate the hot meringue into the boiling cream, pouring slowly and folding* it in carefully.
As soon as the ingredients are combined, line the base and sides of the individual pastry rings with the hot soufflé cream. Scatter wild strawberries inside. Fill the rings with the cream and smooth over. Freeze for a few hours.

Baking and finishing
Preheat the oven to 400°F (200°C). Turn the frozen gratins out of the pastry rings and dust with confectioners' sugar. Bake for 10–12 minutes, until browned. Serve the hot apricot coulis separately.

III. Caramelized chocolate crisp rolls and coconut ivory sauce

Ganache
Bring the cream and the milk to the boil. Pour the hot liquid over the couverture chocolate to melt it. Whisk until smooth, add the softened butter and then the egg yolk. Set aside.

Caramelized crisp chocolate rolls
Cut strips of filo pastry measuring 2 $^1/_2$ in. (6 cm). Baste* them with clarified butter. Place the ganache on the strips and roll them up to form cigarette shapes. Sprinkle with granulated sugar and bake for about 5 minutes at 350°F (180°C). If they have not already caramelized, finish the process under a salamander or with a caramelizing iron.

Coconut-flavored ivory Sauce
Bring the coconut milk to the boil. Add the couverture chocolate and mix until smooth. Heat the glaze to 140°F (60°C) and incorporate it into the chocolate-coconut mixture.

Finish and presentation
Cut the rolled filo. Arrange three crisp chocolate rolls and a ramekin of coconut-flavored ivory sauce on an attractive plate.

Ingredients (II)
Soufflé cream
For the lemon-scented cream
1 cup (250 ml) lemon juice
1 cup (250 ml) whipping cream, 35 percent fat content
12 egg yolks (240 g)
$^1/_2$ cup (100 g) sugar
7 tablespoons (1 $^1/_2$ oz./40 g) cake flour
4 sheets gelatin (8 g), soaked and drained

For the Italian meringue
1 $^1/_2$ cups (300 g) granulated sugar
12 egg whites (360 g)
Wild strawberries as needed for 10 soufflés
A little confectioners' sugar, for dusting
Apricot coulis, to serve on the side

Ingredients (III)
Ganache
Scant $^1/_2$ cup (100 ml) whipping cream, 35 percent fat content
3 tablespoons (40 ml) milk
3 $^1/_2$ oz. (100 g) bittersweet couverture chocolate, 64 percent cocoa
2 teaspoons (10 g) butter, softened*
1 egg yolk (20 g)

Caramelized crisp chocolate rolls
Filo pastry as needed
A little clarified butter*
A little granulated sugar

Coconut-flavored ivory Sauce
3 $^1/_4$ oz. (90 g) coconut milk
4 $^1/_2$ oz. (125 g) white couverture chocolate
1 $^3/_4$ oz. (50 g) clear glaze*

Apricot tartlets ★

Serves 8

Preparation time: 45 minutes
Resting time: 20 minutes
Cooking time: 25 minutes

Prepare the sweet shortcrust pastry (see p. 12).
Sift the flour with the salt. Rub the butter into the flour with your fingertips until you have the texture of coarse crumbs. Incorporate the egg yolk, sugar, and water. Be careful not to overwork the dough, which would make it too elastic, and form it into a ball. Flatten it out with the palm of your hand to ensure it is thoroughly mixed.
Chill, covered in plastic wrap, for 20 minutes.
Preheat the oven to 350°F (180°C).
Roll the dough out with a pastry roller into a circle about $1/10$ in. (3 mm) thick. Cut out circles big enough to line the tartlet molds and transfer them to the molds. Make a decorative pattern around the edges.

Prepare the almond cream (see p. 176).
Cream the softened butter well with the sugar.
Add the ground almonds, and then the eggs, mixing them in one by one.
Add the flavorings and whisk until smooth.
Half fill the tart shells with the almond cream.
Wash the apricots, cut them in half, and remove the pits.
Place an apricot half in the center of each tartlet, pressing it into the almond cream. Bake for about 20-25 minutes. When they are almost done, remove the tartlets from the molds and return to the oven for a few minutes so that the edges of the pastry shells can brown lightly.
Transfer to a cooling rack immediately and brush them with apricot glaze. If you are using apricot preserves, liquefy it a little over low heat first.

Techniques

Shortcrust pastry ›› p. 12
Almond cream ›› p. 176

Ingredients

4 large sweet, juicy apricots
4 $1/2$ oz. (125 g) apricot glaze* or preserves

Sweet shortcrust pastry
2 $3/4$ cups (250 g) cake flour
1 generous teaspoon (5 g) table salt
1 stick (125 g) unsalted butter, softened*
1 egg yolk
3 $1/2$ tablespoons (40 g) sugar
4 $1/2$ tablespoons (50 ml) water

Almond cream
7 tablespoons (100 g) unsalted butter, softened
$1/2$ cup (100 g) granulated sugar
1 generous cup (100 g) ground almonds*
or almond meal
2 eggs
A few drops of vanilla extract
1 tablespoon (15 ml) rum

Serves 8
Preparation time: 1 hour 50 minutes
Cooking time: 10 minutes
Chilling time: 3-4 hours

Ingredients

Bavarian cream mousse
5 sheets (10 g) gelatin*
2 cups (500 ml) milk
1 vanilla bean, slit lengthwise, seeds scraped
10 sprigs of fresh mint
5 egg yolks
2/3 cup (125 g) granulated sugar
1 2/3 cups (400 ml) whipping cream, minimum 35 percent fat content
1 1/3 tablespoons (20 ml) mint liqueur

Joconde sponge
3/4 cup (140 g) plus 1/4 cup (50 g) granulated sugar
1 2/3 cups (5 oz./140 g) ground almonds
4 eggs plus 4 egg whites
8 tablespoons (45 g) flour
1 3/4 tablespoons (scant 1 oz./25 g) butter, melted

Chocolate mousse
4 1/2 oz. (125 g) bittersweet chocolate, 64 percent cocoa
1 3/4 tablespoons (25 g) butter
3/4 cup (150 g) sugar
2/3 cup (150 ml) water
3 egg yolks
3/4 cup (200 ml) whipping cream, minimum 35 percent fat content

2/3 cup (150 g) neutral glaze* (buy at specialty stores)

⌇ Techniques
Joconde sponge >> p. 194
French meringue >> p. 49
Egg-based Bavarian cream >> p. 191
Pâte à bombe >> p. 210

Mint-chocolate entremets ★ ★ ★

Prepare the joconde sponge (see p. 194). Line a baking sheet with parchment paper.
Preheat the oven to 350°F (180°C). Sift the flour and set it aside. Sift together the sugar and ground almonds*.
Beat this together with the four whole eggs until the mixture reaches the ribbon stage*. Fold* in the sifted flour, followed by the melted butter.
Beat the four egg whites until they form stiff peaks. Add the remaining sugar (1/4 cup or 50 g) and beat until the mixture is firm and shiny (it forms a French meringue).
Carefully fold this French meringue into the egg and butter mixture.
Spread the batter on the baking sheet. It should be very thin, about 1/5 in. (3-5 mm) thick. Bake for 8-10 minutes. As soon as it is done, turn it over onto a rack to cool. Cut out eight disks the size of the base of the molds you are using.

Prepare the mint Bavarian cream mousse (see p. 191).
Soak the gelatin sheets in very cold water until they are completely soft.
Heat the milk in a saucepan with the vanilla bean and its seeds and the mint leaves. Leave to infuse for at least 15 minutes.
Energetically whisk the egg yolks with the sugar. Pour half of the hot milk over the beaten egg yolks, beating constantly. Pour the rest of the milk in and then return the mixture to the heat. Heat gently, removing the pan from the heat from time to time, until the cream coats the back of a spoon* or to 185°F (85°C) if you have a thermometer. (It is important that the cream not be subjected to continuous heat, as the egg yolks might coagulate.)
Strain the custard through a chinois* into a bowl. Squeeze the water out of the gelatin leaves and mix it thoroughly into the custard. Cover the bowl with plastic wrap and leave to cool.
Whip the cream until it forms firm peaks, to a Chantilly consistency.
When the custard has cooled to room temperature (about 68°F or 20°C), whisk in the mint liqueur.
Gradually fold in the whipped cream using a rubber spatula, taking care not to deflate the mixture.
Pour the mint Bavarian cream into eight individual molds (with rounded bottoms, for example) and chill to set.

Prepare the chocolate mousse.
Melt the chocolate and butter together over a hot water bath. Do not let the temperature of the mixture exceed 122°F (50°C).
Bring the water and sugar to the boil.
Pour the egg yolks into the bowl of a stand-alone mixer and begin beating them. Gradually pour the hot syrup over the beaten egg yolks (see Pâte à bombe p. 210). Continue beating until the mixture has completely cooled down.
Beat the cream until soft peaks form.
By now the chocolate-butter mixture should have cooled to 82°F-83°F (28°C). Carefully fold it into the pâte à bombe, and then fold in, just as carefully, the whipped cream.

Spoon a layer of chocolate mousse over the mint Bavarian cream. Top with a disk of joconde sponge.
Chill until set, about 2-3 hours, before turning them out of the molds. Coat them with a neutral glaze and garnish attractively before serving.

Desserts

French fruit loaf ★

Serves 8

Preparation time: 20 minutes
Cooking time: 40-50 minutes

Prepare the loaf batter (see p. 33).
Preheat the oven to 300°F-325°F (150°C-160°C). Grease a loaf pan*.
Energetically cream the softened butter with the sugar and salt.
Add the eggs, one by one, mixing thoroughly each time.
Sift 2 ¹/₂ cups (250 g) flour and the baking powder together and stir into the batter. Stir in the vanilla extract.
Add the orange and lemon zests and the ginger.
Lightly coat all the pieces of fruit in the remaining flour so that they don't fall to the bottom during baking.
Pour the batter into the greased pan, scattering the pieces of dried fruit evenly throughout.
Bake for 40-50 minutes. Test for doneness: a tip of a knife should come out clean.
Turn the loaf out onto a cooking rack.

● Did you know?

What the French call a "cake" is more commonly known in the English-speaking world as a fruit cake, originally from Scotland. A raised dough with generous helpings of raisins and rum-soaked, candied fruits make up the basic recipe, and it is usually topped with sliced almonds and bright red glacéed cherries. This multicolored, multiflavored cake was invented by a pastry chef by the name of Michel, who took his inspiration from the Dundee Cake. He owned a tearoom, and Parisians thronged there to taste this new wonder, whose slices displayed cheerily bright fruits. Not only was it attractive, it was also mouthwatering. For added chic, the English word "cake" was used to describe it, and Monsieur Michel's creation became the new "must-have" treat.

Technique
Loaf cake batter » p. 33

Ingredients

1 ¹/₂ sticks (6 oz./175 g) unsalted butter, softened*, and a little extra for the pan
²/₃ cup (125 g) granulated sugar
¹/₂ teaspoon fine sea salt (3 g)
3 eggs
3 ¹/₃ cups (330 g) flour, divided
1 slightly heaped teaspoon (5 g) baking powder
1 teaspoon (5 ml) vanilla extract
Zest of 1 unsprayed or organic orange
Zest of 1 unsprayed or organic lemon
¹/₂ teaspoon (3 g) freshly grated ginger
2 oz. (50 g) dried figs
2 oz. (50 g) candied cherries
2 oz. (50 g) candied pineapple
2 oz. (50 g) candied apricots
2 oz. (50 g) mixed candied fruit

Serves 8
Preparation time: 45 minutes
Resting time: 20 minutes
Cooking time: 1 hour 10 minutes

Ingredients

Sweetened short pastry

3 ²/₃ cups (250 g) cake flour
1 teaspoon (5 g) table salt
1 stick (125 g) unsalted butter, softened*
²/₃ cup (125 g) sugar
1 egg

Lemon cream

1 cup (200 g) sugar, divided
1 ¹/₄ cup (300 ml) lemon juice
3 eggs plus 4 egg yolks
Scant ¹/₄ cup (35 g) cornstarch
Zest of 1 unsprayed or organic lemon
4 tablespoons (60 g) unsalted butter, cubed
³/₄ cup (200 ml) whipping cream, 35 percent fat
content

Lemon garnish

2 unsprayed or organic lemons
1 cup (200 g) granulated sugar

Italian meringue

Generous 1 cup (210 g) granulated sugar
4 egg whites
1 pinch salt
Special equipment: a sugar thermometer

Techniques

Sweetened short pastry >> p. 13
Candying (crystallizing) >> p. 97
Italian meringue >> p. 49

Lemon meringue tartlets ★ ★

Start the garnish. Slice one lemon very finely and dry it in the oven at 200°F
(100°C) for about 30 minutes.
Prepare the sweetened short pastry (see p. 13).
Sift the flour with the salt. Dice* the butter and blend it in with your fingers
until it forms coarse crumbs. Make a well and incorporate the sugar and the
egg until just mixed. Shape the dough into a ball, cover with plastic wrap,
and chill for 20 minutes.
Preheat the oven to 350°F (180°C).
Roll out the dough to form a disk about ¹/₁₀ in. (3 mm) thick.
Cut out disks big enough to line tartlet molds or circles and place one in each
mold. Line them with heat-resistant plastic film or parchment paper and fill
with dry beans so that the sides stay in place during baking.
Bake blind* for about 15 minutes, until the pastry is lightly golden all over.

Prepare the lemon cream.
Bring ¹/₂ cup (100 ml) water, half the sugar, and the lemon juice to the boil.
Whisk the eggs, egg yolks, and the other half of the sugar together until the
mixture is thick and pale.
Whisk in the cornstarch and blend thoroughly.
Pour the lemon syrup over the egg mixture, beating constantly, and then
return all the liquid to a low heat. Add the lemon zest and cook it using the
same method as for a pastry cream, stirring constantly until it thickens and
coats the back of a spoon* or until it reaches 185°F (85°C). Remove from the
heat and whisk the butter in while the lemon cream is still hot.
Transfer it to a bowl, cover with plastic wrap so that it is in direct contact
with the cream, and chill.
When the lemon cream is at room temperature, or 68°F-77°F (20°C-25°C),
beat the cream stiffly. Fold* it carefully into the lemon cream and spoon the
mixture into the pastry shells. Chill.

Using a vegetable peeler, peel off the skin of the remaining lemon for
the garnish. Cut it into fine julienne strips and blanch* them three times,
changing the water each time.
Bring ³/₄ cup (200 ml) water and 1 cup (200 g) sugar to the boil. Add the
julienne strips to the water to candy them (see p. 97).

Prepare the Italian meringue (see p. 49).
Begin heating the sugar with a scant ¹/₂ cup (70 ml) water.
When the temperature of the syrup reaches 230°F (110°C), start beating the
egg whites with a pinch of salt. When the temperature of the syrup reaches
243-250°F (117-120°C), begin pouring it gradually into the egg whites.
Continue beating until the meringue has cooled down completely. It will be
dense and shiny, and will form many small peaks. Spoon it into a piping bag
and pipe out in decorative patterns onto the tops of the tarts.
Set the oven to "broil."
Lightly brown the meringue under the broiler and allow to cool.
Garnish with the dried lemon slices and blanched julienne strips.

Canelés, a specialty of Bordeaux ★

Make a day ahead

Serves 8

Preparation time: 35 minutes
Resting time: overnight
Cooking time: 55 minutes

Melt 3 1/2 tablespoons (50 g) butter in a small saucepan until it browns*.
Slit the vanilla bean lengthwise and scrape out the seeds. Bring the milk to
the boil with the seeds and the vanilla bean.
Combine the flour, salt, and sugar. Pour in the whole eggs and egg yolks
together and whisk vigorously to combine with the flour and sugar.
Pour the boiling milk into the batter and stir to combine. Pour in the melted
brown butter and mix gently. Your batter should be liquid–the texture of a
crêpe batter. Add the orange zest to the batter and stir in the rum.
Chill overnight.
Place a flat baking tray on the center rack of the oven and preheat it to 525°F
(270°C). If you cannot heat your oven to this temperature, the canelés will
bake on a hot tray at 475°F (240°). Butter the canelé molds.
Half fill the molds with the batter and place the pan on the hot baking
tray. Bake for 5 minutes, then lower the temperature to 300°F (150°C) and
continue baking for about 40 minutes.
The canelés should have a brown crust and a nice soft crumb.

Ingredients
3 1/2 tablespoons (50 g) butter, plus a little extra to
grease the molds
1/2 vanilla bean
2 cups (500 ml) full cream milk
1 generous cup (110 g) all-purpose flour
2 teaspoons (10 g) fine salt
1 1/4 cups (250 g) sugar
2 eggs plus 2 yolks
Zest of 1/2 unsprayed or organic orange
1 1/3 tablespoons (20 ml) rum
Special equipment: a canelé pan

Ingredients

¾ oz. (20 g) fresh (compressed) yeast

5 cups (500 g) all-purpose flour

2 teaspoons (10 g) fine salt

1 ⅔ cups (375 g) salted butter

1 ¼ cups (250 g) granulated sugar

1 egg yolk

Scant cup (200 ml) warm water

Kouign Amman, a specialty of Brittany ★★★

Serves 8

Preparation time: 45 minutes

Resting time: 1 hour 45 minutes

Cooking time: 30-40 minutes

Heat the oven to a temperature of 77°F-82°F (25°C-28°C) and place a bowl of water at the bottom.

Dilute the yeast in ¼ cup (50 ml) warm water.

Combine the flour with the salt. Add the yeast diluted in the water and work it in. Slowly pour in ¾ cup (200 ml) warm water and knead* until the dough is smooth, just like a bread dough. If you are using the dough hook of your food processor, knead at medium speed.

Place the dough in the oven to rise until it doubles in volume.

Dust the working counter with a little flour and deflate the dough. Roll it out into a rectangle just under 1 in. (1.5-2 cm) thick.

Cut the butter into small cubes and arrange them on the entire surface of the rectangle. Sprinkle the sugar over evenly.

Using the same method as required for puff pastry (see p. 16), fold and roll it out four times, chilling it 20 minutes between each operation.

Roll out the Kouign Amman dough into a circle and baste* it with beaten egg yolk. Leave to rest for 45 minutes in an unbuttered baking pan.

Preheat the oven to 450°F (230°C).

Bake for 30-40 minutes, keeping a close eye on the color. It should turn a lovely golden color.

When it comes out of the oven, the Kouign Amman is literally swimming in butter, but that will be absorbed as it cools.

● **Did you know?**

Kouign Amman (pronounced "kween a-mun") is a specialty of Brittany. The name comes from the Breton words for "bread" and "butter."

Technique

Puff pastry >> p. 16

Orange liqueur soufflé ★★

Serves 8
Preparation time: 40 minutes
Cooking time: 35 minutes

Prepare a pastry cream (see p. 182).
Slit the vanilla bean lengthwise and scrape the seeds into the milk. Place the milk and vanilla bean in a saucepan to heat.
In a mixing bowl, energetically whisk the egg yolks, sugar, and cornstarch until the mixture is pale and thick. When the milk is simmering, pour half of it over the egg yolk mixture, beating all the time. Pour in the remaining milk and return all the liquid to the heat. Bring to a simmer. Leave to simmer for no longer than 2-3 minutes, stirring constantly so that it does not burn.
Pour it into a mixing bowl and cover with plastic wrap flush with the pastry cream to prevent a skin from forming. Chill rapidly.

Use a pastry brush to grease the molds or ramekins with butter. Then sprinkle the molds all over with 2 generous tablespoons (30 g) sugar. Turn them over and give them a rap to remove any excess sugar.
Stir the Cointreau into the pastry cream.
Whip the 8 egg whites stiffly with the pinch of salt. When they are firm, whip in the remaining ¹/₃ cup (60 g) sugar until the mixture is shiny.
Place a baking tray in the oven and preheat the oven to 400°F (200°C).
Stir the 2 egg yolks into the pastry cream. Carefully fold* in the stiffly beaten egg whites using a rubber spatula.
Fill the soufflé molds to the top and smooth the surface.

Place the soufflé molds on the hot baking pan and bake for about 20 minutes, depending on the size. The soufflés should be well risen, have a nice brown crust, and be soft inside.

Technique
Hot soufflé (pastry cream base) >> p. 202

Ingredients
2 tablespoons (30 g) butter
2 generous tablespoons (30 g) sugar for the molds
plus ¹/₃ cup (60 g) granulated sugar
¹/₄ cup (60 ml) Cointreau or other orange liqueur
2 eggs, separated, plus 6 egg whites
1 small pinch of salt (2 g)

Pastry cream
2 cups (500 ml) milk
1 vanilla bean
4 egg yolks
²/₃ cup (125 g) sugar
¹/₃ cup (2 oz./60 g) cornstarch

Ingredients

Genoese sponge
4 eggs
$^2/_3$ cup (125 g) granulated sugar
1 $^1/_3$ cups (125 g) cake flour, plus a little extra

Orange mousse
3 sheets gelatin* (6 g)
4 oz. (125 g) puréed orange
3 egg whites
3 $^1/_2$ tablespoons (40 g) sugar
A few drops of Cointreau or other orange liqueur
Scant $^1/_2$ cup (110 ml) whipping cream

Syrup
1 $^1/_2$ cups (300 g) granulated sugar
1 $^1/_3$ tablespoons (20 ml) Cointreau
Zest of $^1/_2$ unsprayed or organic orange
$^3/_4$ teaspoon (2 g) ground cinnamon

Passion-fruit mousse
9 sheets gelatin (18 g)
17 $^1/_2$ oz. (500 g) passion-fruit pulp
10 egg whites
$^3/_4$ cup (150 g) granulated sugar
2 cups (500 ml) whipping cream

2 $^1/_2$ oz. (70 g) neutral glaze* (at specialty stores)
1 orange to garnish

Passion-fruit and orange mousse ★

Serves 8
Preparation time: 45 minutes
Cooking time: 35 minutes
Total chilling time: 3-4 hours

Prepare a Genoese sponge (see p. 193).
Preheat the oven to 350°F (180°C). Cover a baking sheet with parchment paper.
Working over a hot water bath, beat the eggs and the sugar together in a round-bottomed mixing bowl until the mixture reaches the ribbon stage*–a temperature of 140°F (60°C).
Sift in the flour in two stages, folding* it in gently each time with a rubber spatula. Work carefully so as not to deflate the batter.
Pour the batter onto a baking sheet to a thickness of about $^1/_8$ in. (4 mm). Bake for 15-20 minutes. Test for doneness (the tip of a knife should come out dry) and turn out onto a cooling rack. Remove the sheet of parchment paper. When it has cooled, cut out a disk just under 1 in. (2 cm) smaller than your ice cream cake or entremets ring.

Prepare the orange mousse (see p. 197).
Soak the gelatin sheets in cold water until they are softened.
Bring the orange purée to boil and simmer for 2 minutes.
Squeeze the water from the gelatin sheets and incorporate them into the orange purée. Leave to cool.
Prepare an Italian meringue with the three egg whites, sugar, and 1 tablespoon (15 ml) water (see p. 49).
Beat the scant $^1/_2$ cup (110 ml) cream until it form stiff peaks.
When the orange purée has reached room temperature, whisk in the orange liqueur. Use a rubber spatula to gently fold the cool Italian meringue into the orange purée. When it is completely incorporated, carefully fold in the whipped cream. Leave the mixture in the refrigerator to chill.

Prepare the syrup (to soak the sponge).
In a small saucepan, bring the sugar, the Cointreau, orange zest, and ground cinnamon to the boil in 1 $^1/_4$ cups (300 ml) water. Place the disk of Genoese sponge at the center of your circle over a flat stainless steel baking dish or rack lined with aluminum foil. Using a pastry brush, soak the disk of Genoese sponge with this syrup.
Spoon in the orange mousse until it reaches quarter way up the side of the ring. Freeze to set.

Prepare the passion fruit mousse (see p. 197).
Soak the gelatin sheets in cold water until they are softened.
Bring the passion fruit pulp to the boil and simmer for 2 minutes. Squeeze the water from the gelatin sheets and

incorporate them into the passion fruit pulp. Leave to cool.
Prepare an Italian meringue with the 10 egg whites, sugar, and scant $^1/_4$ cup (50 ml) water (see p. 49).
Beat the 2 cups (500 ml) cream until it form stiff peaks.
When the passion fruit pulp has reached room temperature, whisk it to ensure it is smooth. Use a rubber spatula to carefully fold the cool Italian meringue into the pulp. When it is completely incorporated, carefully fold in the whipped cream. Leave the mixture in the refrigerator to chill so that it does not melt the first layer of mousse when poured.
Fill the circle to the top with the passion fruit mousse and smooth the surface with a spatula.
Place in the freezer until set, 30 minutes to 1 hour.
When the mousse has set, glaze* it with the neutral glaze.
If you wish, use a colorant for a marbled effect.
Place the mousse on a serving dish and remove the circle with a blowtorch or a hot towel.

 Techniques

Genoese sponge ›› p. 193
Fruit mousse ›› p. 197
Italian meringue ›› p. 49

Assortment of almond macaroons ★★★

Serves 8
Preparation time: 55 minutes
Resting time: 20 minutes
Cooking time: 45 minutes

Prepare the macaroon batter (see p. 195). Prepare a silicone baking sheet or a baking tray lined with parchment paper. If you use parchment paper, drizzle a little cold water between the paper and the tray.

Process the ground almonds and confectioners' sugar finely in a food processor. If the powder is not uniformly fine, you may need to sift it through a fine-mesh sieve. Finely ground almonds are essential to the quality of macaroons.

Add the 2 oz. (50 g) of egg whites and stir in until the mixture reaches a fairly firm texture.

Begin cooking the sugar and 3 1/2 tablespoons (50 ml) water to form a syrup. When it reaches a temperature of 250°F (121°C) prepare an Italian meringue (see p. 49) using the beaten egg white. When it has cooled, carefully fold* the Italian meringue into the almond mixture, taking care not to deflate the mixture. Stir until it reaches a consistency that is firm but still fluid.

Divide the macaroon batter in two and incorporate the red colorant into half of it to make the raspberry macaroons.

Spoon the mixture into a piping bag and pipe out small rounds on to the baking sheet. If you are making mini macaroons, pipe out circles just under 1 in. (2 cm), and for individual desserts, make them about 2 1/2-3 in. (5-8 cm). Leave them out to dry for about 20 minutes. They will form a light crust— make sure it has formed before you bake them!

Ensure that the oven is completely dry (no residue of steam from previous use) and pre-heat it to 300°F (150°C). Cook for 8-10 minutes.

When they are done, leave them to cool on the baking sheet. Transfer them to a rack only when they are cold.

Prepare the raspberry preserves.
Begin cooking the raspberries with the sugar. Slit the vanilla bean lengthwise and scrape the seeds into the mixture. Add the vanilla bean to the pan. Slowly bring the temperature to 225°F (107°C).

Stir in the raspberry brandy or liqueur and crush the raspberries roughly using a fork. Leave to cool completely. Take pairs of raspberry macaroons the same size and sandwich them together with the raspberry preserves.

Prepare the salted butter caramel.
Cook the sugar until it reaches a dark caramel color–350°F (180°C). Remove from the heat and stir in the salted butter. When it has melted, pour in the whipping cream. Return to the heat so that the caramel sauce liquefies. Allow it to cool. When it has cooled, sandwich together pairs of equally sized plain macaroons with the caramel.

● **Chef's note**
This recipe requires precisely measured ingredients and just the right baking temperature.

Ingredients
1 3/4 cup (5 1/4 oz./150 g) ground almonds*
1 generous cup (5 1/4 oz./150 g) confectioners' sugar
1 3/4 oz. (50 g) egg whites
3/4 cup (5 1/4 oz./150 g) caster sugar
Scant 2 oz. (55 g) egg whites, whipped
1 small pinch ground red colorant

Raspberry preserves (with seeds)
1 lb. 2 oz. (500 g) raspberries
1 lb. 2 oz. (2 2/3 cups or 500 g) granulated sugar
1 vanilla bean
1 1/3 tablespoon (20 ml) raspberry brandy or liqueur

Salted butter caramel
2/3 cup (125 g) sugar
3 tablespoons (45 g) salted butter
Scant 1/2 cup (125 ml) whipping cream, minimum fat content 35 percent

Techniques
Macaroon ›› p. 195
Italian meringue ›› p. 49

Ingredients

Puff pastry

2 ³/₄ cups (250 g) cake flour

1 teaspoon (5 g) salt

¹/₂ cup (125 ml) water

³/₄ cup (185 g) unsalted butter

Pastry cream

1 cup (250 ml) milk

¹/₂ vanilla bean

2 egg yolks

¹/₃ cup (65 g) granulated sugar

6 ¹/₃ tablespoons (generous ¹/₃ cup or 60 g) cornstarch

A few drops of bitter almond extract

Almond cream

1 generous cup (100 g) blanched* ground almonds* or almond meal

7 tablespoons (100 g) unsalted butter, softened*

¹/₂ cup (100 g) granulated sugar

2 eggs

For basting

1 egg, lightly beaten

1 ¹/₂ cups (300 g) sugar

2 tablespoons (30 ml) water

Kings' cake (*galette des rois*) ★ ★

Serves 8

Preparation time: 1 hour 30 minutes
Resting time: 1 hour 40 minutes
Cooking time: 50 minutes

Prepare the puff pastry, following the instructions on p. 16. Prepare the frangipane cream (see p. 178).
First, make a pastry cream (see p. 182) and leave it to cool. While it cools, prepare the almond cream (see p. 176).
Stir the bitter almond extract into the pastry cream.
Incorporate the almond cream, and stir energetically.

Preheat the oven to 425°F (210°C).
Roll the puff pastry out: you will have to cut out two circles so make sure it is long enough. It should be about ¹/₈ in. (4-6 mm) thick. Cut out one disk (for the bottom of the cake) with a diameter of just under 10 in. (24 cm). The top disk must be just slightly bigger–just under 1 in. (2 cm)–as it has to cover the low mound of frangipane.
Transfer the smaller circle to a baking tray (lined with parchment paper, if you wish). Baste* the edge of the circumference, no more than ¹/₂ in. (1-1.5 cm) with the beaten egg. This will help seal the cake. Spread the frangipane out evenly on the pastry, taking care not to put any on the egg-painted edge. One way to do this is to pipe it out from a piping bag, starting in the center.
Cover the frangipane with the larger pastry circle. If you are including the traditional lucky charm or trinket, put it in now, pressing it in very lightly. To seal the two parts together, press lightly with your fingers all round the edges. Then take a small, sharp knife and make shallow, angled incisions in the two layers around the edge at fairly close intervals. This will help prevent the frangipane from seeping out as it bakes. You may make a small hole in the center to allow steam to escape during baking.
Baste the top with the beaten egg yolk, but stop short of the edges. Then use the back of a knife (so that you don't cut into the top pastry) to make a decorative pattern, radiating arcs or criss-crossing lines. Chill for 20 minutes.
Place in the oven and bake for 35-45 minutes altogether. While the cake is baking, prepare a syrup with the 1 ¹/₂ cups (300 g) sugar and 2 tablespoons (30 ml) water. When the cake has puffed and started to turn golden, near the end of the baking time, paint the top with the syrup and return it to the oven for a few minutes. Repeat the procedure two more times during the last 5 minutes. The cake top should be golden brown and lightly caramelized. Do not let it get too dark. When it is the right color, transfer it to a rack and allow to cool. Serve the same day.

Techniques

Puff pastry >> p. 16

Frangipane cream >> p. 178

Pastry cream >> p. 182

Almond cream >> p. 172

Mixed berry tart ★

Serves 8

Preparation time: 45 minutes
Resting time: 20 minutes
Cooking time: 45 minutes

Preheat the oven to 350°F (180°F).
Prepare a sweetened short pastry (see p. 14). Place the butter, sugar, and egg
in the bowl of a food processor and cream together until smooth. Sift the
flour and add it with the salt to process for 1-2 minutes further, until smooth.
Press down the dough with the palm of your hand, pushing it away from
you, until the ingredients are thoroughly blended. Chill, covered, for 20
minutes. Roll out the dough very thinly (about ¹/₆ in./3 mm) to form a disk.
Use a rolling pin to transfer it from the working surface to the baking pan
or circle: drape it round the pin and then unroll it in place. Make decorative
patterns around the edge.
Prick the dough with a fork and bake blind* for 20-30 minutes, until it is
a light golden color.

Prepare the pastry cream (see p. 182).
Slit a vanilla bean lengthwise and scrape the seeds into the milk. Place the
milk and vanilla bean in a saucepan to heat.
In a mixing bowl, energetically whisk the egg yolks, sugar, and cornstarch
until the mixture is pale and thick. When the milk is simmering, pour half
of it over the egg yolk mixture, beating all the time. If you are adding a
flavoring ingredient, now is the time to incorporate it, unless you are using
a liqueur, in which case you should add it when the mixture has cooled.
Pour in the remaining milk and return all the liquid to the heat. Bring to a
simmer, stirring all the time. Leave to simmer for 2-3 minutes, still stirring.
Transfer the pastry cream to a mixing bowl and cover it with plastic wrap
flush with the surface. This will prevent a skin from forming. Cool down
rapidly.
When the pastry cream has cooled, spoon it into a piping bag and fill the
cooled pastry shell. Arrange the berries attractively over the pastry cream.
Give them a nice shine by brushing them with the apricot glaze. If using
apricot preserve, liquify a little over a low heat before use. Serve when cool.

Techniques
Sweetened short pastry ›› p. 14
Pastry cream ›› p. 182

Ingredients
A total of 4 ¹/₄ oz. (120 g) of mixed berries,
including:
Raspberries
Blackcurrants
Redcurrants
Strawberries
Wild strawberries
¹/₃ cup (80 g) smooth apricot preserves or glaze*

Sweetened short pastry
1 stick (125 g) unsalted butter, softened*
¹/₂ cup (100 g) granulated sugar
1 egg
2 ³/₄ cups (250 g) cake flour
1 teaspoon (5 ml) salt

Pastry cream
2 cups (500 ml) milk
1 vanilla bean
3 eggs
²/₃ cup (125 g) granulated sugar
6 ¹/₃ tablespoons (generous ¹/₃ cup or 60 g)
cornstarch
A few drops of vanilla essence

Ingredients

Frying batter

2 cups (200 g) all-purpose flour

1 teaspoon (5 g) table salt

2 eggs plus 3 egg whites

1 ¹/₃ tablespoons (20 ml) sunflower seed oil

³/₄ cup (200 ml) milk or beer

2 lb. (1 kg) golden delicious apples (about 5-6 apples)

2 teaspoons (10 ml) calvados or other apple brandy

Scant ¹/₂ cup (80 g) sugar

Generous ¹/₂ teaspoon (3 g) ground cinnamon

Oil for frying

Apricot coulis

1 ¹/₂ lb. (700 g) apricots

1 cup (250 ml) water

3 ²/₃ cups (700 g) sugar

1 vanilla bean

Apple fritters with apricot coulis ★

Serves 8

Preparation time: 50 minutes

Resting time: 30 minutes

Cooking time: 30 minutes

Prepare the batter for frying (see p. 23).

Sift the flour into a mixing bowl and add the salt. Break the whole eggs one by one, and whisk them in to the dry ingredients. Incorporate the oil.

Pour in the liquid (milk or beer) and whisk until the mixture is smooth.

Stiffly beat the egg whites.

Gently fold in* the beaten egg whites using a flexible rubber spatula.

Prepare the apples

Peel, wash, and core the apples. Slice them into disks just over 1 in. (3 cm) thick. Allow 3 slices per person.

Combine the calvados, sugar, and cinnamon and place the apple slices in the liquid to marinate.

Prepare the apricot coulis (see p. 164).

Remove the pits from the apricots. Place them in a saucepan with the water and the sugar over low heat. Add the vanilla bean with its seeds scraped. Leave to stew gently. If you wish, add a few drops of the marinade to heighten the flavor of your coulis. Process the stewed fruit using an immersion blender or juicer.

Strain through a fine-mesh sieve and set aside.

Begin heating the oil bath.

Dip the apple slices in the frying batter.

Fry them evenly on both sides. When they are done, remove them with a slotted spoon and drain on paper towel.

The fritters should be eaten immediately, accompanied by the apricot coulis.

 Techniques

Batter for frying >> p. 23
Fruit coulis >> p. 164

Ingredients

Puff pastry
1 ¹⁄₃ cups (4.4 oz./125 g) cake flour
1 small pinch fine salt
¹⁄₃ cup (70 ml) water
6 ¹⁄₂ tablespoons (95 g) unsalted butter

Choux pastry
1 ¹⁄₄ cups (125 g) all-purpose flour
1 cup (250 ml) water
1 teaspoon (5 g) table salt
1 scant tablespoon (15 g) sugar (optional)
7 tablespoons (100 g) unsalted butter, cubed
4 eggs, plus 1 egg, lightly beaten, for basting

Chiboust cream
5 sheets gelatin* (10 g)
2 cups (500 ml) milk
1 vanilla bean
3 egg yolks (retain whites for meringue)
²⁄₃ cups (125 g) granulated sugar
¹⁄₃ cup (55 g) cornstarch

Italian meringue
8 egg whites
2 ²⁄₃ cups (500 g) sugar
¹⁄₄ cup (60 ml) water

Caramel
1 cup (200 g) granulated sugar
¹⁄₄ cup (60 ml) water

Techniques
Puff pastry ≫ p. 16
Choux pastry ≫ p. 20
Chiboust cream ≫ p. 175
Italian meringue ≫ p. 49

Gâteau Saint-Honoré ★ ★ ★

Serves 8
Preparation time: 55 minutes
Resting time: 1 hour 20 minutes
Cooking time: 50 minutes

Prepare the puff pastry (see p. 16).
Sift the flour and add the salt. Pour the water into the flour and stir with your fingers to combine.
Blend the ingredients together rapidly until thoroughly mixed. You should have a smooth paste, known as the *détrempe*. Form it into a ball, and chill, covered, for about 20 minutes.
Check that the butter has the identical consistency of the dough mixture. Beat it, if necessary, between two sheets of parchment paper, with your rolling pin. This enables it to be incorporated more easily into the dough, and gives it a longer rectangular shape.
Now roll out the dough mixture to form a cross shape, leaving the center–where you will place the butter–thicker (about $^1/_5$ in./5 mm) than the four other parts. The butter should fit over this part of the dough.
Place the butter in the center of the dough and fold over each of the four parts of the cross, similarly to the back of an envelope.
Lightly dust your cool working counter with flour (use as little as possible each time, so that the pastry does not become too hard). Roll out the dough (called a *paton*) to form a rectangle whose length is three times greater than its width.
Fold this into three, starting at each end (three layers). Rotate the folded dough a quarter turn and roll out again to form the same shape as previously, a rectangle three times its width. Repeat the folding operation. Cover with plastic wrap and chill again for about 20 minutes.
Repeat this procedure–rolling out and folding–five more times (a total of six times), chilling for 20 minutes between each step of two quarter turns.
Roll it out and cut out a circle with a diameter of about 8 in. (20 cm), prick it with a fork, and leave in the refrigerator until needed.

Prepare the choux pastry (see p. 20).
Preheat the oven to 425°F (210°C).
Sift the flour. In a saucepan, bring the water, salt, sugar if using, and cubed butter to the boil. Remove from heat.
Pour the flour in altogether. Stir until combined. It should form a thickish paste.
Return to the heat and beat energetically with a rubber spatula until the moisture has evaporated.
Transfer the mixture to a mixing bowl. Spread it out with the spatula so that it adheres (it will not stick, however) to the sides of the bowl.

Add the four eggs, one by one, using the spatula to mix. Stir in thoroughly each time.
Spoon the batter into a piping bag. Take the puff pastry disk from the refrigerator and pipe out a spiral of choux pastry on it, starting from the center, large enough to fit over the disk of puff pastry.
Pipe out eight to ten small puff pastry shapes on to a baking tray. Baste* them with the remaining beaten egg.
Bake all your pastries together for about 20 minutes (for the small puff pastries) to 30 minutes (for the larger piece).

Prepare the Chiboust cream (see p. 175) by first making a pastry cream.
Soak the gelatin sheets in a bowl of very cold water. Slit the vanilla bean lengthwise and scrape the seeds into the milk. Add the vanilla bean to the milk and begin to heat.
Whisk the 3 egg yolks, the sugar, and the cornstarch until the mixture is pale and thick.
When the milk begins to simmer, remove from the heat and pour half of it over the beaten egg yolks. Combine thoroughly. Pour the egg and milk combination over the milk and return to the heat. Bring it back to the simmer and leave to simmer for 2 to 3 minutes, whisking continuously.
Remove from the heat. Drain the gelatin sheets, squeezing out all the water, and fold* into the milk mixture. Mix thoroughly with a whisk.
Transfer to a bowl and cover with plastic wrap flush with the cream. Allow to chill until it reaches a temperature of about 60°F (15°C).

Prepare an Italian meringue (see p. 49) with the 8 egg whites, the sugar, and the water.
When the pastry cream has cooled but has not yet set, smooth it out. Carefully fold in the Italian meringue into the pastry cream to make a Chiboust cream. Spoon the Chiboust cream into a piping bag.
Prepare a caramel with the sugar and the water.
Take a small sharp knife and make a small hole in each of the puff pastries. Fill them with Chiboust cream.
To close the holes you have made, dip each puff pastry into the hot caramel. To cool, place them, caramel side downward, on a sheet of parchment paper.
To assemble the cake, place the choux pastry disk over the puff pastry disk. Once again dip the filled choux pastries into the caramel (it should still be hot; if not, reheat it) and glue them around the edge of the choux pastry spiral. Fill the center of the gateau with the remaining Chiboust cream.
Garnish and serve.

Apple upside-down cake (*tarte Tatin*) ★

Serves 8
Preparation time: 40 minutes
Resting time: 20 minutes
Cooking time: 55 minutes

Prepare the shortcrust pastry (see p. 12).
Sift the flour and add the salt. Blend the butter and the flour together with your fingertips until the mixture forms coarse crumbs. Make a well and incorporate the egg yolk and water. Form a ball with the dough, still working quickly with your hands. Flatten the dough with the palm of your hands, pushing it away from you, until it is quite smooth.
Chill the dough, wrapped in plastic, for about 30 minutes.
Lightly sprinkle the working surface with flour and roll the dough into a disk shape with a thickness of about $1/6$ in. (3 mm).
Preheat the oven to 350°F.
Peel and core the apples. Cut into thick slices.
Place a nonstick cake pan or special *tarte Tatin* pan on the heat and melt the butter. Add the sugar and caramelize over low heat. When the sugar begins to change color, arrange the apple slices in overlapping circles in the pan. Do not leave any gaps between the pieces.
Flatten them slightly using a spatula so that they can poach in the caramel.
Sprinkle with cinnamon. Remove the pan from the heat and cover with shortcrust pastry, pressing down firmly at the edges. Prick the pastry with a fork.
Bake for 35-40 minutes. The pastry will be golden.
Allow to cool a little in the pan before turning the tart out onto a serving plate. Serve it, still warm, with the apples facing upward. *Tarte Tatin* is excellent with slightly sweet whipped cream and vanilla ice cream–a wonderful warm-cold combination.

Technique
Shortcrust pastry ›› p. 12

Ingredients
Shortcrust pastry
2 $3/4$ cups (250 g) cake flour
1 generous teaspoon (5 g) table salt
1 stick (125 g) unsalted butter, softened*
1 egg yolk
4 $1/2$ tablespoons (50 ml) water

10 golden delicious apples
1 stick (125 g) unsalted butter
1 cup (200 g) sugar
Generous $1/2$ teaspoon (3 g) ground cinnamon

Didier Stéphan
presents his recipe

The *verrine*, or shot glass, no doubt still has a bright future, even if—just like the omnipresent macaroons—we seem to see too many of them in France.

There are many advantages to this form of dessert, not the least among them being transparency: we can see—or at least glimpse—what we are about to eat. Next, it allows the pastry chef to make more use of textures that have not set: crispness and melt-in-the-mouth creaminess can be juxtaposed with no difficulty. This gives free rein to the imagination. In my opinion, the *verrine* should be another means of expression for desserts, just like petit fours, the equivalent of a quarter cup containing multiple and short explosions of tasting pleasure.

In this *verrine* recipe, Pineau wine, an aperitif from the Poitou-Charentes region in southwest France, takes pride of place. Pineau is a grape juice whose fermentation is stopped by adding eau-de-vie before being matured in oak barrels, where it acquires its delightful taste. Pineau rosé, in addition, takes on notes of berries. And diplomat cream, much used in the past, seems almost to have come out of a black-and-white film. Today it is making a comeback and its lightness and subtle creamy texture are once again winning it popularity.

Vanilla-Pineau diplomat cream

Jelled Pineau
Soften the gelatin leaf in cold or iced water for 3 minutes. Drain well and dissolve in a few drops of water in a microwave oven for 10 seconds. Combine the Pineau with the gelatin and immediately pour the liquid just under 1 in. (2 cm) deep into each of the 4 glasses.

Diplomat cream
Bring the milk to the boil. Leave the vanilla bean to infuse in the milk for 30 minutes. Beat the egg yolks and sugar together, whisk in the cornstarch, and pour the mixture over the milk. Bring to the simmer and allow to thicken to the texture of a pastry cream. Remove from the heat and whisk in the butter. Cover with plastic wrap and chill for 20 minutes to set.
When it has chilled, whisk the cream stiffly and carefully fold* it in.

Crumble
Cream the butter and sugar together. If you are not using salted butter, add a little salt. Then incorporate the ground almonds* and flour.
Chill for 15 minutes and crumble it onto a baking tray. Bake it at 350°F (180°C) for 5–10 minutes, until it turns a light golden color.

Salted caramel sauce
Caramelize the sugar (use the dry method, i.e. without any water). Heat the cream and add it to the caramel. Remove from the heat and adjust the consistency when cold by adding more cream if necessary, until it is syrupy. Add a pinch of salt.

Glucose bubbles
Preheat the oven to 300°F (150°C). Line a baking sheet with parchment paper or use a silicone baking sheet. Spread the glucose out (if you wish to color it, add a few drops of colorant) and bake for 50 minutes.

To assemble
Pour the Diplomat cream (just over 1 in. or about 3 cm) over the jelled Pineau. Then pour in the caramel sauce.
Sprinkle the crumble on the top and garnish with a sheet of glucose bubbles.

Serves 4
Preparation time: 2 hours
Cooking time: 1 hour 40 minutes

Ingredients
Jelled Pineau
Scant 1/2 cup (100 g) Pineau
1 sheet gelatin* (2 g)

Diplomat cream
1 cup (250 ml) milk
1 vanilla bean, slit and scraped
1/3 cup (60 g) sugar
2 1/2 egg yolks (50 g)
2 tablespoons (20 g) cornstarch
1 1/3 tablespoons Charente butter
3/4 cup (200 ml) whipping cream, stiffly beaten

Crumble
Scant 1/2 cup (100 g) butter
7 tablespoons (100 g) sugar
1 generous cup (100 g) ground almonds
1 generous cup (100 g) cake flour

Salted caramel sauce
1/2 cup (100 g) sugar
Scant 1/2 cup (100 ml) crème fraîche
A pinch of salt

Glucose bubbles
2 oz. (60 g) glucose
Food colorant (optional)

Raspberry charlotte ★★

Serves 8

Preparation time: 1 hour 10 minutes
Chilling time: 2 hours 30 minutes
Cooking time: 35 minutes

Prepare the ladyfingers (see p. 188).
Prepare a French meringue (see p. 49) using four egg whites and the sugar.
Fold* this in with the egg yolks. Sift the flour with the starch directly into
the egg mixture. Carefully fold in using a rubber spatula.
Preheat the oven to 400°F (200°C).
Pipe out the mixture, or spoon it, onto a silicone baking sheet or parchment
paper. Each ladyfinger should be about 3 ¹/₂-4 in. (8-10 cm) long and ²/₃ in.
(1.5 cm) wide.
Dust them with confectioners' sugar and allow it to penetrate.
Sprinkle the ladyfingers again with confectioners' sugar and bake for 10-15
minutes, until a very pale color. Allow to cool.

Prepare the raspberry syrup. Bring the water and the sugar to the boil.
When quite dissolved, add the raspberry liqueur.

Line the charlotte mold with the cooled ladyfingers, packing them closely
together. Use a pastry brush to moisten them well with the warm syrup.

Prepare the raspberry Bavarian cream (see p. 190).
Soak the gelatin sheets in very cold water to soften them.
Bring the raspberry purée and sugar to the boil. Drain the gelatin, wringing
out the water with your hands, and add it to the purée. Combine thoroughly.
Allow the mixture to cool. When the purée has cooled to about 68°F (20°C) or
room temperature, whisk in the raspberry liqueur.
Whip the cream until it forms firm peaks.
Carefully fold in the whipped cream, little by little, using a rubber spatula,
taking care not to deflate the mixture.
Pour it into the mold immediately to set. Cover it well with plastic wrap and
chill for 2-2 ¹/₂ hours.

Prepare the raspberry coulis (see p. 164).
Wash the raspberries and blend them with the lemon juice and sugar.
Strain through a fine-mesh sieve. Cover with plastic wrap and chill until
needed.
Turn the charlotte out of the mold onto a serving plate (use hot tea towels if
necessary). Garnish with raspberries and serve with the coulis.

Techniques

Ladyfingers ›› p. 188
French meringue ›› p. 49
Syrup ›› p. 168
Fruit-based Bavarian cream ›› p. 190
Fruit coulis ›› p. 164

Ingredients

Ladyfingers
3 eggs, separated, plus 1 egg white
¹/₂ cup (100 g) sugar
Generous ¹/₂ cup (50 g) cake flour
¹/₃ cup (50 g) cornstarch
Confectioners' sugar for dusting

Raspberry syrup
¹/₃ cup (60 g) granulated sugar
3 tablespoons (40 ml) water
2 teaspoons (10 ml) raspberry liqueur
4 ¹/₂ oz. (125 g) raspberries, for garnish

Raspberry Bavarian cream
10 sheets gelatin* (20 g)
1 ³/₄ lb. (800 g) puréed raspberries
¹/₂ cup (100 g) sugar
1 ¹/₂ teaspoons (8 ml) raspberry liqueur
3 ¹/₄ cups (800 ml) whipping cream, 35 percent
fat content

Raspberry coulis
7 oz. (200 g) raspberries
1 ¹/₃ tablespoons (20 ml) lemon juice
²/₃ cup (80 g) confectioners' sugar

Special equipment: a charlotte mold, about 8 inches
(18 cm) in diameter, or individual molds

Ingredients

Brioche
$^1/_5$ oz. (5 g) fresh (compressed) yeast
2 teaspoons (10 ml) milk or water
2 $^1/_2$ cups (250 g) all-purpose flour
1 teaspoon (5 g) table salt
2 tablespoons (25 g) granulated sugar
3 eggs
$^1/_2$ cup (125 g) unsalted butter, softened*

Sweet cream
Scant $^1/_2$ cup (100 ml) milk
Scant $^1/_2$ cup (100 ml) whipping cream
2 eggs plus 2 egg yolks
3 $^1/_2$ tablespoons (40 g) sugar
A few drops of vanilla extract, or the seeds from a vanilla bean
A few drops of bitter almond extract
5 $^1/_2$ tablespoons (80 g) butter

Stewed rhubarb
1 lb. (400 g) rhubarb
1 $^3/_4$ cups (350 g) sugar
Scant $^1/_4$ cup (50 ml) water
A few drops of vanilla extract

Techniques
Brioche dough ≫ p. 24
Sweet baked cream ≫ p. 186

French brioche toast and vanilla-scented stewed rhubarb ★★

Serves 8
Preparation time: 50 minutes
Resting time: 1 hour
Cooking time: 1 hour
Refrigeration time: 8 hours

A day ahead
Prepare the brioche (see p. 24).
Dilute the yeast in the milk or water at room temperature. Sift the flour onto a flat surface and make a well in the center. Sprinkle the salt and sugar outside the well so that they do not come into direct contact with the yeast. Beat the eggs and incorporate them into the mixture using a rubber scraper. Knead* the dough energetically to give it elasticity. You may use the hook attachment of an electric beater to do this. If you opt for the electric beater, use medium speed for about 10 minutes. Then knead in the butter until it is completely incorporated and the dough is smooth, and place the dough in a mixing bowl.
Cover with plastic wrap and leave to rise for 30 to 40 minutes at a temperature of 77°F-82°F (25°C-28°C) with a bowl of water. When the dough has doubled in volume, remove from the bowl and turn out onto a lightly floured surface. Flatten it and fold into three. This is known as deflating. Form a ball and shape it to fit the brioche pan. Leave to rise again until it reaches halfway to the top of the mold.
Preheat the oven to 350°F-400°F (180°C-200°C). Bake the brioche. It is done when it is a nice golden color and the tip of a knife comes out dry.

Prepare the sweet cream for baking (see p. 186).
Combine the milk, cream, whole eggs, egg yolks, sugar, vanilla, and bitter almond extract until just mixed. Do not beat until the mixture forms bubbles. Strain it through a fine-mesh sieve, cover with plastic wrap, and chill.

Prepare the stewed rhubarb.
Trim, wash and peel the stalks, pulling off the hard fibers. Cut them into slices just under 1 in. (2 cm) long and blanch* them in boiling water. Drain the rhubarb and rinse it under cold water. Gently stew it over low heat with the sugar, water, and vanilla extract. Test for doneness: it should be soft when pressed between your fingers (allow a piece to cool down before testing). Chill until the next day.

To prepare and assemble
Cut thick slices of brioche, just under 1 in. (2 cm) thick.
Dip them in the sweet cream on both sides.
Melt the butter in a pan and brown the slices of brioche evenly on both sides. Arrange the brioches slices in plates with the stewed vanilla rhubarb. If you like, you may serve it with vanilla ice cream.

Raspberry ganache tart ★

Serves 8
Preparation time: 45 minutes
Resting time: 20 minutes
Cooking time: 40 minutes
Chilling time: 2-3 hours

Prepare the sweetened short pastry (see p. 14).
Place the butter, sugar, and egg in the bowl of a food processor and cream together until smooth. Sift the flour and add it with the salt to process for 1-2 minutes further, until smooth. Remove from the bowl.
Press down the dough with the palm of your hand, pushing it away from you, until the ingredients are thoroughly blended. Chill, covered, for 20 minutes.
Preheat the oven to 350°F (180°C).
Roll out the dough very thinly (about ¹/₆ in./3 mm) to form a disk. Use your rolling pin to transfer it from the working surface to the baking pan or circle: drape it round the pin and then unroll it over the tart mold.
Make decorative patterns around the edge. Prick the dough with a fork, line it with parchment paper, and fill with baking beans. Bake blind* for 20-25 minutes and allow to cool.

In a copper saucepan, cook 3 ¹/₂ oz. (100 g) of the raspberries with the sugar and glucose. Bring to the boil and leave to simmer for a few minutes. Add the cream and butter and bring to the boil again.
Remove from the heat and incorporate the raspberry brandy or eau-de-vie and the chopped chocolate. Mix until thoroughly blended.
Strain through a fine mesh sieve and pour the ganache into the cooled tart shell.
Leave in the refrigerator until set, about 2-3 hours.
Garnish with the remaining raspberries and serve.

Techniques
Sweetened short pastry » p. 14
Ganache » p. 180

Ingredients

Sweetened short pastry (creamed)
1 stick (125 g) unsalted butter, softened*
¹/₂ cup (100 g) granulated sugar
1 egg
2 ³/₄ cups (250 g) cake flour
1 teaspoon (5 ml) salt

Ganache cream
¹/₂ lb. (225 g) raspberries, divided
¹/₄ cup (50 g) granulated sugar
2 oz. (50 g) glucose
1 ²/₃ cups (400 ml) whipping cream, 30 percent fat content
7 tablespoons (100 g) unsalted butter
Scant ¹/₃ cup (70 ml) raspberry brandy or eau-de-vie
1 ³/₄ lb. (750 g) bittersweet chocolate, 64 percent cocoa, chopped

Special equipment: a copper saucepan

Ingredients

10 egg whites
$^1/_2$ teaspoon (2 g) fine table salt
1 $^3/_4$ cups (240 g) confectioners' sugar
4 cups (1 liter) milk
2 $^3/_4$ oz. (80 g) sliced almonds

Custard
$^1/_2$ vanilla bean
5 egg yolks
$^2/_3$ cup (125 g) granulated sugar

Spun sugar
1 $^1/_2$ cups (200 g) sugar

Floating islands with spun caramel ★★

Serves 8

Preparation time: 40 minutes
Cooking time: 30 minutes

Prepare a French meringue (see p. 49).
Use a round-bottomed mixing bowl that is perfectly clean and dry. Beat the egg whites together lightly with the salt using a fork. Then begin whisking them energetically, making sure you lift up the whisk high to incorporate as much air as possible. When the whites begin to form stiff peaks, add 1 $^3/_4$ cups (240 g) sugar, blending it in with a circular movement until the meringue is firm and shiny. It should form small peaks at the end of the whisk.
Bring the milk to a simmer in a fairly large pot or pan.
Dip a soup ladle into the beaten egg whites and form domes using a plastic scraper. Poach the domes in the milk for 1-2 minutes, depending on their size. Turn them over carefully to ensure they are cooked through. Remove the cooked meringue domes, reserving the milk for the custard.
Drain them on paper towel and chill.

Prepare the custard (see p. 172).
Take 2 cups (500 ml) of the poaching liquid and strain it through a fine-mesh sieve. Slit the vanilla bean and place it in a saucepan with the milk to heat. Energetically whisk the egg yolks with the sugar until the mixture is thick and pale. Pour the milk over the beaten egg yolks, beating constantly, and return to the heat. Simmer and stir all the time, removing from the heat from time to time, so that the egg yolks do not coagulate from too much contact with the heat. Continue until the mixture thickens and coats the back of a spoon* (185°F/85°C if you have a thermometer).
Strain through a chinois* and pour the cream into a mixing bowl. Cover with plastic wrap and allow to cool.
When it has cooled, half fill dessert bowls or cups with it. Then carefully place a floating island meringue dome on top of the liquid.

Make the spun sugar: heat the sugar to make a light caramel and allow to cool just slightly. To make the sugar threads, dip a fork in the caramel and whisk it energetically in a round-bottomed mixing bowl. Garnish one of the floating islands. Reheat the caramel just slightly and repeat the operation as many times as necessary, garnishing the desserts each time.
Lightly toast the sliced almonds, allow them to cool, and scatter them over the floating islands. Serve immediately.

● Did you know?

The recipe for floating islands was first written up by La Varenne in his Le Cuisinier Français (The French Cook) of 1651, and is still popular in its original form.

 Techniques
French meringue ›› p. 49
Pouring custard ›› p. 172

Tutti-frutti waffles ★

Serves 8

Preparation time: 40 minutes
Resting time: 30 minutes
Cooking time: 15 minutes

Prepare the waffle batter (see p. 22).
Combine the flour, sugar, salt, and baking powder in a mixing bowl. Make a well in the center.
Break the eggs into the well and whisk them into the dry ingredients with a little milk.
Gradually add the rest of the milk, whisking until there are no lumps.
Stir in the melted butter and orange-blossom water. Leave the batter to chill for about 30 minutes.

Prepare the fruit. Peel and wash the apples and cut them into quarters. Wash all the berries.
Coat the raspberries and strawberries lightly in confectioners' sugar by placing a little sugar on the tip of a knife and blowing lightly down the blade.

Cook the waffles in the waffle maker according to instructions and leave them to cool.

Prepare the Chantilly cream (see p. 174)
Pour the cold cream into a cold mixing bowl or the cold bowl of a food processor.
Whisk briskly or beat at medium speed with the food processor until the cream begins to form peaks.
Sift the confectioners' sugar into the cream and then add the vanilla extract.
Whisk the cream briskly for a few moments until it forms stiff peaks.
Pipe or spoon the cream onto the waffles and garnish attractively with the fruit.

Techniques
Waffle batter ›› p. 22
Chantilly cream ›› p. 174

Ingredients

Waffle batter
3 ³/₄ cups (340 g) cake flour
Scant ¹/₂ cup (80 g) sugar
Scant ¹/₂ teaspoon (2 g) table salt
2 ³/₄ teaspoons (10 g) baking powder
2 eggs
2 cups (¹/₂ liter) milk
Scant ¹/₂ cup (100 g) melted butter
A little orange-blossom water

2 apples
4 ¹/₂ oz. (125 g) blackberries
8 bunches red currants
4 ¹/₂ oz. (125 g) small, tasty strawberries (Mara des bois if possible)
8 bunches (125 g) blackcurrants
4 ¹/₂ oz. (125 g) raspberries
A little confectioners' sugar, for coating

Chantilly cream
1 cup (250 ml) whipping cream, 35 percent fat content, well chilled
¹/₄ cup (35 g) confectioners' sugar
A few drops vanilla extract

Ingredients

1 lb. (500 g) black cherries
¹/₂ cup (100 g) sugar, divided
1 ¹/₃ cups (125 g) cake flour
1 teaspoon (5 g) fine salt
3 eggs, beaten
1 ¹/₄ cups (300 ml) full cream milk
2 tablespoons (30 g) butter, melted
1 vanilla bean, slit, seeds scraped out
Confectioners' sugar, for dusting

Cherry clafoutis ★

Serves 8

Preparation time: 15 minutes
Resting time: 40 minutes
Cooking time: 45 minutes

Wash the cherries and remove the stalks. Sprinkle them with half of the sugar and leave to rest for 30-40 minutes.

Preheat the oven to 350°C (180°F). In a mixing bowl, combine the flour and the remaining sugar. Add the salt and energetically whisk in the beaten eggs so that there are no lumps. Stir in the melted butter and the vanilla seeds. Place the cherries (leave the pits in) in a cake mold or silicone flan mold. Fill it with the batter.

Bake for 40-45 minutes. Test for doneness: it should be very soft, and when you insert the tip of a knife some steam will rise.

Dust with confectioners' sugar as soon as you remove it from the oven and serve hot or warm.

● Did you know?

A clafoutis is a simple dessert that was traditionally made in the country when cherries were harvested. When cherry season is over, the recipe works equally well with many other fruits.

Ingredients
¹/₂ lb. (250 g) bittersweet chocolate, 64 percent
cocoa, chopped
5 ¹/₂ tablespoons (80 g) butter, cubed
3 eggs, separated, plus 3 egg whites
¹/₂ cup (100 g) sugar
2 oz. (30 g) chocolate sprinkles, for garnish

Chocolate mousse ★

Serves 8
Preparation time: 25 minutes
Chilling time: 1 hour minimum
Cooking time: 10 minutes

Melt the chopped chocolate and the cubed butter in a bain-marie* to
a temperature of 122°F (50°C). Remove the mixture from the heat and whisk
in the three egg yolks until the mixture is smooth.
Leave to cool to about 82°F (28°C).
Start whisking the six egg whites. When they start to form firm peaks,
add the sugar and whisk until shiny and compact (see French meringue
technique p. 49).
Carefully fold* the meringue mixture into the chocolate-butter mixture
using a rubber spatula. Take care not to deflate the mixture by breaking the
air bubbles.
Spoon the mousse into a piping bag and pipe into ramekins or shot glasses
(*verrines*). Chill for at least 1 hour, until set.
Garnish with chocolate sprinkles.

● **Did you know?**
*Mousses practically disappeared from classic French cuisine toward the end of
the eighteenth century, only to reappear with the advent of* nouvelle cuisine.
*There was one notable exception: the chocolate mousse, probably the most
popular of all French desserts.*

 Techniques
Chocolate mousse ›› p. 196
French meringue ›› p. 49

Ingredients

5 oz. (140 g) round-grain rice
1 small stick of cinnamon (2 g)
1 vanilla bean
4 cups (1 liter) milk
4 egg yolks
¾ cup (150 g) granulated sugar
1 pinch fine salt (2 g)

Cinnamon-scented rice pudding ★

Serves 8
Preparation time: 20 minutes
Cooking time: 40 minutes

Wash the round-grain rice.
Place the rice in cold water with the salt and bring it to the boil. As soon as it starts boiling, remove from the heat and refresh* under cold running water. Drain.
Preheat the oven to 325°F (160°C).
Break up the cinnamon stick into pieces and slit the vanilla bean lengthwise.
Bring the milk to the boil with the vanilla bean and the cinnamon stick pieces.
If you are not using a saucepan with an ovenproof lid, transfer the milk to a deep baking dish, pour in the rice, cover, and bake for a good hour.
Check for doneness by pressing a few cooled grains of rice between your fingers.
Whisk the egg yolks and the sugar until the mixture is thick and pale.
Remove the rice from the oven and stir in the egg mixture. Place over a low to medium heat and bring back to a simmer.
Arrange the rice pudding attractively in individual dishes and allow to cool rapidly. Garnish as you wish, with mint leaves, a thin piece of vanilla bean, grated lemon rind, etc.

 Technique
Rice pudding >> p. 198

Ingredients

Succès meringue batter

5 egg whites

$^2/_3$ cup (125 g) sugar

$^1/_4$ cup (25 g) flour

1 $^1/_2$ cups (4 $^1/_2$ oz./125 g) ground almonds*

Nougatine

2 oz. (50 g) glucose syrup (from specialty stores or online)

2 $^2/_3$ cups (500 g) sugar

10 oz. (300 g) chopped almonds

$^1/_3$ cup (70 g) unsalted butter, melted

Chestnut butter cream

1 cup (200 g) sugar

Scant $^1/_3$ cup (70 ml) water

2 eggs plus 2 yolks

2 sticks (250 g) unsalted butter

3 $^1/_2$ oz. (100 g) chestnut cream (from specialty stores or online)

1 cup (4 $^1/_2$ oz./125 g) shelled walnuts

Chestnut cream Succès
and caramelized walnuts ★ ★

Serves 8

Preparation time: 50 minutes

Cooking time: 35 minutes

Chilling time: 2 hours

Preheat the oven to 400°F (200°C).

Prepare the Succès meringue batter (see p. 204).

Beat the egg whites until they form firm peaks. Add 1 generous tablespoon (15 g) sugar and beat until dense and shiny.

Sift the remaining sugar, flour, and ground almonds together. Pour into the beaten egg whites and fold* in carefully so that the mixture does not deflate. Immediately spoon it into a piping bag and pipe out sixteen circles (diameter about 5 in./10 cm) onto a baking sheet. Make a close whirl pattern starting in the center.

Bake for 8-10 minutes and transfer immediately to a rack to cool.

Prepare the nougatine. Melt the glucose syrup over medium heat. Gradually add the sugar, stirring constantly. Toast the almonds and keep them warm without burning them or allowing them to darken. When the sugar mixture begins to turn yellow (the temperature will be around 330°F or 165°C), add the still-hot almonds, stirring them in, and then the melted butter. Stir until all the ingredients are well combined. Pour the mixture out onto a silicone baking sheet and roll out thinly between two baking sheets. Allow to cool. Toast the walnuts and allow them to cool.

Prepare the chestnut butter cream (see p. 173).

Prepare a sugar syrup with the sugar and the water and cook until it reaches a temperature of 243°F (117°C). With an electric beater, whisk the egg and yolk mixture until is it foamy.

Pour the sugar syrup over the eggs, and continue beating for a few minutes to lower the temperature of the mixture.

Incorporate the cubed butter using a whisk or an electric beater at medium speed. Stir in the chestnut cream.

Spoon the butter cream into a piping bag. Take a disk of Succès meringue and pipe out the butter cream around the edge of the circle.

Coarsely chop the nougatine and rub the walnuts to remove their skin.

Place the chopped nougatine and walnuts in the center of the piped chestnut butter cream. Top with a second disk of Succès meringue and chill until needed.

 Techniques

Succès >> p. 204

Butter cream >> p. 173

Brown sugar tart ★

Serves 8
Preparation time: 40 minutes
Resting time: 40 minutes
Cooking time: 30 minutes

Prepare the pastry. Dilute the yeast in the warm milk.
Sift the flour and prepare a well in the center. Stir in the egg. Add the salt,
sugar, and the yeast diluted in the milk. Knead* until combined. Then knead
in the cubed butter. Knead vigorously. Use the method for making brioche
dough (see p. 24). Cover with plastic wrap and leave to double in volume for
30-40 minutes at a temperature of 77°F-82°F (25°C-28°C) with a bowl of
water.

Preheat the oven to 450°F (240 °C).
Roll out the dough to fit the tart mold. Sprinkle the brown Vergeoise sugar
inside.
Beat the eggs and butter together. Add the whipping cream and pour the
mixture over the sugar.
Bake for 25-30 minutes, depending on the size of your tart. It should be a
golden color. Serve warm or cool.

● Did you know?

*Until the early nineteenth century, cane sugar was imported into France. Then
Benjamin Delessert succeeded in producing another form of sugar using beets.
The first factory was located just outside what were then the limits of Paris.
The northern regions of France, in particular, made excellent use of the various
types of light-colored and brown sugars, known as Vergeoise or cassonade, in
candies and cakes such as this tart.*

Technique
Brioche >> p. 24

Ingredients
Pastry
¹/₂ oz. (15 g) fresh (compressed) yeast
Scant ¹/₂ cup (100ml) full cream milk, warm
2 ¹/₂ cups (250 g) all-purpose flour
1 egg
1 teaspoon (5 g) salt
¹/₄ cup (50 g) sugar
5 ¹/₂ tablespoons (80 g) butter, softened* and cubed

Filling
5 ¹/₄ oz. (³/₄ cup or 150 g) brown Vergeoise sugar
(soft brown sugar made from beets)
2 eggs
3 tablespoons (40 g) butter, softened
1 cup (250 ml) whipping cream

Ingredients

7 oz. (200 g) faisselle cheese (or drained, smoothed cottage cheese, or quark or cream cheese

Scant ¹/₄ cup (30 g) confectioners' sugar

1 vanilla bean, slit lengthwise, seeds scraped

2 egg whites

¹/₃ cup (60 g) granulated sugar

Scant cup (200 ml) whipping cream, 30 percent fat content

7 oz. (200 g) mixed berries (raspberries, strawberries, redcurrants, etc.)

Cream cheese and berries ★

Serves 6

Preparation time: 35 minutes
Chilling time: 1 hour minimum

If you are using French *faisselle* cheese, drain it well–you might need to drain it overnight. If the type of cream cheese you are using does not have such a high water content, it will not be necessary to drain it so long. Whisk in the confectioners' sugar and the seeds of the vanilla bean.

Beat the egg whites until they form stiff peaks. Add the sugar and whisk until the meringue is firm and shiny.

Prepare the Chantilly cream (see p. 174).
Gently fold* the beaten egg whites into the cheese, and then, equally carefully, the whipped cream. Fold just until all the ingredients are combined.
If you used French *faisselle*, return the mixture to the *faisselle* containers (these are tiny colanders). Otherwise spoon the mixture into ramekins or small bowls. Top with the mixed berries and chill for at least 1 hour.
Serve with a berry coulis (see p. 164) or Breton-style shortbread cookies.

 Technique
Chantilly cream ›› p. 174

Ingredients

1 lb. (500 g) strawberries
$^2/_3$ cup (125 g) sugar
Zest of 1 unsprayed or organic orange
Zest of 1 unsprayed or organic lemon
A few sprigs of lemon verbena, leaves chopped
1 cup or $^1/_4$ lb. (125 g) confectioners' sugar

Sabayon
4 egg yolks
Scant $^1/_2$ cup (100 ml) strawberry liqueur

Strawberry gratin with sabayon

Serves 8

Preparation time: 25 minutes
Marinating time: 30 minutes
Cooking time: 20 minutes

Wash and hull the strawberries. Roll them gently in the granulated or caster sugar. Scatter the grated zest and lemon verbena over the strawberries. Stir gently to combine and leave to marinate for 30 minutes.
Set the oven to "broil."
Prepare the sabayon (see p. 50).
Place the egg yolks in a saucepan. Add the strawberry liqueur and whisk energetically.
Place the saucepan over a low heat. Whisk the mixture continuously until it is creamy. Arrange the strawberries in small, shallow casserole dishes or in a serving dish with handles. Pour the sabayon over the strawberries and broil briefly, or use a torch to caramelize the top. Dust with confectioners' sugar just before serving. Serve warm.

Technique
Sabayon >> p. 50

Mirabelle plum tart,
a specialty of Alsace ★

Serves 8
Preparation time: 40 minutes
Resting time: 20 minutes
Cooking time: 25 minutes

Prepare a sweetened short pastry (see p. 14).
Place the butter, sugar, and egg in the bowl of a food processor and cream together until smooth. Sift the flour and add it with the salt to process for 1-2 minutes further, until smooth.
Press down the dough with the palm of your hand, pushing it away from you, until the ingredients are thoroughly blended. Chill, covered, for 20 minutes. Roll out the dough very thinly (about $^1/_6$ in./3 mm) to form a disk. Use a rolling pin to transfer it from the working surface to the baking pan or circle: drape it round the pin and then unroll it in place. Make decorative patterns around the edge.
Preheat the oven to 350°F (180°C).

Prepare the sweet cream for baking (see p. 186).
Combine the milk, cream, whole eggs, egg yolks, sugar, and bitter almond extract until just mixed. Do not allow the mixture to form bubbles. Pour the Mirabelle brandy in to the batter and scrape the seeds out of the vanilla bean to flavor it.
Strain it through a fine-mesh sieve, cover with plastic wrap, and chill.

Wash the plums. Arrange them at the base of the pastry crust and pour the batter over.
Bake for 20-25 minutes. If you are using a pastry ring, remove it for the last 5 minutes so that the edges can brown slightly.
Remove from the oven and dust with confectioners' sugar.
Turn onto a cooling rack. This tart is best served warm, and is delicious with ice cream.

● Did you know?
Mirabelle plums, a small, very sweet variety of plum, are grown in the Alsace-Lorraine region in eastern France. They are much appreciated for their juicy flesh and are used to make preserves and eau-de-vie. You can use other plums or even other fruit to make this tart—but it will no longer be called a Mirabelle tart!

Techniques
Sweetened short pastry ›› p. 14
Sweet baked cream ›› p. 186

Ingredients
Sweetened short pastry
1 stick (125 g) unsalted butter, softened*
$^1/_2$ cup (100 g) granulated sugar
1 egg
2 $^3/_4$ cups (250 g) cake flour
1 teaspoon (5 ml) salt

Sweet baked cream
1 scant cup (200 ml) milk
1 scant cup (200 ml) whipping cream, 35 percent fat content
4 eggs plus 4 yolks
Scant $^1/_2$ cup (80 g) sugar
A few drops of Mirabelle plum brandy
$^1/_2$ vanilla bean

1 lb. (500 g) Mirabelle plums
Confectioners' sugar for dusting

Ingredients

2 ³/₄ cups (250 g) cake flour
1 teaspoon (5 g) salt
¹/₂ cup (125 ml) water
1 stick plus 4 tablespoons (185 g) unsalted butter

5 sheets gelatin* (10 g)
1 vanilla bean
2 cups (500 ml) milk
3 egg yolks
²/₃ cup (125 g) sugar
¹/₃ cup (55 g) cornstarch
A few drops of orange-blossom water
3 cups (750 ml) whipping cream, 35 percent fat content

1 scant cup (125 g) confectioners' sugar
¹/₂ lb. (250 g) white fondant icing, optional
2 oz. (50 g) chocolate, 64 percent cocoa

Diplomat-filled mille-feuille ★★★

Serves 8

Preparation time: 50 minutes
Resting time: 1 hour 20 minutes
Cooking time: 40 minutes
Chilling time: 40 minutes

Prepare the puff pastry (see p. 16).
Sift the flour and add the salt. Pour the water into the flour and stir with your fingers to combine.
Blend the ingredients together rapidly until thoroughly mixed. You should have a smooth paste, known as the *détrempe*. Form it into a ball, and chill, covered, for about 20 minutes.
Check that the butter has the identical consistency of the dough mixture. Beat it, if necessary, between two sheets of parchment paper, with a rolling pin. This enables it to be incorporated more easily into the dough, and gives it a longer rectangular shape.
Now roll out the dough mixture to form a cross shape, leaving the center–where you will place the butter–thicker (about $^1/_3$ in./5 mm) than the four other parts. The butter should fit over this part of the dough.
Place the butter in the center of the dough and fold over each of the four parts of the cross, similarly to the back of an envelope.
Lightly dust a cool working counter with flour (use as little as possible each time, so that the pastry does not become too hard). Roll out the dough (called a *paton*) to form a rectangle whose length is three times greater than its width (2).
Fold this into three, starting at each end (three layers) (3).
Rotate the folded dough a quarter turn and roll out again to form the same shape as previously, a rectangle three times its width. Repeat the folding operation. Cover with plastic wrap and chill again for about 20 minutes.
Repeat this procedure–rolling out and folding–five more times (a total of six times), chilling for 20 minutes between each step of two quarter turns.

Prepare the diplomat cream (see p. 177).
Place the gelatin sheets in a bowl of very cold water to soften.
Slit the vanilla bean lengthwise and scrape out the seeds. Place them in the milk, together with the vanilla bean, and bring to a simmer.
Whisk the egg yolks, sugar, and cornstarch briskly together until the mixture thickens and becomes pale.
When the milk is simmering, remove it from the heat and pour half of it over the blanched eggs. Mix together. Incorporate the orange-blossom water.
Pour the mixture back onto the remaining milk, return to the heat, and bring back to the boil. Leave to boil for 2-3 minutes, whisking constantly.

Remove from the heat. Wring the water out of the gelatin sheets with your hands. Mix the gelatin in with a whisk until the mixture is smooth.
Transfer to a bowl. Cover with plastic wrap flush with the cream. Cool to about 60°F (15°C).
Using a stand-alone or heavy-duty beater, whip the cream until it is the same consistency as a Chantilly cream.
When the pastry cream is cold but not yet set, mix it again. Delicately fold in* the cold whipped cream with a rubber spatula.

Preheat the oven to 425°F-450°F (220°C-230°C).
Roll the puff pastry out to a thickness of about $^1/_{10}$ in. (3 mm). You will need three equal shapes to make your mille-feuille, so the aim is to cut it into three rectangles. Prick it at regular intervals with a fork and bake for about 20 minutes. To obtain very thin, delicate layers of pastry, place a baking tray over your puff pastry halfway through the baking process. This will deflate the air that causes it to rise. At the same time, when the pastry is barely colored, dust it with confectioners' sugar. Repeat this once more, just before baking is completed. Be careful that it does not burn–it should remain a nice golden brown.
Use a knife with a serrated blade to cut out three rectangles. If you are making eight individual portions, cut out twenty-four rectangles. Spoon the diplomat cream into a piping bag and pipe it out onto the first rectangle of pastry. Place the second rectangle just above this and garnish with more diplomat cream.
Dust the third sheet of pastry with confectioners' sugar and make criss-cross patterns using hot steel skewers, or a caramelizing blow torch. If you prefer, you may coat the top layer with fondant icing. Heat the fondant to 95°F (35°C) and spread it over. Trace a chocolate design on top. Place this third layer of puff pastry on the top of the mille-feuille and chill for 30-40 minutes before serving.

Techniques
Puff pastry ≫ p. 16
Diplomat cream ≫ p. 177

Opéra ★★★

Serves 8
Preparation time: 2 hours 10 minutes
Cooking time: 35 minutes

Prepare the joconde sponge (see p. 194). Line a baking sheet with parchment paper.
Preheat the oven to 350°F (180°C). Sift together equal quantities of sugar and ground almonds: 3/4 cup (140 g) granulated sugar and 1 2/3 cups (140 g) ground almonds.
Beat this together with four eggs until the mixture reaches the ribbon stage*. Fold in* the sifted flour, followed by the melted butter.
Beat the four egg whites until they form stiff peaks. Add the remaining sugar (1/4 cup or 50 g) and beat until the mixture is firm and shiny (it forms a French meringue).
Carefully fold this French meringue into the egg and butter mixture.
Spread the batter over the baking sheet. It should be very thin, about 1/5 in. (3-5 mm) thick. Bake for 8-10 minutes.
As soon as it is done, turn it over onto a rack to cool with the parchment paper.

Make the coffee syrup.
Bring the coffee and the sugar to the boil. Cover with plastic wrap and set aside.

Prepare the ganache cream (see p. 180).
Bring the cream and milk to the boil.
Chop the chocolate and pour the boiling cream-milk mixture over to melt it.
Remove from the heat, whisk in the butter, and stir until smooth.
Leave to cool, stirring from time to time.

Prepare the coffee butter cream (see p. 173).
Prepare a sugar syrup and cook until it reaches a temperature of 243°F (117°C).
With an electric beater, whisk the egg and yolk mixture until is it foamy.
Pour the sugar syrup over the eggs, and continue beating for a few minutes to cool the temperature of the mixture.
Incorporate the cubed butter using a whisk or an electric beater at medium speed. Stir in the coffee extract. Transfer to a mixing bowl and cover with plastic wrap flush with the surface.

Remove the joconde sponge from the baking sheet and cut it into three identical rectangles.
Glaze* the top of one of the rectangles with melted chocolate or glazing paste, using a pastry brush. Allow to set, turn it over, and moisten the other side with coffee syrup. Cover this layer with coffee butter cream and place a second rectangle of sponge over it. Moisten the second layer with coffee syrup and pour over a very thin layer of ganache. Place the last sponge layer over the ganache and moisten it with coffee syrup. Cover it with butter cream and chill.
Slightly heat some glazing paste to smooth over the Opéra, or cover it with a thin layer of ganache. Keep in the refrigerator. It is a good idea to trim the edges with a sharp knife for an attractive presentation. Coffee-flavored custard makes a refined accompaniment.

Ingredients

Joconde sponge
1 scant cup (190 g) sugar, divided
1 2/3 cups (140 g) ground almonds* or almond meal
4 eggs plus 4 egg whites
1/3 cup (45 g) flour
1 1/3 tablespoons (1 oz./25 g) butter, melted

Coffee syrup
3/4 cup (200 ml) strong coffee
1/2 cup (100 g) sugar

Ganache cream
Scant 1/3 cup (70 ml) whipping cream, 30 percent fat content
1/4 cup (50 ml) milk
7 oz. (200 g) bittersweet chocolate, 64 percent cocoa
1 1/2 tablespoons (25 g) unsalted butter

Coffee butter cream
2 cups (400 g) sugar
Scant 1/3 cup (80 ml) water
2 eggs plus 2 egg yolks
2 sticks (250 g) unsalted butter, cubed
A few drops of liquid coffee extract

To finish
4 1/2 oz. (125 g) bittersweet chocolate, 64 percent cocoa, or 7 oz. (200 g) glazing* paste

Techniques
Joconde sponge >> p. 194
Ganache cream >> p. 180
Butter cream >> p. 173

Ingredients

3 egg whites

Generous ¹/₄ cup (25 g) cake flour

2 teaspoons (10 g) unsalted butter, melted

²/₃ cup (125 g) sugar

¹/₂ teaspoon (3 g) vanilla extract

Flavorings–choose from:

4 oz. (125 g) sliced blanched* almonds, or

4 oz. (125 g) toasted crushed pistachios, or

2 oz. (60 g) candied citrus zest, or

Scant ¹/₂ cup (50 g) cocoa powder, or

3 ¹/₂ oz. (walnuts)

or any other ingredient you would like to try!

Citrus lace tuiles

¹/₃ cup (80 g) melted butter

¹/₂ cup (100 g) sugar

¹/₃ cup (1 oz., 30 g) cake flour

Scant ¹/₄ cup (50 ml) orange juice

Zest of 1 unsprayed or organic orange

1 tablespoon plus 1 teaspoon (20 ml) Cointreau or other orange liqueur

3 ¹/₂ oz. (100 g) chopped almonds

Assorted tuiles ★

Serves 8

Preparation time: 35 minutes

Resting time: 40 minutes

Cooking time: 15 minutes

Prepare the tuile batter (see p. 205).

Beat the egg whites lightly with a fork.

Add the rest of the ingredients, except the flavorings, using a whisk.

Chill for about 20 minutes.

Preheat the oven to 350°F (180°C).

Drop thin layers of batter on a silicone baking sheet or baking tray lined with parchment paper and flatten using the back of a spoon. The mixture spreads, so leave plenty of space between the cookies.

Scatter with the chosen flavoring.

Bake for 5-8 minutes, until they are a light golden color.

Take them off the baking sheet immediately (an offset spatula will come in handy) and drape them around a rolling pin while still hot. (If they become too hard to drape, return them very briefly to the oven.) Allow to cool.

Prepare the citrus lace tuiles. Melt the butter in the microwave oven and combine it with the sugar and flour. Stir in the orange juice and zest, flavor with the orange liqueur. Chill the batter for 20 minutes.

Preheat the oven to 350°F (180°C).

Drop thin layers of batter on a silicone baking sheet or baking tray lined with parchment paper. Scatter the cookies with chopped almonds, then bake for 5-8 minutes, until they are the right color.

Remove them from the oven and wait 15-20 seconds before taking them off the baking sheet and shaping them around a rolling pin. Leave them to cool.

 Technique

Tuiles >> p. 205

Bitter almond crème brûlée ★

Serves 8

Preparation time: 20 minutes
Chilling time: 1 hour
Cooking time: 55 minutes

In a round-bottomed mixing bowl, beat the egg yolks and sugar together
energetically until the mixture thickens and becomes pale.

Pour in the milk and whipping cream. Whisk together and add the seeds
from the vanilla bean. Flavor with the bitter almond extract.

Cover with plastic wrap and chill for about 1 hour.

Preheat the oven to 200°F (100°C).

Strain the liquid through a chinois* and pour it into eight small crème
brûlée dishes or ramekins. Bake for 45-50 minutes. Test for doneness: the tip
of a knife should come out clean.

Allow the crèmes to cool. Just before serving them, set your oven to "broil."
Sprinkle the top of each one with brown sugar. Caramelize them briefly in
the oven, or use a caramelizing iron, and serve.

Ingredients

10 egg yolks
Generous 1 cup (225 g) granulated sugar
2 cups (500 ml) milk
2 cups (500 ml) whipping cream, 35 percent fat
content
1 vanilla bean
A few drops of bitter almond extract
A little brown sugar, for caramelizing

Ingredients

1 tablespoon plus 1 teaspoon (20 g) salted butter
1 ¼ cups (125 g) all-purpose flour
1 pinch (2 g) fine salt
4 eggs
½ lb. (250 g) dried plums with their pits
1 cup (250 ml) well-aged rum
½ cup (100 g) sugar
4 cups (1 liter) full cream milk
1 tablespoon (15 g) unsalted butter,
to grease the dish

Breton flan with dried plums (*Far Breton*) ★

Serves 8

Preparation time: 20 minutes
Soaking time: 12 hours or overnight
Cooking time: 40 minutes

A day ahead
Soak the dried plums in the rum.

To prepare
Preheat the oven to 425°F (210°C). Butter an ovenproof dish.
Melt the butter until it browns*. Place the flour and salt in a round-bottomed mixing bowl.
Whisk in the eggs one by one, taking care that they are thoroughly mixed in and that there are no lumps.
Pour in the browned melted butter and whisk the batter again energetically until it has the light texture of a crêpe batter. Whisk in the sugar and the milk.
Drain the dried plums and arrange them in the dish. Pour the batter over the dried plums.
Bake for 20 minutes, then reduce the temperature to 350°F (180°C) and cook for another 20 minutes or so, depending on the diameter of the dish. The tip of a knife should come out dry and some steam will escaped from the small hole when it is done.

● Did you know?

The Breton far *(literally "flour") is a dense custard flan that is popular as a dessert. There is a variation on this Breton* far, *the* farz fourn *("oven-baked* far"), *which is a savory flan served with meats.*

Iced Desserts

Stéphane Augé
presents his recipe

French gastronomy is a combination of tradition and revolution. As the years go by, the great classics remain. It is up to each of us French chefs to transmit our culinary heritage, but we make them our own and give them new life. And so tradition becomes evolution. The Belle-Hélène is a pear sundae that was created around 1864 in honor of Jacques Offenbach's comic opera of that name, and the dessert continues to enjoy popularity. Here, I have reinterpreted what is traditionally served in a sundae glass so that it can be served on a plate. The basic elements—vanilla, pear, and chocolate—are still there, but they are treated differently. The vanilla ice cream has taken in fine leaves of chocolate and becomes a stracciatella (white base with fine chocolate shavings). The poached pears are served in the form of both tiny cubes and jelly, and the crystallized violets have made way for caramelized cocoa nibs and a fantasy caramel-chocolate bow. All the ingredients come together to make up a dessert that is easy to prepare and quick to plate for service. Cold, hot, iced, melting, crisp, crusty, soft, and creamy—here you have an interplay of textures, temperatures, and intense flavors that will enthrall your palate. Bon appétit!

Pear Belle-Hélène, revisited

A day ahead

Stracciatella ice cream
1 cup (250 ml) full cream milk
2 ¹/₂ tablespoons (³/₄ oz./20 g) skimmed powdered milk
Scant ¹/₃ cup (2 ¹/₄ oz./65 g) granulated sugar, divided
³/₄ oz. (20 g) glucose syrup (liquid glucose)
¹/₂ cup (125 ml) whipping cream, 35 percent fat content
³/₄ oz. (2 g) ice cream stabilizer (available from professional suppliers)
1 Madagascar Bourbon vanilla bean, slit lengthwise, seeds scraped
1 teaspoon (5 ml) Morand Williamine® pear brandy
2 oz. (50 g) fine chocolate bits, 70 percent cocoa

Prepare the ice cream mix.
Heat the milk to 77°F (25°C). When it reaches this temperature, mix in the powdered milk. Continue heating. When it reaches 86°F (30°C), add 3 ¹/₃ tablespoons (45 g) sugar and the glucose syrup. At 95°F (35°C), add the whipping cream. At 113°F (45°C), mix in the remaining sugar combined with the stabilizer, as well as the slit vanilla bean with its seeds. Bring it to 189°F (87°C) to pasteurize it as you would for a custard. Process it so that it is perfectly smooth.
Place in the freezer at 39.2°F (4°C) for 1–4 hours. Process again and churn. Then add the pear brandy. When you extrude it, incorporate the fine chocolate bits. Spoon the ice cream into a piping bag fitted with a fluted nozzle measuring ¹/₂ in. (16 mm) in diameter. Store at 10°F (-12°C) until serving.

Cigarette paste tubes
1 ³/₄ oz. (¹/₃ cup/50 g) confectioners' sugar
1 ³/₄ oz. (3 ¹/₂ tablespoons/50 g) butter, softened*
1 ³/₄ oz. (50 g) egg whites (equivalent of approximately 2 egg whites)
1 ²/₅ oz. (6 ¹/₂ tablespoons/40 g) all-purpose flour
¹/₃ oz. (1 ¹/₂ tablespoons/10 g) unsweetened cocoa powder

Sift the confectioners' sugar and cream it with the softened butter. Mix in the egg whites. Sift the flour and cocoa powder together and combine them with the mixture. Leave to chill.
Preheat the oven to 300°F (150°C).
Roll out the mixture very thinly, using a frame if you wish, on a silicone baking sheet to make six rectangles measuring 4 × 5 ¹/₂ in. (10 × 14 cm). Bake for 5 minutes. As soon as you remove the rectangles from the oven, roll the pastry around six 4-in. high (10 cm) tubes with a diameter of 1 ¹/₄ in. (3 cm). When they have cooled, carefully remove the tubes. Store the pastry cylinders in an airtight container.

Pears poached in syrup
3 Bartlett (also known as Williams) pears (10 oz. or 300 g)
³/₄ cup (4 ³/₄ oz./135 g) granulated sugar
1 vanilla bean, slit lengthwise
Scant ¹/₂ cup (100 ml) water

Serves 6
Preparation time: 1 hour 30 minutes
Cooking time: 35 minutes
Freezing time: 12 hours

Peel the pears and dice* them very finely ($^1/_{10}$ in./3 mm cubes) to make a brunoise*. Place them in a bowl with the sugar, slit vanilla bean, and the water. Cover the bowl with plastic wrap and poach the pear brunoise in the microwave oven for 4 minutes. Drain carefully, reserving the hot liquid for use for the rest of the recipe. (The pears will give off some of their own liquid, all of which will be needed.) Set aside in the refrigerator.

Bartlett pear jelly

3 g powdered gelatin, 200 Bloom strength (check with your supplier)
$^1/_2$ cup (125 ml) of the reserved poaching liquid, still hot
4 teaspoons (20 ml) Morand Williamine® pear brandy

Dissolve the gelatin directly in the hot poaching syrup. Flavor with the pear brandy and pour into a shallow tray. Cover with plastic wrap and chill. When the mixture has set, cut out thirty cubes ($^1/_2$ in./1 cm). You will need five per person.

Caramel-chocolate bow

1 $^1/_2$ oz. (40 g) pure cocoa paste (from specialty stores)
1 $^1/_2$ oz. (40 g) glucose syrup
2 oz. (60 g) fondant (from specialty stores)

Chop the cocoa paste finely. Cook the glucose syrup and the fondant to a temperature of 325°F (160°C) and mix in the chopped cocoa paste. Roll it out between two silicone baking sheets and leave to cool. To make the bows, break off pieces and soften them slightly in a heated oven. Roll them out thinly and shape into bows. Set aside in an airtight container.

Polignac cocoa nibs

1 oz. (30 g) cocoa nibs (at specialty stores or online)
1 $^1/_3$ tablespoons (20 ml) pear poaching liquid

Preheat the oven to 300°F (150°C).
Mix the cocoa nibs into the syrup and spread the mixture on to a silicon baking sheet. Bake for 7 minutes, allow to cool, and set aside in an airtight container.

Prepare ahead of serving time

Dark chocolate Chantilly mousse

3 $^1/_2$ oz. (100 g) bittersweet chocolate, 70 percent cocoa
$^2/_3$ cup (185 ml) whipping cream, 35 percent fat content, divided

Melt the chocolate to a temperature of 131°F (55°C). While it melts, begin heating $^1/_4$ cup (65 ml) cream. Remove from the heat before it reaches a simmer. Whisk the heated cream into the melted chocolate. Beat the rest of the cream until it forms soft peaks. When the mixture is at a temperature of 113°F (45°C), incorporate the softly beaten cream. Spoon the mousse into a piping bag and keep in the refrigerator until needed.

Prepare just before serving

Custard-style sabayon

2 $^1/_2$ tablespoons (40 ml) full cream milk
$^3/_4$ oz. (20 g) egg yolk (appr. 1 egg yolk)
$^1/_3$ cup (80 ml) pear poaching liquid

Beat the egg yolk with the syrup until white and pale. Bring the milk to the boil and pour it over the egg yolk mixture. Whisk the mixture over a hot water bath until it reaches a sabayon texture. It should now be served.

To assemble

Fill $^1/_3$ of the tubes with chocolate Chantilly and place one in the middle of each plate. Drain the diced pears well and fill the next third of the tubes with the pears. Arrange five cubes of jelly around each tube. Spoon the sabayon into the base of each plate and scatter it with cocoa nibs. Fill the tubes to the top with ice cream and garnish with the chocolate-caramel bow. Serve immediately.

Rum and raisin profiteroles ★★

Serves 8
Preparation time: 1 hour 5 minutes
Baking time: 25 minutes
Freezing time: 4 1/2-5 hours

Prepare the choux pastry (see p. 20).
Preheat the oven to 400°F (200°C) and ensure there is no residual steam in it. (Choux pastry has to dry out well.)
Sift the flour. Bring the water, salt, and cubed butter to the boil in a saucepan. Remove from the heat and pour in all the flour at once.
Return the saucepan to the heat and stir the mixture energetically with a spatula to dry it out. When the moisture has evaporated, put the batter into a mixing bowl.
Mix in four eggs, one by one, stirring well each time with the spatula.
Spoon the choux batter into a piping bag with a plain tip and pipe out small choux pastries with a diameter of just under 1 in. (1.5 cm).
Beat the remaining egg and, using a pastry brush, baste* the choux pastries. Dip a fork in water and press down lightly on the surface of the pastries with the tines to make a grid pattern. This will help them bake evenly.
Bake for 25 minutes. When the choux pastries are done, leave the door ajar for a few minutes to allow the steam to escape so that they can dry out completely.

Prepare the rum and raisin ice cream (see p. 209).
Macerate the raisins in rum (just enough to cover them in a small bowl).
Slit the vanilla bean lengthwise and place it in a saucepan with the milk and cream. Bring the mixture to the boil.
Beat the egg yolks with the sugar until the mixture is thick and pale. Pour the hot milk and cream over the eggs, beating constantly, then return the liquid to the saucepan. Heat it as you would a custard, to a temperature of 185°F (85°C), or until it thickens and coats the back of a spoon*.
Chill the custard cream rapidly over ice and then pour it into an ice cream machine. Follow the instructions for the time, but it will take a minimum of 3 hours.
Remove the ice cream from the ice cream maker and stir in the macerated raisins. Place in the freezer for 1 1/2-2 hours.

Prepare the chocolate sauce (see p. 166).
Heat the milk and cream on low heat. The temperature of the mixture should not exceed 130°F-140°F (55°C-60°C) (it will be hot but should not burn the tip of your finger).
Remove the saucepan from the heat and, using a spatula, incorporate the chopped chocolate until the sauce is smooth. Keep it warm over a bain-marie*.
Slit the profiteroles in half horizontally. Fill each one with a scoop of rum and raisin ice cream.
Arrange them on a dish and drizzle with the warm chocolate sauce.

🥄 **Techniques**
Choux pastry ›› p. 20
Custard-based ice cream ›› p. 209
Chocolate sauce ›› p. 166

Ingredients

Choux pastry
1 cup (250 ml) water
1 teaspoon (5 g) fine salt
7 tablespoons (100 g) unsalted butter, cubed
1 1/4 cups (125 g) all-purpose flour
4 plus 1 eggs

Rum and raisin ice cream
1/2 cup (3 oz./80g) raisins
Rum (sufficient to soak the raisins)
1 vanilla bean, slit lengthwise
1 2/3 cups (400 ml) full cream milk
Scant 1/2 cup (100 ml) whipping cream, 35 percent fat content
6 egg yolks (4 1/4 oz./120 g)
1/2 cup (100 g) sugar

Chocolate sauce
1 cup (250 ml) full cream milk
3 1/3 tablespoons (50 ml) cream, minimum 30 percent fat content
6 3/4 oz. (190 g) bittersweet chocolate, 64 percent cocoa, roughly chopped
Special equipment: a sugar thermometer

Acacia honey parfait ★

Serves 8

Preparation time: 20 minutes
Cooking time: 10 minutes
Freezing time: 30 minutes

Using the method for pâte à bombe (see p. 210), heat the honey to 244°F (118°C). Pour the honey over the egg yolks, beating constantly, until the mixture cools down completely.
Whisk the cream until it forms stiff peaks and carefully fold* it into the honey pâte à bombe.
Pour the mixture into ramekins or shot glasses (*verrines*) and leave to set in the freezer for 2-3 hours.

● Chef's note

Lightly oil the measuring cup with a neutral oil when measuring the honey so that you can pour it out without any waste.

Ingredients

Scant ¹/₃ cup (3 ¹/₂ oz./100 g) acacia honey
4 egg yolks
1 cup (250 ml) whipping cream, minimum 30 percent fat content
Special equipment: sugar thermometer

Techniques
Pâte à bombe ›› p. 210
Iced parfait ›› p. 210

Iced hazelnut parfait ★

Serves 8

Preparation time: 20 minutes
Cooking time: 10 minutes
Freezing time: 3 hours

Using the method for pâte à bombe (see p. 210), begin cooking the water and sugar.
Place the egg yolks in the bowl of a heavy-duty mixer and begin beating them. When the syrup reaches a temperature of about 243°F-250°F (117°C-120°C), begin pouring it over the egg yolks as the mixer continues to beat. Continue beating until the mixture has reached room temperature. It will be dense and shiny, and form a mousse-like ribbon.
Whip the cream until it forms stiff peaks and fold in* the hazelnut paste. Carefully fold the flavored whipped cream into the pâte à bombe.
Spoon the parfait mixture into molds or small shot glasses (*verrines*) and freeze for 2 ¹/₂-3 hours.
Garnish with toasted sliced hazelnuts.

Techniques
Pâte à bombe ›› p. 210
Iced parfait ›› p. 210

Ingredients

¹/₄ cup (60 ml) water
²/₃ cup (4 ¹/₃ oz./120 g) granulated sugar
5 egg yolks
1 ¹/₂ cups (375 ml) whipping cream
2 oz. (50 g) pure hazelnut paste (from specialty stores or online)
Toasted hazelnuts, for garnish
Special equipment: sugar thermometer

Ingredients

1 ²/₃ cups (400 ml) whipping cream,
minimum 30 percent fat content
1 lb. (500 g) puréed strawberries

Italian meringue
¹/₄ cup (50 ml) water
³/₄ cup (140 g) granulated sugar
3 egg whites (70 g)
1 pinch salt
Special equipment: sugar thermometer

Iced strawberry mousse ★

Serves 8
Preparation time: 20 minutes
Cooking time: 10 minutes
Freezing time: 3 hours

Prepare the Italian meringue (see p. 49). Begin cooking the water with the sugar. When the syrup reaches a temperature of 230°F (110°C), begin beating the egg whites with the pinch of salt in the bowl of a stand-alone mixer. (The bowl should be perfectly clean.) When the syrup reaches 243°F–250°F (117°C–120°C), pour the syrup over the stiff egg whites. Continue whisking until the meringue mixture has cooled down completely. It will be dense, shiny, and form many small peaks.
Beat the cream stiffly to a Chantilly texture. Fold* the strawberry purée into the Italian meringue using a rubber spatula. Then carefully fold the whipped cream into the mixture, taking care not to deflate it.
Spoon the mousse into shot glasses (*verrines*) or ramekins and freeze for 2–3 hours.

> **Techniques**
> Italian meringue >> p. 49
> Iced mousse >> p. 211

Ingredients

1 ¹/₄ cups (300 ml) tangerine juice
³/₄ cup (200 ml) water
1 cup (200 g) granulated sugar
3 cups (700 ml) champagne

Champagne granita ★

Serves 8
Preparation time: 20 minutes
Freezing time: 2 hours 15 minutes

In a saucepan, bring the tangerine juice to boil with the water and sugar. Boil for 3 minutes and allow to cool, either on its own or over ice.
Prepare the granita. Add the champagne to the cool syrup. Pour the mixture into a large, shallow dish so that you have a shallow layer of liquid. Place it in the freezer for 15 minutes. With a fork, scratch the surface and stir it to break up any lumps. Return the granita to the freezer and repeat the procedure every 25 minutes for 2 hours.
Just before serving, scratch it well again with a fork to lighten the texture.

Iced blackberry *vacherin* ★ ★

Serves 8

Preparation time: 45 minutes
Baking time: 1 hour 30 minutes
Freezing time: variable, approx. 6 hours for a classic ice cream maker

Prepare the blackberry sorbet (see p. 209).
Wash the blackberries.
Bring the water to the boil with the sugar.
Process the blackberries in a juicer and add the juice to the syrup. Cool rapidly over ice and then pour into the ice-cream maker.

Prepare the meringue shells (see p. 49).
Preheat the oven to 200°F (90°C). Line a baking sheet with parchment paper. Ensure that a round-bottomed bowl is perfectly clean and dry before you pour the egg whites in. Beat the egg whites together with a pinch of salt lightly with a fork. Then begin whisking them energetically, making sure to lift the whisk up high to incorporate as much air as possible. When the whites begin to stiffen, add the sugar, incorporating it with a circular movement until the mixture is firm and shiny. The meringue should be compact and smooth, and should form stiff peaks from the whisk.
Spoon the meringue batter into a piping bag and pipe out the shells onto the baking sheet.
Dry the meringue shells out in the oven for 1 1/2 hours.
When the meringues are perfectly dry and cool, form the sorbet into a single cake shape, or eight individual cylinder shapes, and press the meringues into it around the sides.
Decorate with Chantilly cream (see p. 174) and garnish with the blackberries.

Techniques

Sorbet ›› p. 209
French meringue ›› p. 49
Chantilly cream ›› p. 174

Ingredients

Blackberry sorbet
2 lb. 4 oz. (1 kg) blackberries
1 1/4 cups (240 g) sugar
2 cups (500 ml) water

Meringue
7 egg whites (200 g)
2 cups (400 g) sugar
1 pinch salt

Chantilly cream
1 cup (250 ml) whipping cream, minimum fat content 30 percent
1/3 cup (40 g) confectioners' sugar
A few drops of vanilla extract

8 blackberries, for garnish

Ingredients

Scant ²/₃ cup (120 g) sugar
2 tablespoons (30 ml) water
3 egg yolks (60 g)
10 oz. (300 g) mashed banana
Juice of 1 lemon (to squeeze over the mashed banana to prevent it from going black)
1 ²/₃ cups (400 ml) whipping cream

Italian meringue
1 ¹/₄ cups (220 g) granulated sugar
Scant ¹/₃ cup (70 ml) water
4 egg whites (110 g)
1 pinch salt

Iced banana soufflé ★★

Serves 8

Preparation time: 40 minutes
Freezing time: 3 hours

Prepare the pâte à bombe (see p. 210).
Begin cooking the water with the sugar. Start beating the yolks in the bowl of a stand-alone mixer. When the syrup reaches a temperature of 243°F-250°F (117°C-120°C), pour it over the beaten egg yolks. Continue beating until the pâte à bombe has cooled down completely. It will be dense and shiny, and form a mousse-like ribbon.
Mix in the mashed banana (with or without the lemon juice).
Stiffly whip the cream and set aside in the refrigerator.

Prepare the Italian meringue (see p. 49). Begin cooking the water with the sugar. When the syrup reaches a temperature of 230°F (110°C), begin beating the egg whites with the pinch of salt in the bowl of a stand-alone mixer. (The bowl should be perfectly clean before you begin.) When the syrup reaches 243°F-250°F (117°C-120°C), pour it over the stiff egg whites. Continue whisking until the meringue mixture has cooled down completely. It should be dense, shiny, and form many small peaks.
Fold* the meringue into the pâte à bombe, then fold in the stiffly whipped cream.

Line the inside of eight soufflé molds with strips of parchment paper 6-8 in. (15-20 cm) high, depending on the size. Keep the paper in place with paper clips.
Pour the soufflé mixture into the molds and freeze for 2 ¹/₂-3 hours.

Techniques
Pâte à bombe ›› p. 210
Italian meringue ›› p. 49
Soufflé ›› p. 211

Baked Alaska ★★

Serves 8

Preparation time: 50 minutes
Baking time: 25 minutes
Freezing time: 5 1/2–6 hours, depending on the ice-cream maker

Prepare the vanilla ice cream (see p. 209).
Slit the vanilla bean lengthwise. Bring the milk and cream to the boil with
the vanilla bean.
Beat the yolks with the sugar in a mixing bowl until they are thick and pale.
Pour the milk and cream mixture over the egg yolks, beating constantly,
then return all the liquid into the saucepan.
Heat it as you would to make a custard, to a temperature of 185°F (85°C).
Cool rapidly over ice and then transfer to an ice-cream maker for 2 1/2–3
hours.

Prepare a Genoese sponge (see p. 193).
Preheat the oven to 350°F (180°C).
Beat the eggs and the sugar together in a round-bottomed mixing bowl over
a bain-marie* until the mixture reaches the ribbon stage* and a temperature
of 140°F (60°C).
Sift in the flour and pour half of it in to the mixture, folding* it in gently with
a rubber spatula. Pour in the remaining flour and fold it in, working quickly
and carefully so as not to deflate the batter.
Spread the batter out to a thickness of about 1/8 in. (4 mm) on to a silicon
baking sheet or baking pan lined with parchment paper. An offset spatula
will come in handy here to smooth it. Bake for 10-12 minutes.
Test for doneness–it should be a light golden color–and turn it out onto a rack
to cool.
Remove the vanilla ice cream from the ice-cream maker when it is ready, and
shape it into a cube 15 × 4 × 4 in. (40 × 10 × 10 cm).
Cut out the Genoese sponge so that you have two layers, each the same size
as the vanilla ice-cream cube (15 × 4 in./40 × 10 cm).

Prepare the Italian meringue (see p. 49). Begin cooking 1/2 cup (120 ml) water
with the sugar in a saucepan. Check that the bowl of the heavy-duty mixer is
perfectly clean before you pour the egg whites in.
When the temperature of the syrup reaches 230°F (110°C), begin beating the
egg whites with a pinch of salt. When the temperature of the syrup reaches
243°F-250°F (117°C-120°C), begin pouring it gradually into the egg whites.
Continue beating until the meringue has cooled down completely. It will be
dense and shiny, and will form many small peaks.
Place the ice-cream cube on one layer of the sponge base and then place the
second layer on top.
Spoon the meringue into a piping bag and decorate your dessert.
Freeze for at least 3 hours.
Preheat the oven to 400°F (200°C). Just before serving, place the dessert in
the oven until the meringue browns. Flambé it with the fruit brandy just
as you serve.

Ingredients

Italian meringue
1 3/4 cups (360 g) sugar
6 egg whites (180 g)
1 pinch salt

Vanilla ice cream
1 vanilla bean
1 2/3 cups (400 ml) full cream milk
Scant 1/2 cup (100 ml) whipping cream, minimum
fat content 30 percent
6 egg yolks
1/2 cup (100 g) granulated sugar

Genoese sponge
4 eggs
2/3 cup (125 g) granulated sugar
1 1/3 cups (125 g) cake flour, plus extra for the pan
A little butter to grease the pan
Fruit brandy, such as orange or cherry, to flambé*

Techniques

Custard-based ice cream >> p. 209
Genoese sponge >> p. 193
Italian meringue >> p. 49

Ingredients

Nougatine
5 ¼ oz. (150 g) glucose
½ cup (100 g) sugar
1 cup (125 g) chopped almonds

Ice cream
Scant ⅓ cup (3 ½ oz. or 100 g) honey
¼ cup (55 g) granulated sugar
4 egg whites (120 g)
2 cups (500 ml) whipping cream 35 percent fat content, well chilled
¾ cup (125 g) assorted candied fruit, cubed
¼ cup (125 g) roasted unsalted pistachios
¼ cup (125 g) chopped nougatine
¾ cup (125 g) candied orange peel, cubed
1 ½ tablespoons (25 ml) Cointreau or other orange liqueur

Raspberry coulis
4 ½ oz. (125 g) raspberries
2 teaspoons (10 ml) lemon juice
Scant ½ cup (60 g) confectioners' sugar

Iced nougat and raspberry coulis ★★

Serves 8
Preparation time: 35 minutes
Freezing time: 2 ½–3 hours.

If preparing homemade nougatine, melt the glucose in a saucepan, add the sugar, and cook until it forms a light caramel. Lightly toast the chopped almonds and mix them into the caramel. Pour the caramel on to a silicon baking sheet, spreading it out. When it has cooled, chop it up.

For the ice cream, cook the honey and sugar together until the mixtures reaches a temperature of 243°F (117°C). While the mixture is cooking, beat the whites stiffly. Pour the cooked sugar/honey mixture over the beaten egg whites using the method for an Italian meringue (see p. 49), until it has cooled.
Beat the well-chilled cream in the bowl of a heavy-duty mixer. Fold* it into the Italian meringue. Then stir in the cubed candied fruit, roasted pistachios, crushed nougatine, and cubed candied orange peel. Stir in the orange liqueur.
Pour the mixture into stainless steel dessert circles or other shaped silicon molds.
Place in the freezer until it hardens, 2 ½–3 hours.

Prepare the raspberry coulis (see p. 164).
Wash the raspberries and blend them with the lemon juice and confectioners' sugar. Strain through a fine-mesh sieve.
Cover with plastic wrap and chill until needed.
Turn the iced nougat out of the molds or circles and serve it with the raspberry coulis.

● **Did you know?**
Nougat is a specialty of the south of France and Montélimar is particularly well-known for its nougat. The iced version combines all the basic ingredients of the traditional recipe.

 Techniques
Italian meringue >> p. 49
Fruit coulis >> p. 164

Index

506
Index

DVD Contents

The sequences show professionals at work and therefore the quantities, cooking times, and other specifics may vary slightly from the recipes in the book, which have been adapted for use in the home. When putting techniques into practice or making recipes, follow the precise indications given in the book.

To follow along in the book, the page numbers indicated below refer to the corresponding technique.

Eggs
    Scrambled eggs, 42
Fish
    Filleting a fish (flat), 71
    Filleting a fish (round), 70
    Fish fumet, 139
    Shallow poaching, including
        how to prepare a parchment
        paper lid, 108, 112
Garnishes
    Dicing, 54
    Peeling tomatoes, 61
    Turning vegetables, 65
Meat
    Dressing and trussing poultry, 82
    Jointing rabbit, 77
    Mousseline stuffing; boning and
        stuffing a chicken leg, 89; 157
    Preparing a rack of pork, 83
Pastries, cakes, and desserts
    Bread dough, 28
    Choux pastry, 20
    Fruit mousse, 197
    Genoese sponge cake, 193
    Italian meringue, 49
    Madeleines, 35
    Pastry cream, 182
    Pouring custard, 172
    Puff pastry, 16
    Shortcrust pastry, 12
Sauces
    Béchamel sauce, 131
    Hollandaise sauce, 148

Selected Bibliography

Child, Julia, Louisette Bertholle, and Simone Beck. *Mastering the Art of French Cooking*, vol. I. New York: Alfred A Knopf, 1970.

Child, Julia, and Simone Beck. *Mastering the Art of French Cooking*, vol. II. New York: Alfred A. Knopf, 2009.

Davidson, Alan. *The Oxford Companion to Food*. Oxford: Oxford University Press, 1999.

Greenspan, Dorie. *Paris Sweets*. New York: Broadway Books, 2002.

Kamman, Madelaine. *When French Women Cook: A Gastronomic Memoir*. New York: Macmillan, 1996.

Keller, Thomas. *The French Laundry Cookbook*. New York: Artisan, 1999.

Larousse des Cuisines Régionales. Paris: Larousse, 2005.

Larousse Gastronomique. New York: Clarkson Potter, 2009.

Pépin, Jacques. *La Technique*. New York: Times Books, 1976.

Rombauer, Irma S., Marion Rombauer Becker, and Ethan Becker. *Joy of Cooking*. New York: Scribner, 2006.

Schneider, Elizabeth. *Vegetables from Amaranth to Zucchini*. New York: William Morrow, 2001.

Scotto, Les Soeurs, and Annie Hubert-Baré. *L'Héritage de la Cuisine Française*. Paris: Hachette, 1992.

Willan, Anne. *La Varenne Pratique, The Complete Illustrated Cooking Course*. Toronto: Macmillan of Canada, 1989.

http://www.epicurious.com

http://www.joyofbaking.com

Acknowledgments

The authors are very grateful to the Lycée Hôtelier de La Guerche, Brittany, for supplying the materials and location featured in this work.

They would also like to thank the many partners and suppliers who made this work possible:
- Les vergers Boiron (frozen fruit)
- Boursault (cheeses—Paris 75014)
- Bragard (chefs' clothing)
- Cefimev (training center for meat professionals)
- Céréco (organic cereals)
- Ducros (spices, herbs, condiments)
- Emeraude Marée (fish and shellfish)
- Ercuis (tableware)
- Eurolam (knives)
- Gama 29 (cleaning products)
- Gatine viandes (pork)
- Janzé Volailles Tradition (poultry)
- Lactalis (dairy products)
- Louaisil (fresh fruit and vegetables)
- Panzani food service (pasta)
- Loïc Raison (cider and apple juice)
- Raynaud (Limoges porcelain)
- Société Ricard (alcoholic beverages)
- Super U (groceries)
- Tendriade (veal)
- Triballat Sojasun (dairy and soy-based products)